MW00981812

Village of Unsettled Yearnings

Copyright © 2002

All rights reserved. No part of this publication may be reproduced, stored in a retrieval system or transmitted in any form or by any means — electronic, mechanical, audio recording or otherwise — without the written permission of the publisher or, in the case of photocopying, a licence from CANCOPY, Toronto, Canada, except for brief passages quoted by a reviewer in a newspaper or magazine.

TouchWood Editions is an imprint of Horsdal & Schubart Publishers Ltd.
Victoria, BC, Canada.

This book is distributed by The Heritage Group, #108-17665 66A Avenue, Surrey, BC, Canada, V3S 2A7.

Cover and book design by Retta Moorman.

TouchWood Editions acknowledges the financial support for our publishing program from The Canada Council for the Arts, the Government of Canada through the Book Publishing Industry Development Program (BPDIP) and the Province of British Columbia through the British Columbia Arts Council.

This book is set in AGaramond.

Printed and bound in Canada by Friesens, Altona, Manitoba.

National Library of Canada Cataloguing in Publication Data

Village of unsettled yearnings: Yarrow, British Columbia: Mennonite promise / editor, Leonard N. Neufeldt; managing editor, Lora Jean Sawatsky; assistant editor, Robert Martens.

Includes bibliographical references and index.
ISBN 1-894898-01-X (Village of unsettled yearnings) — ISBN 1-894898-001 (Before we were the land's)

1. Yarrow (B.C.)—History. 2. Mennonites—British Columbia—Yarrow—History. I. Neufeldt, Leonard, 1937- II. Sawatsky, Lora Jean, 1935- III. Martens, Robert, 1949-
FC3849.Y37V54 2002 971.1'37 C2002-911294-X
F1089.5.Y37V54 2002

The Canada Council for the Arts | Le Conseil des Arts du Canada

BRITISH COLUMBIA ARTS COUNCIL
Supported by the Province of British Columbia

Village of Unsettled Yearnings

Yarrow, British Columbia: Mennonite Promise

Editor: Leonard N. Neufeldt
Managing Editor: Lora Jean Sawatsky
Assistant Editor: Robert Martens

Contents

Dedication

With gratitude and affection this volume is dedicated to the founders of Yarrow and to Jacob A. Loewen, founder of the Yarrow Research Committee.

Acknowledgments

Generous contributions from the Jacob H. Enns Estate, Henry and Margaret Neufeldt Fund, and Vine and Branch Foundation (Arthur J. and Irma Block) have assisted in the preparation of this volume. Much of the research was supported by Jacob A. Loewen and the Quiring-Loewen Trust. We are also grateful to the many contributors of essays for this volume, whose writings have formed a new Yarrow community, as it were, even as they recall a community largely vanished. Audrey Beaumont deserves special thanks for serving as final reader of manuscripts for both this volume and *Before We Were the Land's*. The editors are also indebted to Vivian Sinclair and Brenda Martin, who served as editors of our project for The Heritage Group, and to publisher Rodger Touchie, who unflinchingly demonstrated his faith in this project — *omnibus modis.*

* * *

The Yarrow Research Committee is an affiliate of the Chilliwack Museum and Historical Society.

Preface

It has always been difficult to follow up invitations of African American friends to define whiteness after they have discussed in some detail what being black means to them. Defining contemporary Mennonitism may be relatively easier than explaining whiteness, but considerably more difficult than defining the Mennonites of early Yarrow. As *Before We Were the Land's* explains, most of the adult founders hoped to re-establish a Mennonite village culture that had forcibly been taken from them in Russia. This statement, however, should not be taken to mean that village and colony life in Russia had been homogeneous. Individuals, families, and villages had been less than unanimous in their responses to cultural and political changes in late 19th-century and early 20th-century Russia, especially in such matters as following a single church model and authority, continuing the time-honoured vocation of farming, adopting the Russian language, pursuing higher education, performing alternative (non-combatant) military service, and, more generally, adjusting to native and imported forms of cultural modernism.

Nonetheless, one can cite many similarities between the way Mennonites lived their lives in early Yarrow and in Russia before that. These include: differentiation from the people around them, efforts to establish and foster their own institutions, close ties between civic and religious life, the simple biblicism of the church, the primacy of farming, marrying fellow Mennonites, using Low German as vernacular and High German in church services, maintaining their traditional ethnic foods, and celebrating and mourning as a community.

Yet even in their biblicism, often cited as one hallmark of Mennonitism, Yarrow settlers were, and were not, one. They loved the Bible, and some owned extensive collections of translations. Those with libraries took pride in their Bible dictionaries, concordances, atlases, and commentaries. In meetings large and small, when interpretations were at variance with one another, one could expect a gesture of respect to each view, perhaps even a bearhug. When interpretations deviated too far from settled opinion, one could anticipate attempts to cajole or coerce the deviant back to more acceptable views. At periodic conferences devoted to explication of a book or several books of the Bible, men in the audience responded to formal presentations with a range of questions and views more unlike each other than the different translations they brought to bear on the discussion. Guest presenters responded variously to this divergence of opinion: some with long-fingered irritation, some with the indifference of a station stop for the presenter's train of thought, some with obvious delight in the large menu of response. In the end, the pastor would declare the contributions as valuable before leading in a closing hymn and prayer. Then the parishioners left these *Bibelbesprechungen* as one — and as many.

Of course, such intellectual give and take around a text revered by almost everyone is hardly unusual in a literate community and surely did not signify cultural stress lines capable of fracturing what would be from what had been. Yet the Yarrow settlement that saw itself as a unified community was also at odds with itself and with the pressures of acculturation. In this respect, the biblical conferences can be viewed as a metaphor for the coexistence of unity and difference in behaviour, practices, beliefs, and aspirations. This coexistence, indeed reciprocal goad, of consensus and dissent, persistence and rapid change, was at the heart of Yarrow's rich cultural life with its large capacity for hope, strong personal investments, and tensions. These tensions, including above all the inevitability of assimilation, walked hand in hand with the young pioneer settlers, born in Russia, and especially with the next generation, born in Canada. There was no possibility that the new generation would be absorbed into a Russian colony ethos or would move elsewhere in order to perpetuate it.

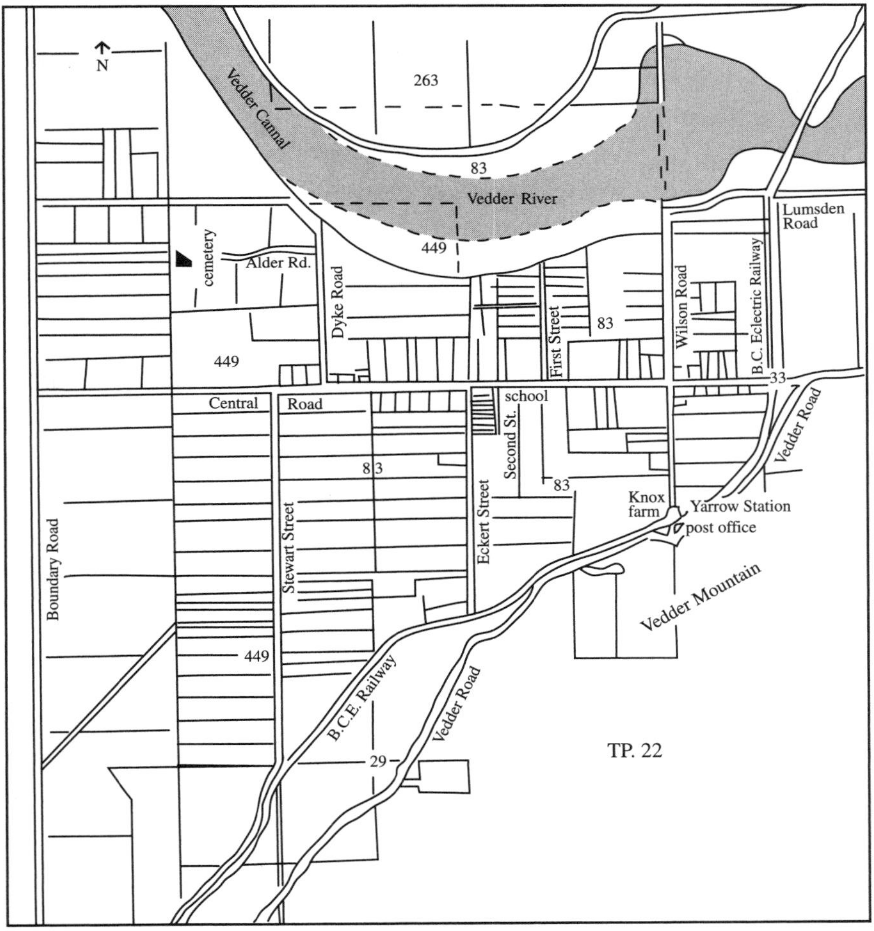

Surveyor's Map of Yarrow, ca. 1939

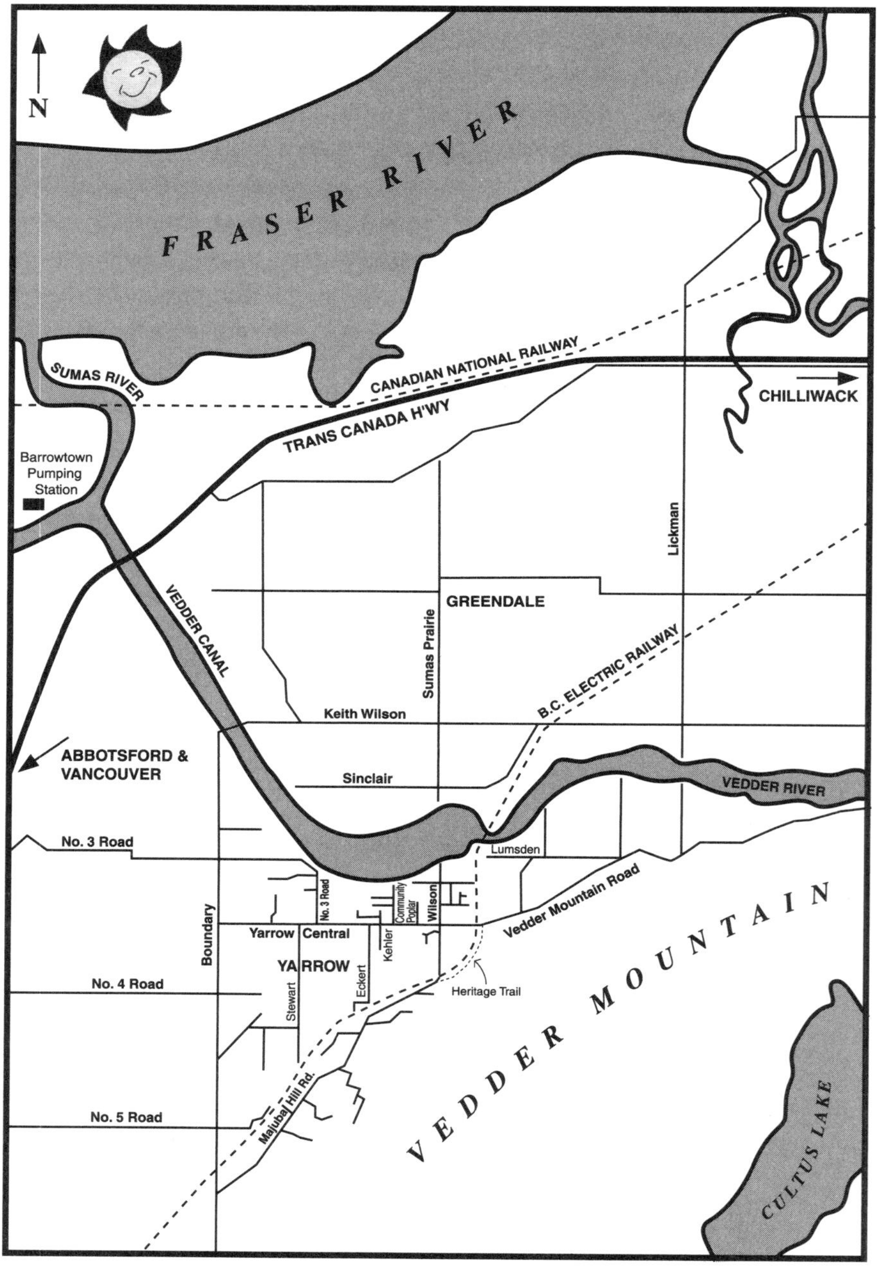

Modern Yarrow and Area

Part One

A Cultural Mural of Yarrow

Central Road, looking west (probably from the upper storey of the roof of the Co-op department store), late 1940s.

Rites of Dying, Death, and Burial

By Esther Epp Harder

Much of our understanding of death and dying, our attitudes and response to these final life experiences, have been influenced by Mennonite faith and the surrounding community. … We seem to be generally unaware of the radical change in our attitude toward death as a result of changing practices around us."[1]

Walking through the new brick gates of the Yarrow Cemetery on a beautiful, warm November day, I was reminded of what we had been taught as children and had heard at funerals in our early years: that the many Yarrow people resting here today would one day rise from the

Recently renovated gate of Yarrow Cemetery.

dead. As a child, I imagined what this would be like. Now, years later, I tried to imagine it again. The trumpet would sound, the graves would open, the dead would rise up, and we would all be caught up to meet the Lord of life and death. I noticed how the wind was blowing leaves among the graves, and I distinctly recalled my step-grandmother, Helena Janzen (1890-1985), who used to say, "When the leaves fall from the trees again, I will be under them." On my way toward the row farthest back, where the oldest graves are, I passed by her grave and then older ones. The inscriptions on some of the headstones are no longer readable; time and weather have obliterated them. Others still show the names and dates of saints and sinners, young and old, as they were buried one by one in 17 straight rows in the Yarrow Cemetery. So many changes have taken place in Yarrow in the span of years during which this place, close to where I lived as a child, has been used as a burial ground.

After leaving the burial ground, however, I began to reflect on how this quiet place is linked to a history of changes in Mennonite rituals, particularly those associated with preparation for death, death itself, funerals, and burials. Prior to the Mennonites' arrival, some of the earlier settlers were buried on Marshall Knox's property, then in the Carman United Church graveyard. The graves on the Knox farm were relocated when the B.C. Electric Railway laid tracks through the Knox property for its new line.[2]

Before a church was built, Yarrow Mennonite families gathered in their homes or out in the open, weather permitting, for church services, weddings, and funerals, as many of them had done in Russia in new colonies. Understandably, Yarrow Mennonites wished to bury their dead in their own community or church cemetery. However, they needed official government authorization to do so. In 1928, the closest burial ground was the small cemetery on Promontory Road in Sardis. The first birth and death in Yarrow was that of infant George Giesbrecht, the last child born to Elizabeth Wittenberg Giesbrecht and Peter Giesbrecht, Sr. This child, born on July 28, 1928, was buried at the Carman United Church Cemetery on August 2.

After inquiries to provincial offices and formal applications, the Mennonite settlers in Yarrow received official British Columbia government authorization in May 1931 to establish a cemetery. The plot approved is the current site of the burial ground, still the only community cemetery in Yarrow's relatively brief history. It is located

George Giesbrecht's grave marker, Carman United Church Cemetery.

about two kilometres from the town centre on a short reach of land slightly higher than most of the surrounding land. The slight elevation of this property and several other nearby spots is due to alluvial deposits built up along the shore close to the mouth of the Vedder River—that is, at the place where it formerly flowed into Sumas Lake. Johann Braun, one of Yarrow's earliest Mennonite settlers, was instrumental in establishing the cemetery, and for many years he was gravedigger and keeper of the grounds. Area maps called the short road leading from Dyke Road to the cemetery grounds Alder Road; later the name was changed to Hare Road. But for decades the Mennonites called it simply *Kirchhofstrasse* (Cemetery Road). Today the visitor will notice a sign when turning into this road from No. 3 Road (formerly Dyke Road) — NO EXIT.

Most Yarrow Mennonites lived with the expectation of death and with constant reminders to be prepared for life after death. "The old must die, the young may die," was a well-rehearsed saying. Many expected to die at home with family around them. Often, caskets were built as part of this preparation, and people took the caskets with them when they moved to another house, storing them in attics, sheds, or, if space was limited, under their own beds. A casket was a reminder of an inescapable moment at the end of one's life, as well as a practical preparation for a funeral and burial.

More important than having a family member or acquaintance construct a casket was the state of one's soul—that is, a readiness for what lay beyond death, in eternity, and indications of this readiness to family members and friends around the deathbed. The last words of the dying frequently suggested an open portal or way, or a peaceful journey, or Jesus waiting with open arms, or angels hovering overhead, waiting to take one home. Many times these last words were spoken as a prayer, with folded hands and resounding amen. Families usually shared these final moments of the deceased at the funeral as words of comfort and with the hope that one day they would see their loved one in eternity.

The story is told of one unusually lively Yarrow woman, known for her outrageous sense of humour and for playing tricks on her family. She had no fear of her casket, which had been waiting for many years in the shed behind her home. Eventually she retired to a personal care home in Abbotsford, taking her casket with her and storing it under the bed in her small room, as other residents had done. Several years later, at age 92, although still feisty and in love with life, she complained to her great-grandson that she didn't enjoy sleeping in her bed. When asked what was wrong, she told him with a serious face that she didn't like having her casket under her bed: she feared that if she died in her sleep, they would simply pull the casket out, roll her into it, and close the lid.

In Yarrow there was more to dying than that. Grandmother Katherine Enns Janzen (1875-1940) died at home in February 1940. Her husband, Jacob K. Janzen (1874-1960), usually built caskets for the family in his workshop, and he was skilled at this work. But, as his daughter, Elizabeth Janzen Epp (1909-), recalls, the prospect of making a casket for his wife, Katherine, made him too sad. There were numerous casket builders in early Yarrow, including Johann Braun, Gerhard Hooge, John Toews, and later Henry Spenst. (Spenst built caskets both for individuals and, after 1965, for the North Vancouver Funeral Home.) When it became obvious that Katherine Janzen would not recover from her cancer surgery, Jacob Janzen approached his friend Gerhard Hooge to build a new-style half-open casket for her.

After Katherine Janzen died, her daughter Helen and a neighbour, Mrs. Susanna Dyck, a midwife, took care of her. It was customary for midwives in early Yarrow to prepare the bodies for burial, which included closing the eyes and tying a scarf under the chin to keep the mouth closed. This had to be done immediately, before rigor mortis set in. They washed the body with alcohol to clean the skin and prevent an odour, then packed the body in ice. A loved one usually spent that first night sitting beside the body, keeping watch out of devotedness and custom, but also, apparently, in case the deceased were to awaken from a coma. In Grandmother Janzen's case, the midwife dressed her the next morning in a traditional black dress with a white collar and placed her in the casket. The coffin stood in the unheated living room of her home until it was time to take it to the funeral service that afternoon. (Given the lack of embalming in those days, funerals were usually held within two days of a death, or sooner if there wasn't enough ice for packing the body.[3] After the body was removed from the house, it was customary to ignite a small amount of sulphur in a spoon and walk through the home, letting this burning sulphur cleanse the air.)

A friend took pictures of the Janzen family standing around the casket. The women were dressed in black, and the men and children had black armbands sewn around their sleeves. The casket was placed on a horse-drawn wagon for the journey to the church, and the family walked behind the wagon. Other people joined the procession for my grandmother's final service in the church. The theme of our mortality in the funeral sermons and songs emphasized that the Creator had granted us this life as an opportunity to live to His glory by serving His purposes and had given us a life beyond as a confirmation of our faith and His grace. After the service, family and friends followed the wagon carrying the casket to the cemetery for the burial service.

The casket of Katherine Enns Janzen. The coffin and hearse are typical of the early years of Mennonite Yarrow.

In 1947, a doctor informed my grandfather Jacob G. Epp (1882-1949), a respected Mennonite Brethren minister in Yarrow, that he had approximately two years to live due to severe arteriosclerosis and that he could, in fact, die of a heart attack at any time. He had been the only ordained minister among the first settlers. Jacob Epp wished to go to sleep in Yarrow and wake up in heaven. On March 1, 1949, after he had been taking out posts in his raspberry field, he came in complaining of not feeling well and so went to lie down. When his daughter checked on him, she noticed his breathing—and realized that he was dying. She ran next door to telephone the doctor and my father, then hurried to the home of Reverend Petrus Martens (1887-1969), a friend and neighbour, to request that he attend her father in his hour of death. After they arrived at the bedside, Martens asked Grandfather if he was in pain; Grandfather shook his head. "Is the way up open?"Martens asked. Grandfather nodded his head and folded his hands. The reverend asked if he should pray, and again Grandfather nodded. After responding with a loud "amen" at the end of the prayer, Grandfather was gone.[4] The doctor arrived somewhat later.

When my father arrived home, he took me to view Grandfather's body. Since it was Wednesday night, Father stopped at the church and interrupted the regularly scheduled prayer meeting to tell the pastor that Grandfather had died and to ask him to notify the people, many of whom were Grandfather's friends. I recall Grandpa lying in his bed as if asleep, his hands folded as though in prayer. I was amazed to see a book stuck under his chin to keep his mouth closed. The doctor had called Henderson's Funeral Home, a Chilliwack business established in 1919, to pick up Grandfather's body. The undertakers placed the body on a stretcher, carried it out to the hearse and drove away. We returned home.

As Grandfather's eldest child, my father had the customary responsibility of making the funeral arrangements. He met with the pastor to decide on a day for the funeral. I had to help him write the *Zettel*, a letter of announcement in German, to notify everyone in Yarrow of Jacob Epp's death and the day and time of the funeral, and to invite everyone to refreshments after the burial at Yarrow Cemetery. The *Zettel* was the common method used in Yarrow to notify people of a church or community event to which all were invited. For funeral announcements, the letter and envelope were edged in black to signify a death in the community. Written on the envelope were instructions as to which streets the letter was to be delivered to, and it would be passed along from household to household. Usually the family made several copies of the letter so that the news would spread quickly.

There were other preparations. When an ordained Mennonite minister died in those days, it was common practice to invite other ministers who were friends and/or associates to take an active part in the funeral service and to be recognized and thanked by the family for their influence on the life of the deceased minister. Since Reverend Gerhard Regehr of Seattle had ordained Grandfather as a minister in Russia in 1913 and was a good friend of the family, Father invited him to speak at the funeral. Father also helped his mother and sisters compose the obituary. It was written in the usual form of a historical document to be read at the funeral and then sent to the *Mennonitische Rundschau* in Winnipeg. The obituary appeared in the *Rundschau* and the *Zionsbote*, another Mennonite weekly newspaper.[5]

As tradition dictated, the refreshments after the funeral were coffee and zwieback (two small buns stuck together, the top one somewhat smaller than the one beneath it). Wedding zwieback was quite sweet, but zwieback for funerals had only enough sugar to make the yeast rise. Mother mixed the dough according to Grandmother's recipe and brought batches of dough to neighbours and friends with the request that they bake the zwieback and bring them to the funeral reception. She also asked them to help with the serving and cleaning up.

The family considered it important for Grandmother Elizabeth Paetkau Epp (1886-1949), at the time recovering at home from recent cancer surgery, to say her personal farewell to her deceased husband. My father made arrangements for Grandfather's body to be brought to their home by Henderson's hearse. Reverend Petrus Martens came to the house to conduct a short service for the family. Then everyone but Grandmother went to the Yarrow Mennonite Brethren Church for the funeral.

The funeral service was traditionally Mennonite. My father, his brothers, and brothers-in-law served as pallbearers. They carried the casket up the stairs of the church. Had it been a decade earlier, they would have carried it all the way to the chancel area, below the pulpit. But now funeral-home personnel transported the casket down the aisle. The ministers and the family, including 20 grandchildren, walked into the church behind the casket. The family sat in the front centre pews, and the grandchildren sat with their parents. As for the many others present, the men and boys sat on the right side of the church, and women and girls on the left side. The closed casket was placed in front of the family. The casket floral spray was carefully arranged on top of it, and the other flowers were placed on special stands nearby. Reverend Abram Nachtigal from Yarrow and Reverend Gerhard Regehr from Seattle delivered messages in German. The obituary was read by one of the ministers. The men of the Sunday School class that my grandfather had taught sang the song my father had requested—"*Selig in Jesu Armen*" ("Safe in the Arms of Jesus"). Vocal solos or a women's choir at funerals were a later innovation; in earlier years the church choir usually provided the music with moving renditions of hymns such as "*Dann, ja dann, wird mir alles klar/Was hier nieden dunkel war*" (Then, yes then, all will be clear/what here below was obscured in darkness).

After the closing prayer, the funeral director repositioned the casket, removed the flower spray, opened the top half of the lid, and invited the people to pay their last respects to Jacob Epp. (In the 1940s and '50s, the casket remained half-open throughout the service; in the very early years it was usually fully open.) After the viewing, the casket was closed and wheeled out of the church, the ministers and family following it down the aisle. The bearers carried the casket down the stairs of the church and placed it inside the hearse. The family and friends got into their own cars, turned on their headlights as a sign of respect and honour to the deceased, and followed the hearse in a slow procession to the cemetery.

At the Yarrow Cemetery, the bearers carried the casket to the gravesite. Reverend Heinrich Bartsch conducted a short service in German that included a hymn and reading of the traditional New Testament passage: "We believe that Jesus died and rose again and so we believe that God will bring with Jesus those who have fallen asleep in him. According to the Lord's own word, we tell you that we who are still alive, who are left till the coming of the Lord, will certainly not precede those who have fallen asleep. ... And so we will be with the Lord forever. Therefore, encourage each other with these words" (1 Thessalonians 4:14-17). A prayer was spoken, then Grandfather's casket was lowered into the ground with two ropes held by four men. They then pulled out the ropes and placed the lid over the coffin. (Often, at this point, someone had to step down into the grave to straighten and secure the lid.) A family member threw the first shovel of dirt into the open grave, then the other men took spades in hand and filled the grave with earth and mounded it while the others watched. In a final act, the family placed the flowers on top of the mound. As we walked back to our cars, we heard in the far background our uncle Peter Epp (1923-1990), playing one of the deceased's favourite hymns on his trumpet. Everyone returned to the church for refreshments.

The Epps had two more family funerals in this same year: Grandmother Elizabeth Epp died on May 2, and our baby sister, Dorothy Susan Epp (born May 15, 1948), died on August 16, 1949. Dorothy's funeral was particularly sad for my family because she died so young and as a result of an accident on our farm. Although most of the funeral preparations and the services themselves were conducted in much the same way as Grandfather Epp's, there were differences. Both caskets were purchased at Henderson's Funeral Home. Grandmother's coffin was half-closed, but Dorothy's was a shallow open coffin, similar to the traditional caskets used by Mennonites in Russia and for the first decade in Yarrow. Flowers from my school garden were pinned around the inside of my sister's casket, and a tiny bouquet of baby's breath and stock was placed in her folded hands. Mother made a casket spray of gladioli and ferns from her garden, in keeping with the custom in Russia of using whatever flowers were in season. At Dorothy's funeral I found it extremely unsettling to listen to the thud of the spaded earth hitting the casket as we stood at the very edge of the burial site. This experience must have been difficult for others as well.

Early Yarrow Mennonites brought very strict rules from Russia. Some of these pertained to funerals for people who had not been church members, particularly those who had been excommunicated from the church and those who had committed suicide. The ministers would not allow these people's caskets to be brought into the church, and they sometimes refused to conduct a funeral service. If burial of such individuals in the Yarrow Cemetery was permitted, the grave was placed just outside the burial area proper. Many people suffered not only the loss of their loved one, but also public shame and indictment because of these rigid rules. Families of suicides usually made arrangements for a private family service at a funeral home or at the burial site to avoid the emotional pain of dealing with the harsh practices of the church.

Over the years, Yarrow Mennonites have abandoned many of their rites and rituals connected with death in favour of practices common in the culture around them. Those attending a gravely ill individual at the hospital or at home summon emergency medical personnel, whereas they used to call a minister and the immediate family to the bedside.

Today one hopes that medical intervention may grant the loved one a reprieve. If the person dies, we encounter the world of the modern funeral home with its professional staff, impressive casket showrooms, meticulous preparations, and chapel-like room for viewing. Few people wear black to a funeral; even black hats and armbands have disappeared. The hearse for the casket and a limousine to transport the family to the funeral service and burial site are provided by the funeral home. The burial of the body takes place in the morning, usually in a private service, with a public memorial service later in the day. At the burial site, the casket rests above the grave. All the mourners are asked to leave the graveyard before someone comes to lower the casket and close the grave with earth.

At the church service that follows, a large photograph of the deceased is often on display with the flowers. In the foyer of the church or at the reception following the memorial service, some families display items such as needlework, a photo album, or a collage of pictures from the life of the deceased. Both the service and the reception usually include a celebration of the deceased's life. The obituary, now commonly read by a family member or close friend, is a personal tribute to the person memorialized rather than a formal historical document read by a minister. The sad, tear-filled funerals I attended as a child, where no one dared smile, are gone. To some extent, perhaps, so is the reality of death.

When I walked through the Yarrow Cemetery, I noticed many recent improvements. A committee that includes Mary Ratzlaff Froese and Susie Giesbrecht Derksen has been working hard to renovate and beautify it. One cannot help but notice the brick entrance, large gate, and immediate park-like area beautifully landscaped with evergreen shrubs and purple heather. Until recently, all grave markers were simple concrete slabs, identical in size and shaped in the form of beds, with a concrete pillow as a headstone. Perhaps this was symbolic of a frugal people, simple and equal in death if not in life. Perhaps it signified that they are asleep and resting. The concrete slabs are being removed, and many burial sites have new headstones. But one notable burial custom has not changed: the age-old Christian convention of burying the corpse on its back with the head to the west so that on the day of resurrection the dead will rise and face the morning sun in the east. Memorial benches are being placed around the cemetery so that people may rest while visiting burial sites of loved ones. I couldn't help but wonder if the masses of violets I had seen blooming in the cemetery in spring began with those my mother and I planted long ago near my sister's grave. But on this November day there were no violets blooming—only silk and plastic flowers, some of them anchored to a headstone, others blown about by the wind. There was a freshly mounded gravesite with real flowers, and these were wilting.

Midwifery: A Ministry

By Irma Epp, Lillian Harms, and Lora Sawatsky

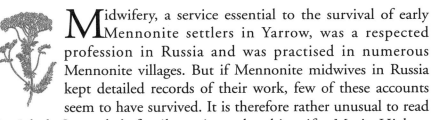

Midwifery, a service essential to the survival of early Mennonite settlers in Yarrow, was a respected profession in Russia and was practised in numerous Mennonite villages. But if Mennonite midwives in Russia kept detailed records of their work, few of these accounts seem to have survived. It is therefore rather unusual to read in Jakob Sawatzky's family register that his wife, Maria Hiebert Sawatzky, born 1842 in Schönfeld, Bergthaler colony, began practising midwifery in 1865 in Wiesenfeld. Jakob goes on to record that 43 years later she had delivered 1,013 babies. In addition, by 1899 she had administered medical care other than delivering babies to 400 individuals.[1]

Even more unusual is the detailed account written by Sara Dekker Thielman in which she records 1,448 births at which she presided between 1909 and 1941. Born April 14, 1878 in Kleefeld, southern Russia, she moved with her family to Samara, where she appears to have trained as midwife. In 1919 she and her husband, David Thielman, moved to Siberia, "where she delivered babies not only for Mennonites but also for Russians and other peoples in that country." In 1929 she and her husband moved to Glenbush, Saskatchewan, then later to Beamsville, Ontario, where she died in 1968.[2]

Few historians of Russian Mennonites have included information on the training and careers of midwives. This is the case even with historians in Russia, although P.M. Friesen notes the Mennonite hospitals in the Molotschna—Muntau, Waldheim, Ohrloff, Halbstadt, and Neu Samara, among others—and, in Chortiza, the district hospital and the Alt Kronsweide mental hospital. In 1909, the Moria Society of

Evangelical Sisters of Mercy, principally a school of nursing, was opened in Neu Halbstadt, Molotschna.[3]

Lack of information on training centres for midwives does not mean such centres did not exist. Apparently in 1907, at age 18, Aganetha Dueck Brucks was sent by her parents to train as midwife at the Muntau Hospital under the administration of the head doctor, Erich Tavonius.[4] Several Russian Mennonite midwives refer to Riga, Latvia, as the training centre for their career. While living in Alexanderkrone, Molotschna, Katherina Born Thiessen (1842-1915) studied midwifery with the aid of textbooks from Prussia to Germany. She and her husband, Abraham, immigrated to the United States in 1874 and 11 years later moved to Hoffnungsfeld, Manitoba (near Winkler), where she served as midwife and medical practitioner. Here, the Thiessens soon discovered that their ideas and lifestyles were too liberal for the Old Colony Mennonites, who feared learning and acculturation. Adding to Katherina's difficulties, her medical colleagues shunned and ridiculed her, and in 1895 the American Medical Association sued her for practising without a licence. A subsequent court order prohibited her from charging fees for practising medicine.[5]

But such hostility to an educated midwife was hardly typical among Mennonites in the New World and not at all the case in Russia. In Russian Mennonite villages, the practice of midwifery continued to be popular, particularly in areas geographically removed from hospitals or doctors. In the Siberian settlement of Blumenort, where Margaretha Klippenstein Enns practised as midwife, the closest hospital was in Slavgorod, a day's journey by horse and wagon.[6] In Franzthal (southern Russia), where midwife Elizabeth Harder Harms worked, the nearest hospital was Muntau, a two-day journey by horse and buggy. Not every village had a midwife, Jacob Martens observes, and the mortality rate for both mothers and babies was high.[7]

By the time the first Russian Mennonites arrived in Yarrow, midwifery had already been practised for many years in the Upper Fraser Valley, beginning with Mary Ann Nelmes, who arrived in New Westminster in 1865 and moved to the Chilliwack Valley after marrying Isaac Kipp. "Not only was she the first white woman to reside in the Chilliwack Valley, but she was also the first and for many years the only trained medical person in the area." Her training consisted of a two-month course in Ontario in fundamentals of medicine and Latin; the rest she learned on her own.[8]

McGill graduate Dr. John Cotter Henderson was the first physician to arrive in the Chilliwack Valley, in 1887.[9] In 1912, Chilliwack opened a 12-bed hospital; another wing was added within two years, increasing its capacity to 28 beds.[10] Robert McCaffrey, Lee Alfred Patten, and later George F. Enns and J.D. Moore were some of the physicians practising in the Chilliwack area, and they were well known to the early Yarrow Mennonite settlers who benefited from their medical expertise.[11] In 1934-35, civic leaders in Yarrow negotiated a group health plan for Mennonite residents[12] and hired Dr. Henry Epp, a Sardis resident, to make weekly visits to Yarrow under this plan. He set up his practice in the John G. and Caroline Kroeker residence on First Street (G.F. Enns later replaced Epp). Beginning in the late 1930s, David Epp, a dentist from Vancouver, practised dentistry in the Kroeker residence approximately once every second week.[13] During this time, Chilliwack physicians such as J.D. Moore also made house calls in Yarrow to treat the seriously ill.

Although Chilliwack physicians made house calls in Yarrow, midwives were essential because doctors were not available on a regular basis. Settlers usually had no way to travel over the primitive roads to Chilliwack for medical attention, and even if they had transportation, most were too poor to pay for medical services. Midwives consulted with Chilliwack doctors, who, after making a diagnosis, often left specific instructions with midwives for the continuing care of patients in Yarrow.

The Mennonites who emigrated from Russia and eventually settled in the Fraser Valley brought with them numerous midwives. Elizabeth Rabsch (1884-1978) had practised midwifery both in Russia and on the Prairies, but it seems she largely discontinued her practice after moving to Yarrow.[14] Anna Reimer Peters (1881-1971) trained as midwife in Riga and was a practising midwife when she met her husband, Cornelius C. Peters, a teacher in the Kuban region. After emigrating from the USSR, she practised in Saskatchewan in Herbert, Langham, and Davidson, and later in Agassiz, B.C.[15] Anna Dick Nachtigal had worked for many years in the Muntau Hospital and in private practice as a practical nurse and midwife in the Molotschna when her career was interrupted by marriage to Abram Nachtigal, the father of 11 children. She was 50 years old at the time. The Nachtigals emigrated in 1924 and settled in Arnaud, Manitoba, for 11 years. In Arnaud, she continued to practise midwifery using the only supplies available to her: scissors and hot water. Occasionally she received gifts of eggs and chicken for her voluntary service. After the Nachtigals moved to Yarrow in 1935, she discontinued her practice for the most part but occasionally delivered a baby.[16]

Aganetha Dueck Brucks (1889-1972), born in Klippenfeld, Russia, had trained both as midwife and tailor. She practised midwifery in Orenburg, Russia, and, after 1926, in Coaldale, Alberta. After she moved to Yarrow in 1939, she practised midwifery only sporadically, serving families who had settled east of the B.C. Electric Railway tracks, where she herself lived.[17]

Mathilda Lehn Hildebrandt had trained as a midwife in both Leipzig and Dresden, where her husband Dietrich, a chiropractor from Russia, had studied herbal healing. In 1904, while still in Russia, she and her husband had been presented with a choice by her parents: they would pay for a traditional large wedding celebration, which usually continued for about three days, or finance one year of studies in Germany. The Hildebrandts opted for the year of medical studies in Leipzig and Dresden. Mathilda developed an extensive midwifery practice in Nikolaipol, Russia, where she and her husband built a private sanitarium, and she also practised when they moved to Rosthern, Saskatchewan.[18] After they moved to Yarrow in 1935, Mathilda assisted her husband in his chiropractic practice.

Other practising midwives in early Yarrow were Susanna Decker Dyck (1902-1971), Margareta Wieler (1889-1961), Elizabeth Harder Harms (1887-1983), and Margaretha Klippenstein Enns (1888-1977). All but one of the children of Peter and Elizabeth Giesbrecht, two of the first settlers to arrive in 1928, were delivered by Margareta Wieler. Their last child, George, was born in Chilliwack Hospital in 1928, with Dr. Patten in attendance, but died a few days later.[19]

Yarrow midwives kept no written records of the number of babies they delivered, the kinds of medical problems they encountered, or the total number of people to whom they offered medical care. Although Yarrow midwives may have thought it unimportant to keep records, the stories of two principal midwives in early Yarrow, Elizabeth Harder Harms and Margaretha Klippenstein Enns, illustrate that midwives considered their calling a ministry. Furthermore, midwives were as dedicated to their patients as were the church leaders to their parishioners, often at the expense of their own family lives.

Elizabeth Harder Harms, 1887-1983

By Lillian Harms, with Lora Sawatsky

Elizabeth Harder studied the serious, determined blue eyes of her slender, dark-haired daughter in disbelief. "You are going to the city of Riga to study as midwife? I hear it is an ungodly and dangerous city." But since her youth, Elizabeth Harder Harms had been interested in caring for the sick, and God had recently given her a dream in which she was called to Riga to study midwifery. Why then should Riga be dangerous?[20]

Elizabeth, a practical 24-year-old, pursued that dream. Her father, Johann Harder, a carpenter, had died at age 35, leaving her mother with seven children. Five of the children were given to various relatives. The mother, together with her eldest, Elizabeth, and her youngest, a baby, were taken to another village. Because of poor health, Elizabeth was unable to seek employment for a few years, but when her health improved, she worked as a maid for estate owners until she left to study midwifery.

Having grown up in poverty, Elizabeth was unable to finance her studies. Undaunted, she approached one of her relatives, who owned a substantial estate in the Molotschna colony, to request a loan. He was reluctant to lend her money for studies, but offered to finance her wedding or assist in establishing her own home. When he noticed her determination, he reflected, "On the other hand, you haven't done anything foolish yet." In the end he agreed to finance her studies, and in 1911 Elizabeth left to begin her studies in Riga.

Midwife Elizabeth Harms.

There, she studied in a German hospital, finishing her program in one year. Working long hours, she completed courses in midwifery, first aid, diagnosis of medical conditions, and administration of medications. All of these courses were necessary, as it turned out, as she would soon be employed in a village where doctors were not available. For her practicum, she was sent to patients' homes to deliver babies, submitting written

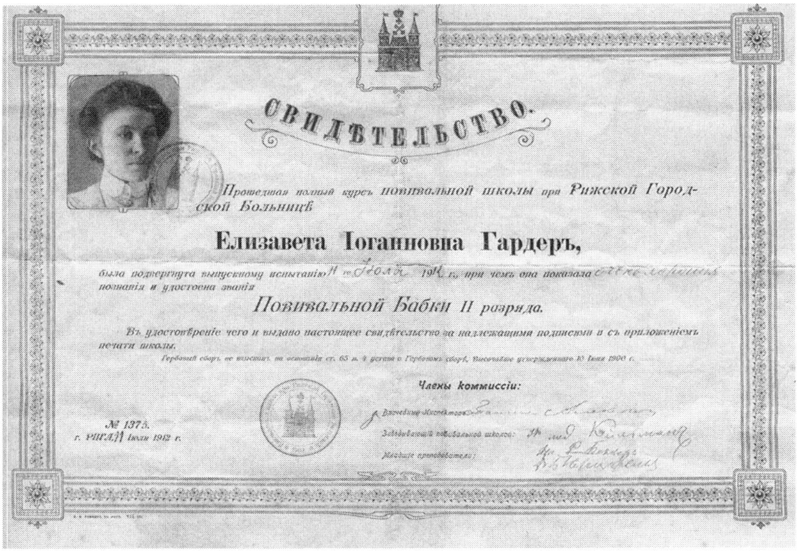

СВИДѢТЕЛЬСТВО.

Проведшая полный курсъ повивальной школы при Рижской Городской Больницѣ

Елизавета Іоганновна Гардеръ,

была подвергнута выпускному испытанію 11 Іюля 1912 г., при чемъ она показала отличныя познанія и удостоена званія

Повивальной Бабки II разряда.

Въ удостовѣреніе чего и выдано настоящее свидѣтельство за надлежащими подписями и съ приложеніемъ печати школы.

Члены коммиссіи:

№ 1375.
г. РИГА 11 Іюля 1912 г.

Diploma certifying Elizabeth Harms as a midwife.

reports to doctors in charge. Her practicum also included experience in the hospital delivery room and on the obstetrical and surgical wards.[21] On July 11, 1912, she received her certification as midwife, signed by inspector Alekseew, director Keljman, and instructor Bekker.[22]

She was hired as the village midwife in Schönfeld, Ukraine, in 1913. After 1917, the Ukraine experienced chaotic conditions resulting from the Russian Revolution. First a Ukrainian peasant leader, Nestor Makhno, together with his militia of anarchists, and then the White and Red armies overran the Ukraine. From 1918 to 1920, Makhno and his followers looted and sacked Mennonite villages, often raping women and girls and murdering villagers, particularly landowners and older boys. Batjko Pravda, one of Makhno's henchmen, established his troop headquarters in Schönfeld. Elizabeth lived on the high-school campus in the home of teacher Gerhard Schroeder and his wife, Truda. Because Makhno's militiamen and the villagers needed the teachers and medical personnel, their lives were spared. Elizabeth not only delivered babies but also assisted when called by Mennonite villagers and Makhnovists who were ill, wounded, or dying.[23] "One evening," Elizabeth recorded, "I thought anytime it could be my turn to lose my life. I felt deeply that I was a lost sinner. I prayed, 'I will not leave you Lord unless you bless me.' That evening I received assurance that I had been saved from eternal death."[24]

In spite of the conditions in Schönfeld, Elizabeth stayed as resident nurse at least until after New Year's of 1919. Then she left for Franzthal, Molotschna colony, where she continued to work as a midwife, was baptized, and joined the Mennonite Brethren Church. She and her sister, Anna, taught Sunday School and organized a club for 13- and 14-year-old girls, a new initiative for that area.[25]

Heinrich (Henry) Harms, who taught Sunday School and led a youth choir in Franzthal, was attracted to Elizabeth, and she, feeling that the Lord had a new assignment for her, prepared for her marriage to this man. The wedding took place in Franzthal in 1924. But at the same time, preparations of another kind were underway: Mennonites were arranging to leave for Canada. Elizabeth and Henry Harms did not hesitate to leave, although they knew they would probably never see their parents and siblings again. In 1925 they landed in Quebec, and then settled briefly in Plum Coulee, Manitoba. They moved on to Drake and then to Nokomis, Saskatchewan.[26] They were anxious to have a family, but Elizabeth had several miscarriages. She jokingly used to say, "I guess it was too cold"—and cold it was in their little house: water left in containers would freeze during the night. As Elizabeth had 12 years of experience as a midwife, a doctor offered her work in the hospital. She wanted to accept this position, but her husband listened to the advice of his friends, who didn't think it proper for wives to work outside the home. Although he disallowed her to work in the hospital, she continued to practise midwifery in the communities in which she lived.[27]

In 1928, Henry and Elizabeth noticed an advertisement for land in mild British Columbia. Henry had heard that his cousins, Nickolai and Sara Reimer, had already settled in Yarrow. Henry was an employee of the Canadian National Railway at that time, and in October he and his wife boarded the train and left for Yarrow. They bought 10 acres on Central Road from Chauncey Eckert and, like other early settlers, built a house consisting of one room and a small kitchen.[28]

Less than one year after they had arrived, Elizabeth was ill and pregnant, and her doctor ordered her to stay in bed. Elizabeth commented, "The move to B.C. did it [produced a child]."[29] August 18, 1929, was a special day for Henry and Elizabeth. Forty-two-year-old Elizabeth, who had miscarried several times, gave birth to a daughter in Chilliwack Hospital, with Dr. Patten in attendance. Henry Harms recorded that this was a difficult birth and that Dr. Patten fought to save the lives of both mother and child while Harms pled with God.[30]

The daughter, Lillian, states:

I was named Lilly Annie. According to my father's memoirs, there were only two cars in Yarrow in 1929. Because people were too poor to pay a doctor, my mother's expertise … was in demand. My father, a kind man, saw the need for her services and this time did not object to his wife working outside the home. She was happy to help and, in addition to delivering babies, she was required to give other kinds of medical assistance.

My mother remembered well the pharmacist at Hipwell Drugs in Chilliwack, where she shopped for her supplies. He allowed her to read his pharmaceutical book so she could find the necessary ingredients and mix her own compounds. In doing so, she managed successfully to treat an infection under the fingernails. Girls and young women who worked as domestics in Vancouver developed this infection as a result of too much scrubbing using strong solutions. Sometimes Mother allowed me to assist when she treated boils by applying sterile cotton soaked in iodine to the boil, which killed the infection. Continuing her career as midwife helped my mother adjust to life in Canada, whereas my father was unable to continue his career in Russia as teacher.

Mother tried to schedule her visits to patients in the evenings when father and I were asleep, which meant walking along dark, unlit and unpaved streets. In spite of her efforts, her career affected our family. At times, babies were delivered in the homes of the midwives. When this occurred, the children of midwives were sent to neighbours. Babies, of course, arrived day or night, but as a young child, it seemed to me that babies liked to arrive mostly at night. When this happened at our home, I often resented having to spend the night at one of the neighbours except when I stayed at Olga Rempel's house. She didn't tease me; she was kind. When a baby was born at our house, mother and infant stayed for at least one week. Mother, having delivered many babies for others and having experienced loss through miscarriages, understood my longing to keep at least one of these babies. "How do you know that the angels did not bring this baby for us?" I used to ask my mother. Nevertheless, after a brief convalescence, mothers left our home taking their babies with them. When Mother, who was often sick, became

> bedridden, I was a happy child because now she might give birth to a baby like the other women who stayed in bed at our house. Although my mother was a skilled midwife and indulgent parent, she could not diminish my longing for siblings.
>
> Like other Yarrow midwives, Mother kept no records of the many babies she delivered. ... Ironically, like most women in Yarrow, she kept mental records of preserving food: 60 quarts of cherries, 48 quarts of raspberries, 36 quarts of strawberries, tomatoes, raspberry juice, jams and jellies. She collected recipes from other women in Yarrow and enjoyed trying them. She sewed clothes for both of us, as well as some casual shirts for my father, but she did not have time to crochet and embroider or to teach Sunday school as she had in Russia.[31]

Elizabeth Harms was always prepared to sacrifice her time when she saw someone in need. Hilda Baerg later paid tribute to this midwife who had come to her house one hour every day to look after her baby, who had acute eczema, so that Hilda could rest. Every morning, Elizabeth started a fire in the wood and coal stove for an elderly woman who was ill. Once a week she visited a woman who was housebound with a handicapped child.[32] "Elizabeth Harms saved my mother's life in Drake, Saskatchewan," comments Mary Froese. "It was a difficult delivery for my mother, Katherina Wedel Ratzlaff, who likely would have died without the help of this midwife." On the other hand, although Elizabeth was kind and understanding with her patients, she became quite annoyed with husbands who fainted during childbirth.[33]

With economic improvement in Yarrow, the place for children to be born gradually shifted from the home to the Chilliwack Hospital, with a physician rather than a midwife attending. In 1957, the Harms family moved to Vancouver, where Elizabeth pursued her hobby of nurturing houseplants. By the late 1960s, she had to stay indoors and in bed much of the time because of heart disease. In 1970, her husband died of cancer. Elizabeth, who had always dreaded becoming a widow like her mother, lived another 13 years. "Women from church sacrificed their time to stay with her just as she had sacrificed her time to care for people in Yarrow," Lillian recalls. "She never complained even though she was blind the last year of her life, and she remained independent for as long as possible. She died in 1983."[34] John Dyck, a former resident of Yarrow whose spouse was delivered by this midwife, was one of the speakers at her funeral. His biblical text, taken from

Revelation 14:13, was: "...that they may rest from their labors, for their deeds follow them!"[35]

Margaretha Klippenstein Enns, 1888-1977

By Irma Epp

Darkness had fallen on the desolate Kulundian Steppes of Siberia. Six children had been bedded down for the night in a two-room sod hut in the village of Petrovka, also known as Lichtfelde. Margaretha and Heinrich Enns were speaking in subdued tones so as not to wake their three daughters, who were sleeping across the room on a handcrafted pull-out bed. They had much to talk about. Margaretha was just recovering from typhoid fever. So far, the rest of the family had been spared. It seemed to her the right time to raise the question again.

"Are the children all asleep?" she asked.

Heinrich quietly made his way across the room and checked on the girls. "Yes," he whispered, "they are all asleep."

"Will you let me go to do the work that the Lord wants me to do?" Margaretha asked.

"Margaretha," he answered, "when we were married I thought I was getting a housewife, not a career woman." Heinrich knew what life was like in his mother-in-law's home. Helena Klippenstein was a midwife; she came and went as circumstances demanded. This was not what he had in mind for his family. But his wife was determined and sure of her calling. Choosing his words carefully, he added, "If you think this is what must be, I will let you go."

Midwife Margaretha Enns.

Later, after the birth of a fourth daughter in Petrovka, the Ennses moved to Blumenort, a day's journey by horse and wagon. Here a fourth son, Jacob, was born in 1924, but he died at five months of age. After his death, Heinrich, true to his promise, took his wife by horse and sleigh to the village of Saratov, commonly known as "Number 89," to the home of Anna and Frank Duerksen.[36] Margaretha Enns had the highest regard for Anna, a professional nurse. With her widowed mother's blessing and finances supplied by a wealthy estate owner, Anna had completed her midwifery degree in Riga, Latvia, and later worked under the direction of the well-known Dr. Tavonius at the large Muntau Hospital in the Molotschna colony. What really intrigued Margaretha was that, in addition to being an acclaimed midwife and chiropractor, Anna Duerksen also had the ability to set broken bones and use splints to restrict mobility until the bones had mended.[37]

Leaving her seven children and the running of the household to the care of her 14-year-old daughter Margaret, assisted by 13-year-old Helen, Margaretha became an apprentice of Anna Duerksen, accompanying her on her medical visits. Only once during the next three months did she have an opportunity to go home to see her family. But this work was the beginning of the fulfillment of a dream she had nurtured since childhood.[38]

Margaretha's journey had actually begun 36 years earlier on April 19, 1888, in Alexanderwohl, a village in the Molotschna colony. Her parents were Johann and Helena Wall Klippenstein. Nine children were born into their family; she was number seven. From Alexanderwohl the Klippensteins moved to Logovsk, a village in the Neu Samara Colony, which had been established in 1891 for landless families in Molotschna.[39] In this village, Margaretha Klippenstein spent her youth, received her education, and joined the flourishing Mennonite Brethren congregation.[40]

Margaretha was a striking young woman. Tall and slender with a mass of curly brown hair framing her face, she exuded confidence wherever she went.[41] Heinrich Enns, who attended the same church, fell in love with this attractive, confident young woman. They were married February 14, 1908, in the village of Donskoye with Abram Martens, the leader of the Logovsk Mennonite Brethren Church, officiating at their wedding.[42]

Shortly after their marriage, Margaretha and Heinrich left southern Russia and homesteaded in Petrovka, a newly established Siberian village in the Slavgorod Colony.[43] It was a very difficult beginning. Growing seasons were short, markets far removed, and winters brutal. Adding to their difficulties was the death of their first-born, Helena, who died of whooping cough at nine months. Hers was the first grave in the Petrovka cemetery. But seven additional children were born to Heinrich and Margaretha in Petrovka: Margaret, Helen, Sarah, Henry, John, Peter, and Anne.

During the hardships of the First World War, when all able-bodied men were drafted for military service in Russia, Heinrich Enns could depend on his wife's determination and independence. He chose the forestry service as an alternative to combat, leaving his wife to run the farm. Even though the birth of another child (Henry) was imminent, she hired a young man to ride the horses while she walked behind the plow, preparing the fields for seeding. "I don't want everything to go to weeds," she would say. "We need to have a living when my husband comes home." With most of the men gone, someone had to direct the church choir. She packed up her three daughters on a small sled, hitched the horse to the sled, and off they went to choir practice. At first she conducted a women's choir. Later, when some of the men who had remained in the village asked why they couldn't sing in the choir, they were invited to join.

In 1923 the Enns family moved to Blumenort, where Margaretha began her midwifery studies. After completing her training, she worked as a midwife in the Blumenort area for two years. Her oldest daughter recalls how Margaretha used a protective measure that she had learned from her own mother, Helena Klippenstein. When she returned from a medical visit, she would light some wet straw outside the house and stand in the smoke.When she entered the house, she would put some garlic in her mouth. She believed this regimen would protect her family from dangerous microbes that she might be in danger of transmitting.[44]

In October 1926, the Enns family, convinced that political and economic conditions in the USSR would only become worse, left Russia for Canada, arriving in Quebec on November 21. From there they traveled by train to Zeneta, Saskatchewan, where Margaretha's skills as a midwife were much in demand. There were no doctors or cars in this village, which consisted of a train station, post office, and a grocery store. Traveling by horse and buggy in the summer and by horse and sleigh in the winter, she administered medical help and delivered all the babies that were born to Mennonite families in Zeneta.[44] During this time she gave birth to another son, named after the infant Jacob she had lost in Russia.

After three years of struggling to make a living on the bleak Saskatchewan prairie, Heinrich and Margaretha and their eight children, moved to Yarrow. They arrived on February 20, 1929, and immediately purchased 10 acres of land at 1191 Stewart Road. Two years later a ninth child, George, was born with midwife Elizabeth Harms in attendance. (Following in the footsteps of mother and grandmother, George and two of his sons, Gordon and Robert, eventually became medical doctors.)

Until the 1940s, Margaretha delivered many babies in Yarrow and was frequently called to the neighbouring village of Greendale. She was well accepted as a midwife because she had a large family of her own. She knew the pain of losing children and understood immigrants who struggled against poverty. In the early years, when people were too poor to pay for her services, she never demanded payment. At times families sent foodstuffs, including fresh fruits and vegetables, in lieu of money.

Irma, Margaretha's oldest granddaughter, has vivid memories of her grandmother inviting her, a young girl, into the bedroom where the mother and infant were being cared for. She watched her grandmother pick up the little bundle and gently stroke the sleeping child's cheek with the tip of her finger. She realized that this was her grandmother's domain; this is what she had been called to do.

Often a woman waiting to give birth was brought to Grandmother's house by a friend who had use of a car. Back in Russia, whenever women had given birth at this midwife's home, the children had been sent across the street to the home of her sister, Anna Isaak. In Yarrow, the children were sent across the street to the Braun household while a bed was set up for the patient in the Ennses' living room. When bedrooms were added to this home, the former bedroom of the two daughters still at home was used as the birthing room.[46] When the Ennses built a new and larger house, they added a guest room that doubled as a care facility. Patients usually stayed for 10 days. Sometimes husbands argued persistently that their wives come home sooner because they were desperately needed, but Grandmother stood her ground. Often, their time here was the only respite from hard work that these women had. A close relationship developed between patient and caregiver, and the midwife often became a woman's confidante and counselor.

Margaretha was not only a midwife but also a nurse in Yarrow and Greendale. She was well known to Chilliwack physicians, especially Drs. McCaffery, Moore, and Patten, and she regularly consulted with them. They gave her an official brown bag embossed with the initials *M.E.* and any medical supplies she needed. Among the items in this bag were disinfectant, a thermometer, a pair of glasses, a stethoscope, syringes, string, birth registration cards, needles for injections, enema equipment, a circulatory and respiratory stimulant (injection solution), and various medications for relieving pain and such problems as diarrhea, dysentery, cholera, menstrual discomfort, and constipation. When doctors made house calls in Yarrow, they frequently asked Margaretha to continue injections as needed and report on the patient's condition. People trusted her judgment and often consulted her on medical conditions before they contacted a doctor.[47]

A similar kind of trust seems to have carried over into her involvement with the church, which in essence became her community. Soon after their arrival in Yarrow, Heinrich and Margaretha Enns were appointed deacons in the Yarrow Mennonite Brethren Church. All women and girls sat on one side in this church, and Margaretha sat near the back of the women's section, where she kept an eye on the comings and goings of the women and girls. Her two trademarks were her distinguished hats, emulating those of the Queen Mum, whom she admired, and her genuine-leather purses, in which she kept her peppermint candies. When someone became ill at church, she was tapped on the shoulder. If someone needed help or advice, she gave it gladly.

The medical bag of Margaretha Enns, given to her by Chilliwack physicians.

Margaretha's work as a midwife and nurse did not come without sacrifices from her family. Her husband was aware of the consequences of his decision to allow his wife to pursue her career. Even though he was very proud of her, he and the children sometimes resented the impositions her career made upon the family. Because the three oldest daughters were needed to run the household and look after the children, they were deprived of the advanced education they longed for. Being awakened at night and whisked away was not a pleasant experience for the children, or for the neighbours who received them—space for the children had to be found at a moment's notice. Picking up neglected housework on weekends after a week of hard labour in the hopyards was difficult, particularly for the oldest daughter still at home after her two older sisters had left to work as domestics in Vancouver and Chilliwack, and had then married and moved into their own homes. The family often felt that everything revolved around their mother's career; family birthdays and Christmas gatherings were frequently interrupted when she was called away. Relatives who attended these gatherings recall her being summoned while she was in the midst of distributing Christmas gifts and homemade fudge to the grandchildren. She would drop everything, pick up her brown bag, and leave on her mission.

At her funeral at the Mennonite Brethren Church in Yarrow on February 10, 1977, Reverend Peter D. Loewen emphasized that it was Margaretha's love for the Lord that had motivated her in her ministry. Following the service, a large funeral cortege made its way down Alder Road to the Yarrow Cemetery, thus bringing to an end a journey that had spanned three continents and many years of service.

* * *

A former Yarrow resident has noted that the often-unremunerated labours of the midwives deserve special recognition. One midwife, after delivering a baby in Yarrow, discovered that the family had no bed sheets and nightgown for the mother and no diapers for the newborn. The midwife rushed to a neighbour for help. Although this family was also poor, the mother offered one of her two well-worn nightgowns and a much-used sheet for the bed, and she cut another old sheet into squares for diapers. Though all were poor, the poor shared with the poorer. Essential to the survival of mother and infant was the kind of mutual aid exemplified by midwives in early Yarrow. In serving many people without remuneration, they epitomized the determination, dedication, and obligation to others so fundamental to the pioneer community in Yarrow.

Living East of Eden

By David Giesbrecht

In the early 1930s, Mennonites first began settling east of the B.C. Electric Railway track that marked the border of Yarrow. This tract of land, bounded, like Yarrow, on the north by the Vedder River and on the south by the Vedder Mountain, had considerable swampy subsoil and extensive woods and was often subject to seasonal flooding.

This enclave and Yarrow had only very recently been occupied by non-Aboriginals. Not until after the 1858 Cariboo gold rush did European settlers first begin "laying claim to the lands along the Lower Chilliwack River."[1] In 1898, the Marcy family moved from Lynden, Washington, to homestead on 169 acres between what are now Brown and Martin-Simmons roads.[2] According to the Marcys, only two other settlers lived near them at the time. Then in April 1905, *The Chilliwack Progress* informed its readers of the arrival of Mr. Knox, with family and stock, who "purchased the Lumsden property of 1200 acres."[3] That property included most of the land later known as Yarrow, but also a number of acres just east of the community. The area to the east, and the community that developed there, is the subject of this essay.

The scarcity of white settlers did not translate into a welcome for Mennonites moving into the Yarrow area in the 1920s and '30s. The *Progress*, for example, wrote condescendingly and demeaningly of them. As late as 1938, it allowed that the Mennonites of Yarrow "have created new problems in education, politics, labor and administration in the Chilliwack valley," but "are gradually taking their place in the general picture."[4]

As for the area east of Yarrow, in the 1930s some of the destitute Mennonite arrivals began to purchase land there. This group of east-enders had to deal with condescension not only from the established

Anglo settlers of Chilliwack and Sardis, but also from the economically improving Mennonites within Yarrow. While the attitude of Yarrow Mennonites to east-siders was friendlier than that expressed in the *Progress*, it was hardly free of prejudice.

There were notable exceptions to this attitude. Ben Schmidt, a member of a Mennonite family living east of Yarrow, recalls that the Simmonses, a local Anglican family, were a great encouragement to the early Mennonite settlers. "Not only would they show interest in the land-clearing efforts, but they would bring fresh garden produce when our gardens were not yet producing." When the Simmonses subdivided their property, they sold most of their lots to Mennonites and then "annually invited the newly settled families to their home for a Christmas party."[5] However, such personal warmth toward and concern for Mennonite settlers in this area was probably more the exception than regular practice.

A significant factor in the social geography of the early Greater Yarrow area was the B.C. Electric Railway, a major transportation corridor through Yarrow that was completed in 1910.[6] This link connected the Fraser Valley communities between New Westminster and Chilliwack, allowing for reasonably inexpensive transportation of passengers and goods. The tracks not only marked the eastern border of Yarrow; they also served as something of a social boundary separating east-siders from their friends in the core part of the community. Farmers on the east side had settled in an area proverbially known as "the Bush." In terms of the way status was assigned in the Mennonite community, these east-siders were often viewed as having "landed on the wrong side of the tracks." Few among this group were in the Yarrow leadership circle, and none were considered well-to-do.

Yarrow Mennonites were, for the most part, farmers who had recently arrived in Canada only to discover how difficult it was to make a living in the harsh environment of the Canadian Prairies. The comparatively inexpensive land east of the Yarrow railway tracks offered impoverished Prairie Mennonites the prospect of an affordable new beginning. But owing to the many social dislocations and considerable turmoil they had experienced, few east-siders had been well-educated or trained in the skills and awareness that getting established in British Columbia would require of them.

On the other hand, it was not lost on these east-siders that the very rapid growth of the Mennonite Brethren Church in Yarrow tended to preoccupy the leaders and that the leaders usually addressed pressing issues close to the centre. For instance, leaders were focused on developing the structure of the young congregation in Yarrow or attending to troublesome disciplinary cases that took much time and attention to resolve. Because leaders themselves were unsalaried and had to make their daily living just as their lay constituents did, they simply did not have time to do all the desired house visitations or to cultivate the personal contact necessary to understand the nuanced separation of east-siders from the others. This perceived neglect by the leaders, sometimes interpreted as disinterest, resulted in some marginalization of the members geographically farthest from the church, a distancing that perhaps shaped perceptions on both sides of the tracks.

Economically, the roughly 30 family units in the eastern enclave struggled to make ends meet. Mortgages were out of the question during the first years, as these new settlers had nothing to offer as collateral to secure a bank loan. Consequently, some of them had no option but to live in chicken coops until they could afford houses. The settlers were mainly subsistence farmers who relied on low-scale mixed farming. None of the farms were large by Yarrow standards. Typically, as was the experience of the Jacob Janzens on Ford Road, a family farm included a small dairy operation supplemented by a few chickens, pigs, a raspberry patch, and an assortment of fruit and nut trees. The difficulty of generating enough income to make a living while at the same time developing their farms (which included manually clearing old-growth trees and their enormous root systems) meant that farming had to be supplemented by employment wherever paid work could be found. Thus Jacob Janzen was employed as a construction assistant for the City of Chilliwack. Henry Penner supported his family by tilling raspberry fields with his horse-drawn cultivator, and later he worked as custodian at Sharon Mennonite Collegiate. During harvest season, all able-bodied people laboured at picking hops, beans, raspberries, or strawberries. A few first-generation men, such as Peter Wolfe and John Klassen, became successful carpenters. While the economy of east-siders gradually stabilized during the 1940s, this group never did realize the affluence of its Yarrow compatriots. The limited land base simply did not support major agricultural development. Furthermore, in the 1950s, second-generation residents joined the urban exodus that was also occurring in Yarrow proper, and this migration further worked against east-siders achieving economic and social parity, if only belatedly, with their friends in Yarrow.

On a more personal level, Mennonites often tagged people with nicknames. While such naming might quite innocently be intended as humorous, some nicknames also served as a convenient way of distinguishing between people with similar names. After all, there were at least three Dyck families living east of the tracks. However, tagging could also be a crude means of social control. Jacob Loewen recalls that shortly after he arrived in Yarrow, his childhood zeal for memorizing Bible verses soon earned him the unflattering label *Schriftgelehrte* (biblical and temple scribe), conveying a sense of precocious biblical literacy. In reality, his friends were telling him that his piety was insufferable.[7] East-siders were proverbially known as "bush-Mennonites." This label served not only to identify the area in which they lived, but also to remind the people that they were of lesser status and significance in public esteem.

Whatever sense of marginalization existed, the east-side settlers shared a community of values with their Yarrow cousins. Very close to the top of the list of virtues was hard work. Economic improvement was a cherished goal regardless of the paucity of money, employment opportunities, and employable skills. A particularly high value was placed on "getting by" without governmental or church financial aid. Indeed, receiving any form of public assistance was frowned upon. Because economic independence was such a priority, idlers were caricatured in stories and anecdotes that reflected fundamental convictions regarding the sanctity of hard work. Given this aggressive work ethic, it followed that some east-side parents considered athletic activities for their children a frivolous use of time and perhaps even viewed them as antithetical to the Christian way. Being labeled idle or lazy was a severe indictment.

Religiously, the majority of the first-generation adults in the eastern enclave had their faces set toward the church in Yarrow. To many, the house of worship represented a spiritual Eden, if not in terms of the real, surely of the ideal. Most families affiliated with the Mennonite Brethren Church and several with the United Mennonite Church. In both of these congregations, and in the homes of numerous members, deep concern for loved ones still in the USSR, many in the Gulag Archipelago, lent poignancy to conversations. This shared concern was one of many bonds between Yarrow residents and the east-siders. Moreover, whether Mennonite Brethren or United Mennonite, those from the east side and those from Yarrow alike tended to be loyal to the ideals and teachings of the believing community. Thus east-siders participated assiduously in the activities of their local congregations. For example, Henry Penner was a long-time member of the Sharon Mennonite Collegiate board of trustees. Peter Wolfe served on the church council. John Giesbrecht, an ordained minister, took his turn preaching intermittently, and John Klassen was involved in the music ministry of the church. Moreover, deeply grateful for the assistance that the Mennonite Central Committee had lent them and their parents in earlier years, most of the adults strongly supported this organization and welcomed opportunities to be actively involved with it.

For east-side settlers, as for most of the Yarrow Mennonites, the church became both the centre of their spiritual lives and the hub of their social activities. Attending two services on Sunday, morning and evening, and Sunday School in the afternoon was normal. A church business session, a choir rehearsal, a special-interest meeting during the week to hear a missionary report, and a Saturday-evening prayer meeting left little room for non-church-based activities. In addition, some families met weekly during winter months for home Bible study. The spiritual zeal exemplified by their elders was not lost on some of the second generation. During the 1950s, several young men who lived east of Eden organized a Christian club (dubbed "the church in the wildwood") that met in an abandoned building on the Jacob Janzen farm. Perhaps the club was an alternative to the popular but somewhat distant gathering of young people at the Alexander Voth place in Yarrow.

Despite their limited economic means, east-siders promoted and encouraged the education of their children. Indeed, education, particularly Christian education, was a paramount goal, evident in the strong east-side support of Saturday German Religious School as an important extension of children's religious education. (This tutelage was often resented by students from the east side and Yarrow alike.) Many east-siders also enthusiastically supported the construction of Sharon Mennonite Collegiate in Yarrow and found ways to pay the high cost of tuition for their children to attend this school. Interestingly, east of the tracks everyone seemed to know which children went to public schools and which attended the private institution.

Of course, Mennonites in Yarrow and on the other side of the tracks encountered difficulties common to any strongly ethnocentric immigrant population that suddenly finds itself thrust into a new and largely alien environment. These newcomers were called on to negotiate a host of first-generation issues of adaptation, such as understanding prevalent Canadian social structures and cultural institutions, learning a new language, becoming knowledgeable about new crops, and learning to trust local, provincial, and national governments. Filling out government statistical forms might ignite fears that government inventories of agricultural production could be a precursor to the appropriation of these assets, as had been the case in Russia. There was also the exasperating problem of not adequately understanding non-Mennonite neighbours or of being misunderstood by them. Almost always troubling to the Mennonite parents was the marriage of their children to non-Mennonites; even more disconcerting was marriage to non-Christians. Consequently, it did not take long for a sharp cultural divide to develop in some families. The social division between the east side and Yarrow proper sometimes accentuated this divide.

Difficulties notwithstanding, the families on the east side of the tracks tended to exhibit resilience more than equal to the burdens of cultural adaptation. In part, their strength derived from a capacity to pool resources and work together at common tasks such as making hay, slaughtering pigs, removing stumps, and cultivating larger fields. Sharing a vehicle to attend church services was a form of mutual assistance one could always count on. Mutuality also included occasional financial loans to individuals who could not afford the high interest charged by banks. In such circumstances, a handshake rather than a contract would seal the conditions of a loan.

Most fundamentally, these families viewed themselves as rooted in a practical Anabaptist faith tradition. They longed for a spirituality that had sustained them through some of the worst horrors and indignities the 20th century had meted out. Ben Schmidt recalls that the great desire of his parents was to "bring their children up in the Lord. … We were 'poor' materially, as were all families east of the tracks, but we had a sure foundation of faith."[8] And that perspective helped him and many other east-siders retain a confident Christian worldview.

The Early Years of the Mennonite Brethren Church

By David Giesbrecht

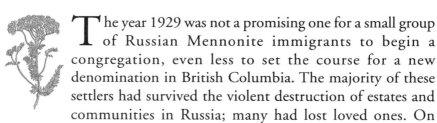

The year 1929 was not a promising one for a small group of Russian Mennonite immigrants to begin a congregation, even less to set the course for a new denomination in British Columbia. The majority of these settlers had survived the violent destruction of estates and communities in Russia; many had lost loved ones. On arriving in Canada, most had settled in the Prairie provinces, where they were greeted by several years of miserable weather, crop failures, and a farming recession. They were also regarded with suspicion owing to their Germanic roots and immigrant status. As a result, these Mennonites developed a deep-seated determination to succeed in their new country and rebuild a community-based congregational life they had once known.

Soon after their arrival in Yarrow, they began meeting for worship services and Sunday School "in the old farmhouse on Majuba Hill that had accommodated the first six families that arrived in Yarrow in the Spring of 1928."[1] With the construction of a number of family residences shortly thereafter, meeting sites for worship alternated in individual homes.

The subsequent rapid arrival of Mennonites from the Prairies quickly made such small meeting spaces inadequate. In the summer of 1928, this problem was temporarily alleviated when a one-room public school was built in Yarrow. Here was a public facility that allowed both Mennonite Brethren, led by ministers such as Peter Dyck and Jacob Epp, and United Mennonite believers, led by Nickolai Bahnman, to worship together, "taking turns at leading and preaching."[2] In this schoolhouse, Yarrow Mennonites marked their first Thanksgiving and missions celebrations on Sunday, November 4, 1928. According to a report in the denominational newspaper, the little schoolhouse was brightly decorated with an assortment of garden vegetables, including corn "that reached almost to the ceiling."[3] On this festive occasion, morning and afternoon services featured a Bible lesson, four sermons, and some rousing choir music. One of the speakers, Reverend Nickolai Bahnman, urged his hearers to be grateful for the abundance and beauty in their new homeland. The donation to missions that afternoon amounted to $10.

As the community infrastructure of Yarrow began to take shape, the desire among Mennonite Brethren to organize formally as a congregation led to a charter meeting of 96 members on February 3, 1929. The minutes of that first meeting indicate that a well-organized five-point agenda was presented to those assembled. The issue of formal organization was quickly resolved with unanimous affirmation. Similarly, the selection of the first leading minister elicited very little discussion. The aging Peter Dyck, an experienced ordained minister, had shown a gift for preaching and leadership, and so he was elected without any opposition. At the same time, Kornelius Klassen was elected his assistant and recording secretary.

Earliest Mennonite settlers, Good Friday, 1928. Back, l-r: Jacob Dyck, Aron Jantzen, George Epp, David Rempel, Nickolai Reimer, Jr., Jacob Krause, John Braun, Isaak Sawatsky, Peter Giesbrecht, Sr., George Doerksen, John Jantzen, Jr., John Bargen, George Hooge, David Giesbrecht. Front, l-r: Nickolai Reimer, Sr., Gerhard Hooge, Johann Jantzen, Sr., Reverend Jacob Epp.

However, the weighty issue of who qualified for immediate membership was more difficult to resolve. After a lengthy discussion, the people at this meeting agreed to include three classes of individuals: those who had a membership certificate in hand from another Mennonite Brethren congregation; those who were members of a Mennonite Brethren congregation elsewhere and were taking steps to secure a transfer to Yarrow; and any person who was a member of an evangelical church, had been baptized by immersion, and now wanted to join this congregation. After the reading of three passages from New Testament epistles concerning God and the church (Colossians 1:18, 1 Corinthians 1:27, and 1 Corinthians 3:11), the members agreed to become an independent congregation, "solemnly promising to abide by the confession of faith of the Mennonite Brethren Churches of North America."[4] A year later the Yarrow church was officially accepted into the Northern District Canadian Conference of Mennonite Brethren Churches.

From the outset, leading ministers in this church were elected by a majority of those voting (all males) at membership meetings. Within a year of the charter meeting, Peter Dyck moved from Yarrow. The church now prevailed upon a young, energetic, and talented man to accept pastoral leadership. In 1931, Reverend Johann A. Harder commenced a ministry that was to continue for 18 years, the longest pastoral tenure in the history of the church. Harder was a natural leader and administrator who combined a gift for preaching with an enormous capacity for work. In addition to his heavy pastoral duties, he taught in the Elim Bible School and for many years held offices in the Northern District Canadian Conference and on both the Canadian and the North American Mennonite Brethren Board of Missions. Because work in the church was unsalaried, he was at the same time obliged to earn his living by farming.

The spiritual nurturing of members under his charge was Harder's greatest concern. Although he worked with a team of ministers, including Abram Nachtigal, Petrus Martens, Peter D. Loewen and Aron Rempel, his frustration with the burdens and overwhelming tasks thrust on his shoulders grew as the membership continued to increase. Torn by inner conflict, he informed the church in September 1940 that he could no longer live with his conscience while he was neglecting the spiritual care of individual members. His unexpected resignation sent shock waves through the church and community.

Those assembled pled with him to reconsider. After "intense inner agonizing," he agreed at a subsequent meeting to continue as pastor on condition that his tenure be understood as only temporary—that is, until a replacement could be found—and that Abram Nachtigal be appointed to assist him in the pastoral care of the church. Such was the regard of the congregation for their leader that, on receiving this news, they responded "with joy and thanksgiving to God for this victory." Harder served for another nine years, greatly influencing the development of the church and its ministries.

While this young church elected its leaders by male-membership vote, church governance was vested mainly in the non-elected church council, or *Vorberat*, a term literally meaning "an advisory council charged with bringing matters forward." During the first decade of the church, this leadership group consisted of all the ordained ministers, of which there were a dozen or more at any given time, but no lay members. These men deliberated on all issues of interest to the church, including very delicate matters of personal behaviour, prior to forwarding the results of their discussions to the voting members of the church. Such a tightly controlled leadership structure soon caused unrest. The problem of governance came to a head at a church business meeting on August 16, 1937, when members openly questioned who should serve on this council and how large it ought to be. The congregation urged that only a few ministers henceforth be included and that the majority on the council be elected from the membership. In an extraordinary development at this meeting, all the existing members of the council tendered their resignations. It was further agreed that the council would henceforth consist of 15 members and that the majority of these would be elected on an at-large basis. Thus a more representative governing body emerged within the first decade of the church.

The congregation flourished. Membership statistics show that in its first two decades the church grew by an average of 50 members a year, although growth patterns tended to be erratic, especially toward the end of the 1940s. The congregation reached an all-time high of 971 members in 1948. The pre-eminent place this church now held within the Provincial Mennonite Brethren Conference and the Canadian Conference, largely because of its numbers, was not to last. The following year saw a notable decrease in membership, and this decline has continued unabated into the 1990s.

Yarrow Mennonite Brethren Church Growth (1929-1949)

Year	Membership
1929	96
1935	237
1940	434
1945	740
1948	971
1949	875

The well-being of the rapidly growing church called for a carefully regulated order of services. By decision of the membership, Sunday-morning worship services were to begin at 9:30 a.m. with an invocation and a call for public prayer. Two sermons and stirring choir renditions were always considered central to the program. The principal feature in the Sunday-evening service was another sermon. Furthermore, the first Sunday evening of each month was set aside for a communion service. Until 1955, common communion cups were used in this service and "the brotherly kiss" at the conclusion was accepted practice (men kissed men and women kissed women). Every third Sunday evening featured a youth program. Sunday School classes were convened in the afternoon, partly to resolve the pressing problem of inadequate space and partly to keep children (students) and young people (teachers) engaged in the life of the church.

The Yarrow Mennonite Brethren Church's second building, dedicated in 1938. Within less than a decade, its seating capacity of almost 1,200 was inadequate.

Church seating arrangements were deemed critical to preserving proper decorum and order, especially after the new sanctuary was built in 1938. It was formally decided that families were not to sit together but would have their assigned areas in the four long series of pews separated from each other by aisles. Women sat on the far left side, facing the choir. Girls sat in the left-of-centre pews, and behind them, women with very young girls. Boys were required to occupy the front pews just right of the centre aisle, where appointed monitors would keep a sharp eye on the sometimes-inattentive ones. Behind them sat the men with younger boys. Older men were assigned to pews on the far right, where they faced the "preacher's loft containing thirty to forty men, most of whom had at one time or another preached the Word."[5] In practice, this arrangement no doubt served tradition more than decorum.

A rapidly growing congregation generated a full and varied business agenda. Consequently, congregational meetings serving many purposes were frequently called; there were 19 such meetings in 1930, and 24 in 1931. At one meeting, all candidates for membership were obligated to share their personal testimony as a way of ensuring that only those who professed a personal faith in almighty God and in Jesus as God's son and saviour of humankind were admitted to membership. Then there were many housekeeping issues to be decided, such as determining the date of the next Sunday School picnic or the speaker for a forthcoming Bible-exposition conference (*Bibelbesprechung*).

On June 26, 1932, members considered how to cover the cost of bringing Dr. Abraham Unruh, the noted Bible expositor from Manitoba, to present lectures in Yarrow. Because such expenses could not be drawn from the meagre church budget, it was agreed at this meeting that 15 members would each contribute one dollar, and 30 members 50 cents each. Not to be left out, one member pledged to add 25 cents to ensure Dr. Unruh's appearance. Significantly, the financial plight of individual members was often sympathetically addressed at membership meetings. The congregation would agree, for example, to pay the medical costs for an impoverished parishioner or to provide a so-called love offering for someone in need whose service was particularly appreciated.

But it was also at these meetings that all manner of ethical behaviour was examined with pontifical concern. No known infraction seemed to escape censure. At the meeting on August 16, 1937, council members were admonished for their indiscretion in publicly discussing what had been a very private council matter. On another occasion, Reverend

Harder expressed his grave concern that during public prayer time in the worship services "many brothers were not praying in a worthy manner." Displeasure was frequently voiced over inappropriate dress in general and at weddings in particular. At the meeting of April 15, 1939, married women were reminded to attend church services with their heads covered. It was further stipulated "that in regards to clothing for both brothers and sisters, the church expects all members to respect the Holy Spirit, whereby it is understood that brothers as well as sisters will be so attired that all parts of the body, including arms for sisters, will be covered."[6]

As a result of discussions at these meetings and the admonitory sermons preached during worship services, members clearly understood that wearing gaudy or overly fashionable dress, bathing at public beaches, attending theatres, and belonging to secret societies were strictly prohibited.

Church business meetings were also the venue for settling serious doctrinal differences, often through a ruling. One case, which carried on over numerous meetings, involved a member who questioned the customary reference to the Bible as "God's Word," arguing instead that the Bible refers to itself as Scriptures. He also questioned the view that every word of the Bible as we have it is accurate. Several official delegations visited this member to admonish him as well as assure him of the church's continuing prayers for him; then the visitations were suspended. Eventually he sent word that the church was no longer to trouble God on his account as he had now come to the correct understanding of this matter of his own accord.

In the interest of fostering faithful discipleship (as members understood this important Mennonite teaching), much time and energy at church membership meetings were devoted to matters of discipline. In some ways these meetings served a function similar to the confessional in the Roman Catholic Church. Individuals would appear before the congregation, tearfully express repentance for having shamed the Lord, and, by extension, the church, and then beg the forgiveness of those assembled. The infractions in these cases included serious disputes between individuals, taking unfair economic advantage of others, misappropriations (as in the case where a member confessed to having illegally tapped into a source of electrical power), consumption of alcohol, and, frequently, matters of sexual indiscretion. Marriage to someone outside the Mennonite Brethren fold was frowned upon; marriage to an unbeliever or to someone assumed to be an unbeliever invariably resulted in excommunication.

Disciplinary action could take one or more of several forms. The mildest censure consisted of a "wait-and-see" period of time, especially for cases in which the congregation was uncertain that repentance had been genuine. A more severe response required that the erring member withdraw from serving in a church-related function. In addition, the erring member might be barred from participating in communion and, perhaps, also be asked not to attend any services for a stipulated period of time. The severest form of discipline was excommunication from membership. Excommunication customarily included a social ban that in the earlier years prohibited even conversing with the banned individual. In all cases, once the form of discipline was decided, several male members of the congregation were personally authorized to deliver the verdict, which was usually buttressed by several pertinent passages from the Bible. As intended, such methods of discipline caught the attention of all members, not only those being disciplined. However, these measures seem rarely to have achieved their intended purpose. With a few notable exceptions, there is scant evidence in the minutes that individuals were brought back into good standing of the church after having been thus publicly censured.

Vital to the life of this congregation from its earliest days was the development of strong ministries within the church. The importance of nurturing children was signaled when on February 10, 1929, exactly one week after its inaugural meeting, the church elected Johann Neufeld as Sunday School superintendent. With the election of Peter D. Loewen to this position in December 1937, the Yarrow Sunday School began to flower. At its crest in 1953, this Sunday School "included 461 students with forty classes being taught by seventy-two teachers."[7] Loewen served the Yarrow church as Sunday School superintendent for 26 years.

As evident in the objectives of the Sunday School, the Yarrow church placed a premium on knowing the Bible. Thus, austere conditions notwithstanding, within a year of the organizational meeting members viewed the establishment of a Bible school as a priority. In 1930, the church launched its own Bible-training school, eventually named Elim. Enrollment peaked at 152 students in the winter of 1941-42. However, the founding of Sharon Mennonite Collegiate Institute in the mid-1940s introduced competition for students and finances that Elim could not withstand. Given the dwindling enrollment, the church had no alternative but to close its Bible School in 1955.

The Yarrow Mennonite Brethren Church was synonymous with excellence in choral music. Mennonites seemed to have arrived in Yarrow singing. Over the years, this church was nurtured by a rich assortment of musical groups and gifted musicians. In time Yarrow became known for its choral festivals (*Sängerfeste*). George Reimer, who directed the church choir for 24 years, cultivated a love for choral music that saw the church through times of joyous celebration and rancorous struggle. This musical tradition included, at various times, a large youth choir, a male choir (first organized by Rudy Boschman), a woman's choir (directed by Anna Bartsch), and a men's quartet.

Central to the congregation's purpose, which in 1937 was defined as "But we preach Christ crucified," was the desire to offer a public witness to its understanding of the Christian faith. This desire was translated into support for "home" and "foreign" missions, with a clear division between them. By the early 1940s, the enthusiasm for home missions resulted in local outreach activities in communities such as Haney, Pitt Meadows, and Hope. Active in these evangelistic and educational ministries among the "unchurched" were Abram Esau, Jacob Loewen, Henry Brucks, Frank Peters, Peter Neufeldt, and Nick Dyck, to name only a few. With the growth of the West Coast Children's Mission, which had its headquarters in Yarrow, members of the church became widely involved both in administering this outreach and conducting Daily Vacation Bible Schools throughout the province, from the Fraser Valley to the central and northern Interior. Thus, within a relatively short time, this ministry was not restricted to children. These early outreach efforts set an evangelistic agenda for Mennonite Brethren in the province that continues to this day and has contributed significantly to the establishment of almost 100 Mennonite Brethren congregations throughout British Columbia, which hold services in more than a dozen languages.

But it was in the promotion and advocacy of global missions that the Yarrow church singularly applied its energies. The need to fund such outreach was the catalyst for scheduling frequent missions auctions. Women's fellowship groups were particularly active in contributing crafts and baking to these auctions, thereby garnering significant financial support for missions. Another strong agent on behalf of the foreign missions commitment was the Elim Bible School, which inculcated in its students the importance of proselytizing and evangelism. Consistent with its stated mission and priorities, the congregation sent many of its members on overseas assignments through agencies such as the Mennonite Brethren Board of Missions or the Mennonite Central Committee. Among the large contingent of career missionaries that set out from Yarrow were Susie Brucks (Congo), Henry and Elsie Brucks (Congo), Jacob and Anne Loewen (Colombia), Abe and Sarah Esau (Congo), Anne Friesen (Japan), Irma and Walter Sawatsky (Congo), Elsie Peters (South Africa), and Harold and Alma Hide (Nigeria).

The settlers who met on February 3, 1929, to organize the Yarrow Mennonite Brethren Church could not have imagined that they were laying the foundation for what would become, by the end of the century, one of the rapidly growing denominations in British Columbia. In beliefs, they adopted the creed of the Mennonite Brethren Conference; in practice, they and their children sought to develop a version of a 20th-century Anabaptist spiritual community, even if, during its first several decades, this congregation reflected many of the characteristic features of the renewalist southern Russian Mennonite churches to which it was historically linked.

History of the Yarrow United Mennonite Church

By Veronica Barkowsky Thiessen

The first group of Mennonite settlers in the Yarrow area, 16 families, came in 1928 from Saskatchewan, Manitoba, and Mexico, where Mennonites emigrating from Russia had settled. Many others followed during the next 20 years, mainly from the three Prairie provinces: Alberta, Saskatchewan, and Manitoba. The early settlers belonged to two Mennonite denominations: the United Mennonites and the Mennonite Brethren, with a larger number in the latter.

Although these two organizations had become separate denominations in Russia in 1860, little thought was given to this division during the pioneering years of the Mennonite Yarrow settlement. Religiously, the settlers had one common goal: to meet for worship. At the outset it was decided to meet in homes, primitive as these were. But they needed someone to lead them in worship services. In Johann Braun they found a member of the United Mennonites capable of leadership. Later Jacob Epp of the Mennonite Brethren served the group. Services were conducted exclusively in the German language, which was the official church language of the settlers and was used in the United Mennonite Church until the end of 1979. In January 1980, this congregation made the change to English, with some opposition.[1]

With the influx of additional settlers in 1928, even the largest house was no longer adequate for church services. The municipal school board granted permission to use the new one-room elementary school building on Central Road for religious services. The Mennonite Brethren and United Mennonites held joint services in this little schoolhouse until 1930, when a second one-room school building was constructed next to it. Subsequently, the two denominations separated, each using one of the school buildings for its services.[2]

It was at this time that Nickolai W. Bahnman, an ordained Mennonite minister and *Ältester* (elder) from Kansas, came to Yarrow to assist Johann Braun in preaching and teaching in the United Mennonite Church.[3] As an elder (a title of distinction and elevated responsibility and authority accorded to a small number of ministers in the General Conference Mennonite Church), Bahnman was a welcome addition to the tiny population of Mennonite settlers. His tenure, however, was brief. Because land in nearby Greendale was less expensive than in Yarrow, he moved to Greendale and established a United Mennonite congregation there under his leadership. But until 1943, he continued to serve the Yarrow United Mennonite group as elder whenever he was needed. Because the Yarrow group remained small in the early years, it affiliated with the Greendale church, although it met independently in Yarrow for Sunday services. In 1930, Aron Jantzen was selected as the Yarrow congregation's first deacon.[4] When Johann Braun transferred to the Mennonite Brethren Church in 1931, the group was without a pastor; they chose Aron Jantzen and Wilhelm Schellenberg to serve as leaders. When Jantzen relocated to Langley, B.C., Gerhard Loewen was selected to assist Schellenberg. But because

The original Yarrow United Mennonite Church meeting house, built in 1938.

Loewen resided in Greendale, weekly transportation to Yarrow became an insurmountable obstacle. Even the modest fare of 35 cents for a return-trip ticket on the B.C. Electric train was difficult to raise in those days.

Early in the spring of 1938, the Yarrow United Mennonite group completed plans to construct a church on Eckert Road on an eighth of an acre acquired from Dietrich Hildebrandt. A modest 40- by 28-foot building was erected by means of donations and volunteer labour. Only the chief carpenter, Mr. Goetz, was paid for his services—a sum of $50.00.[5]

In October 1938, the building was dedicated, and on October 25 the congregation, numbering 31 members, officially organized as the Yarrow United Mennonite Church and simultaneously joined the Conference of Mennonites, British Columbia. Elder Bahnman made this possible by providing leadership and counsel. Cornelius Janzen was chosen as deacon, but he resigned shortly thereafter because he felt that he was not suitable for this position. At the same time, the first church council was selected: Johann Dyck, Johann Toews, Peter Klassen, and the first treasurer, Abram Thiessen. At the conclusion of this historic meeting, the congregation sang *"Schenk uns Vater Deinen Segen"* ("Father, grant us your blessing").[6]

Elder Bahnman, who had served as instructor in the Swift Current Bible School, assisted in filling the position of pastor by encouraging Johann Julius Klassen, a teacher at the Swift Current school, to come to Yarrow. After much deliberation, Johann Klassen and his family moved to Yarrow in March 1938. His ordination and dedication as leading minister took place in a special service on December 26 of that year, with Elder Bahnman officiating.[7]

Sunday School instruction and a youth program were begun almost from the time the congregation was organized. In 1940, Wilhelm Schellenberg was appointed the first Sunday School superintendent. In the preceding year, Franz Klassen had been elected as deacon to replace Cornelius Janzen. Mathilda Lehn Hildebrandt soon established the first women's missionary circle (*Frauenverein*).

Since in those days everyone was poor, the women's circle could raise only two dollars in two collections. This was forwarded to the Eaton's mail-order service with a request to send the maximum amount of sewing material that two dollars could buy. Eaton's sent ten dollars' worth of material, and the women were ecstatic. Immediately they began to prepare items for an auction. The first auction produced $140. These proceeds were allocated mostly for care parcels shipped to Mennonites in Russia.[8] As the minutes of the sewing circle note in plain and poignant words: "Although they were struggling with poverty themselves, they still remembered the poor and needy of the world." In 1961, the women's circle numbered 44 members, and it continued to offer help to the needy until the late 1980s, when it was dissolved due to the advanced age and poor health of its remaining members.

During the annual convention of the Conference of Mennonites of British Columbia in January 1939, discussion among some of the women revealed an interest in organizing a meeting of all the churchwomen's clubs. In sharing their experiences and voicing problems, they felt they would benefit from each other and learn how they, as women, could participate more effectively in the Lord's work. The response to a proposal that such a meeting be arranged was favourable, and an invitation by the Yarrow sisters to host the meeting at their church was accepted. The very next month, 125 women met, enthusiastic and keenly interested in their common work. They chose as their motto "My grace is sufficient for thee" (2 Corinthians 12:9), which remains their motto to this day. When this historic meeting day concluded, individual clubs banded together in one overall women's conference now known as the B.C. Mennonite Women in Mission. Meta Regier Bahnman, spouse of the well-known elder, served as the first president of the women's conference and continued in this position for 20 years. Elizabeth Schmidt Dueck served as first vice-president, Mathilda Lehn Hildebrandt as treasurer, and Irene Thiessen as secretary.[9]

From 1938 to 1948, the United Mennonite congregation experienced growth in many areas. In 1942, hymnals and a pump organ were purchased. In the same year a choir was formed, and Peter Martens was appointed director. In October 1944, the congregation was able to pay the Canadian Conference the final loan installment of $65 for the church building. With this payment the church was debt-free.[10]

At this time, Elder Bahnman was no longer able to serve the Yarrow congregation in important functions. Thus the congregation requested that Elder J.B. Wiens of Vancouver assume the role of elder in the Yarrow congregation in matters such as communion and baptism (since these functions were reserved for elders, and Yarrow's leading minister was not an elder). Elder Wiens willingly accepted this invitation.[11] The congregation continued to grow and improve its financial condition.

The minutes of the 1945 annual business meeting report that the congregation sent a contribution of $25 to a Mennonite church in Winnipeg for its building, along with this note: "If we are faithful with our little things God will honor this and bless us."[12]

The post-Second World War years saw a number of changes, including the addition of several ordained ministers for service in the church: in 1946, Isaak Penner; in 1948, Peter J. Klassen (a renowned essayist, poet, and storyteller known as "Onkel Peter"); and in 1954, Martin Unrau. In 1954, Peter Kehler and Henry Claassen were also elected as candidates for the ministry. In 1955, Henry J. Friesen was ordained as deacon and served the congregation for 19½ years. For a brief period in the 1950s, Henry P. Neufeldt of the Mennonite Brethren Church directed the church choir and trained a new young conductor to assume this role. In the summer of 1957, after 19 years of continuous service, Pastor Johann Klassen notified the church of his imminent resignation from his position in order to further his education. A month later Pastor Peter W. Dyck of Chilliwack accepted the position of leading minister. He was installed as pastor in November and served as senior pastor until the end of 1970 and as elder from 1959 to 1979. In 1958, the former ministerial candidate Henry Claassen was ordained as minister. Claassen, who would eventually serve as senior pastor (1971-1979), was one of many European war refugees who had come to Yarrow and joined the United Mennonite Church (Claassen arrived in 1951). In 1979, Henry H. Epp, senior pastor, was given the authority to perform the duties of elder.[13]

In the late 1940s, the membership had increased so rapidly—mainly because of the influx of Mennonite refugees from war-ravaged Europe—that the sanctuary had to be expanded by 20 feet. The enlarged and renovated building was dedicated on December 11, 1949.[14] Less than four years later, the congregation purchased adjoining land to the north to solve the ever-worsening parking problem, and in 1956 land was acquired on the south side of the church property in order to create yet more parking space. By 1957, attendance at Sunday School had increased so much that a new building program had to be undertaken. Since 1938, the membership had increased from 31 to well over 200. Some 130 children now attended Sunday School, 20-40 participated in the young adults' Bible-study class, and enrollments in catechism instruction were substantial. The following year the membership voted almost unanimously to construct a new church. The

New Yarrow United Mennonite Church building.

sod was turned on October 20, 1958, and the dedication of the newly completed church building was held on June 21 of the following year. Significantly, this service was also the occasion for the ordination of Reverend Peter W. Dyck as elder. Finally the congregation had a new, modern building, sufficient Sunday School space, and its very own elder. In October 1963, the church celebrated its 25th anniversary, at which time the mortgage papers on the new building were ceremoniously burned. By this time, church members numbered fewer than 200, and membership continued to decline as Mennonites left Yarrow in increasing numbers to find employment.

But the church continues to be a strong local institution, offering regular worship services, Sunday School instruction, Bible studies, Bible conferences, young people's activities, women's societies, and home and foreign missions endeavours. It vigorously promotes and supports the work of the Mennonite Central Committee and the Red Cross. Other ministries include inter-church Vacation Bible School, clubs, community-oriented worship services in the Yarrow Park, and the inter-church seniors' festival (*Altenfest*). Its presence is also evident in its volunteers for the fire department, Yarrow Waterworks, and various charities, and in its support of the annual Yarrow Day celebrations.

The Foreign Missionary as Hero

By Peter Penner

In the 1950s, when I was much younger, I sometimes changed the topic of conversation with the flippant statement that I wished I could be either a guest conductor or a missionary on furlough. What lay behind that remark? Both the conductor and the missionary seemed to get a lot of adulation from their audiences. I had frequently observed that the missionary on furlough was a person who got special treatment. In contrast to home missionaries, once "foreign" missionaries (those working abroad) had been ordained—in the case of women, commissioned after 1957—the structures in the constituency kept them in highest esteem unless there was a "fall from grace."

The Missionary on Furlough

Esther Epp Harder remembers some of the occasions when missionary heroism was fostered: annual missions conferences; harvest festivals; and reports by missionaries on furlough or by members of the Mission Board to Sunday school, collegiate, and Bible school classes. These meetings would end with a prayer that God would call someone in the audience to work in the far-flung mission field. On such occasions, even though few missionaries went abroad primarily for adventure, a sense of adventure was strongly present, which supporters—family, friends, and congregation—shared vicariously. Those attending would be rewarded with an illustrated report, curios, and colourful attire from the foreign country. They reacted with wonder at the objects and with reverence for the speaker. Esther Harder remembers how Susie Brucks, for example, loved to gather the children around to help her "unroll this thing—[the] skin of a very large snake … and she also showed us 'lantern pictures'. ... Undoubtedly, children especially were awed. All of this was a bit scary."[1]

This view of the missionaries was reinforced by the Board of Foreign Missions, which sent solicitous letters of concern and requests for financial support. The board, too, enjoyed an elevated status in the Conference. When a board member such as the spellbinding John B. Toews came to Yarrow to speak, he could make people believe that the mission effort formed part of the bulwark against the powers of hell. When he spoke at special conferences in his inimitable rhetorical style about their missionaries, people believed God's hand was on these missionaries in a remarkable way.

Many in the constituency gave generously to make the missionaries' work possible. For example, the Riediger family of Morden, Manitoba, gave Henry and Elsie Brucks a new vehicle during their first furlough in the mid-1950s and paid the extra expenses when the Bruckses had to change this vehicle for another. When it required certain modifications, these were also taken care of. When they were back home in Yarrow, the Bruckses represented the Foreign Missions program, the board that supervised them, and the church that was being formed in the Congo mission compounds. During the missionaries' furlough, the congregation gave them a residence and helped with their living expenses. Thus it is not surprising that missionaries were thought to receive special treatment.

Although few people probably realized how minimal the missionaries' pension expectations were, everyone knew missionaries' earnings were relatively low and thus deserved to be supplemented in tangible ways. Yet there were other important reasons behind such assistance. The missionary was the congregation's representative or substitute, going to foreign countries on its behalf. Jacob Loewen reflected in the late 1960s that some church members saw their missionaries "as a kind of substitute for [them] in service, suffering, and sacrifice." Many experienced qualms for evading similar self-sacrificing service, so were prepared to give money in support of others. In this sense the member "vicariously participate[d] in the [missionary's] self-abnegation and thus atone[d], at least in part, for his own selfish life."[2] No doubt there was also vicarious participation in the missionaries' adventures. Their travelogues were eagerly read in the church papers of the day. They had ventured to exotic places halfway around the world, a rare and enviable experience for the average church member in Yarrow during that period. Who else in Yarrow in the 1940s went to distant schools and thereafter even farther afield to work with people whose way of life was alien yet fascinating to those who heard the reports with rapt attention? Identifying with the missionaries encouraged the congregation to support them financially.

To come home on furlough confirmed that the missionary family or single person was committed to returning abroad for another term. Everyone knew that returning missionaries had already served six years in a radically different culture, that they had been forced to acquire another language or two, as in the Congo, and that they had laboured in a climate and human environment where the mortality rate was high. The Congo was administered in French, and learning this language proved most difficult for many missionaries—in some cases, more difficult than learning a tribal language. Henry Brucks once admitted to Susie that he had been almost "done in" by French-language studies. The dedication needed to fulfill the missionaries' commitment elicited prayers on their behalf, for they would in all likelihood continue to be subjected to greater risks than in mission endeavours at home. Missionaries thus became the recipients of special attention in the prayers of family, friends, and congregation.

Susie and Henry Brucks as Types

While noting other foreign missionaries from Yarrow, I have selected the missionary members of the Brucks family as my principal examples on the grounds that they best represent the reverence in Yarrow for foreign missionaries during the 1940s and '50s. Siblings Henry and Susie Brucks were in fact idealized and by some perhaps idolized.

Their father, Henry Brucks, Sr., had been a teacher, preacher, and artist in Russia. In 1926 he and his wife and their eight children immigrated to Canada. After 12 years in Coaldale, Alberta, where another child was born, the family moved to Yarrow. Two of the children, Susie (1909-1983) and Henry (1918-1987), felt personally called to go abroad as missionaries. Without much educational preparation, Susie went to the Belgian Congo in 1944 under the Board of Foreign Missions. After five years there, she proceeded to Belgium for French-language studies. Henry, on the other hand, enrolled at the Mennonite Brethren Bible College in 1946, during John B. Toews's tenure as president. While there, Brucks and Henry Poetker launched a radio program that became the Gospel Light Hour and, subsequently, Mennonite Brethren Communications.

At the Mennonite Brethren Bible College, Henry met Elsie Hiebert, and they were married in 1948. By that time they were candidates for work in the Belgian Congo, a field adopted by the Board of Foreign Missions in 1943. Henry was ordained in Yarrow in August 1948, the year of the great Fraser Valley flood. Before leaving for their assignment, Henry and Elsie attended Tabor College, Hillsboro, Kansas. Then they traveled by ship to Belgium for about a year of French-language studies. Their work with the mission in the Congo was interrupted by revolutions, first in 1960, then in 1964. As a result, the Board of Foreign Missions returned Susie, Henry, and Elsie to Canada. Elsie, now widowed for some years, lives in retirement in Kelowna.[3]

It should be acknowledged that Susie and her brother were not the only missionaries associated with Yarrow. They were only the first of a small cavalcade of missionaries who had resided in Yarrow, some from the beginning. Abram Esau and his wife, Sarah Martens, were both baptized into the Yarrow congregation, and in 1948 they went to the Belgian Congo.[4] While Heinrich Bartsch and his family had gone to the Congo from Manitoba more than a decade earlier, they eventually settled in Yarrow, where he promoted missions for a number of years. Herman and Tina Lenzmann followed the Bartsch family to the Congo in 1937, but stayed only two years. Yet as the pastor who succeeded John A. Harder, Lenzmann promoted mission efforts abroad and at home in the West Coast Children's Mission. As for Harder, he was an influential member of the Board of Foreign Missions.

Nor should one overlook two other Yarrow couples, both of whom went to South America: David and Annie Peters Nightingale, and Jacob and Anne Enns Loewen. Following some years of preparation, the Nightingales went to Quito, Ecuador, where they served on the staff of the international religious radio station HCJB, beginning in 1953. Jacob and Anne Loewen went to Colombia in 1947. A very young convert, Jake was ordained to the ministry in Yarrow at age 22. He served among the Noanama Natives in Colombia, where he soon demonstrated linguistic and translation talents. These abilities and interests also led him to Panama and Paraguay to study the languages of other tribes, then to graduate studies in linguistics and anthropology, and finally to translation work with various Bible societies. Later in his career, he also wrote as a Christian anthropologist and missiologist about the concept of the foreign missionary as hero.[5]

But for our purposes, Susie Brucks is the central character because she is the best example of status-granting by the community (as distinct from status-seeking by the individual). Her correspondence with A.E. Janzen and John B. Toews during her years as a missionary in the Belgian Congo (1945-1960) and her autobiography, *To God be the Glory*, make it clear that she looked back on her role as that of God's special emissary. The very specific call to missions she received in a sugar-beet field and an equally specific call to Africa through a visit a few years later by three members of the Mennonite Brethren Church in Coaldale were recognized by leaders in Yarrow and elsewhere and became known in the Yarrow community. Soon her call was widely accepted as something worthy of support. When given the opportunity for assignment by the Board of Foreign Missions, she accepted and was officially ordained for missionary service in 1944.[6]

In recent times, the authenticity of this kind of call has been questioned.[7] Yet it is clear that without such a special summons, Susie would never have applied for overseas service, and without it she would never have waited a number of years to be accepted, sent, or kept on the field. With very limited educational and professional qualifications, this God-fearing, determined young woman, certain of her call to missionary service, was totally dedicated to that service and willing to study hard to acquire languages in order to bring the Christian message to those she was convinced were lost.

There were, of course, many splendid examples in the annals of evangelical missions of selfless persons, especially single women, for Susie to follow. She would have known about several from the history of Mennonite Brethren missions, such as Katharina Lohrenz (1882-1913), who died in India in the midst of her duties, and Anna Epp (1878-1915), who went from Russia a single woman, consented to become the second wife of Daniel Bergholdt, and died in childbirth 10 years later. Their stories of risk, sacrifice, and seemingly premature death would have been read in the pages of the ubiquitous *Zionsbote*, both in Russia and in North America. Susie's autobiography offers evidence that she saw herself in such heroic company; the Yarrow Mennonite Brethren Church certainly viewed her in that way.

Like many of her predecessors, Susie Brucks was a single woman called to foreign missionary service. There were virtually no single men on the field. It is widely acknowledged that without the work of single women (who outnumbered men on almost any field by two to one or close to that) the history of evangelical missions from 1850 to 1950 would look quite different.[8] Until 1957, such women in Mennonite Brethren missions were accorded the same ordination service as male missionaries, almost identical to the service for a man being ordained as minister in the church. When the ordination of women was changed to commissioning—supposedly in line with a biblically based gender principle as it applied to the ministry—in the Mennonite Brethren North American General Conference mission policy revisions ratified at the Yarrow Conference in 1957, the change being signaled was significant. No single women would henceforth be granted the "wide privileges usually assigned to a minister" or male missionary, as J.B. Toews admitted to Susie's brother Henry in 1960.[9] But even without ordination, women, like married men, were considered apostles of the church sent to the "heathen," as the indigenous were usually referred to then. There was no greater calling.

Susie's Work in the Congo

It is doubtful that the local church was ever well informed about the realities of the mission field. Indeed, home congregations rarely heard details of problems that missionaries experienced. The humanity of people on the field was seldom, if ever, brought to light. Whatever could unduly embarrass the work, the worker, or the Mission Board, was kept from the constituency.[10] As long as the missionaries did not create problems for the board, board members would help keep them on the pedestal. If missionaries *did* cause difficulties, as often happened, the board made sure that the constituency heard its position, especially if the field council had convinced the board of that position.

To board members, Susie must have seemed a model missionary, someone they could always count on to be deferential and submissive to policy, yet courageous in the face of what appeared unwise or wrong to her. For example, unlike Anna Sudermann in India, who openly complained about the transportation policy with respect to single women on the field, Susie, as much in need of a car as anyone in the Congo, concealed her feelings when she was told in 1952 that cars were only for the person "in charge" on each station, and that such a person had to be a married man.[11]

During her first year in Africa, Susie wrote A.E. Janzen in Hillsboro an unusual letter. Declaring that she did not want all of her letters to appear in the *Zionsbote*, only those that would be a blessing, she told of her upbringing in a godly family. "My parents taught us children to share everything with them so that they could help and discipline us. I loved to have fellowship with my parents. My mother is my friend and means much to me. But now you [A.E. Janzen] are my spiritual father as I could wish, and I will try to be your child [here in the jungle]. I want to write you quite often, though I do not expect you to answer all of [my letters], only when you think it necessary [for my discipline]."[12]

Although reluctant to raise issues, Susie Brucks had profound concerns in 1947 about a fellow missionary because of his inordinate love of big-game hunting. As a result of pursuing his passion, he accidentally shot and killed a Congolese tribal person while out hunting for elephants after dark. Susie was more than worried about the negative impact on their work of this accidental homicide. She felt she must admonish the hunter and report him and his excesses to the Board, which she did. But this incident was never reported in the wider constituency. The hunter/missionary got off by appearing before a tribal chief and paying a fine.[13] Twelve years later, in the year before the Congo's independence, Susie reported on serious dissension among six missionaries at Matende, very likely about broken-down vehicles. This dissension had been going on for years. She was there when attempts were made to heal the rifts through the mediation efforts of missionaries in charge of various nearby stations. The work had been suffering because of the dissension.[14]

As a result of J.B. Toews's visits to the missionaries on the field, who often felt burned out, Susie experienced renewal and rededicated her life to the work. Yet by late 1956 or early 1957, she was much in need of a furlough. While waiting for permission to leave, she was requested to bring many pictures of her work home with her. These were to be used by the Board in their publicity department.[15]

Susie's commitment to her work was total, and this commitment was known and admired. She sought to upgrade her French. She sought to acquire two or three tribal languages. She respected those official bodies that made such demands. *My Utmost For His Highest!*, the title of Oswald Chambers' bestselling book, seemed to be her motto. She was not a certified registered nurse, and at one point she seemed so discouraged about her lack of certification for maternity/obstetrical work that she considered returning home rather than being transferred to another station. Yet she persevered until she acquired a legitimate certificate for her obstetrical work. She wanted to work with and assist those who needed medical attention. After some months she was granted permission to do so. "Isn't this nice?" she wrote friends at home.[16]

Susie Brucks had to leave Africa twice: in 1960 because of the revolution that created the independent nation of Zaire, and in 1966 because of the Biafran War in Nigeria (she had gone to Nigeria to assist the World Wide Mission in 1964). She returned to Zaire two more times to work: once under a different mission, and once independently with $500 to her name. She married in 1968 and a second time in 1972. Her first husband, Fred Reimer, died soon after the marriage; her second husband, Cornelius Dyck, a widower who had raised seven sons and five daughters, supported her continuing interest in Africa. Together they made five visits to her last place of work, the Bible School at Idiofa.[17]

Henry Brucks

Like his sister Susie, Henry Brucks was in many ways a model missionary. His Congo correspondence files indicate that he worked with his wife Elsie in the Congo field from 1950 to 1961, at places whose names became familiar to home congregations: Matende/Kafumba (where he did his Kituba language studies), Panzi, and Kipungu. At the time of their first furlough, they had four children: Florence, born in Belgium, and Naomi, Paul, and Joanne, born in the Congo.

While Henry's main assignment was fostering the work of Bible training for converts, the correspondence indicates that so much time was consumed in administrative questions and legal representation that the Bible-school work was seriously weakened. Generally speaking, his and Elsie's autobiography passes over the serious problems raised in his correspondence files.

Henry's initial hurdle was language. He found language study very hard, especially his French studies in Belgium—and French was a requirement by then for missionary work in the Belgian Congo. By Easter of 1950, his year of language study, he felt the strain on his heart. He told his sister Susie when they were together at Kafumba that his application to his studies "had taken his health. His heart had been so affected that while walking on the street he had to stop and take a rest." Susie wrote her friends: "He still suffers from [his over-exertion or anxiety]."[18]

If Henry's Congo experiences were to be summarized in a few words, these would be "mainly station busywork." His correspondence is filled with concerns about missionary vehicles. How were missionaries to get around? What make of car or truck should be purchased, and where should it be purchased? To whom did the vehicles belong? While he argued for the theoretical corporate mission ownership, some individuals strongly defended personal priorities. Another of his assignments, when the Congo mission was short-staffed, was dealing with legal and political matters. Again and again these matters fell into his lap, and they continued to do so until he had to leave the Congo. Although he seemed to have very little time for the Bible School at Kafumba, the principal station of the mission for many years, he had to deal with the issue of a second school that some people wanted to the south at Panzi, near the Angolan border. He could not stay out of tension-filled situations, much as he may have preferred to.

Yet all the tensions that he experienced in the 1950s pale by comparison with the coming of the Congo's independence and new nationhood in 1960. The prospect of anarchy and violence in the region of the mission made it necessary to evacuate the entire field and its personnel. He was asked to remain to the very last because he was trusted to deal with the many extraordinary situations that arose. Though he fretted over questions of fairness and almost succumbed to exhaustion in those last months, he appears to have had the Board's strong support to the end of his Congo experience.

What becomes clear is that J.B. Toews thought of Henry Brucks as the best person for many tasks, including overall administration and, especially, overseeing the Bible School. Brucks never seemed to be afraid to present his views to the board members, even when these differed from theirs. He had a way of presenting different views without giving undue offence. The community of Yarrow was not familiar with many of the details of his work in the Congo, but like his sister Susie, Henry was held in the highest regard. Indeed, after he returned to Canada, the Yarrow Mennonite Brethren Church urged him to become pastor of their congregation, which he served from 1962 to 1966. His subsequent career as Evangelism Secretary and Canadian Conference Minister confirms the high status that he had been accorded as missionary.

Jake Loewen

It is instructive to note how Jacob Loewen's status in Yarrow as a missionary compared with that of Susie and Henry Brucks, especially since Loewen himself wrote about the problems that arose from the "near perfect saint" status to which the missionary was elevated at home.[19] According to Harvey Neufeldt, Loewen and his wife Anne, who had served a decade in Colombia and Panama, were well received when they returned home in 1958. Loewen was particularly admired and lauded in 1957 for climbing the Andes Mountains in Colombia to identify and bury his friends and colleagues John and Mary Dyck, missionaries from Saskatchewan who had perished in a plane crash. This certainly made Loewen a hero with the young people. To Harold Dyck, a university scholar and political consultant who is related to John Dyck, "Jake is a hero to this day."

Loewen had the strong support of John Harder, his former pastor. Harvey Neufeldt's father, Peter P. Neufeldt, an ordained minister in Yarrow, also was a close friend and thought highly of Loewen. Unlike Susie Brucks, however, Loewen was never known to be deferential and submissive. His contemporaries remember that Loewen had antagonized some of the Yarrow ministers and other church members as a teenager and as a young preacher prior to becoming a missionary. They did not appreciate his sharp tongue. During the 1950s, differences of opinion developed between his administrative superiors and him regarding his work as both missionary and Bible translator. Moreover, he had enrolled in graduate school, intent on getting a doctorate, and was told by a board member (probably J.B. Toews, who had faced the same difficulty) that there was no place in Mennonite Brethren missions for a person with a PhD.[20] Had Loewen's writings of the 1960s and '70s—for example, his "Message for Missionaries from Mopass"[21]—been known in Yarrow, they would have been viewed by many as too critical. For these reasons Loewen did not attain the same status in the church as the Brucks siblings. Nor did the Yarrow church give him the same financial support.

On the other hand, Abram and Sarah Esau, like the Brucks siblings, were regarded as model missionaries. As in the case of Henry Brucks, Esau's services were in demand in the Mennonite Brethren Church of Canada when he returned from Africa. There was deep affection and high respect for him in Yarrow in the years following his long foreign service, and he, like Brucks, was offered the pastorate by the Yarrow Mennonite Brethren Church.

The Widespread Use of Myth

The veneration of foreign missionaries during the 1940s and early '50s came to be seen about two decades later as too hagiographic (literally "hallowed writings or characters"). When missionaries on furlough spoke at special conferences to highlight their missions and to point to the acute needs in the field, they relied on stock phrases based on certain biblical texts useful for their purpose. They used such phrases as "the field is white unto harvest" or "now we have an open door for the Gospel" in order to raise the sense of urgency. Or, in the case of a country and people undergoing major change, they warned of "the fast-closing door." Seeking to reinforce this sense of urgency, mission boards would make requests of the missionaries such as: "Send us pictures or letters that illustrate the terrible plight of your objects of mission." After Henry Brucks had been in the Congo for one term, he felt constrained to write at least one letter in this genre before leaving for home, a letter of no administrative or historical significance and intended solely for publication in the church paper. His letter was entitled "The Spiritual Cry in the Congo."[22] His implied message was that "the heathen are crying for the Gospel."

As the colonial period ended in the 1960s, the missionary experience increasingly became the focus of criticism from journalists, social scientists, historians, and missiologists. One of these, an evangelical missiologist named J. Herbert Kane, offered a moderately critical analysis of elements in the missionary mythology that should be regarded as less than acceptable. Although there had been instances of a spiritual cry, Kane has pointed out, this overt expression or manifestation of spiritual hunger seldom occurred. Massaging the truth in reports and articles by or about missionaries was clearly excessive.[23]

Reflection

Massaging the truth aside, it was widely believed that missionaries were agents of the one message that would bring the "heathen" a true spiritual life of the heart similar to ours as Christians of North America—the kind of life that was viewed as the only passport to the divine kingdom. They were a small number of persons doing what most could not or would not do. And theirs was regarded as the genuine gospel, not to be confused with the message of Catholicism or liberal Protestantism.

The story of Christian missions has fascinated supporters and critics for more than a century. The Mennonite Brethren Church, founded in 1860, developed a very close identity with the evangelical missionary movement launched in the 18th century. That strong identity seems to have peaked in the mid-20th century, when Mennonite Brethren in

North America sent out one foreign missionary for approximately every 120 members, a phenomenal statistic. It was not surprising, therefore, that Yarrow, with a congregation of almost 1,000 members, should have witnessed the departure of a cavalcade of foreign missionaries who periodically returned to report on their work and, for the most part, were highly honoured by the Yarrow church community.

Reflections on Growing up as a Pastor's Daughter

By Mary Lenzmann Braun

In January 1950, on a day like any other, our parents, Herman and Tina Lenzmann, calmly announced to us children that beginning on Sunday we would see Dad in the chancel (the church platform). He now would be the church leader. We had lived in Yarrow for about seven years. Dad was teaching at the Elim Bible School in Yarrow and tending our several acres of raspberries. Because the Bible school year was short, he worked at other jobs during the spring months; he was also involved in the West Coast Children's Mission. We ranged in age from 2 to 13. We were missionary kids, preacher's kids, and now we would be the pastor's kids.

After that low-key announcement, we expected little to change in our day-to-day life. However, that was not to be, and the changes that came taught us a lot. We learned from our parents what it meant to serve, to be committed to helping others, and to be thorough in preparing for public ministry. We learned from the church community that there were many kind and generous people in the Yarrow congregation. And we also learned from a few of them that henceforth we were expected to be role models and that our parents were expected to exemplify child-raising standards for the community. In short, life in the fishbowl had just begun. This was the difficult part about growing up in a pastor's home in the '50s.

Our dad ministered to a church of good people who showed us much kindness. As children, we knew nothing about pastoral salaries or stipends. Nor did we know that the previous pastor had been unsalaried. Our basic physical needs were met, and we were not concerned about where the money came from. But because we lived off the income of a small raspberry farm and Dad's part-time salary from the church, we learned at an early age that we had to be careful about spending money and that priorities had to be set. So it was that we had a piano and money for piano lessons, but no refrigerator. We had a small cellar in which we stored the food Mom had canned, and I recall that on rare occasions, on a hot summer day, one of us would be sent to the store just before supper to pick up a one-pound brick of ice cream. This would be placed on the floor of the cellar, the coolest place in the house, and covered with a pillow. We ate our supper more quickly than usual so that the ice cream would not be too soft by dessert time.

It happened that one summer, when Dad was away at a conference, a Yarrow businessman showed up at our house. He said something to Mom about wanting to take some measurements in the house. We paid little attention to him, but I vaguely remember words to the effect that someone else was building a house similar to ours, and therefore he wanted to do some measuring. Mom left it at that. What a surprise it was when shortly thereafter a refrigerator was delivered to our house. Some very kind people (to this day I don't know who they were) had bought a refrigerator for us. It made life easier, but I do not recall our consumption of ice cream increasing after that.

Another incident related to transportation. When we arrived in Yarrow in the early 1940s, Dad rode a bicycle, since owning a car was out of the question. On Sunday mornings, he would ride his bicycle to church and take two children with him. Mom and the baby would ride with neighbours who owned a car. Then, for a short time, we had the use of the West Coast Children's Mission car because Father did field work for them. Eventually he bought that old Mission car. As the pastor, he had a lot of driving to do: many afternoons and evenings were spent visiting the sick and elderly nearby, as well as driving to Chilliwack, New Westminster, and Vancouver to visit church members in various hospitals. He refused an increase in salary because he did not want to offend anyone or have the issue of money compromise his ministry in any way. One year, just before Christmas, our car was at the local garage for servicing. After repeated phone calls to inquire whether the car was ready, Dad finally was told he could pick it up. When he arrived at the service station, he was handed the keys to the car. However, they were not the keys he knew; they were keys to a brand-new car. A very generous group of people had purchased a new car for us. Who were they? We are not sure. But we were deeply touched by this act of love by members of our church.

There was another act of generosity I will never forget because of its strong visual image. One evening when our parents were out, we answered a knock at the door, and a grateful church member presented us with fresh meat—a rabbit stretched out on a cookie sheet, ready for the oven. I don't recall how our mother served it; I do recall it tasted like chicken. But its resemblance to a small human body gave me no small discomfort.

As children we learned that members of the congregation would differ on various issues and that adjustments would have to be made. Very early in his public ministry, our father realized that in the future a good command of the English language would be necessary for an effective ministry. With that in mind, our parents, after their return from Africa with three preschoolers in tow, spent a winter at the Prairie Bible Institute in Three Hills, Alberta, where all classes were taught in English. Sure enough, the transition from German to English in the Yarrow Mennonite Brethren Church took place during Dad's tenure as pastor. A substantial number of church members vehemently opposed any use of English in church. Nevertheless, Dad was determined to improve his competency and comfort level in English, and so we spoke it in our home. We children knew German well, so it was deemed a priority for Dad and Mom to improve their English. But we were told to be discreet about this matter and not mention it to our friends. It would be unkind to antagonize the pro-German-language faction of the church by flaunting the fact that we spoke English in our home. To do so would hurt those who attached spiritual value to the use of German in our services, and the apostle Paul had clear advice about not offending those who saw things differently than we did. We learned that principle in a very practical way.

We also observed first-hand what a pastoral couple does in the church. Father's "church office" was our living room. A lot of counseling happened in that room. Young people came to announce that they wished to be baptized. Young couples showed up to announce that they were engaged and wished to set a wedding date. Wayward youth came for help to get right with God and the community. Adults came with their spiritual problems; women came for counsel regarding their very difficult marriages and problems with their children. Frequently people would simply show up at the door, requesting to speak with Father. Thus it was that we saw a steady flow of people through our house. We were not told the subjects or details of the sessions, but we often drew our own conclusions.

I vividly recall a woman showing up in our home early on a Sunday morning. On her way home from our place she was involved in a traffic accident, and I remember thinking that her preoccupation with her problem may have caused the accident. Although I did not know her and could not begin to understand what she was going through, my teenaged heart went out to her in sympathy.

Often counseling and other forms of pastoral care took place in others' homes. Of course, the personal communication technology of that time was the telephone, and ours was used to schedule these many visitations. It was used, moreover, to arrange for various other meetings. Our telephone rang a lot, and Mom was a principal monitor. She would be called upon to listen to women, many of them needing a sounding board, a sympathetic ear, and perhaps a word of encouragement or advice. When she was called to the phone, she quickly discerned whether this would be a long conversation. We knew it would be if she signaled us to bring her a chair. She might as well get off her feet and rest a while as she listened and listened and listened.

Dad's work in the raspberry field was mostly done in the early morning hours, before the rest of us had started our day. He would turn the soil with a tractor and cultivator, cut out last year's growth, trim the tops of the new growth, check posts and wires, and apply fertilizer. We would be called upon to help with the very prickly job of removing the trimmed stalks from the raspberry rows and piling them up for the bonfire and marshmallow roast that would be the reward for our hard work. We were also called upon to help hoe the berries. No doubt many a sermon, Bible study lesson, or church problem was mentally framed and thought through as Dad worked outdoors by himself in the cool of the morning. Beginning his day so early also freed him for counseling and visitations during the rest of the day.

Before Dad became the pastor of the church, I would hear preachers say, "*Der Herr gab mir dieses Wort*" (the Lord has given me this word), and I would think that they were receiving the word right then and there behind the pulpit. When Dad became the pastor of the church, I realized that this was not the case. Preaching involved a lot of study and careful preparation. I can still see Dad coming into the kitchen to share with Mom his sermon text, outline, and summary. Then he would give her a detailed illustration that he planned to use and ask for feedback as to the suitability of the story. Many were the discussions in our kitchen. Mother was an excellent critic: she had taken four years of Bible school in Manitoba beyond her regular schooling in Russia. We realize now that she would have made a fine scholar.

We also learned from our mother that we owe it to those who are going to listen to us to prepare well and do our best. On Sunday mornings, she taught a class of women in the church nursery. Women with babies came to this class, and they remained in the class long after their babies had left for Sunday School classes of their own. During those years, we would come home from church, Mother would serve Sunday lunch, and, since Father had declared Sunday to be her day off, we would clean up the dishes while she began preparing next Sunday's lesson. She would continue her preparations every day of the week. Even in her later years, women were pleased to have her as their Bible teacher.

Dad's preparations included typing the weekly church bulletin. Several daughters proofread the master copy, then it was printed. If we missed a typographical error, we could expect to get up early on Sunday morning to correct all the bulletins.

Then there were the many visiting ministers and missionaries who entered our home for meals, for coffee after a service, or for overnight stays. Sometimes, during special services, a minister would be in our home for a whole week. Because our house was small and our grandmother lived with us, there was little room for extra people, but somehow we managed. On the whole, these were positive, enriching experiences for us children, although I do remember that occasionally I thought a visitor was simply too inquisitive about my personal life.

When we hosted visitors, Mom would cook a "company" meal, often consisting of roast chicken and a wonderfully tart lemon pie. No prepackaged mixes were allowed. She would be quite nervous about hosting strangers, especially if they were not German-speaking people, yet she would manage the occasion with warmth and ease. No doubt the experience she had gained as a new immigrant in Winnipeg, working as domestic help in wealthy homes, served her well as a hostess in her own home.

Our parents regularly entertained widows as well as families who were without means and somewhat marginalized. One Sunday, when a very poor family was invited to our home, I was apprehensive about how the afternoon would go. Yet what a highlight this visit turned out to be. These kids knew how to have fun with one another and with us. Never had climbing trees been so enjoyable. Our toys were superfluous.

Perhaps one of the most valuable lessons we learned was that of caring about others. Early on in Dad's pastorate, we were awakened in the middle of the night by a knock at the door. A very distraught widow reported that her son had not come home and that she was sure he was experiencing great difficulty somewhere. Perhaps he had driven his bike off a mountain road; perhaps he was in more serious trouble. Who might he be with, and what might they be doing to him? I remember trembling with fear in my bed, hoping that Dad would not go out to search for this irresponsible young man. But Dad went, and even today I hope the outcome was good.

Because he was absent each summer during part of the raspberry-picking season, we were expected to manage the harvesting, and thus we learned to labour diligently and hard in the raspberry fields. While he attended the Canadian or North American Mennonite Brethren Conference, berry picking was underway. We teenagers would weigh, load, and haul flats filled with raspberries to the cannery. As the berry yield increased, so did the number of flats filled by pickers. We transported the berries in the trunk of our car, so sometimes the daily harvest required us to make several trips daily to the cannery. Mom supervised the pickers.

The events I have described are the kind we as siblings reflect on now—they help us to understand how they influenced our lives. However, as teenagers we did not value these events as tutors as much as we resented living in a fishbowl. Time has a way of changing our perspective on what we have experienced. What seems unfair, even traumatic, to a young teen, may seem comical or insignificant to an adult. Nonetheless, I now offer a teenager's perspective on being the pastor's daughter in Yarrow in the '50s. Three examples will suffice.

At age 12, I entered Chilliwack Junior High School, and here I was introduced to Physical Education, known to the students as P.E. Because we were expected to wear shorts to this all-girls class, we shopped for a pair of gym shorts, and I merrily went to class wearing the required gym outfit. But Yarrow would not allow a pastor's daughter to dress like *that.* Shortly thereafter I had to switch from shorts to slacks—a most unpleasant experience. The other Yarrow girls, who were not in the public eye as we were because of my father's position, continued to wear shorts.

On the other hand, it did not take long to be introduced to the soon-familiar rubrics, "If the Lenzmann girls can do it, so can you," or "If the Lenzmann girls can't do it, neither can you." It was June, and my sister was in Grade Six. A group of friends who had been together for six years were ending a chapter in their lives. In the fall, they would be separated: some would attend Chilliwack Junior High School, others would attend Sharon Mennonite Collegiate in Yarrow. A sleepover party was planned, and my sister was invited to attend. It must have been the first event of its kind, for there was controversy over it. Parents had to decide whether to allow their daughters to go to a slumber party. When my sister was asked if our mom was willing to let her go, she responded in total exasperation, "Doesn't your mom have a mind of her own?" Rather than making decisions based on her own convictions, this mother let her children blame the pastor's children for restrictions she put on their behaviour. "Doesn't your mom have a mind of her own?" is something we laugh about now, but not without some remembered pain.

My sister Elvira tells this story. One Sunday morning a woman in the church handed her a note and asked her to take it to a certain young woman in the choir. She dutifully complied. Later, when members of the choir talked to my sister, we discovered that the note was anonymous and non-complimentary. Understandably, the recipient of the note wanted to know who its author was. Since we were on very good terms with the young woman, she likely did not suspect that it was our mother. We can only assume that the message was about the way the young woman was dressed. The pastor's daughter had been used as unknowing courier for an anonymous admonition.

These were experiences we had to struggle with. But pastors' kids also struggle with their faith, as most others do. Elvira remembers thinking, "Other kids can see their pastor for counsel and assurance. To whom can I go?" When it came to baptism, the candidates would come to see our parents and discuss their spiritual journey with them. When we became candidates, we had to go to another minister's home. Consequently, when Elvira decided to request baptism, she went to the home of the former pastor, Johann A. Harder. She remembers being deeply moved when, after praying with her, Mrs. Harder gave her a warm hug and a kiss.

From a teenager's perspective, growing up in the pastor's home in Yarrow had its frustrating moments. Looking back on it as an adult, I realize we learned many positive lessons from being in that situation. I also wonder whether we would have learned those lessons without being a pastor's kids. How often back then I wished and dreamed that my father had an occupation like other fathers in Yarrow, perhaps farming or carpentry or teaching. Auberon Waugh, the son of Evelyn Waugh, once observed, "A child hopes for parents who will be inconspicuous." Not all children can be that fortunate.

PETER DANIEL LOEWEN AND RELIGIOUS EDUCATION

By Dorothy Loewen Derksen

Peter Daniel Loewen (1902-1993) had a marked influence on the development of Christian education in Yarrow. He had always wanted to be an educator. Even during his youth in Russia, he seemed to anticipate, however vaguely, his course of life. He was an excellent student and looked forward to a teaching career. When the events of the First World War and the Russian Revolution interrupted his post-secondary studies at the Institute of Science, he continued his studies under the tutorship of professors who found refuge in the Loewen home. In the first aftermath of the Revolution, he and his twin brother Wilhelm were held hostage for several days by the Makhno anarchist militia. Later, the revolutionaries murdered his older brother, Daniel. These events deeply troubled and angered Loewen, and he turned to the Scriptures for understanding. He attended catechism classes in the Mennonite church. His devout mother, discerning her youngest son's desire to know God, encouraged him to attend Bible study at the local Mennonite Brethren Church. His life changed when he committed his life to God and began to express his faith openly, although timidly at first. He joined the church in 1923, shortly before the family left for Canada.

Peter and Wilhelm were fortunate to find jobs and, with their first summer's earnings, pay the family travel debt and provide for the family. Whereas the twins pondered their future in Canada, their mother believed that God had given her two boys, one to support the parents and the other for the Lord's calling. After much prayer she announced that the twins would draw lots. Peter drew the straw to pursue his own career. His studies, his interest in religious education, and his sense of adventure eventually led him to move from Manitoba to Yarrow. He never doubted that move, and years later, he wrote in his memoirs about his joyous sense of having come home.

Shortly after arriving in Yarrow in 1930, he began his teaching career as an instructor in the new Elim Bible School. In the ensuing years he established a highly successful Sunday School Christian-education program in the Mennonite Brethren Church, served as instructor in the Saturday German Religious School, and helped to launch a kindergarten program.

Gerhard J. Derksen and several others in Yarrow headed the effort to found Elim Bible School, the first Mennonite Brethren institution of its kind in British Columbia. They then asked Loewen, a recent graduate of Winkler Bible School, to launch the school. Although young in years, he had already demonstrated ability and enthusiasm for both teaching and the ministry, and this opportunity would include both kinds of work. His decision to accept the invitation shaped the rest of his life. Working without the benefit of a mentor or any history of such a school in Yarrow, he defined his curriculum, developed the courses, and performed all the administrative duties associated with starting and operating this institution. In addition, he taught most of the classes. The Gerhard Derksens' living room served as the first classroom.

Because of severe economic hardships in Yarrow during this time, the young men of the community sought work wherever they could find it, often in the hopyards. The young women found employment mainly in Chilliwack or Vancouver. Initially, therefore, all classes were taught for two hours in the evening, five nights per week. In the first winter (1930-31), more than 30 male students attended the school. To accommodate the range in age and maturity, the group was split into two classes. Johann Harder helped teach some of the subjects. Although it was difficult for the students to do homework after a long day of hard physical labour, most were interested in their studies. Students were charged a nominal tuition fee, but inability to pay did not preclude anyone from attending classes. The initial salary for the teacher was $20 per month over the span of two six-week terms. Out of that income, Loewen had to pay $18 per month for room and board plus the cost of textbooks and other related expenses. It was assumed that his summer income would make up the shortfall.

In the first year the curriculum consisted of courses in biblical doctrines, biblical history, Sunday School methodology, and the German language. The curriculum was continually revised and expanded, however. By the third year, daytime courses were introduced; these included several new subjects, including music, Christian ethics, biblical exegesis, and homiletics. In 1934, Abram Nachtigal joined Harder and Loewen. Once the school had matured into a viable daytime institution, Cornelius C. Peters, Gerhard Sukkau, and others joined the staff.

As a Bible-school instructor, Loewen was expected to assume other duties in the work of the local Mennonite Brethren church. In 1930, he was appointed chairman of the Youth Endeavour program. He was expected to teach Sunday School. He also served as church librarian and church secretary, and he agreed to teach in the Saturday German Religious School.

Loewen soon distinguished himself as educator and friend of young people. At the annual year-end congregational business meeting in December 1937, he was elected Sunday School superintendent. He served as such for the next 26 years. Visionary and innovative, he organized the Sunday School according to age and maturity levels and moved instruction to Sunday morning. In the early years, Sunday School had been for children only, but he insisted that it be for everyone and gradually introduced adult classes. He also started special classes for mentally and physically challenged children. During the mid-1940s, he introduced monthly children's worship sessions for each age group or level. Conducted mainly in English, these sessions served as a bridge from the German to the English language in the church as a whole. In addition, they provided teaching opportunities for younger church members not proficient in German. With many Mennonite war refugees arriving from Europe after the Second World War, the German language could not be discarded. Over the next decade, however, he facilitated a smooth transition in the Sunday School from German instruction to bilingual to mainly English.

Concerned about adequate preparation of teachers and the quality of instruction, he assiduously trained his staff through staff meetings, class visitations, and teacher-development clinics. To accomplish the latter, he offered teacher-training courses and organized conventions, often bringing in outside specialists to conduct seminars. He worked closely with the Bible School because of its vital role in preparing and training Christian educators for the church. In order to elevate the level of instruction, he introduced a unified and graduated curriculum, student homework, and, as a measure of student progress, report cards.

He also became deeply involved in developing the curricular materials and lesson plans. Cornelius C. Peters, a member of the Elim Bible School faculty, wrote many of these materials in collaboration with Loewen and others.

For many years, Loewen also taught in the Saturday German Religious School, an institution established for all the children of Yarrow that emphasized both religion and the German language. Peter Reimer started the school in 1929 and was succeeded by Johann Janzen. Then, for many years, Petrus Martens, Cornelius C. Peters, and Peter Loewen complemented each other as instructors. Martens loved to sing with his students; Loewen was a thorough German grammarian; Peters had an extraordinary sense of humour and knew how to create an enjoyable environment for learning.

As already implied, the purpose of the school was to reinforce religious and cultural values, especially since the language of worship in the community was German. Although instructors differed somewhat on questions of content and teaching methods, these differences did not seem to present problems. By the mid-1940s, however, the interest in the German language and in German-language instruction had begun to wane in Yarrow.

In the late 1930s, together with Aron Rempel, Loewen started a kindergarten in the church facilities. These two men and their wives were concerned about the creative development of their children, but kindergarten was not yet available in the public school system. Annie Hepting (who later married Henry Enns) was the kindergarten's first teacher. Daily three-hour sessions were held in the morning during the late spring. By the second year, enrollment had increased to almost 40. As the number of participants increased, Sarah Martens, Anne Friesen, and Anne Enns were added to the teaching staff. Classes were conducted at two levels—three-to-four-year-olds, and five-to-six-year-olds—and instruction was entirely or almost entirely in German. During the 1940s and early '50s, most of the kindergarten instructors were students of Elim Bible School with training in Christian education. Principally religious in nature, kindergarten classes included Bible stories, much singing, games, pantomimes, and handicrafts, especially drawing and cutting out images for mural-like displays on a board.

Early in his career, Loewen had vowed to teach and encourage others, build their self-esteem, nurture their capacity for hope, and foster their sense of spiritual obligation. This commitment became the fulcrum of his life and work. He maintained a keen interest in Christian education until his death in 1993. After he retired, for example, he continued to teach Bible classes and deliver sermons, frequently speaking in Yarrow even after he had moved to Clearbrook. He also served on the board of the Mennonite Educational Institute (Mennonite High School in Clearbrook) until he was almost 90 years old. But he is best remembered for his work as an educator in Yarrow, especially in the formative decades when he was a member of the core leadership group and pastor Johann Harder's friend and confidant. Their mutual trust and support were crucial in nurturing the young community. Loewen's high sense of calling as an educator helps to explain his influence on religious education and the Mennonite Brethren Church in Yarrow.

We Dare Not Lose Our Language: The German Religious School

By Agatha E. Klassen

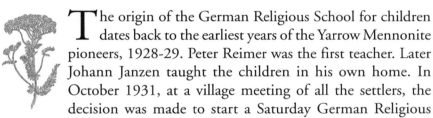

The origin of the German Religious School for children dates back to the earliest years of the Yarrow Mennonite pioneers, 1928-29. Peter Reimer was the first teacher. Later Johann Janzen taught the children in his own home. In October 1931, at a village meeting of all the settlers, the decision was made to start a Saturday German Religious School for all children in the community aged 6 to 14. For several years thereafter the Yarrow Elementary School was used for classes. At that time, the school day lasted from 9:30 am to 3:30 pm. Petrus Martens was appointed teacher-principal. The community paid 50 percent of the operating expenses of the school, and the parents contributed the balance on a per-capita basis. Eventually the foyer of the Mennonite Brethren Church was also utilized for classroom space. After 1944, the Saturday school was relocated to the new Elim Bible School building. When the Sharon Mennonite Collegiate was built on Stewart Road in the early 1950s, it became the home of the Saturday school, from 9:00 AM to noon.

The Saturday German Religious School offered three levels of instruction: beginner, intermediate, and advanced. The teaching material was the *Fibel* (primer) for the younger students, and the *Deutsches Lesebuch* (German reader), steps 1, 2, 3, and 4, for intermediate and advanced students. The *Wartburg Fibel* (primer) introduced students to Gothic letters (old German script). These German readers, chosen in part for their literary value, contained both poetry and prose, including humorous works. Teaching was done by a phonetic method, as this approach was the most effective for teaching the German language.

Students were thoroughly schooled in German grammar, writing dictation, reading, and penmanship. One of the instructors, Anna Bartsch, experimented with another method: teaching by recognition and repetition. This was one of the approaches used to teach English in Canadian schools. In her classes, she used a text she had authored. She also changed over from the Gothic script to Latin letters. Whether her success was due to her method or her skill as a teacher was a matter of debate. Bible stories were also taught, and all students became familiar with the classic *Biblische Geschichten* (Bible stories). Children were expected to memorize and recite passages or complete stories from the Bible.

In the early years, most children, especially those who spoke German in the home, quickly learned to read and write German. Those children whose mother tongue was Low German found German study more difficult. A few years later, when most children spoke more English in their homes and with each other, teaching and learning German presented more of a challenge. In addition, many, perhaps most, children were reluctant to give up their whole Saturday, or even half a day, for German school. But parents persisted with the program, and nearly 100 percent of the village children attended the German Religious School for seven months each year.

For many years the staff consisted of three to four instructors, but with time this number increased to eight. In addition to instructors already mentioned, teachers included Peter D. Loewen, Sara Riesen, a Mr. Thiessen, Johann Toews (who also taught at the Elim Bible School), Cornelius C. Peters (also a Bible-School instructor), David J. Klassen, Margaret Binder, Cornelius Regehr, Martha Goosen, Linda Falk, Frida Nightingale, Anne Janzen, Ann Andres, Arthur Janzen, David Giesbrecht, Linda Matties, Erna Barwich, Werner Holtz, and Heidi Schilling. For many years teachers were paid five dollars per Saturday.

Anne and Susie Funk, who attended the German School during the 1930s and '40s, have offered reminiscences of those days. Apparently, strict discipline was very important. Parents expected this, and instructors attempted to carry out their wishes. Anne remembers her teacher breaking a yardstick while disciplining a group of boys who had been passing notes to each other. A female instructor confronted cheeky students by calling them *Naseweiss* (White Nose). When recess was over, all students in her class returned to the room with white noses, thanks to their ingenious application of the blackboard chalk brush. No one was called *Naseweiss* again. Susie recalls that one of her teachers was very gentle and soft-spoken. Some of the children took advantage of him by being particularly unruly. One day he remarked, deadpan, "Is it possible that there may be a few doves among all these crows?" Anne and Susie both remember a teacher who presented excellent religious meditations. There were no discipline problems in his class. All too keenly do Anne and Susie remember *Prüfung* (examination day). All parents of students, as well as school board members and friends of the school, were invited to attend the closing ceremonies. Teachers had collected and compiled in a booklet various samples of the students' work, including dictation and penmanship exercises. The booklet was passed around to all the parents. The program also included a question-and-answer period in which several Bible stories were reviewed. Some of the students were petrified when the teacher called them by name to answer a question in this totally unrehearsed event.[1] The school choir also sang a number of hymns and folk songs. Comments by a parent or school board member concluded the *Prüfung* and the school year, which ran from October to the end of April.

One individual whom I interviewed confided, "I would have broken or given away my best doll in exchange for not having to attend German Saturday School." Another former student, Edward Klassen, who attended in the 1960s, remembers that one of his instructors, no doubt a decent and kind-hearted person, coped with student behavioural challenges by being overly authoritarian, frequently "losing her cool" in the process. When a student requested permission to leave the room, she would walk briskly to the student's desk and twist his or her ear until it hurt. Her motive was to discourage the students from repeatedly leaving the classroom without reason. "Generally speaking," Ed Klassen observes, "the atmosphere in the classroom was hardly conducive to good teaching and learning."[2]

Lillian Harms remembers that she generally enjoyed the German School very much. A good student, she quickly learned to read and write. She too remembers some of the students' shenanigans, but she also remembers that she didn't let these bother her, since she was so eager to learn German. She recalls an incident in which an older student, usually "full of beans" and constantly exasperating his teacher, was sent outside to get a switch with which he would be punished. After a long time, he returned with a cedar fence post. "Here's your switch, sir," he said, grinning widely. The classroom erupted in laughter, and no further action was taken.[3]

Katie and Cornelius Regehr, who had four children in the German School during the 1950s and '60s, noted in an interview that their children seldom complained about this school. They suspect that their children were not angels, but nothing about them ever leaked out. All four children have remembered the German they were taught, speaking, reading, and writing it to this day, but, as the parents point out, German was spoken in their home when their children were growing up.[4]

From its official beginning until the mid-1960s, the German Religious School was responsible for the annual Christmas Eve program in the Mennonite Brethren Church. This production, well planned and rehearsed, delighted the community. Usually the program included some kind of dramatic presentation of the Christmas story as well as recitations, dialogues, and musical numbers by the school choir. At the close of the program, bags of nuts were distributed to all the children, including those who did not attend the German School. For the children, of course, the bag of goodies was the highlight of the evening. Frequently, bags were also slipped to occasional visitors, especially individuals of few means.

By 1954, the Mennonite Brethren congregation had assumed sole responsibility for the German Religious School, although students were accepted regardless of denominational adherence or church attendance. When the German School no longer served the needs of the majority of the children in the community, the Sunday Schools of the Mennonite Brethren and United Mennonite churches assumed the responsibility in their respective congregations. The influx of European refugees in the late 1940s and early 1950s and the entry of some German-speaking Mennonites from Paraguay in the 1950s and '60s helped enrollments somewhat in these years.[5] Nonetheless, the student population continued to decrease. Most of the students knew very little German. There was also the increasingly difficult problem of finding qualified teachers. The last year of instruction was 1970-71.

Looking back on the 40-year history of the German Religious School in Yarrow, one can draw a number of conclusions. Obviously, understanding German and developing competence in the language were assets for children as long as German was spoken in homes and used in Sunday School and church services. Most of the individuals I interviewed expressed appreciation for the opportunity they had to learn the German language. One of them remarked, "Knowing your mother tongue is a priceless inheritance and would be the envy of many who are not so fortunate." Former instructors of the Yarrow Mennonite Brethren Sunday School, Elim Bible School, and Sharon Mennonite Collegiate (high school) have observed over the years that students who received training in the German School had a marked advantage over those who did not receive this formal instruction in biblical knowledge and the German language. Both kinds of knowledge were held in high regard by many parents.

One suspects, however, that there may have been another agenda in the almost fanatic attempt to hold on to the German language. In the volume of essays *P.M. Friesen & His History*, John B. Toews observes: "There appears to have been an almost instinctive understanding that 'Germanness' was basic to Mennonite survival in an alien culture."[6] Such Germanness was obviously a survival strategy for Mennonites in 19th-century Russia, and it may well have been repeated for the same reason in the early decades of Mennonite Yarrow. As one of the interviewees for this essay put it, "By giving up the German language, many of us strongly felt that we were in danger of losing our cultural and spiritual values."

Glimpses of Elim Bible School, 1930-1955

By Peter Penner

Between 1925 and 1950, some 20 Bible schools were founded across Canada by Mennonites who, like the Yarrow Mennonites, had emigrated from Russia early in the 20th century. These institutions were sponsored by church congregations or special societies interested in fostering religious education and Mennonite values among their people. Specifically, the Bible school had two important and closely related purposes: to keep the youth loyal to the church, and to provide a substitute for or counter to secular learning in high school.[1]

No doubt Mennonite Brethren Church leaders preferred to have their youth attend school at home or at a Mennonite Brethren institution like Winkler or Hepburn rather than go off to interdenominational schools such as those in Three Hills, Alberta or Caronport, Saskatchewan.

Bible school at Gerhard Derksen's home.

Thus it is not surprising that early on the Mennonite Brethren constituency in Yarrow decided to establish its own Bible school.

Much credit for establishing the Bible school in Yarrow is given to Gerhard J. Derksen. He had resided in Winkler when its influential Bible school was founded in 1925 by three teachers who brought their experience from the Tschongrow Bible School in the Crimea: A.H. Unruh, Johann G. Wiens, and Gerhard Reimer. Derksen's own son Jacob had attended this school in Winkler. In 1929, Derksen brought his family to Yarrow. Eventually dubbed the mayor of the B.C. Mennonites because he was foremost a man of practical affairs, he saw the need for a Bible school that would bring to Yarrow the spiritual impact he had noted in Winkler. His purpose was realized, and Peter D. Loewen, who had become acquainted with the Derksen family while he was a student in Winkler, became the first teacher of the Yarrow Bible School.[2] A few years later the school was named "Elim," an Old Testament word derived from a Hebrew term meaning "springs of living water."

To begin with, classes were held in the evenings, first in a home and then in the men's coatroom of the newly built Mennonite Brethren Church. These classes, eagerly attended by young men, allowed them to continue their all-day employment. Given the practical needs of the fledgling community, young people needed to work during the day in hopyards or in other jobs. At first, relatively few young women attended, not because of segregation, but because many of them were in Vancouver or Chilliwack doing housework in order to supplement the family income. In many families, part of this income had to be allocated—in some instances, for many years—to paying off their *Reiseschuld* (costs incurred in the Canadian Pacific Railway passage from Russia to Canada).

The Winkler Influence

The influence of Winkler Bible School extended to the school in Yarrow and to most other Bible schools that followed.[3] Elim showed its strong Winkler influence in its teaching staff. Peter Loewen, the first teacher at Elim, was one of the early graduates of Winkler (1929). Undoubtedly he set the agenda and tone by emphasizing the values he had learned from noted instructors at Winkler. The first courses taught were Bible Doctrine, Bible History, Sunday School Methodology, and German. Leading minister Johann A. Harder, who assisted from the beginning, was not a Winkler student, but his successor at Elim, Gerhard H. Sukkau, attended Winkler in 1931-32 and 1933-35. Sukkau served as principal of Elim from 1939 to 1943 and again from 1946 to 1952 and was an instructor in the intervening years. Herman Lenzmann, a student at Winkler from 1930 to 1935, taught at Elim from 1942 to 1952.[4] The Winkler influence brought with it an emphasis on training workers for Sunday schools—that is, for local religious education. This religious education assumed a larger purpose with the founding of the West Coast Children's Mission (WCCM) in the 1940s, since it widened the focus at Elim beyond the local church or even the Mennonite Brethren churches of the region to outreach in the immediate area. *Randmission* (church extension to communities outside the local perimeter) was the name given to this effort.[5]

A Telling Interlude, 1942-44

Due to the increasing number of wartime enrollments, Elim faced a potentially embarrassing problem. Herman Lenzmann, at the age of 90, recalls the situation, which he describes with some delight. During the 1942-43 academic year, when Johann ("*Väterchen*") Toews, Gerhard Sukkau, Cornelius C. Peters, Jacob H. Epp, and Lenzmann were the instructors, about 20 to 22 young men came to Elim, ostensibly to study. But in time they were perceived as behaving much like a gang bent on mischief in the school and in the community, a development most unbecoming to a Bible school. The leader was Peter Wolfe, who later became a well-known figure in the area. The "gang" created so serious a problem that a decision was pending to expel them en masse. While Toews stated that if Wolfe remained, he would leave, not all teachers agreed with him. Indeed, Peters' attitude as principal was that "out of this wolf something good would come" (*Aus dem Wolf gibt es noch einst ein Löwe*!). The teachers had failed to reach a decision late in the appointed week, but they were met with an entirely new situation on Monday. Two preachers had come to Yarrow for weekend services, and all members of the troublesome group had converted on the weekend. On Monday Peters' view seemed entirely vindicated.[6]

According to Lenzmann, the instructors faced a more serious problem during the 1943-44 school year. Critics of the practice of conscientious objection charged Elim with harbouring young men who should be joining the military forces. Elim staff deflected the criticism by pointing out that many young Mennonite men had joined the forces.

Construction of spacious new building for Elim Bible School.

Rise and Decline

As the Yarrow Mennonite community slowly began to prosper in the late 1930s and early '40s, attendance at Elim increased significantly. Before Yarrow launched its own secondary school, Sharon Mennonite Collegiate Institute, in 1945, most parents shied away from sending their youth to Chilliwack High School. They still feared dangerous cultural influences, and as new immigrants their young people lacked the self-confidence to make a wholesome adjustment there. Besides, as revealed by several articles in *The Chilliwack Progress*, memoirs by Yarrow settlers, and anecdotal reports by early Yarrow Mennonites, a number of residents in the greater Chilliwack area, as well as some teachers and students, found strangers like the immigrant Mennonites hard to accept. Given the negative wartime feelings in nearby communities toward the pacifist-minded, German-speaking Mennonites of Yarrow, church and Bible school formed a bulwark against the hostility, often openly expressed, to Yarrow's way of life.

Elim grew from an evening class to two levels or grades in 1937 and to four levels, requiring four staff members, in 1940. Then, again in emulation of Winkler, a fifth class level was added in 1941. Classes migrated from the church foyer to a two-room school building located on the church property on Central Road. The additional classes moved into the basement of the new church, completed in 1938. As enrollments burgeoned in proportion to the rapid growth of the congregation, by

1942 it seemed imperative to construct a six-classroom Bible-school building on the church lot. Enrollments approached 150 in the later years of the Second World War, 1942 to 1945. During the war, the majority of Yarrow's young people attended Elim for at least one year, if not more. Among the teachers, in addition to those already mentioned, were several who came to play a prominent role not only in the local church and community, but also in the Canadian Mennonite Brethren Conference. These included Jacob H. Epp (1942-44), and Henry Bartsch (1945-47). Younger instructors, such as George Konrad and Henry Warkentin, came to Elim several years later, following training at the Mennonite Brethren Bible College (MBBC) in Winnipeg.

A panoply of courses was offered and divided among the five or six teachers who served each year. Choir, music, homiletics, and child psychology were significant components. The students' interest in serving in the WCCM increased, as did their willingness to serve in Daily Vacation Bible School, conducted during the summer in various communities in the Fraser Valley and beyond. Student participation in these two related programs reached its peak in the 1950s,[7] despite the fact that total student enrollments were already declining.

By the time Henry Warkentin from Abbotsford began to teach in Yarrow in 1950, the graduating class was half as large as in peak years, and total enrollment was down by about two-thirds. The teaching program was kept intact, but other nearby Bible schools had opened, in Abbotsford in 1945 and in East Chilliwack in 1947. Warkentin supplemented his income by helping to administer the WCCM during the years he taught at Yarrow.[8] He had to compete for students with MBBC, as well as with high schools and universities.

Peter Harder, son of Greendale minister Jacob B. Harder, who taught at Elim for one year (1948-49), vividly remembers attending Elim during the last year of the war, 1944-45. Classes were entirely in German. Cornelius D. Toews was there that year to teach music, while Sukkau taught church history, and Cornelius C. Peters was in charge of biblical history. Peters' lively sense of humour included self-deprecation, even to the point of comparing his rotund figure with the grill of his Willys Jeep. The most popular teacher at the institution, he also gave rudimentary lessons on how to present oneself as public speaker and preacher by speaking convincingly on topics and using short sentences.

In 1945, the new Mennonite high school opened with the enthusiastic and sacrificial support of leading minister Johann A. Harder.

Peter Harder noticed how C.C. Peters now sought to rise to the challenge of educating a different kind of student, one who in all likelihood was a returning conscientious objector or war veteran interested in moving on to university or settling into the work force. A similar change was evident in the school's social life, which was not as carefully and specifically controlled as it had been a few years earlier. Because social contact was quite limited in a non-residential school like Elim, according to Peters there was no great need to enforce rules. All students were highly motivated to support the church and its programs, missionaries abroad, and those closer to home. Celebration focused on banquets for special occasions such as Christmas and on graduation ceremonies.

It was clear to Peter Harder that the purpose of Elim was to prepare young people to be faithful church members, effective Sunday School teachers, and supporters of mission endeavours. From Peter P. Neufeldt, a member of the WCCM who served as a monitor of the particular student "mission circle" to which Harder belonged, Peter Harder learned how to prepare a program as though he was about to embark on a mission to a rural area. The main question was "*Wo sind die Schnitter?*" (Where are the reapers?). Students like him required songs, poems, displays, maps, and short sermons—in other words, readiness to do the work of an evangelist.[9]

Sharon Mennonite Collegiate Institute (SMCI)

Although Johann A. Harder assisted with Elim Bible School in the formative years of the community, he soon had reservations about its direction under the influence of North American evangelicalism. This influence had entered Winkler Bible School when A.A. Kroeker, the only Canadian-born instructor on the staff, joined five years after the Winkler school was founded. His interest in and support of the Canadian Sunday School Mission led to an emphasis on work among children through Daily Vacation Bible School and the use of summer camps to attract children.[10] The training for a children's crusade that Winkler graduates took to Mennonite centres such as Coaldale, Alberta (Bernard Sawatsky), Hepburn, Saskatchewan (G.W. Peters), and Yarrow (Peter Loewen) included the requisites of child psychology courses, an emphasis on child conversions, and certification from the Evangelical Teacher Training Institute. (In its early years, even the Mennonite Brethren Bible College issued this certification to those who completed the Bachelor of Religious Education degree program.) Such reception of American evangelical influence did not please Johann A. Harder. In his view, popular American evangelicalism was compromising the core Mennonite faith tradition (both Anabaptist beliefs and traditional Mennonite practices). As the Second World War progressed, he began to agitate for the creation of a high school that would prepare students for the postwar world.

Apparently Harder hoped Sharon Mennonite Collegiate Institute would be a Canadian adaptation of the Russian Mennonite *Zentralschule*. What undoubtedly reinforced his thinking was the knowledge that, as in Winkler in the 1930s and '40s, no one at Elim seemed to have thought it crucial to teach Reformation, Anabaptist, Mennonite, and Mennonite Brethren history. Knowing the contents of the Bible was sufficient for life. When Elim came under criticism for encouraging students to apply for the status of conscientious objector, it became evident that the Mennonite principle of non-resistance had been dusted off only when conscription of Mennonite young men for the war effort became imminent. This was Jacob A. Loewen's experience. He was carefully coached to tell the draft board examiner: "My conscience does not allow me to take up arms to kill other people." Only then did he begin to think deeply about whether his "professed peace position was really a personal conviction or merely an oddity I followed because of tradition and pressure."[11]

Notwithstanding the importance and successes of Elim at the community level in the first decade or two of the Mennonites in Yarrow, the war experiences and developments after the war suggest that the school, like the community, had not prepared Yarrow's young people for the rapidly changing world into which most of them would soon be moving. Elim suspended operations in 1955 and did not reopen.

They Had to Learn to be Canadian: Carl Wilson and the Yarrow Mennonite Community

By Harvey Neufeldt

Several decades after leaving the principalship of Yarrow Elementary School, Carl Wilson returned to the community to attend the Yarrow Day festivities at the Yarrow Mennonite Brethren Church. When he was publicly introduced, the audience responded with a round of applause. Yet the views of Carl Wilson had contrasted sharply with those of Yarrow's early Mennonite settlers. The latter endorsed an education that would help preserve their Mennonite identity, including language and religion. Wilson, on the other hand, had sought to use the schools to promote assimilation of the Mennonites into Canadian culture and society. Whereas many Mennonite settlers viewed Anglo-Canadian culture and the English language with suspicion, Wilson equated these with good citizenship. How was it possible for the Yarrow settlers to disagree with Wilson on such a fundamental issue and yet view this long-time local educator worthy of special public recognition?

Wilson arrived in Yarrow in 1929 at the age of 23. His heritage, Wilson emphasized, was Canadian. He pointed out that he, as well as both of his parents, had been born in Canada. His father claimed Irish heritage, his mother German. His paternal grandfather had emigrated from Ireland and eventually settled near Watertown, Ontario. Wilson's parents moved from Ontario to Arden, Manitoba, where he was born in 1906. After building a flour mill at Arden only to see it destroyed by fire, the Wilsons moved to British Columbia in 1911. Here the father found employment with the B.C. Electric

Railway, first as assistant stationmaster at New Westminster, then as stationmaster at Sardis.[1]

Carl Wilson loved the outdoors. After graduating from high school, he spent two years hunting, trapping, and fishing. But then he complied with his father's wishes that he prepare himself for a career by entering the Vancouver Normal School. Throughout his adult life, however, he retained his love for mountains, streams, and lakes, and for hunting and fishing. He fell in love with Mildred Behrner from Seattle, who shared his appreciation for nature. They met in 1929 while he served as a guide for a party of Americans attempting to climb Mount Liumchen, some 10 miles southeast of Cultus Lake. When dense fog set in, Wilson became lost. Friends later called the place where the party had to settle in during the fog "Camp Cuddle." In 1930 the same mountain plateau, 6,000 feet high, served as the site of Carl and Mildred's wedding.[2] (Fifty years later, they returned to the same site in a helicopter chartered by their son in honour of their golden wedding anniversary.)

Carl Wilson, whose educational mission was to turn Mennonite children into good Canadians.

Following their wedding, the Wilsons rented the house of Yarrow postmaster Eva Siddall at the south end of Wilson Road before moving to a newly built house at Cultus Lake. For several years they rented out their Cultus Lake home in July and August while they lived in one of George Lindemann's cabins at Chilliwack Lake. Lindemann, an American immigrant of Pennsylvania Dutch ancestry, shared the Wilsons' love for the outdoors.[3]

Wilson fished and hunted after work hours and in the summers. He caught—actually gaffed—his first steelhead in 1922, but for the next 15 years had little time for steelhead fishing. Winning the Vedder River Steelhead Derby in 1937 whetted his appetite for the sport; it made him "pretty nuts about steelhead fishing."[4] His diary reports a one-week period in 1941: fishing after school on Thursday, on Saturday, Sunday, fishing after school on Wednesday. He caught up to105 steelhead in the Chilliwack River in a single year. His largest catch included a 25-pound steelhead and a 66-pound spring salmon. Winter weather did not deter him from fishing, as revealed by his diary entry for January 15, 1943: "The wind changed to the North East and continued so for two weeks. Three feet of snow and down to -3 (F). Fishing was very, very good." His love for fishing was gradually tempered once he came to realize that extensive sport and commercial fishing was endangering the steelhead.[5]

Along with being "Canadian," Wilson identified himself culturally and economically with the middle class. His father, Wilson recounted, had the means "to give me anything I wanted in the way of education." Being station agent in Sardis was an "important job."[6] Wilson's post-secondary education and entrance into a profession, which his father valued highly, served as a marker of middle-class status. This status was reinforced by the contacts he made as a fisherman. He was a guest of A. R. McMillan, who took Wilson in his airplane for a three-day fishing trip. In addition he fished with "Budge" Bell-Irving, lieutenant governor of British Columbia, and John Buchan, the son of the Governor General of Canada.[7]

As a teacher and principal, Wilson enjoyed an income that contrasted sharply with the poverty experienced by the Yarrow Mennonite settlers during the Great Depression. When he left the school at Kispiox on the Yukon Telegraph line some 30 miles north of Hazelton to teach in the Fraser Valley, he gave up a salary of $120 a month, which, as he pointed out, was "substantial in those days." His starting salary in Yarrow in 1929 was $100 per month. During the Depression, the Chilliwack School Board proposed cutting his salary by 20 percent. When Wilson responded by threatening to seek a teaching position up north, the board actually raised his salary for the next year to $110 per month, making him one of the highest paid teachers in the district. The Yarrow families, on the other hand, were poor, "desperately poor," he recalled, and their children seemed destined to fill the ranks of unskilled labour. Consequently, he advised a teacher not to waste too much time on promoting intellectualism.[8]

Wilson never questioned the fact that leadership in the public sphere was a male prerogative. Since he was the only male in a family of three children, it was assumed that he should receive an education that would help ensure his economic mobility. When he arrived in Yarrow in 1929, Ella M. Currie, who had previously taught in the Majuba Hill School, was already teaching in the little village school. However, others presumed—and he as well, it seems—that he would serve as principal, although at first he was not officially designated as such.[9] In this respect he and the Yarrow immigrants were in agreement: women were not expected to take a leadership role in the public sphere. Indeed, the Yarrow Mennonite Brethren Church did not extend the vote to its female members until the late 1950s.

The Yarrow school to which Wilson was assigned in 1929 was one of two public schools in Yarrow. In 1903, a school later named the Hillcrest School but commonly referred to as the Majuba Hill School was built on the hill. With the influx of early Mennonite settlers and the rapid growth of the Mennonite community, the Hillcrest School was by far the smaller of the two. When a new and much larger Yarrow Elementary School opened in the village in October 1937, the Hillcrest School ceased operations.[10]

When describing the Yarrow people, including the children, Wilson emphasized that they needed to be assimilated into the dominant Anglo-Canadian culture. Their parents, he recalled, were "keen on having them come to school." Looking back 30 years after being transferred from Yarrow to the Chilliwack Elementary School, he paid tribute to the

Carl Wilson's first class in Yarrow, spring 1930.

Yarrow Elementary School May Queen celebration: Hilda Neufeldt and princesses elected by each class to complete the Queen's court.

Mennonite children. Teaching in Yarrow had been a delightful experience "because the kids were good kids. ... You wouldn't find kids like that anywhere now in Canada, I'm sure."[11] On one occasion Wilson asked a schoolboy to wash his car. He used that opportunity to encourage this student not to drop out of school as soon as he came of age (John Ratzlaff, Jr., oral communication). He found the pastor of the Mennonite Brethren Church, Reverend John Harder, to be "very cooperative in every way." There would be occasions when some parents would register a complaint, as was the case when one of the teachers voiced his support for the theory of evolution.[12] But Mennonites, in Wilson's opinion, had to learn what it meant to be Canadian, and this requirement largely defined his educational purpose. He recalled that he had recommended the transfer of one or two teachers who were not a good fit for the school. Fitting in included accepting his mission for the school. Teaching in Yarrow, he felt, was somewhat different from teaching in another school within the Chilliwack district. As he later recalled: "I somehow got the feeling, I don't know why, I not only had to teach them that one plus one makes two, but I had to teach them to be Canadians. ... Well they had to be Canadians, that's all. They had to learn how Canadians live, how Canadians do things, how Canadians think."[13]

Acting and thinking Canadian, in Wilson's view, included a number of stipulations. One was minimum dress standards. He appreciated the fact that families' budgets were extremely limited; nevertheless, he insisted that all children wear shoes. He informed the students: "You can come any way you like, but you must have shoes when you are in the schoolroom itself." Being Canadian also meant speaking English. In the early 1930s, many of the children arrived at school with fluency in German but no knowledge of English. Wilson immediately sought to enforce the English-only rule on school premises. If children inadvertently blurted out something in German, he would, as he recalled, scold them and get after them. He informed the community: "Don't drop the German, don't forget German, but you're living in Canada now. We speak English; we do things in English and you're going to have to learn and you might as well start now and work hard at it."[14] As for himself, Wilson never felt the need to learn German.

Wilson agreed with the school board's policy of hiring few, if any, Mennonite teachers. While this policy never became an issue in the 1930s—very few Russian Mennonites had English-language proficiency or held British Columbia teaching credentials—things changed during the 1940s. He later observed that he was not opposed to hiring Mennonite teachers provided there were not many on the staff. They could even be useful in assisting the children in language acquisition. But he also observed, "I don't think it was the finest thing in the world to hire Mennonite teachers."[15]

Being Canadian also meant participation in extra-curricular events. Since the school lacked an auditorium, Wilson made arrangements with the Yarrow Mennonite Brethren Church to use its sanctuary for a black vocal quartet he wished to bring to town. One assumes that much of their music was religious in nature and that Wilson was after a larger audience than merely his students. Imitating other schools that sponsored school picnics, Wilson arranged with Henry Neufeldt of the Martens & Neufeldt trucking firm for the provision of two trucks to transport the students to Cultus Lake. He was pleased that the children enjoyed the picnic, but for him such a picnic involved more than having a good time: "It was part of Canadian life." Surprisingly, although many children went swimming or wading in the lake, Wilson received no criticism from the community and the church leaders. Yet for at least two decades, going to a public beach had been a sign of worldliness in the Yarrow Mennonite Brethren Church. In a similar vein, he interpreted the annual sports day in terms of being Canadian.

The races, running, jumping, skipping, hopping, baseball, and softball, he observed, were "fun; well that's Canada."[16]

The difference between the views of Mennonite settlers and Wilson regarding education and assimilation became especially evident in 1945 with the opening of Yarrow's first private high school in the facilities of the Mennonite Brethren Church. Within a year, the Mennonite Brethren churches in Greendale and East Chilliwack formally joined the Yarrow church in constructing a new school on Wilson Road. The project soon proved to be too burdensome for the three congregations. With the collapse of the raspberry market in 1948, the forced liquidation of the Yarrow Co-op in 1949, and the steep decline in student enrollment, the school closed its doors in 1949 and was sold in 1952 to the Chilliwack School Board.[17]

Wilson was in his final years as principal in Yarrow when the Sharon Mennonite Collegiate Institute was established, and for him this private school constituted a direct challenge to his views on assimilation. He respected the Yarrow Mennonites not only for what they were but also for what he envisioned they ought to become. Looking back in the mid-1980s, he still insisted that the Mennonite high school had been a mistake: "No, no, I didn't think they needed that Mennonite school at all; ... they had enough Mennonitism. If they were going to live in Canada, let's become Canadians, because this is where they were going to live and move and have their being. ... What they need is Canadianization, not Mennonitization. ... I was quite pleased when the school could not carry on."[18]

In 1950, Wilson left Yarrow to become principal of the Chilliwack Elementary School. Although he found the students at Chilliwack to be "totally" different from those in Yarrow, he felt that the Yarrow children were nevertheless being Canadianized. This progress, however, ushered in new problems. In Yarrow he had begun to notice an increase in fistfights and petty theft and a slight decrease in honesty as the children became more assimilated. Despite this trend, he never questioned the need for Yarrow Mennonites to be absorbed into mainstream Canadian society. Although he knew nothing about the Mennonites before he arrived in Yarrow in 1929—"Didn't know what the word meant"—he never questioned his qualifications to serve as an educator of the Mennonites and as an agent of the Anglo-Canadian society in bringing the Mennonites into the culture in which he was at home. When asked to list his greatest accomplishment, he replied: "Trying to have

Mennonite children become Canadian children. That was my job, and I think I did not do a bad job at it. I think that was the biggest thing that happened."[19]

At a funeral service in Yarrow in 1985 for one of his former students, Wilson was heard to remark that teaching in Yarrow had not been viewed by many elsewhere as a desirable appointment. He, however, did not share that view. The Mennonites were fine people who happened to be stuck in the previous century. It had been his life's work to "drag them into the 20th century." Reflecting now on what had become of the Yarrow people, he concluded, "I think I can honestly say, by God, I did it" (Jacob Loewen, oral communication).

How then could Wilson be viewed as an exemplar by the very people he sought to "drag" into the modern Canadian mainstream? He is hardly a model for educators in contemporary multicultural education. One could cite several reasons for his stature in Yarrow. The Mennonite community realized that he respected them and that he could be trusted. He was willing to consult with the unofficial school board organized by the immigrant community. In addition, he and the Mennonites agreed that children needed strict discipline, including corporal punishment when deemed necessary. Community leaders rarely, if ever, complained about the harsh punishment he occasionally meted out to those students who, while not delinquents in behaviour, appeared to be social misfits who for various reasons had trouble assimilating. But in the main, he respected the settlers and their children, and he received their respect in return. The Mennonite community realized that its children needed the education that Wilson's school offered. On the other hand, they hoped to negotiate some of the conditions under which it would be appropriated. What they received instead was Wilson's brand of assimilationist instruction. That said, it is probably fair to add that the Yarrow settlers were considerably more willing to become productive and respected Canadian citizens than many of their Anglo neighbours in the Chilliwack district had surmised.

YARROW'S SOLDIERS

By Harold J. Dyck and Marlene A. Sawatsky

Prime Minister Mackenzie King announced Canada's declaration of war in early September 1939. Within weeks, a committee was organized in Yarrow under the auspices of the Red Cross to assist in raising funds for medical supplies in the Canadian armed forces. Women from Majuba Hill and Yarrow village, as well as the local Mennonite church ministers, initially led Yarrow's response to the Second World War. The postmaster, Eva Siddall, chaired the Red Cross committee of young women from the community's Mennonite population.[1] Before the end of the first month of the war, the Yarrow Mennonite churches had conducted special collections to support the wartime preparations of the Red Cross, and their leaders had met in a day-long conference and emerged to "[pledge] their loyalty to Canada and the British Empire" as well as to reaffirm the historic Mennonite principle of non-resistance.[2]

After this early support, Yarrow's contribution to the war effort and to subsequent war-related humanitarian projects continued to be generous and timely. Throughout the war, Yarrow met its annual sales quotas for Victory Bonds and did so on time.[3] In fact, quotas were usually surpassed before their due date. Contributions to the various funds to help those suffering the effects of war—the Milk for Britain Fund, for example—were encouraged. Children grew "victory gardens" and donated the harvest. Large numbers of Christmas parcels were assembled, packaged, and mailed to servicemen and -women. And after the end of hostilities in 1945, tons of clothing were collected and large amounts of locally grown and processed fruit were donated and sent to wartorn areas in Britain and Europe.[4]

Yarrow's most significant contribution to Canada's effort in the Second World War was, however, the military and alternative service provided by 96 young people—66 in the military, including one woman, and 30 in the Alternative Service Corps. Seven non-Mennonite enlistees from Majuba Hill and Vedder Flats joined infantry battalions: Gordon Cameron, Charles Sabo, the two Rexford brothers (Douglas and Thomas), and the three Nowell brothers (George, Norville, and Reuben). Another non-Mennonite enlistee, Geraldine Nowell, was the first woman from the Chilliwack area to join the Royal Canadian Air Force.

Of the other 58 Yarrow enlistees, who were all members of recently settled Mennonite families, there were 37 in various infantry battalions; 17 in the non-combatant Royal Canadian Army Medical Corps; two in the Air Force; one in the Merchant Marine; and one in the United States Signal Corps (Harry Dyck, a student in the United States when that country declared war, was haplessly pressed into its armed services).

Thirty young men, all Mennonites, declared themselves conscientious objectors (COs) and performed alternative service in such

Table 1
Military Service and Municipal Location of Yarrow's Enlistees

Municipal Location	Army	Air Force	Other	Totals
Mennonites				
Yarrow	48	2	2	52
Sardis	2	0	0	2
Sumas	4	0	0	4
Non-Mennonites				
Majuba Hills – Vedder Flats	7	1	0	8

Sources: This numerical compilation and analysis draws from Helen Epp's pioneering compilation of data on Canadian Mennonite military service personnel during the Second World War (taken from "Canadian Armed Forces Records," National Archives of Canada). Epp's data are described from a somewhat different vantage point in T.D. Regehr's "Lost Sons." We owe a debt to T.D. Regehr for providing Epp's unpublished compilation, which lists 34 Yarrow Mennonite enlistees in the Canadian Army. This essay includes an additional 19 such enlistees: 6 of these attended Yarrow Mennonite churches but lived in the adjacent municipalities of Sumas and Sardis, including Vedder Flats; 3 originally enlisted in Saskatchewan, but their families relocated to Yarrow early in the Second World War; and 11 were identified in local newspapers and interviews. Our analysis also draws on reports in various issues of The Chilliwack Progress, 1939-1946, as well as A.J. Klassen's Alternative Service for Peace in Canada during World War II, 1941-1946. In addition, we are grateful to various members of the Yarrow Research Committee (2000-2001) for providing the names, dates, and anecdotal information used in this essay.

essential industries as forestry, agriculture, and health, a choice made available to COs by the Canadian government.

When Canada declared war on Germany and its allies, residents of Majuba Hill and the Vedder Flats responded promptly to the call for military service. Within weeks Douglas Rexford joined up, and within a few months Norville Nowell, Gordon Cameron, and others followed suit. The young men from Yarrow's Mennonite community enlisted for military service more reluctantly. Of the 40 for whom there is information, only 9 enlisted before the end of June 1942, when the war was already half over. By the end of June 1943, 20 of these 40 men had joined the armed forces. The time from the date they were eligible to enlist to the time they actually enlisted was 2.7 years on average (see Table 2).

A number of reasons have been suggested for this hesitancy. The generation to which these young men belonged was in many respects transitional. Many had been born in Russia and had come to Canada with their parents in the 1920s. All spoke German in the home; most knew very little English until they began attending Canadian schools. However, many dropped out of school, usually by age 15, to assist in the family economy. Their disrupted educations and their later job experiences away from their home community resulted in considerable inner conflict for them. Though they may have wished to integrate with the larger society, generally speaking this generation did not have the means to bridge the cultural divide. Entering the military was a very

Table 2
Yarrow Mennonite Military Enlistment by Year, 1939-1945

	Oct 1939-Sept 1940	Oct 1940-Sept 1941	Oct 1941-Sept 1942	Oct 1942-Sept 1943	Oct 1943-Sept 1944	Oct 1944-April 1945
Medical Corps	0	0	1	2	10	1
Infantry	1 (6)	1 (1)	6 (1)	10	5	3
Total	1	1	7	12	15	4

* Estimates for non-Mennonite enlistments are given in parentheses.

large step into the world of the wider society, one that many Mennonite young people of that generation were hesitant to take.

Another struggle was taking place in Yarrow's Mennonite community. There was considerable disagreement and confusion among Yarrow's Mennonite church and civic leaders concerning the application of the principle of non-resistance to the current crisis, a disagreement that led to uncertainty in those who had to decide on military service. Several leading members of the Mennonite community had distinguished records in the Tsarist military, in infantry or Red Cross divisions. Some had been pressed into service to fight with the White counter-revolutionary army during the Russian civil war. And others had participated in the armed self-defence militias organized by various Mennonite communities and districts to protect their families and property from roving bands of brigands during the aftermath of the Russian Revolution. Most of those who had taken up arms were not opposed to military service in principle. However, other leading members of the community, particularly the ministers in the Mennonite churches, were generally opposed to bearing arms of any kind. This group held to the historic principle of non-resistance and urged the young Mennonite men to declare themselves COs when appearing before draft boards. As COs, or "conchies" as they were often referred to in *The Chilliwack Progress*,[5] the draftees would be able to serve their country in alternative essential services.

The non-resistance principle was, therefore, a fragile one for those of Yarrow's Mennonite young men eligible for military service. Only 47

Conscientious Objectors: Camp Q3, Campbell River, B.C.

of Yarrow's 88 Mennonite draftees chose the CO option; and only 17 of the 58 who joined the military chose it, considerably fewer than might be expected. Moreover, convictions about the legitimacy and relevance of non-resistance appear to have eroded during the war. For example, 10 men who originally were accepted by the military draft authorities as COs in alternate service decided after some months to join the armed services (see"Yarrow Military Enlistment"at the end of this essay). Although service in the non-combatant Medical Corps was acceptable within the framework of the Mennonite belief in non-resistance, 7 of the 10 men who left the CO camps joined the infantry and only 3 enlisted in the Medical Corps. As COs, all 10 had worked for varying periods of time on farms and ranches, in mines and forestry camps, and in industries that had been approved for alternate service. Dissatisfied with their work or their working and living conditions, they reconsidered their earlier decision to perform alternative service and joined the military. A number of these men had changed their attitudes toward the principle of non-resistance.

There is some anecdotal evidence for Mennonite resistance to serve in the military. In one case, a young man simply ignored his summons to appear before the military recruitment authorities. It took a visit by the police to his parents' home, a chase around the farmyard, and an arrest to press him into the army. In another incident, a Yarrow soldier is said to have taken an extended absence without leave, evading the police and military authorities by spending his days on Vedder Mountain and in the orchards and fields around Yarrow. He slept in the barns, sheds, and attics of his relatives and friends but was later apprehended and sentenced to a term in military prison. Another young enlistee from Yarrow is said to have shot off one of his big toes to avoid being posted overseas.

Any tentative assumptions about reluctance to join the military and changing attitudes toward non-resistance are further complicated by age and enlistment data. Table 2 shows that those who joined the Medical Corps enlisted later than those who joined infantry units. Although this may suggest a greater hesitation by the medical corpsmen to join up, they actually enlisted at a younger age (21.4 years) than the infantrymen (22.7 years). Also, other data suggest that the infantrymen actually waited slightly longer to enlist after they became eligible for the draft (2.9 years) than did the medical corpsmen (2.5 years). However, if those who eventually joined the Medical Corps appear to have been relatively more hesitant to enter the ranks of the military, they may have waited to serve until the call for a non-combatant Medical Corps was heeded—a corps that had no requirement to bear arms, even in training. In addition, those joining infantry units were, being somewhat older in age, possibly more independent of or opposed to the religious and ethnic values of their families and community.

Fifty of the 66 young people from Yarrow who eventually joined the armed services were posted overseas; 16 performed their entire military service in different parts of Canada.[6] The length of service overseas varied considerably, from 11 months (Frank Froese) to 4.5 years (Gordon Cameron and Victor Wiens). A number of others served overseas for about 4 years: Peter Letkeman, Henry Fast, Peter Falk, Peter Peters, and Henry and John Wiens (Victor's brothers, and sons of Mrs. Elizabeth Wiens). These men all belonged to infantry units. In fact, of the 19 infantrymen and 10 medical corpsmen for whom data are available, the infantrymen served overseas for an average of 3.4 years while the medical corpsmen were abroad for 2 years on average. (The average overseas tenure was 3 years.) Apparently, the Mennonites' reluctance to join the military resulted in their time in Britain and Europe being reduced. Those from Mennonite homes were overseas for an average of 31 months; those from non-Mennonite backgrounds served there for an average of 40 months.

Henry Froese, RCAF wireless operator, Watson Lake, Yukon Territory.

The overseas experiences of Yarrow's servicemen and servicewoman were as diverse as the military at war can offer. They were stretcher-bearers, orderlies, nurses, troopers, paratroopers, signalmen, tank commanders, gunners, dispatch drivers, foresters, infantrymen, anti-aircraft gunners, radio operators, and navigators. Henry Froese, for example, became an effective wireless radio operator.[7] Soldiers were stationed in Asia, Africa, Europe, and North America. Their duties took them to hospitals and anti-aircraft defences in England; to lumber camps and ports of Scotland; to killing fields in France, Belgium, and the Netherlands; on allied bombing missions in Germany; to house-to-house battles in Italy; intelligence gathering in India; jungle marches in Burma; several sea battles on the north coast of Africa; and to the South Pacific to assist American troops against Japan. Yarrow's soldiers did not escape casualties. Local newspapers reported that Abe Wittenberg and Norville Nowell were killed in Italy, Rudy Goetz in Holland, and Doug Rexford in England; Peter Falk, Henry Ratzlaff, Peter Bargen, and Peter Isaak were injured in battle; and Jacob Klassen, a paratrooper during the invasion of Normandy, was captured in August 1944 and held as a prisoner of war until June 1945.

The hardships and horrors of war demanded that servicemen and -women be granted appropriate amounts of leisure time. Yarrow's servicemen enjoyed sightseeing and sought out companionship, socializing with other servicemen and local residents. The more evangelically oriented young men organized singing groups—small choirs and quartets—and conducted services for their fellows in the armed services; they traveled the English and Scottish countryside participating in gospel meetings.[8] Others were more interested in sports and games of skill and chance.[9] Yarrow's young men seemed to adjust well to military life and to use it to further their interests.

Although the Yarrow community had little specific knowledge of what its sons were experiencing abroad, there was much concern for their safety and spiritual well-being. Weekly, during the Sunday-morning church services, prayers were offered for the return of Yarrow's soldiers and for their salvation.

Hostilities in Europe ended in April 1945. Of the 66 young people from Yarrow who had enlisted, two medical corpsmen and four infantrymen had been discharged for medical or family-hardship reasons before the war's end. The remaining members of the forces, now veterans, were discharged during the next 17 months. Their return was gradual, sporadic, and quiet. They came home in no particular schedule—an infantryman now, an airman then. The community, however, wanted its sons back as soon as possible to assist in the local economy. Some Yarrow employers gave signed assurances to the military authorities that certain of these young men were essential to the peacetime economy of their community.[10] For some of Yarrow's soldiers, these assurances hastened their discharge and return.

Only 14 of the 36 soldiers for whom there is information were home for Christmas in 1945, a full eight months after hostilities had ended. As members of infantry units, they had served in the military an average of three years. Another 11 came home by Easter 1946, and the rest, mostly members of the non-combatant Medical Corps, returned over the next five or six months. If some of Yarrow's young men delayed their enlistment during the war, the Canadian military establishment was not in a hurry to let them re-enter civilian life after the war. Neither was the government in a hurry to discharge those in alternative service. It took 15 months after the fighting ended before the COs were returned home.[11]

Although some of Yarrow's servicemen were shellshocked or otherwise traumatized by their war experiences, most came back healthy. Some returned to sweethearts they had left behind; two or three returned with English war brides. Some may have left sweethearts behind in Britain, Holland, or Germany. Many came back to Yarrow without job prospects or definite plans for their postwar lives. They were three years older than when they had left for war, and most now intended to establish homes, families, and vocations. They expected to improve on the lives they had had before leaving for war and hoped the country would help them.[12]

Typically, the veterans came back to their parental homes, stayed for a few days or weeks, and then departed. Some looked for employment in the area; some worked for those who had arranged for their early release from duty. But most left the community soon after their return, unable to find suitable work in Yarrow. Some may have felt confined by a still inward-looking village. Some were stung not only by the absence of any public recognition in Yarrow for their service to Canada, a service of which they were justifiably proud,[13] but also by the belligerent and harsh words in the regional media and in public discussion against the attitudes of Yarrow's Mennonites toward the war.[14] Most of the returning veterans quickly left Yarrow for Vancouver and the rapidly growing towns of coastal, northern, and interior British Columbia.

But a number of the returning veterans remained in Yarrow or its vicinity. John Hepting established a used-car sales business in Yarrow because as a veteran he had first purchase rights on used cars.[15] With the help of a Veterans Affairs support program, Frank Sawatsky and others bought farms. Similarly, John Harder and Jack Block were assisted in furthering their formal education.[16] Herb Guenther pursued professional education in dentistry.[17] Henry Ratzlaff, Peter D. Friesen, and Peter Bargen used their entrepreneurial skills to expand existing family businesses and to develop highly successful new enterprises. Seemingly, Yarrow's veterans adjusted to civilian life quickly and successfully. Ultimately, however, most such businesses moved away, resulting in a considerable loss of leadership talent in Yarrow.[18]

No official homecomings greeted the return of Yarrow's soldiers; no community celebrations acknowledged their bravery in dealing with fear, loneliness, and desperation while in the service of their country. The community, it seemed, took little pride in the way its young people had conducted themselves on the war fronts, behind the lines, or at

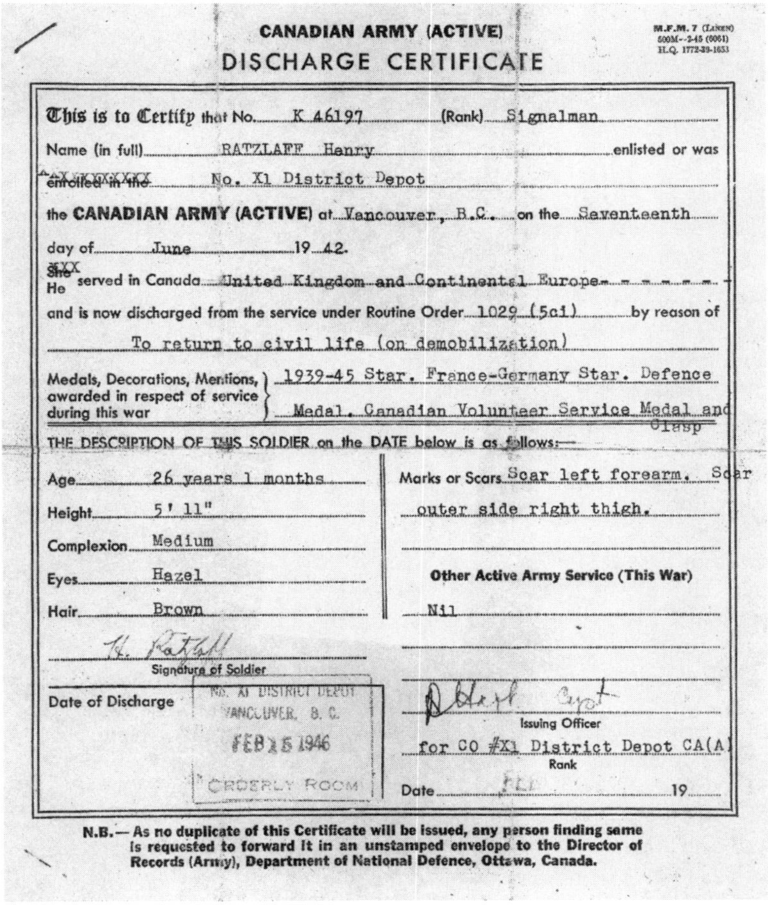

CANADIAN ARMY (ACTIVE)

M.F.M. 7 (Linen) 500M--2-45 (6061) H.Q. 1772-39-1653

DISCHARGE CERTIFICATE

This is to Certify that No. K 46197 (Rank) Signalman

Name (in full) RATZLAFF Henry enlisted or was ~~enrolled in the~~ No. X1 District Depot

the CANADIAN ARMY (ACTIVE) at Vancouver, B.C. on the Seventeenth

day of June 1942.

~~She~~ He served in Canada United Kingdom and Continental Europe

and is now discharged from the service under Routine Order 1029 (5c1) by reason of

To return to civil life (on demobilization)

Medals, Decorations, Mentions, awarded in respect of service during this war: 1939-45 Star. France-Germany Star. Defence Medal. Canadian Volunteer Service Medal and Clasp

THE DESCRIPTION OF THIS SOLDIER on the DATE below is as follows:—

Age 26 years 1 months

Height 5' 11"

Complexion Medium

Eyes Hazel

Hair Brown

Marks or Scars Scar left forearm. Scar outer side right thigh.

Other Active Army Service (This War)

Nil

H. Ratzlaff

Signature of Soldier

Date of Discharge: No. X1 DISTRICT DEPOT VANCOUVER, B.C. FEB 15 1946 ORDERLY ROOM

Issuing Officer

for CO #X1 District Depot CA(A)

Rank

Date FEB 19

N.B.—As no duplicate of this Certificate will be issued, any person finding same is requested to forward it in an unstamped envelope to the Director of Records (Army), Department of National Defence, Ottawa, Canada.

Henry Ratzlaff's military discharge certificate, February 15, 1946.

Henry Ratzlaff's Second World War medals. Ratzlaff, a dispatch rider, was involved in the liberation of the Bergen-Belsen concentration camp by British forces.

Yarrow Military Enlistment

Peter Bargen
Jack Block
Gordon Cameron
Julius Derksen
Harry Dyck
Abe Enns
John W. Enns
Henry Epp
Jake Epp
Jacob Epp
Peter Falk
Bernhard G. Fast
Henry Fast
Peter D. Friesen
Frank Froese
Henry Froese
Henry Giesbrecht
Jake H. Giesbrecht
Rudy Goetz
Herb Guenther
Jacob Hamm
John Harder
Nicholas Harder
Alex Hendricks
Helmuth Hendricks
Julius Hendricks
John Hepting
Cornelius C. Isaac
Peter C. Isaak
Frank Kehler
John Kehler
Jacob Klassen
John Letkeman
Peter Letkeman
Abe Loewen
Dave Nachtigal
Jack Nachtigal
George Nowell
Geraldine Nowell
Norville Nowell
Reuben Nowell
Peter Paetkau
Frank Penner
Peter G. Peters
Henry Ratzlaff
Henry A. Reimer
Douglas Rexford
Tom Rexford
Frank Sawatsky
Charles Sabo
Peter Schellenberg
John Siemens
Dan Thiessen
Nicholas A. Thiessen
Jake Toews
Henry Wall
Jake Wiebe
Peter Wiebe
Henry Wiens
John Wiens
Peter I. Wiens
Victor Wiens
Jacob Willms
Abe Wittenberg
Jake Wittenberg
John Wittenberg

home while in training. Instead, it appeared to find something shameful in having gone to war. Indeed, many people felt that the veterans had participated in some sort of evil. Yet some of Yarrow's soldiers received medals for their outstanding service; Henry Ratzlaff, for example, was awarded five.[19] Closer examination of the experiences of Yarrow's soldiers in war and military life, and of the Yarrow from which they came, may allow a more full comprehension of this climate of moral judgment.

Common Cause: Abram and Anna Wiens and the Mennonite Relief Centre

By John Wiens

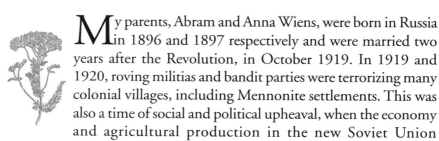

My parents, Abram and Anna Wiens, were born in Russia in 1896 and 1897 respectively and were married two years after the Revolution, in October 1919. In 1919 and 1920, roving militias and bandit parties were terrorizing many colonial villages, including Mennonite settlements. This was also a time of social and political upheaval, when the economy and agricultural production in the new Soviet Union collapsed and widespread famine set in. In the early 1920s, American Mennonites rallied to the support of their Russian co-religionists, and thus the Mennonite Central Committee (MCC) was founded. In Russia, Mennonite leaders, including my parents, did what they could to assist in this relief work. My parents are remembered mainly for their work in organizations associated with the MCC.

After escaping from Russia in 1925, my parents lived in Ontario for a while, then moved on to Manitoba and finally to British Columbia. During those early years in Canada, most of the newly arrived Mennonite immigrants lived on the edge of poverty. Although my parents were no exception, even during the worst years in Manitoba they assisted others who were struggling with impossible mortgages, unfamiliar customs, and expensive health-care systems.

By the end of the Second World War, my parents had relocated to Yarrow. Like many other Mennonites from Russia, they knew almost nothing of the whereabouts of friends and relatives who had remained in Russia. I can remember their excitement and concern when news reached Canada that thousands of Mennonite refugees from Russia had surfaced in western Europe.

Rescuing these refugees became the top priority of many Canadian Mennonites, and my parents were involved in this effort from the start. My father was the executive secretary of the provincial Mennonite Relief Committee of British Columbia in 1945. This committee and its equivalent chapters in other western provinces were now reorganized and strengthened to serve as subsidiaries of the Canadian Mennonite Board of Colonization. In those days, most Mennonite families in British Columbia had relatives or friends among the Mennonite refugees in Europe. But to bring refugees to Canada, these families had to comply with strict government regulations. They had to provide suitable housing, offer employment, pay the transportation charges, and guarantee that the immigrants would not become public charges in Canada. In British Columbia, my father coordinated the effort of bringing émigrés from Europe, personally assisting everyone who applied to relocate refugees and guiding each applicant through what sometimes seemed like endless red tape.

In 1947, 542 Mennonite refugees arrived in Canada. In the next year that number grew to 4,227, one-quarter of whom came to British Columbia. Nearly 2,000 arrived in 1949—again, about 25 percent of them to B.C. In all, more than 3,000 Mennonite refugees from Europe came to B.C. after the Second World War.

The majority of these immigrants and their sponsors were eager to comply with Canadian regulations, but some made things difficult for those directly concerned. A few were simply dishonest, and more than a few made promises that they failed to honour once they had arrived safely in Canada. Some had been involved with the National-Socialists in Germany and tried to deny this involvement. More than a few refused to remain with their employers for a year, as they had promised. Others did not repay their transportation debts even when they were in a position to do so, leaving this responsibility to the Canadian Mennonite Board of Colonization. These problems created a great amount of unnecessary labour for my parents, and my father spent much time working with immigration officials to ensure that these few bad apples didn't ruin the attitude of Canadian officials toward the Mennonites.

A specific example involves a man and his family who had originally been placed on a dairy farm in Saskatchewan with the understanding that he would remain there for the year required by immigration law. Almost immediately after arriving on the farm, the man had disagreements with his sponsor and demanded a new placement. The

Board reluctantly moved him to B.C., where he again became disenchanted. He left his employer without notice and then took a series of jobs, all of which ended when he either left or was dismissed. He refused to pay off any of his debts to the Canadian Pacific Railway although he had earned enough money to pay cash for a car. The Canadian Mennonite Board of Colonization therefore had to assume responsibility for the payments. Eventually the Canadian immigration authorities asked my father for a detailed report concerning this man's activities. An immigration inspector then interviewed the man in the presence of my father and a witness, who was a member of the Chilliwack Municipal Council. The interview concluded with a warning that Canada was under no obligation to permit people like him to remain in Canada.

Among those who made things most difficult was a small minority of refugees from Danzig. These were the descendants of Mennonites who had remained in the Vistula and Nogat regions of Prussia when so many of our people emigrated from there to Russia some two centuries ago. As ethnic Germans, these Prussian refugees did not qualify for immigration under the normal regulations applied to the other refugees. Indeed, many of them were refused entry into Canada because they had been members of Hitler's National-Socialist Party. Of the ones who were admitted into Canada, the majority became good citizens. But there were also those who made their sponsors sorry that they had ever become involved in rescuing them.

At the other end of the spectrum were those who made my parents' work a pleasure. One such group had fled to the east to escape Russian tyranny and eventually surfaced in China. In late 1947 or early 1948, the chairman of the Canadian Mennonite Board of Colonization informed my father that there was no prospect of these people being allowed to come to Canada. But he was unaware that my father, in response to a request from a British Columbia resident, had already conducted preliminary work with immigration officers on the Pacific Coast on behalf of these people. The first six members of the Chinese Mennonite group arrived in British Columbia in 1948. Another group of 14 arrived in San Francisco the same year. They were put on a train to Portland, where Father met them and escorted them to Canada. Two more came from China later that year, and a final four arrived in 1949.

For reasons of health, many refugees were unable to enter Canada; most of them made their way to other countries. Several thousand, including a large contingent involved in a sensational escape from the

Russian military in Berlin, went to Paraguay. For many of these people, Canada remained the hoped-for destination, and so almost immediately upon arriving in Paraguay they renewed efforts to enter Canada. For those wishing to come to British Columbia, applications and negotiations involved working through my father. But now a new problem arose. In part because of their hasty exit from Germany, these refugees included some who had supported the Hitler regime. Because Canadian authorities were well aware of this fact, entering Canada from Paraguay became much more difficult than entering from Europe. Unfortunately, this led to efforts to circumvent normal channels. Even some well-meaning Mennonite leaders were caught up in these efforts. When this sort of thing occurred, Father had to deal with the consequences, as Canadian immigration authorities became highly suspicious whenever a prospective Paraguayan (European Mennonite) immigrant sought to enter Canada without going through the Canadian Mennonite Board of Colonization. More than once my father had to tell his own people that pious words accompanied by misrepresentations to immigration authorities were unacceptable.

Another challenge my parents had to cope with was the appearance of Mexican Mennonites at British Columbia border crossings. These were descendants of a group that had left Canada for Mexico during the 1920s in search of greater religious freedom and cultural autonomy. Their life in Mexico had been difficult, and as a result many of the poorest among them began to drift back to Canada, usually without proper documentation and sometimes literally on the brink of death. More than once my parents had to take a telephone call in the middle of the night because a distraught border customs officer did not know what to do with a destitute Mennonite gypsy (as the immigration authorities termed these people). On at least one occasion, a customs officer bundled one such family into his own vehicle and transported them to Yarrow, where my mother had to take charge of a mother and her newborn baby, both near death, and rush them to the hospital.

When the volume of Mexican returnees became unmanageable, the North American Mennonite community sent my father to Mexico to consult with Mennonite leaders about the circumstances of their people and to advise them on proper legal procedures when seeking to enter Canada. For a while things proceeded more smoothly, but then the problem returned. People in Mexico apparently were being advised, "Just go. Once you reach the Canadian border, people will help you." A number of would-be returnees were turned back at the Canadian border, and on one occasion Father personally had to escort a family all the way back to Mexico.

As is often the case, a minority of people created most of the work for my parents—and for others in similar positions in other provinces. This was discouraging at times, but it was more than offset by the gratitude and cooperation of the majority of the new Canadians.

With the sudden influx of thousands of immigrant Mennonites unaccustomed to the Canadian way of life, my parents and other Canadian leaders took steps to ensure that these people became citizens whose loyalty would be to their new home. They encouraged the newcomers to start the formal process of becoming citizens, and they advised them in whatever way they could along the way. My father's efforts in this regard were aided considerably when the government learned of his efforts. In November 1950, the lieutenant-governor of British Columbia, Clarence Wallace, appointed him a commissioner to receive affidavits and affirmations concerning citizenship proceedings in the courts of British Columbia. This appointment was made in November 1950.

By the mid-1950s, the flood of immigrants had slowed to a trickle, but then the Hungarian Revolution brought a new opportunity for the

A.A. Wiens advising new immigrants after the Second World War (Jack Wittenberg assisting).

Mennonites to assist refugees—in this case, people who were not part of the Mennonite religious community. The numbers were not large, but once again my parents were instrumental in welcoming and placing these people.

By 1957, other needs had begun to preoccupy the British Columbia Mennonite community and the provincial relief committee. Many of the recent immigrants were widows, and there was urgent need to assist them with housing. Support was also needed for the mentally ill. Furthermore, after the Korean War new areas requiring help emerged overseas. Consequently, financial and material assistance was garnered from Mennonites throughout Canada. Material assistance consisted mainly of clothing, and the strong interest in British Columbia in this kind of assistance led to the establishment of the Clothing Depot at my parents' property in Yarrow.

By this time, my parents had reached an age when they could reasonably be expected to retire. Nevertheless, they now decided to begin a major expansion of what had until then been a sideline. With the opening of the Yarrow Clothing Depot, Mennonite women's societies from all over British Columbia provided so much support that the centre had to be expanded, the first of several expansions over the years. Soon the depot was sending more clothing, blankets, and other materials overseas than any other Mennonite centre in Canada. The Mennonite Central Committee headquarters in Akron, Pennsylvania, made use of the depot to send bales of goods to Hong Kong. Shipments were also sent to such places as Jordan and Korea. In the case of Korea, the depot was responsible for clothing 200 boys in an orphanage twice a year.

Each year the operation grew larger. In May 1963, my father reported that the depot employed four individuals full-time and two half-time, with others employed or volunteering as needed. He also reported that in the preceding year, 581 women from various women's societies in the province had come to assist with mending, sorting, and packing. And so in 1963, yet another expansion of the facilities was undertaken. At this time, Father wrote to his friend C.A. DeFehr of Winnipeg: "Who wants to dam up the stream of mercy? Not we. We had dedicated ourselves to this work and we are happy in it. This new building program is completely our own undertaking and we are making it available to the 'Hilfswerk' [relief effort] without asking for anything."

At this time my mother was approaching her 66th birthday, and my father his 67th. It was time to stop. Arrangements were made to find successors for this work, and in 1964, Mr. and Mrs. R. Bauman of Ontario arrived to take over the relief work.

Today a reorganized Mennonite Central Committee, with many branch offices throughout North America, continues the work begun by our pioneers. Hence the practical Christian expression of caring people continues to give life and hope to suffering people around the globe. I believe my parents would be proud of those who have succeeded them and expanded the work into a multi-faceted service to people in need.

Displaced Lives: Influx of European Refugees after the Second World War

By Selma Kornelsen Hooge

Only 12 when my family arrived in December 1948, I had no idea how hard some people in Yarrow had worked to make it possible for us to come to Canada. Nor did I realize how many times our family could have been permanently separated, or that our fate could have been to freeze in Siberia or burn in the "green hell" of the Chaco in Paraguay. Many miraculous events were required in order for all of my father's siblings and my mother's sister and their families to end up in Yarrow after the war. I will mention but two.

For many years, the most indelible memory from my early childhood in the Ukraine has revolved around making a confusing trip to a train station, spending several cold nights in a field of stubble, and then returning to our village, which looked a mess. Much later, as an adult in Canada, after asking questions and reading about the war, I was overwhelmed to learn the significance of that incident in October 1941 involving a train station.

In the summer of 1941, when news reached us that the German army had crossed the border from Poland into the Ukraine, most Mennonites in the Ukraine secretly hoped that the Germans would soon get to our villages. Surely that would mean the end of the oppression of Communism and a return to private property and religious freedom. The Communists, however, had other plans. They ordered the evacuation by train of all German-speaking colonists in the Ukraine to Kazakhstan or Siberia. Their plan succeeded only partially, because of the speed with which the German forces moved eastward. Our village of Marienthal missed by a mere half-hour the last train to stop at the station. My aunt Mary claimed that we could well have been on another train that shot past the station ahead of the advancing Germans as we waited for the train we had missed.

The next morning, after our night in a freezing stubble field, the stationmaster approached Aunt Mary, the only one who had come to the station with her own horses and wagon. Old Ukrainian men had brought the rest of us, because all the Mennonite men, wagons, and horses had already been taken away by the Red Army. The stationmaster asked for one of Aunt Mary's horses to make his getaway before the Germans came. In those days, asking for a horse was almost like asking for a car today. But the man explained, "I'm asking you for a favour because I did you a favour. I could have stopped that last train, but I figured you would rather wait for the Germans than go east." Had this man really held our fate in his hands?

Later, a Red Army soldier came to ask for civilian clothes. "You might as well go home," he said. "The Germans are already in your villages." But we didn't go home immediately: the women were probably afraid, the one horse and one wagon we had couldn't take many people home, and the walking distance was 15 kilometres. Finally, my older sister and a friend rode the one horse to the nearest village to find another horse. Then they began taking one wagonload of people at a time. It took them three days to transport all the women and children back to our village. A few weeks later, there was great joy when some of the men and women who had been digging trenches at the Dniepr River returned. My father and a number of others whom the Russians had sent east with herds of cows and pigs also returned. But the rest of the men were not seen again.

For almost two years thereafter, the Mennonites in the Ukraine lived under German rule, hoping for a quick end to collective farming. Their hopes for the normal village life Mennonites had known before Communism, however, were dashed in 1943 because the once-mighty Germans were thoroughly defeated at Stalingrad and began their retreat back across the Ukraine. All the Mennonite villagers in the Ukraine were evacuated in order to be resettled west of the Dniepr River, then farther west again, and again. Some families made the trip to the west by train, but our family and thousands of others trekked with horses and wagons through fall and winter on muddy roads to the Polish border. In the spring of 1944, we were resettled in Poland, where we resided for the next 10 months. In January 1945, with little warning or time to prepare, we had to flee westward once again, this time in an open wagon. We were among the fortunate ones to make it safely to the west; thousands of other fleeing Mennonite families were intercepted by Russian forces, identified as citizens of Russia, separated from each other and from masses fleeing westward, and sent back to Russia. Most never again saw each other or their former homeland, the Ukraine.

With this evacuation of our villages in September 1943 came the end of the 150-year history of Mennonite settlements in the Ukraine. Then, in 1945, as German forces were being crushed by the fast-advancing Russians, another historical chapter also came to an abrupt end: the 400-year-old history of Mennonites in Danzig and Poland. Most of the fleeing *Danziger* Mennonites were evacuated by ship. Many lost their lives when their ships were sunk in the Baltic Sea.

When Germany surrendered in May 1945, there were thousands of homeless Mennonites in bombed-out Germany. Through the efforts of the Red Cross, the International Relief Organization, the Mennonite Central Committee, and other agencies, refugees found temporary shelters in schools, barracks, or crowded houses. None wanted to go back to his or her former home, which once again was under Communist control. Many who feared forceful repatriation emigrated to Paraguay or Uruguay, the only countries that at the outset accepted refugees.[1] Later, individuals like C.F. Klassen, Peter and Elfrieda Dyck, A.A. Wiens of Yarrow, and many generous sponsors all over Canada helped to bring more than 8,000 Mennonites to Canada by 1952.

During those first postwar years, only healthy persons with close relatives in Canada willing to sponsor them were allowed into Canada. Hardly any of the refugees in Europe, however, had written addresses for their relatives who had come to Canada in the 1920s. It had been a crime under Communist rule to be in touch with the western world. Making contact was impossible—but sometimes the impossible happened. Jacob Quapp and his sisters, Tina and Mary, were among the thousands of homeless in Europe. They knew they had a brother, David, in Canada, and Jacob remembered a Kitchener, Ontario. So Jacob addressed a letter to "David Quapp, Kitchener, Ontario." David Quapp had indeed lived in Kitchener when he first came to Canada in 1926, but subsequently he had moved to Brazil for two years. Upon his return to Canada, he lived at several addresses in Vancouver before moving to Yarrow. Jacob's letter traveled for six months from Ontario to several addresses in Vancouver with "Try this, try this ... " on the envelope. Eventually, in 1947, it reached David Quapp in Yarrow. He quickly filled out the necessary papers to bring his siblings to Canada.[2]

Not only were his family members—Jacob, Mary, and Tina Quapp—the first postwar immigrants to arrive in Yarrow, but they were also probably three of the first five Mennonite émigrés from the USSR to arrive in Canada since 1930. The next war refugees from Europe to arrive in Yarrow were Agatha Rempel with her two sons and two daughters, in September 1947. The Johann Harders in Yarrow and Nick Rempels of Chilliwack sponsored them.

My family had neither close nor distant relatives that we knew of in Canada, but my dad refused to immigrate to Paraguay. We conjectured that perhaps once Agatha Rempel, my mother's immigrating sister, was established in Canada, she could sponsor us. It turned out that "Taunte Gat" did play a role in our coming to Canada, but not as my parents expected. Another miracle, it seemed to us, brought us in touch with our sponsors in Yarrow.

When reports had come to Yarrow Mennonites at the end of the war that thousands of Mennonite refugees from the Ukraine were scattered across Europe, they wondered if their relatives might be among these refugees. Many Yarrow settlers who had left the Soviet Union in the 1920s had left behind brothers, sisters, parents, sons, and daughters. Most of them had had no contact with lost relatives since 1930. At the end of 1945, C.F. Klassen of the Mennonite Central Committee came to Germany to assess the refugee situation. He sent regular reports, "*Brüder in Not*" (brothers in distress), to a number of German newspapers in North America, including *Die Mennonitische Rundschau*. Newspapers like the *Rundschau* also featured columns under the title of "*Verwandte gesucht*" (searching for relatives). People on both sides of the Atlantic were placing items in these columns.

The three Reimer sisters—Gertrude, Elizabeth, and Sarah—who were among the first settlers in Yarrow, heard about the need for sponsors of refugees. They wanted to help, yet they didn't know of any close relatives that they had left behind in the 1920s. Fortunately for our family, they remembered an aunt who had married a Jakob Kornelsen of Pordenau. They wondered if any of his children or grandchildren might be among the refugees. Gertrude Reimer asked educator and minister Cornelius C. Peters to submit an item for her to one of those "Searching for Relatives" columns.

Our aunt, Agatha Rempel, had lived near us for a while back in Germany, but when rumours spread that the Russians were taking Soviet citizens back by force, she fled to Holland. We remained in Germany. Aunt Agatha was soon in touch with her husband's relatives in Canada, the Harders and the Rempels. They sent her parcels, letters, and the *Rundschau*. When she spotted the little item that Gertrude Reimer had placed, she sent the article to us in Germany. Although the Jakob Kornelsen whom Gertrude Reimer had referred to was only my dad's father's cousin, we ardently hoped this distant relationship would be close enough. What a surprise the Reimer sisters must have had when they received my mother's letter informing them that there were 23 of us who would dearly love to come to Canada.

The Reimer sisters prayed to God, asked their brother Nickolai Reimer for advice, and went to several other people in Yarrow for help. They had to. Canadian officials would not allow the three sisters, with their few acres of mixed farming, to sign for 23 refugees. A niece of the Reimer Aunts, as we later called them, remembers how they scrimped and saved those years to pay for our fare. "One year they only allowed themselves $100 for groceries," Gertrude Martens recalls.[3] Through their sacrificial efforts and with help from others, all 23 of us were in Yarrow by December 1948.

Our family arrived at Pier 21 in Halifax in late November, boarded a Canadian Pacific train, and finally transferred to a Canadian National train in Winnipeg. "After Winnipeg came all that flat land which reminded my parents of the steppes of the Ukraine. Then came those mountains the Reimers had written about—what grandeur, but how frightening. At times the river seemed a long way down. Suddenly the mountains parted and stood aside so river and flat land could lie between them. And there between the river and the mountains was Chilliwack."[4] That's where the Reimers met us.

Other relatives sponsored as refugees by the Reimers had already settled in Yarrow. For example, Mary Goosen had arrived with her six children on December 24, 1947; the Bachmans, with five children, had come in April 1948. Our family (the Kornelsens) and Onkel Jasch were the last of the relatives to come. For a while the 23 of us lived in renovated chicken barns at Reimer's Nurseries and on the nearby yard of the Reimer sisters on Dyke Road.

When we arrived in Yarrow on December 2, 1948, Mother was delighted to find that we would have a private place for our family, next

Chicken barn owned by Gertrude, Elizabeth, and Sarah Reimer, which these sisters had converted into apartments for immigrants.

door to Aunt Mary. The Reimer sisters had scrubbed and papered the old chicken barn to make two small apartments. Downstairs was a sleeping area for my parents, a corner pantry stocked with staples, a table and chairs, and a stove. Upstairs was a bedroom for the rest of us. When Mother saw the wood-burning stove, she quoted the German saying "Your own stove is worth gold." She had not had her own stove since September 1943.

Few families were as fortunate as ours to come as a complete unit—that is, with father and brothers present. Typically, families arriving in Yarrow were in similar circumstances as the rest of our relatives: Aunt Agatha had lost her husband and one son in Siberia, and another son in the German army; Aunt Mary did not know her husband's whereabouts (he came to Canada from Russia 22 years later); Onkel Jasch had lost his wife and four children on the flight from Poland to Germany (his oldest son came here from Russia to visit after 35 years of separation).

While we were getting used to our new home in Canada, Danzig and Polish Mennonite refugees were still waiting in Europe. They had more difficulty entering Canada because they were classed as German Nationals.[5] Even though Canada had lifted the "close-relative" requirement for immigration, it was not until 1950 that any *Danziger* came to Canada. Henry Claassen, senior pastor of the Yarrow United Mennonite Church from 1970 to 1979, was among those who came from Danzig (1951). After his family—mother, brother, and two sisters—arrived safely in the British Zone in Germany, they found their way to one of the oldest Mennonite congregations in Germany, Hamburg-Altona. There they met C.F. Klassen and Peter Dyck and learned about the possibility of going to Canada as farm workers. In Canada, the Claassen family was sponsored by the John Esau family of East Chilliwack, who provided well for the Claassens' physical and spiritual needs. A year later the Claassens moved to Yarrow, where they bought a hobby farm and attended the United Mennonite Church. The presence of other *Danziger* families in Yarrow made their experience feel like a homecoming.[6]

Although immigration authorities still required that Canadian sponsors provide Mennonite refugees with housing and help in finding jobs, sponsors no longer were required to be relatives of the immigrants or to pay their fare. The Canadian Mennonite Board of Colonization and the Mennonite Central Committee took responsibility for transportation costs.[7] The immigrants were expected to repay the fare after they were settled in Canada. Susie Derksen and her late husband Jacob sponsored seven such families.

Other Mennonite newcomers to Yarrow during those years came from Mexico, Paraguay, and China. Some immigrants arrived with preconceived ideas and expectations. One émigré brought jewelry from China that he hoped to sell here at a great profit. Another one stocked up on scissors and razors in Germany. He thought he could make money in Canada by selling items on the black market as he had done in Germany. It is safe to say, however, that most immigrants who came to Yarrow after the Second World War were like my parents: they simply wanted jobs to pay off the *Reiseschuld* (travel debt) and to buy a home of their own. In most cases, families accomplished that and much more, thanks to economic opportunities and their hard work.

The Yarrow school quickly realized that a bumper crop of foreign students had appeared in 1948. Starting in January 1949, many of us who spoke no English sat in Mrs. Burgess's class. Mr. Wilson, the principal, had given firm instructions that no one be permitted to speak German at school. Some who didn't like us "DPs" (displaced persons) gleefully followed the rules. When I would ask what a certain word meant, they would respond, "Look it up in the dictionary." Little good that does if the student understands only a few words of English. Others, like Johnny and Violet Kaethler, Bertha Harder, and Hilda Reimer, were kind and always sought to help us out. In other words, for those of us enrolled in school, arrival in Yarrow did not mean having truly arrived there.

As for the older immigrant girls, most of them, including my unmarried sisters, immediately went to Vancouver to do housework, despite being trained teachers, nurses, or secretaries. Some of the young men found employment in Yarrow. My sisters and brother brought most of their money home until the travel debt was paid and my parents were able to purchase their first house. As far as I know, the travel debt for all 23 of us was paid within a year of our arrival.

Not all sponsors worked as hard as the Reimer sisters to prepare homes for the new immigrants. And not all immigrants were as conscientious and grateful as my parents were. Every year my mother reminded us to be grateful to "the aunts." As long as the aunts were alive, Mother or one of my sisters would call them or bring them flowers on the anniversary of our arrival. Several times Mother even wrote them poems and tributes. It was the least we could do.

Artisans and Art

By Lena Isaac, Gladys Loewen, and Lora Sawatsky

When Mennonites fled from Russia, among the items they commonly brought with them were clothing, a Bible, a songbook, a large woven basket (for transporting food), needles, thread, a portable sewing machine, and often a Kröger clock. In most cases, they also brought a determination to create or refashion goods they would need, and they knew their crafts. Governed largely by life's necessities, these crafts were cultivated for years in Yarrow. Craftsmanship was not an instance of enlightenment coming to frontier villagers, but an attempt to recover or continue life as these immigrants had known it. While utilitarian in purpose, crafts and artisanship also served creative impulses and an aspiration to reach beyond the struggle for daily survival. Thus these endeavours tended to erase the lines between high and low art and between fine and practical crafts.

For example, men in Yarrow perfected their skills in carpentry and upholstery, and in building houses, cabinets, tables, chairs, bed frames, rocking chairs, bookcases, chests, spinning wheels, cradles, toys, picture frames, wall decorations, fences, gates, swing sets, arbours, trellises, and workbenches. Sometimes they crafted these benches using wooden dowels and glue rather than nails and screws. They also repaired and refaced Kröger clocks and built new ones. A few worked with leather. John Reimer often welcomed children of the village into his shop to observe a blacksmith at work. Before the days of indoor plumbing, several of the men demonstrated their artistry by crafting fancy outhouses. Gerhard Hooge, Henry Enns, Henry Harms, and others wove attractive baskets for use in the home and on the farm.

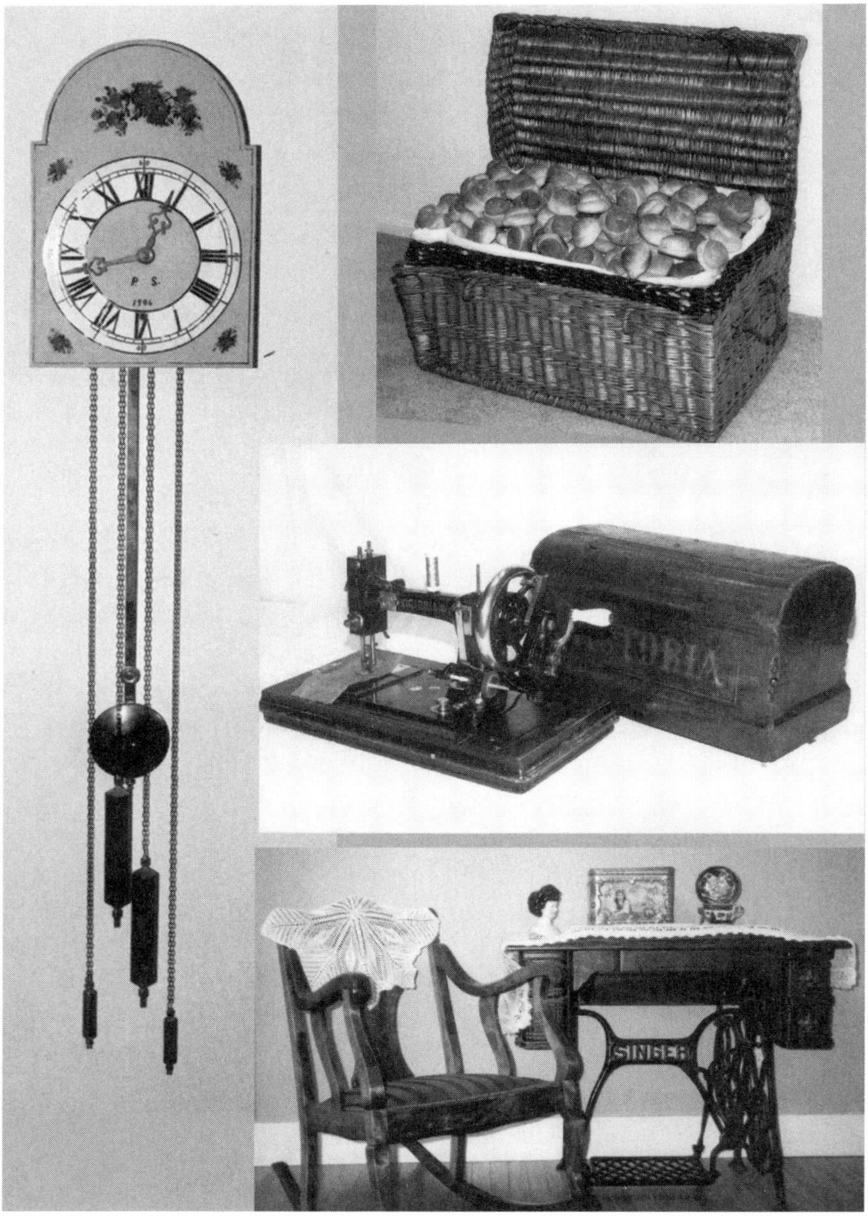

(Clockwise from top left):
Jacob Sawatsky's Kröger clock, brought from Russia in 1926, still loudly sounds the hours today; wicker chest woven by Heinrich Enns, brought from Russia in 1926 (this basket was filled with food for the trip from Russia to Canada); Buschman sewing machine, brought from Russia; Katherine Loewen's treadle machine and rocking chair.

Margaret Enns Neufeldt notes, "My father was a craftsman. In addition to woodwork and carpentry, he wove baskets, some large with handles to carry straw to the kitchen for heating the oven, other smaller ones for knitting supplies and other household items. Baskets were woven with willow branches. To make white baskets, willow branches were soaked in hot water, peeled, dried and woven. He made a wicker chest for our travels from Russia to Canada. It was filled with roasted Zwieback and home cured ham."[1]

Women brought with them the knowledge of spinning wool and silken threads, sewing, knitting, crocheting, and embroidering. Sewing classes were offered by accomplished seamstresses such as Helen Froese Quapp (1899-1986), who came to Yarrow around 1934, and Anna Sukkau (1907-84), who moved to Yarrow in 1941.[2] Helen Quapp's 52-page *Instructive Guide*, which provides detailed instructions for designing and modifying patterns for both women's and men's clothing, reveals her extraordinary creativity as a seamstress. In her published article, Rose Friesen Buschman pays tribute to Helen's talent and generous spirit. Rose recalls a moment in her childhood when she and the rest of her impoverished family received unexpected gifts on Christmas Eve: several beautifully crafted items from their friends Helen and David Quapp, who at that time were deacons in the Yarrow Mennonite Brethren Church.[3]

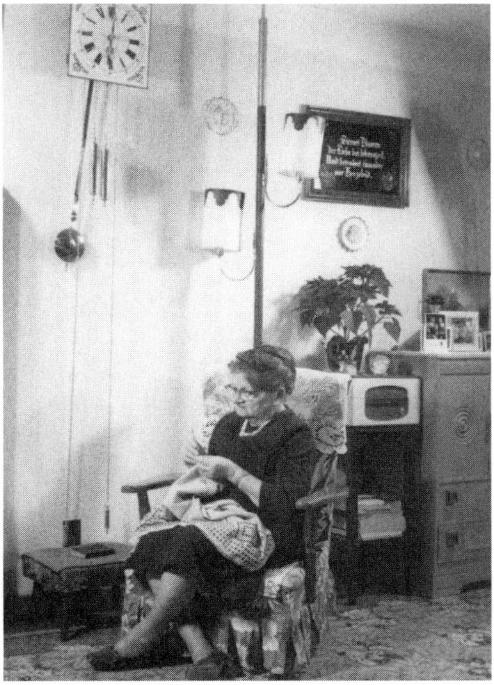

Helen (Friesen) Neumann, known for her fine crocheting, died in 1987 at 100 years and six months of age.

The resourcefulness and talents Rose describes in her story were not unusual for early Yarrow settlers. During the early pioneer years, the only fabrics affordable to most women were unbleached cotton flour sacks or discarded clothing. At home, women took personal pride in cleaning and trimming discarded materials and uniquely and serviceably redesigning them, thereby giving them a new life. But they did so collectively as well. As early as January 26, 1930, Mennonite women of Yarrow organized a Ladies' Aid Society under the leadership of Elizabeth Friesen Klassen.[4] Until 1934 there was only one such group in Yarrow, but by 1954, 12 different groups met weekly. While the women of this society did not confine themselves solely to practical work, their records reveal that in one year they prepared close to 1,000 canned goods, sewed 15 quilts for the Vancouver City Mission, and prepared Christmas hampers for 11 families. They also sewed 108 items for the Chilliwack Hospital and 320 for the Red Cross and purchased $385.97 worth of materials from the Mennonite Central Committee (MCC), from which they sewed 95 blankets and 654 additional items for the MCC. In addition, they mended, restored, and cleaned many other items to send to needy people.[5]

Having become personally acquainted with poverty after difficult relocations, first from Russia and then from the Canadian Prairies, settlers of early Yarrow had to cope with another trial—a decade of international economic depression. Yet the two accounts that follow pay tribute to individuals determined to use their creativity and ingenuity and to share what resources they had with others. This they did in spite of the limitations imposed on them by their condition as immigrants.

Grandmother's Nimble Fingers

By Gladys A. Loewen

My paternal grandmother, Katherine Quiring Loewen (1902-1975), was a resourceful woman who contributed in a major way to the survival of her own family. In Russia, she had grown up in a family of 22 children (with four mothers, three of whom died, and one father). Her first husband died, leaving her with a three-month-old son who was covered with eczema, a condition that seemed beyond medical remedy. After her husband's death, she became her father's caregiver in exchange for a place to live. She cared for him until he died.

Mennonite and other colonial women in Russia were not allowed to own land, so Grandmother decided, upon her father's death, to find a second husband who would agree to move into their family home and accept her sickly child. That man was Abram A. Loewen, and she and he had two daughters. They came to Canada in 1930 after a long and arduous journey through Europe, during which their daughters had died. In 1934, this family of three survivors moved from Manitoba and settled in Yarrow. Her new husband was a gentle person. But his limited education and work experience made his prospects for finding a job bleak. Grandmother was a bright, intelligent woman who desperately wanted to be educated, to read, gather information, and understand new ideas. Schooling was not an option for her because she needed to help support the family. This she did in many ways: sewing, canning, maintaining a huge garden, and sometimes working outside the home when the only employment her husband could find was as a temporary farmhand or a janitor at the church. With these kinds of jobs, my grandparents often lived at the workplace, and Grandmother helped with the chores, thereby adding to the family's income.

Without spending any money, Grandmother also created a huge garden of flowers, fruit trees, vegetables, and grapes. She would take leaves and roots from other people's gardens and nurture the cuttings into mature, healthy plants. In this way she was able to put fresh food on the table and preserve food for the winter. Even though gardening was a means of surviving, she spent hours creating a garden that was remarkably beautiful. I loved walking through it with her. She didn't know most of the flowers by name; nonetheless, they thrived under her care.

My grandparents built a lean-to at the back of the garage, and here Grandmother sewed with her treadle sewing machine for hours each day. When the cuffs and collars of Grandfather's shirts wore out, she would remove them, turn them inside out, and sew them back on, extending the life of the shirt. When the cuffs and collars wore out again, she would turn the shirt into a blouse for me. I loved my blouses: the fabric was soft and well worn. My sisters and I were the pride of the neighbourhood when we each received a bride doll from Grandmother, complete with a wardrobe (pajamas, dresses, a coat), as well as pillows and mattresses for the beds Grandfather had crafted for us.

For her creative work with fabrics, Grandmother collected fabric scraps from friends, but her main source was the garbage dump. She visited it weekly, bringing home discarded clothes, cleaning them, and literally sewing new life into the materials. In her sewing shed, she stored fabric in approximately 25 boxes, all of them labeled and sorted by colour. In addition, she had several boxes that contained buttons, lace, rick-rack, and other types of trimming taken from old clothes.

As we grandchildren grew up, she turned her attention to sewing and donating dresses to the Mennonite Central Committee (MCC) to send to countries where relief was required. When she had completed her first project, Grandfather drove her to the MCC office, where she proudly presented 100 dresses, all of them made from scraps of fabric. Lace and trimming covered the many seams, as each dress was a patchwork of fabric scraps. Some dresses had 20 pieces. One can imagine her shock when the person at the MCC office refused to accept the dresses because they were too fancy for starving children. Grandmother telephoned me in Vancouver to report what had happened, her voice breaking as she cried. I telephoned the person responsible and asked him, "Why can't girls in poverty-stricken countries wear dresses similar to the ones I have worn? Why should girls in other countries not have fancy dresses? Did you realize that all these dresses were made from recycled fabric?" He grudgingly agreed to take them. For many years, Grandmother poured her creativity into these dresses, sewing for hours on the treadle machine and then sitting in her rocking chair, hand-stitching the hems and buttons.

Grandmother died in 1975, but her treadle sewing machine and rocking chair are now part of my home.

Raising Silkworms

By Lena Giesbrecht Isaac

My mother, Elizabeth Wittenberg Giesbrecht, born November 13, 1884, in Altonau, Molotschna colony, was an enthusiast who was always eager to start a new venture. Settling in Yarrow in 1928, however, and raising a family of 10 during the miserably lean years of the Great Depression, meant endless hours of demanding chores. Yet the hard work did not quash her creative energies. Invariably she found the time and passion for unique projects. One such project early on was learning the English language. What could better facilitate this than using the Eaton's catalogue as a textbook? Many an hour was spent with the postmaster, Eva Siddall, writing out catalogue orders, and the two developed a close friendship. During one of their sessions, Mother was encouraged to take up silkworm cultivation, a hobby she had practised back in Russia.

The silkworm industry had been strongly promoted among the Mennonites in Russia by Johann Cornies (1789-1848), a successful farmer, businessman, and political leader. By 1845 some 207 families in 35 colonies were involved in this enterprise. Cornies invested much of his own time and money to further the silkworm industry, including building a special girls' school in Ohrloff, in the southern Ukraine, that offered instruction in silk reeling. Eventually, however, competition from the French and Italians and a silkworm plague resulted in the death of the industry.[6]

After settling in Yarrow, Father, always ready to cooperate with Mother's ventures, responded to her new interest by planting a hedge of some 20 mulberry bushes. These grew very quickly, and within two to three years the leaves were ready for harvesting. In 1940, Eva Siddall contacted government officials in Ottawa, who then ordered and imported silkworm eggs from Japan. Mother was able to start her project.

There are four stages in the life cycle of a silkworm: egg, larva, chrysalis, and adult. The eggs are round, somewhat flattened, and about the size of a turnip seed. Mother kept the eggs in cold storage until the greening of the mulberry bushes in spring, then placed them in the rearing room, where the temperature was 70 to 75° Fahrenheit. The eggs hatched within 10 days. The larvae, about one-eighth of an inch in length, were immediately ready to receive food. To prepare for feeding them, Father had constructed a raised platform of about 3 ½ by 15 feet in a small farm building. Here, the larvae were placed on trays with fresh mulberry leaves. Since the larvae fed most of the time, the leaves were quickly devoured and needed replenishing three or four times daily.

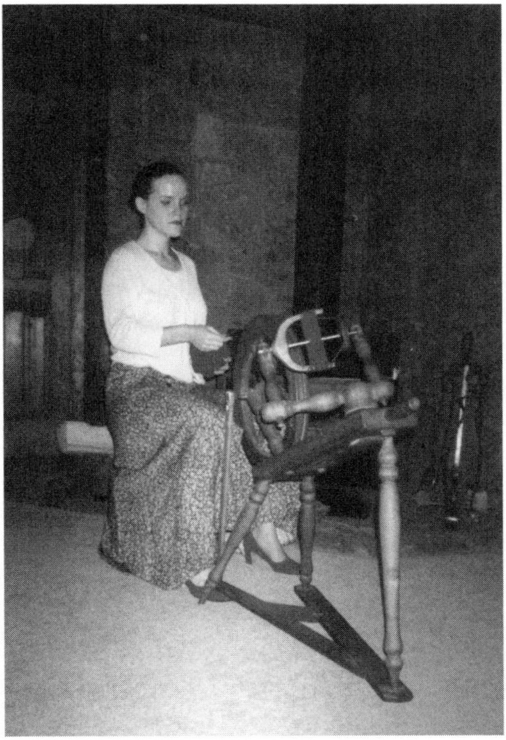
Elizabeth Giesbrecht's spinning wheel, built by Yarrow craftsman John Ratzlaff, Sr. Giesbrecht's great-granddaughter, Tina Derksen, is at the wheel.

The worms grew rapidly, until they were about three inches long. This period of growth lasted 30 to 40 days, during which time the larvae underwent four stages of molting. During each stage, they held their heads up, were motionless, and appeared to be asleep, indicating that feeding would cease for at least 24 to 26 hours. The final molt was the most critical, and any disease lurking in the worms would manifest itself at this time. While the worms were molting, special precautions had to be taken: the worms could not be disturbed or fed stale, damp leaves, and trays had to be cleaned twice daily.

When the worms were ready to form cocoons, they crawled over the leaves, shrank somewhat in size, and became transparent. Restless now, they raised and waved their heads as if searching for something to climb upon. And they began to throw out threads of silk. When she noticed these signs, Mother would place branches with small twigs on the trays so the worms could mount the twigs and spin between them. It took three days for the worms to surround themselves with silken strands. The outer threads, known as floss, were spun first to serve as a network. After securing the network, the chrysalises discharged from their inner spinnerets yard upon yard of silken strands, winding the threads around themselves until they finally became invisible in their cocoons.

Eight days after the first worms had begun their spinning, a number of cocoons were set aside to allow moths to emerge, thus ensuring a supply of eggs for the following season. The chrysalises in the rest of the cocoons were then destroyed using one of several methods: placing the cocoons for several hours in an oven set at 70 to 75°, exposing them to the hot rays of the sun, or steaming them. After this, the silken cocoons were ready for reeling.

In the summer of 1942, Mother raised 400 cocoons and experienced much pleasure from the use of her spinning wheel, which had been handcrafted by John Ratzlaff, Sr. of Yarrow.[7] After the silk had been spun into thread, she knitted socks, stockings, scarves, sweaters, and shawls for members of the family. These were always very much appreciated.

While Yarrow settlers did not always consider the fine arts necessary for survival, craftsmanship was both necessary and acceptable. Individuals of this immigrant pioneer community reached back into their pasts to reclaim the beauty they once had known, but they also reached into the future. In their arts and crafts, they combined what they had fashioned in the past with what they envisioned for their future life in their new cultural environment. At a time when work regimes in Yarrow were strictly governed by the clock and fine arts were often considered superfluous, if not detrimental, to survival, many individuals found ways to practise crafts as art, and art as a means toward a richer life—but one that would also connect with the past.

Erna Ewert, an artist who for years was co-owner and co-manager of a store on Yarrow Central Road before developing her talents as a painter, uses her contemporary watercolours and acrylics to "freeze the past." Her paintings include a tribute to Aberna's IGA, "a … store that she and her husband Abe (now deceased) operated for 26 years."[8] For part of that time, her store had been the only outlet in Yarrow to offer basic supplies for sewing and needlework.

"Pick the Berries, Don't Paint Them": The Odyssey of Three Artists in a Mennonite Lotus Land

By Ruth Derksen Siemens

Midday sun, nut-brown earth, and green leaves frame the crimson berries against the sky. Two little granddaughters in faded dresses and sunbonnets hold baskets half-filled with the deep-red berries. Mesmerized, Henry Brucks sets up his easel, brushes, and paint and begins to capture the image. For the moment, he forgets about the duress and anxiety of immigrant life: never enough money, not enough bread on the table, and almost enough clothing. In this moment, he forgets about the Co-op fees, church fees, travel fees owed to the CPR, and loan payments. He forgets that paint, paper, and brushes might be seen to be an irresponsible, indulgent waste.

His wife, Aganetha, is aghast—overworked, too many children in too short a time, too many bills to pay, and never enough to clothe, feed, and house them. She never wastes time pursuing frivolous hobbies. She darns and patches, rather than crocheting or embroidering. She knits because it provides socks, mittens, and toques. She teaches her daughters to darn and patch.

Life in Russia had been comfortable. She was an educated, practising midwife, raised in a relatively prosperous household and married to a schoolteacher and village preacher. They had been able to employ one housemaid and one farmer's helper. Their destiny seemed secure. But leaving Russia had been unavoidable. Her parents had warned her that if she left for Canada, she might find herself living like her maid—cleaning other people's floors.

As Aganetha observed the events in the berry patch, she was overwhelmed with the responsibility of nine children and the attendant poverty. The conflict was always present: her husband's disinterest in financial success, his lack of material ambition, and his passion for art grating against the need to pick and market the raspberries. And now Henry had set up his easel in the raspberry row and was painting! She shouted as she ran, "Henry! You have to pick the berries, not paint them!"[1]

Henry's love of art began early. He was born in Ladekopp, southern Russia, in 1880. Although it is not clear if he studied art formally in his early school days, those who knew him recognized his interest in sketching, lettering, and painting. His mother had died when he was a young, dependent boy. He and his brother cared for their father, who succumbed to the despairing life of alcoholism. Others in the village noticed the boys' misfortune and financed their education. Both young men graduated from Teacher's College in Halbstadt, Russia. Henry left Ladekopp and traveled north and east to Kubanka in the distant colony of Orenburg, where he assumed the responsibilities of village teacher and ordained minister.

Although his professions would have demanded most of his time, Henry's paints, brushes, and easel were not dormant. His artistic ability served the need in the community for banners to celebrate weddings, anniversaries, and funerals. Always a practical people, the Mennonites in Russia and later in Canada recognized that his calligraphy provided

Henry Brucks with one of his landscapes.

an essential service. With his brushes, he combined names and dates with aphorisms. For funerals, the common maxim was *Ruhe Sanft* (rest in peace). His community, which shunned graven images, valued his grave inscriptions.

Some of Henry's art materials traveled with him and his family to Canada in 1926. But with eight children on the voyage and Aganetha pregnant with the ninth, artistic pursuits were not primary; survival was. Because his teaching credentials were not recognized in Canada, their poverty was soon overwhelming; time and money were inadequate to supply even the most basic needs of the family. In a desperate attempt to survive the winter, Henry suggested they move from their rural Alberta location to the town of Lethbridge, so that their plight would be visible. Here they lived in an abandoned rail car and owed their survival that winter to the generosity of a bank manager, who, after accepting Henry's total deposit of five dollars, sent a truckload of food, clothes, coal, and toys to their rail-car house. How could an artist even dream of pursuing his passion in these circumstances? Yet later, as their living conditions in Lethbridge slowly improved, Henry registered for an art course with an American college of art.

Although few in the Mennonite community knew of his artistic passion, Henry's calligraphic talent was again useful for celebratory events in the church. So long as it could be used for the church community, time and effort could be justified. But he also managed to find the time and resources to continue sketching and painting. He became particularly skilled in capturing the stature and movement of horses.

With the family's move to Yarrow in 1939, their living conditions improved. They were able to buy a small parcel of land "in the bush" east of the village, build a house, and plant a berry patch. The art course with the American college continued. In the attic of their house, Henry set up his easel, charcoal, paints, pens, paper—his studio. This was a place for works in progress and some completed paintings. But the studio was also a place for privacy and reflection. One of his granddaughters recalls seeing a poem on the wall of this attic room. It was not a soothing Bible verse or religious maxim so common in Mennonite homes of that era. Hanna remembers some of the words: "Fear came walking in my room/Fear took flight." Perhaps the poetry reflected Henry's optimism, perhaps it reflected the unremitting struggle of financial and familial pressure, or perhaps the unrelenting effort needed to succeed in his new country. Whatever its presence implied, it remains significant that poetry was displayed on the wall of an aspiring artist's studio in the Mennonite community of Yarrow.

From his studio, Henry continued to supply printed banners for celebrations and funerals. One particularly noteworthy ensign was his framed motto that hung in the Girls' Home, a Vancouver residence and centre for Mennonite domestic workers living away from their families. On a large poster board, he crafted and framed a maxim that expressed the Home's guiding principle: *Heim für Heimatlosen* (home for the homeless). Was the maxim also symbolic of his love of art that was always searching for a place to belong? Did it represent his own plight: misunderstood by his family, unable to continue a career for which he had trained, prevented by his culture and immigrant life from realizing the potential he may have had as teacher, preacher, and artist?

Some said he was "ahead of his time." Others said "he had his head in the clouds" or "he stuck out like a sore thumb." One said he was "different" than other Mennonite men, rather strange. His sermons were "not like others'—they were quite short and expressive." His prayers were also unique: "He often prayed for the Jews."[2]

Henry Brucks continued to paint and draw until his death in 1951 at age 71. Although his studio and portfolio have both disappeared, his daughter Sarah recalls that they contained a large self-portrait (15" by 15"), numerous sketches of horses, and many paintings of mountains, forests, streams, lakes, and meadows.

* * *

Sarah Brucks Kaetler's unpretentious apartment showcases significant photographs on one wall. All other walls are richly textured with her paintings and her crewel embroidery, a gallery of landscapes with cedars, tall mountains, lakes, a quintessential canoe, and a portrait of her husband's nephew. Sarah apologizes for her work: "It's not that good. I really enjoy writing." She has written and recently published a series of children's books. Significantly, her short stories are accompanied by 13 of her illustrations.

Born in Orenburg, Russia, in 1923, Sarah immigrated to Canada with her family and attended school in Coaldale, Alberta, and Chilliwack, B.C. Although there was little time to pursue personal ambitions, particularly artistic ones, she recalls the pleasure she felt in drawing for school assignments. Like the other Brucks children, she watched her father as he designed, sketched, and painted. When the family relocated to Yarrow, she watched her father set up a studio space in the draughty attic of their house.

Even though she had the desire to pursue artistic projects, other concerns dominated her life. Her family was in the grip of poverty. For young women in Yarrow, employment was seasonal. To compensate, Sarah and her niece, Hanna Nikkel Sims, worked for one winter season

Horses in the Snow, *by Sarah Brucks Kaetler.*

at St. George, a Catholic residential school for boys in Vancouver. Both were exhausted by the physically demanding work, and Sarah had little time or energy to paint.

Other concerns continued to take precedence and crowd out artistic work. Aspiring to a career, Sarah attended the Mennonite Brethren Bible College, Vancouver Normal School, and the University of British Columbia. On receiving her teaching certification (which included several fine-arts courses), she taught in elementary schools in Vancouver, Richmond, and Abbotsford. She recalls being always aware that she was instructing impressionable children, and she did not take her role lightly. She attempted to transfer her knowledge, passion, and creativity to all aspects of the classroom. Her music classes, dramatic presentations, visual art displays, Christmas programs, spring fairs, and other public shows were rich statements of her creative ability and artistic talent.

In 1951, however, Sarah's artistic odyssey took a new direction. The Abbotsford School District awarded her a scholarship to study at UBC for one year. Here she completed her Bachelor of Education with a major in fine arts. And it was at UBC that she met Verilynn, a colourful, adventurous young woman who persuaded Sarah to go to Paris for the summer to study art. The class was held on the north bank of the Seine River, across the street from the Louvre, one of the largest and most influential art museums in the world. Every day, the students attended lectures and wandered through some of the world's greatest art treasures with their instructor. Even the design of the building complex and the architectural detail were an inspiration for Sarah.

Although the professor viewed historical paintings and sculpture as "dead art," Sarah was not disheartened. She continued to be enthralled with the exhibits. In a modernist mode, the instructor directed the class to create "living art" and to pursue "relativity." In pursuit of this objective, the class worked with the medium of stained glass. Sarah cut panels of coloured glass and reassembled the pieces to form a decorative design: flowers in vivid reds and greens. She was attracted to contrasts in colour and preferred the brighter tones and dramatic hues. As the design was enhanced by illumination, she attached a light to simulate natural daylight and so brighten the work.

Sarah no longer owns her stained-glass artwork, but she has sketched and painted in a variety of genres. *More Stories From Grampa's Rocking Chair,* her second book in a series, includes 13 of her illustrations, and she designed the cover. Some of her paintings hang on her apartment wall, but she has also given paintings to family members. And like her father, she has maintained her own art studio. When she married in 1977, she and her husband moved to Mission, B.C. When she noticed a small shed on the property and recounted her dream of having her own art studio in which to work, her husband repaired and transformed the small shed. Realizing the importance of natural light, he replaced the small, inadequate windows with large, luminous glass.

An attitude toward art is not easily given words, but Sarah expresses hers lucidly:

> Art is so enjoyable, enriching. Of course in the church, music is more useful than art—art is not specifically evangelistic—but art is pure pleasure, pure enjoyment. Art does not have a direct purpose; rather it is an expression of inner desire, a desire that only God can fully satisfy. Artists are always seeking ways to improve what they are creating, whether they are sewing quilts, painting, or playing a piece of music. But it is only God, the creator of all things who can say: 'And God saw everything that He had made, and behold, it was good.'[3]

* * *

The fire and the flood: Hanna Nikkel Sims depicts the dual tragedy of her family in a charcoal "story drawing." Recently completed, it represents a succession of catastrophes. A fire destroyed her family's home in Yarrow in December 1947, and a flood washed away their house in May 1948. In five months, the Nikkel family had twice lost everything. Hanna recalls the loss and the resulting years of poverty: "We were so poor, so limited in materials. We made paper chains and other baubles for the Christmas tree with whatever was available in the house."[4]

One of her earliest memories was seeing her grandfather Brucks's art studio. She knew it was unusual to have such a room, an attic room filled with colour. She saw brushes, paints, an easel, and some completed paintings, including one of Vedder Mountain and the surrounding landscape.

Hanna's own awareness of her artistic desire began when she was in the fourth grade. She always noticed vibrant colours and was particularly attracted to the hue of brilliantly coloured flowers. Her teacher, Ms. Edmundson, expressed pleasure in her art, and Hanna remembers being asked to sketch a background for a class calendar.

Flowers continued to delight Hanna. Although there was little time and energy for cultivating anything other than vegetables in the garden, she recalls that "we had daisies ... they grew along the pathway. I always liked daisies ... was always aware of them. Now when I get a flower, I feel the compulsion to draw it. Why? I don't know."

The beauty and design of flowers were not directly reflected in the interior space of the Nikkel family home. The furnishings and walls of their house were plain, with only the occasional framed plaque displaying a biblical maxim. According to Hanna, however, her mother had "an eye for design and colour" that found expression in her artistically crafted needlework. Within the limits of her meagre financial resources, she knitted, crocheted, and sewed exquisitely. Hanna recalls yellow sweaters that matched yellow and brown plaid skirts, Christmas dresses and Easter outfits that rivaled the store-bought clothes of the more prosperous families. The poverty of the Nikkel family and the frugality of Hanna's mother resulted in beautifully designed clothes made from second-hand fabric and clothing that others had discarded.

Although keenly aware of her mother's talents, Hanna observed that this form of artistic expression was not affirmed, or for that matter valued, in the greater community. She realized early that musical

Fire and Flood, *by Hanna Nikkel Sims.*

competence was validated at family gatherings, community events, and church meetings. Singing, playing an instrument, conducting a choir, or participating in an ensemble were the approved mediums for artistic expression. In high school, Bible school, and the Mennonite Brethren Bible College, music continued to be the preferred and almost sole aesthetic expression available to students. Although Hanna joined the choirs and ensembles, she inhabited a space outside of this activity and poignantly felt her alienation.

But other communities provided a place for Hanna to explore and expand her artistic aspirations. During her teacher's training at UBC, she enrolled in "Art Methods" courses. Later, when she taught in Kamloops, B.C., her private art instructor provided further instruction and moral support. In the classroom, whether instructing students in social studies and science or in thinking about ways to embellish the classroom walls, she encouraged children to express themselves through the medium of art.

Although her artistic ability lay dormant for many years, Hanna's zeal for studying art and her passion for aesthetic expression has been renewed. In 1994 and '95, she studied at the Emily Carr Institute of Art and Design. The foundational courses defined her strengths and narrowed her interests to a particular field. In May 1997, she participated in her first art show, with the Burnaby Artists Guild. Her exhibits have continued as semi-annual events. In addition, she continues to study with artists in private design studios. Her project in a recent summer was an exploration in "Mysteries of Light and Shade." As a supporting member of the Federation of Canadian Artists, she has found a community that both challenges and affirms her work.

In cultivating her talent, Hanna has worked in a variety of mediums, particularly oil and acrylic, but she prefers watercolour. "I even like the smell of the wet paper," she chuckles. Although not her primary choice, charcoal has proven to be malleable and effective in sketching large movements and shaped lines. She has also experimented with life drawing, expressing "an awe in the line and design of our bodies, the beauty of the human form." She recounts the thrill experienced "when you feel confident to execute lines and mirror what you see and feel as an artist—to experiment with form." She also finds pleasure and artistic expression in being able to capture "a moment in time": kids in a canoe, reflections in the water, evening light on a flower.

In searching for a representative mode, Hanna has gravitated toward impressionist painting and the artists who have embodied this perspective. She is intrinsically drawn to the paintings of Georgia O'Keeffe and Emily Carr. In several of her trips to the American Southwest, carrying art materials in the trunk of her car, she has retraced the steps of O'Keeffe, who found most of her inspiration in desert flowers and arid landscapes. Hanna has visited areas near Abique and Taos, New Mexico, and the desert of southern California. Here she has found inspiration in the variegated hues and strong vibrant colours of the desert and its flowers and has replicated them.

* * *

Raspberries and horses, stained glass and cedars, fire and flood, poverty and passion—for Henry, Sarah, and Hanna, they are the expressions of a desire that has been both repressed and shaped by an immigrant community that struggled for survival.

A Community of Verse

By Marlene A. Sawatsky

The experience of living in the Mennonite community of Yarrow inspired an astonishing range of poetic work. Many of Yarrow's poets emulated traditional forms, favouring pietistic poetry and simple lyric verse forms found in hymns. Their fondness for meditative introspection and didactic purpose often found expression in poems written for special occasions, such as weddings and funerals. These "occasion poems" feature personal, domestic, and spiritual life-journeys of the people of Yarrow. They also reveal long-held community traditions and values, some of which have persisted to the present despite a recent trend toward avant-garde writing. It is impossible to represent adequately this range of work in a brief survey. Longer collections of poetry include Johann A. Harder's handwritten poems (1907-1919); Margaret Penner Toews' *Five Loaves and two small fishes …* (1976); Leonard Neufeldt's *A Way of Walking* (1972), *Raspberrying* (1991), *Yarrow* (1993), and *Car Failure North of Nîmes* (1994); and Robert Martens' *Full Moon* (1998).

The poems discussed in this essay represent the work of 17 poets who lived in Yarrow at one period in their lives. Some of these poems have been published in handsome collections; others are recent retrievals from dresser drawers and storage trunks. We might ask, as we read these poems, from what need were they born? Did bilingualism and the cultural hybridism of the growing community of Yarrow influence poetry writing? One might wonder whether the inroads of North American evangelistic Protestantism challenged a traditionally sterner theology and much more radical Anabaptism. The tradition-bound church, a significant indicator of community membership for the Mennonite émigré, may have furnished important subject matter. Was the experience of migration from Russia to Canada a factor? Were poets invoking some kind of community by seeking transpersonal subjects and language?

One of Yarrow's early writers and one-time bookstore owner is Peter J. Klassen (1889-1953). Klassen's extensive background in German literature is readily discernible in his verse fables (see "*Der Greis und der Tod*" and "*Der Wolf und der Kuckuck*," which imitate the style of Russian writer I.A. Krylow, 1768-1844). More evocative of Yarrow's community life, however, are his lyrics and meditations, several of which depict the experience of migration within the larger context of war.[1] "*Mein Bekenntnis*" ("My Confession") begins with a declaration of loyalty, "*Mit Wort und Tat und Leben*!" ("with word and deed and life"), to the adopted home, Canada—a vast domain where there is freedom to worship God in prayer. By stanza seven, however, the speaker's opening patriotic intentions waver. "*Doch soll ich dir von Nutzen sein,/Darf ich mich nicht verlieren*" launches what appears to be the poem's counterargument: civil rights and freedoms are reconsidered in the context of civic duties and obligations. The poem concludes with the speaker's renewed pledge to serve Canadian aspirations; however, personal identity, including that of future generations, is determined by "*Mein Blut und meine Sprache*" (ethnicity and the German language).

In contrast, personal feelings of dislocation, estrangement, and loneliness are expressed in Klassen's "*Nicht allein*" (Not Alone). Interestingly, this poem interweaves the image of the stranger, walking alone, with an understanding of transnational identity—one that encompasses both "the dear Northern homeland" and "we Germans," who remain true. "*Nicht allein*" perhaps anticipates the concept of the imagined (transnational) community, an idea that would capture the attention of anthropologists and sociologists in years to come.

These poems depict the displacement that Mennonite émigrés may have experienced as a result of crossing political borders; yet relocation in a foreign place did not mean withdrawing from one's heritage. Memories of the Russian experience would be kept alive (see Klassen's "*Sanitar Mennonit bei Imenji*"). And this long memory has continued in more recent poetry—for example, Robert Martens' "March 3, 1991: Grandpa in Russia Before 1917" and "August 23,1996: immigrants" as well as Harold J. Dyck's "A Lament."[2]

Dyck's poem was written in commemoration of the execution of 80 Mennonite men in a Russian village some 80 years ago. Epic-like in its elevated style and solemn tone, the poem confers enduring honour on those who died, while also defining the Brotherhood in terms of this test of faith. The poem's introductory reference, Genesis 4:10, instructs us to consider the story of "mass butchery and terror" on the evening of October 26, 1919, by the Makhno partisans in terms of Cain's vengeful act. The biblical story and the historical event merge in the haunting and incantatory phrase, "When Cain rose up in Eichenfeld." The poem ends with the singer's pledge: "Cry on, kind father ... /That we might know your dreams, your faith and gentle cares/And not forget our loss that tragic night."

A community's past is also preserved in master metaphors, which, like myths, arise from and reiterate communal values and assumptions. Dyck's "A Lament," like many other poems by Yarrow writers, includes the images of exile, the stranger, the brotherhood, the martyr, the survivor. The image of suffering survivors in "War Aftermath," by Lydia Regehr (1903-1991), is another important metaphor extending back in time. Regehr's speaker asks, "Who's crowned with laurels of the war?" A second speaker, "Grim Hunger," responds, "The toll I take/Of those who're dying in my wake/Exceeds the victims war has felled." In its closing emphasis on nonviolence, the poem echoes Anabaptist convictions: "Ban war from inner, outer space!/Change swords to ploughshares on earth's face."[3]

Personal loss, a common motif in poems that recall past hardships in Russia, is also a recurring theme in both the early and more recent Yarrow poems. Dietrich Aron Rempel (1866-1951) wrote his "Mourning Song" on the day of his wife's passing in 1946. Abrupt and simple phrases outline in sensuous detail the loved one's eyes, chestnut hair, and rosy lips as the speaker listens for the sound of her footsteps. This mourner, "*von Liebe ganz bemeistert*," is overcome by love but bereft of consolation.

Similarly personal in tone, Harold Dyck's untitled 1995 tribute, written shortly after his wife's funeral, contains commonplace images that depict the loved one's character—her endurance and fragility. Standing alone, the mourner addresses his beloved: "You were a diamond in our summer's sun." With few exceptions, images of romantic love are most often found in poems about death and loss.

Elegiac verse often attempts to reconcile the sense of personal loss with God's divine plan. For instance, Aron Dietrich Rempel (1903-1981) interweaves religious subjects and autobiographical details in his farewell poem *"Mein letztes Zeugnis an meine lieben Lebensgefährten"* (1968). Addressing the members of his family, the poet reminds them that "there'll be no tears in heaven,/nor parting pain." Similarly, Lena Giesbrecht Isaac's "*Der Abend*" (Evening), written in 1981 on the evening of her brother's death, includes a second speaker, "*mein Heiland*" (my saviour), whose words and presence bring comfort. "*Kind komm wieder!/Komm Heim an deines Vaters Brust!*" reminds the mourner of the Father's love, His gift of redemption (see also Isaac's *"Mein Heiland Weiss"*).

For many of the Yarrow poets, the elegy served to bring the bereaved closer to acceptance of death and loss. Today, when I head out of the city to the Yarrow cemetery to visit my father's grave—Abram J. Sawatsky, one of Yarrow's spirited youths of the 1930s and 1940s—I go in search of quietness, and there I find "grave covers grass high,/like covers of discarded books."[4] The delicate alliterative sound of "grave" and "grass" and the soft echo of "covers" drifting over the line end lends my experience of grief a peaceful finish.

Meditative and devotional poetry was favoured by many of Yarrow's women poets (see Isaac's "*Mein Heiland Weiss*," "Gossip," "The Other Cheek," and "Thankfulness" and Toews's "Mothers Only").[5] Yet, pragmatic to a fault, they also combined spiritual genres with verses for special celebrations. For instance, "*Herzlichen Segenswunsch zur goldenen Hochzeit*," a "blessing" written by Anna Bergman (1905-1979) for the golden anniversary of Heinrich and Margaretha Enns, is clearly devotional and didactic: "*Verlasse uns im Alter nicht*!" ("Forsake us not in old age!") punctuates each stanza. The concluding quotation, "Lord, thou hast been our dwelling place … " (Psalm 90:1), extends the poem's meaning, one in which prolonged trials of life—loss of friends, sight, hearing, strength, and the burden of sorrow—are viewed, surprisingly, not as frailties but as the passing of life's vanities.

Bergman's impulse toward meditative introspection is also found in "*Jesaja 40:31*" and "*Zur Diamanten Hochzeit*," by Louise Buhr Rempel (1894-1985). Both poems were written to celebrate Heinrich and Margaretha Enns's silver and diamond wedding anniversaries. Intriguing details about significant family (for example, the devotion shown by "brother Jake" when their parents were ailing) serve to illustrate the ideals of steadfast Christian patience, endurance, graciousness, and generosity (see also Rempel's "*Das Alter*" [Old Age]).

Women poets of early Yarrow tended to focus on eternal rewards in poems written to honour parents, whereas male poets were more likely to associate service in the church and community with God's kingdom in similar "occasion poems." In his sonnet "Psalm 101" (1940), Pastor Johann Harder (1897-1964) acknowledges the valued contributions of a beloved songleader and youth-choir conductor, Henry Neufeldt (and those of his wife, Margaret). Likewise, Aron Dietrich Rempel's "*Gewidmit unsern lieben Diakonengeschwister Heinrich Enns zur DIAMANTENHOCHZEIT 1968*" (a diamond wedding anniversary dedication), describes the Enns's valued service as deacons in the church: "*Edle Steine sanft behauen*" ("Precious stones, gently cut"). These poems invoke long-held Mennonite values such as independence, hard work, and self-sufficiency; they also reinforce church traditions and the notion of the church community. What emerges in this small sampling of poems is the faint imprint of gendered roles.

Mennonite traditions, Christian imperatives, and family histories are tightly entwined in the unpretentious "occasion poem," a form prominent in the work of Yarrow poets. What is significant about this poetry is that ceremony of various kinds seemingly provides opportunity to see evidence of God's grace and grandeur in the simple and ordinary; it also reveals a communal acquiescence in God's dealings. The predominance of this poetic form clearly signifies the high value placed on the family and kinship ties. And versification serves to give reality and importance to that value.

Family history is often a colourful, highly personal, and entertaining poetic form. Jacob Boldt uses a mock-epic tone to tell "a tale of life/of a simply super man and his lovely wife" in his tribute entitled "Mom and Dad" (1992, written for the occasion of his parents' 59th wedding anniversary). J.C. Krause (1894-1970) similarly uses dramatic realism in his long poem "*Erinnerungen aus einer 40jährigen Wanderschaft: 1918-1959*" ("Remembrances from 40 Years of Wandering"). Interestingly, Krause requisitions images of social and economic progress to describe the wandering of his family, over mountain and valley, and their arrival in the Fraser Valley, where the Vedder River runs at the edge of a mountain and where clouds pass over. The speaker declares, "We built our home together with our children, and it was wonderful." The foundation stone was laid, and quietly the idea of Yarrow was born. Though it wasn't always comfortable and encouraging to experience the pain associated with trial and error, Krause's speaker insists, "always we went ever further, and we had courage." The poem lends nobility to the Krause family for whom it was written; it also contributes to the larger narrative of the communal family.

In a different vein, Abram Nachtigal's (1876-1950) "*In der Hopfenernte*" ("In the Hop Harvest") paints the socio-economic landscape of the community of Yarrow. We see Yarrow's farmers, including their wives and children, scurrying about in the early morning hours to finish the farm work so that they can join the pickers already waiting on the street for the arrival of the "fire-truck." For the pickers, life consisted of grueling, ongoing work; yet the sound of the pickers singing soulful melodies gives momentary relief.

Church meetings in early Yarrow occasionally provided opportunities for the reading of poems on issues facing the church community. Nachtigal's "*Schlussgedicht*" (Closing Poem), written for the "*Jugendverein*" (church meetings of young people), emphasizes the importance of music in forging unity, mediating differences between the generations, bringing healing and salvation—*"Und ihr durch Gesang das Heil zu bringen.*" Yet we sense the poet's underlying uneasiness about the future. Perhaps the spirit of North American evangelicalism, so attractive to many younger people in the Yarrow community at the time, threatened the community's cherished traditions. Interceding between elders and youth and their diverse interests, the poet suggests, "*Musst ins Kämmerlein ihr gehn.*" These words advise young people that such conflicts are resolved through prayer.

As in early New England Puritan poetry, poetry writing is often viewed by the Yarrow poet as a gift of God to be turned to God's service. Poems are therefore dedicated to understanding and praising God. This is especially so for many of the poets of early Yarrow. It is not surprising, therefore, that the use of Christian Scriptures far outstrips that of any other source material.[6] "The Fraser Valley Flood of June 1948" (unpublished), by Helen Matties Jantzen, assumes a context wherein natural phenomena are treated as metaphorical evidence of divine judgment. The poem describes how all who lived in areas surrounding Yarrow were forced to watch helplessly while "the fruit of their hard labour/Disappear[ed] before their eyes,/Swallowed by the swirling water...." Jantzen's speaker asks, "Does God not notice.../Why does He not stretch out His hand/Like at the Red Sea, stop the waters?" Yet the historical event, one etched indelibly in the communal memory, is used to illustrate a biblical truth—that eventually "all things work together for good to them that love God... " (Romans 8: 28).

A growing body of recent work from poets who grew up in Yarrow provides the most convincing evidence of a communal memory still at work. These poets, like those of early Yarrow, are committed to the role of language and writing in shaping and embodying the community: "It was the lost letters we most wanted/to answer," recalls the speaker in "The Cannery Manager, Mr. Penner."[7] What distinguishes these poems from earlier work is an avant-garde quality—that is, a self-conscious concern with the shape of the poem, the visual effect of words on the page. Robert Martens, who frequently incorporates a dated title as part of the poem's first sentence, uses the free play of words and phrases to determine the shape of the poem:

February 21, 2001: yarrow, vedder mountain
it seemed bigger in the morning, as though it had
grown while we slept. sharp and clear as a
blade of grass, so close you could feel it
on the skin. by afternoon, a simple
existence. it could be climbed. the mennonite village
below went about its business. when the sun
set, it faded, hovered, a dusty red. (unpublished)

Any certainty we might feel in this familiar landscape slides away in the gentle flux of the poem's second section, where

one day, the streets are empty, the magic
blown away into land unknown, eastward.
our village of impossible yearnings, gone.

Impossible yearnings back then, perhaps, but not necessarily now. Larry Nightingale's "riding freehand" preserves quintessential Yarrow in verbs that, like memory, extend backward and continue in the present:

Quick on
the heels of
summer-Sunday morning,
.....
still hungry, up on our pedals and ram's-horn handlebars,
white shirts
billowing, cuffless and tieless now,
.....
Free-wheeling on, just out of the guilty reach,

out of guilty sight. Riding sun-blind,
sneezing at the shadows. Our souls (about to shine)
singing, shouting the freehand gospel.
Good news! Good news! Good news![8]

Nightingale's "Aganetha Against the Wind (Lines on Paging Through the Family Albums)" (*The Dry Wells of India*, 65) similarly succeeds in capturing time: "Seemed some wind was always about carrying up/Slip, skirt and apron, big gust catching/At the black flapping of her coat."[9] His whimsical verse anecdotes—for example, "Little Ballad of the Raspberry Road," "The Noon Hour (Husband and Wife)," and "A Soliloquy of the Carpenter Shusta Toews")—recall the particular innocence of Yarrow's bygone days.

The ongoing preoccupation with language and writing in recent poetry (see Leonard Neufeldt's "Paul Celan," *Car Failure North of Nîmes*, 42-44) can be compared to the strong convictions about the power of the spoken word, as expressed by one of Yarrow's earliest poets. Johannes A. Harder's "*Ein Wort*" (A Word) exhorts us to reconsider "*Das flüchtige Wort*" (the fleeting word), which appears soon dissipated but works on and shows itself in the beyond.[10]

Poems written by Yarrow's poets in some way act together to conserve the community's past. We hear many different voices inhabiting the early Yarrow community. Yet to some extent, the past is transmitted in shared and abiding metaphorical images that preserve moments of deep suffering or unshakable perseverance. Poems act to convey stories about migration and faith history; they record and preserve family histories; they reveal religious disputation, individual and group tension. Perhaps much of the poetry also seeks and finds some rootedness in the past without being dominated by it.

I would like to thank Lora Neufeldt Sawatsky, whose invaluable assistance and research made this essay possible.

The Dynamics of Business in Yarrow

By Leonard Neufeldt, with Arthur Block and Jack Derksen

In the years that Yarrow was populated almost entirely by Mennonites, its chief business was farming. As the memoirs excerpted in *Before We Were the Land's* reveal, some berry growers, orchard keepers, chicken and egg producers, dairy farmers, and cattle raisers developed and managed their farms in a businesslike manner. They studied the marketplace and their own capabilities and plowed their profits back into their farms in order to expand, modernize, increase efficiency, alter their products and marketing, and realize larger profits. But this essay focuses on private business ventures by Yarrow Mennonites, and on how these were received in a community that initially sought to continue a Russian Mennonite village culture.

Mennonite entrepreneurship in early Yarrow is to some degree an extension of the history of Mennonite agrarian culture in Russia and the emergence of a class of business entrepreneurs there. In the late 1820s, encouraged by the Russian governmental bureau in charge of colonial affairs, the Mennonites in Russia organized an association called The Agricultural Improvement Society. Johann Cornies, a progressive, wealthy farmer and a politically skilled and authoritarian leader, was its first president. Until his death 20 years after assuming that position, he exerted much influence as its head. His agenda did not die with him.

Cornies envisioned an efficient colony- and village-based agrarian way of life for Mennonites, whether they were large landowners or small farmers. Land ownership would be encouraged, and personally working the land and remaining close to it within a Mennonite community structure in the Russian colonial system would ensure an industrious, thrifty, moral, and mutually supportive people.

Industries and crafts were assumed important insofar as they supported this agrarianism. Thus farm machine and equipment manufacturing, crafts such as those practised by wheelwrights, blacksmiths, and leather-harness makers, and businesses such as wind- and water-run mills and village general stores were encouraged, but as important adjuncts to an agrarian way of life. Cornies himself had gained business experience before taking up his large-scale farming, which we today would refer to as an agribusiness.

The agrarian culture Cornies and other leaders envisioned was taken for granted, if not always adhered to, by Mennonite colonies in Russia. Closely linked to this high view of an agrarian culture was a notably lower view of the trader, influenced, no doubt, by a traditional identification of trader as pariah in much of European and North American Christianity. This view sometimes took anti-Semitic forms. Indeed, Russian Mennonites tended to associate agrarianism with godliness, since agrarian life was seen as nurturing good stewardship of time and labour, prudence, frugality, and prosperity free of exploitation. The Mennonites' agrarian agenda had the strong endorsement of the imperial government.

By the middle of the 19th century, however, success in modern farming among Russian Mennonites was a mixed blessing in that it created a rapidly increasing "landless" population among the Mennonites. Despite the establishment of a succession of daughter colonies to make more land available to Mennonites who wished to farm, one result of the land crisis was an increase in Mennonite tenant farmers and labourers. Increasing numbers of Mennonites also migrated into crafts, small businesses, and farm-related services. But many of these entrepreneurially minded Mennonites undoubtedly would have been drawn into business pursuits regardless of the land shortage. Especially in the latter decades of the 19th century, a substantial number of Mennonites pursued small local businesses, larger commercial ventures, manufacturing, and, in a few cases, import/export trade as a way of life. Although they were a minority, Mennonite entrepreneurs began to show the same degree of success that farmers had exhibited for decades. In many cases, this business development was not directly linked to an agrarian way of life. At the same time, the industrial prowess of Mennonites became a source of pride for many.

Not surprisingly, this development of commerce and industry was viewed as dubious in some quarters of Mennonite civic, religious, and educational life. Thus tensions developed in Russia between Mennonite entrepreneurs and the tradition-minded majority engaged in agriculture. Despite their success, entrepreneurs could not entirely escape the images of pariah and rascal. Understandably, while most church leaders were well-to-do farmers, wealthy Mennonite manufacturers and merchants were rarely conscripted for important church work.

With the settling of "Russian" Mennonites in Yarrow, similar tensions quickly surfaced as the sum and size of business ventures increased. Yet this interest in business enterprise was hardly surprising. Many of the Mennonite settlers of Yarrow came from Mennonite Brethren constituencies in Russia with sizable numbers of labourers, craftsmen, and business entrepreneurs, or descendants of these, as well as former tenant farmers and long-time landowners. Indeed, from the outset, the membership of the Mennonite Brethren Church in Russia included successful businessmen.[1] Since the large majority of Yarrow Mennonite settlers were Mennonite Brethren, and both landless and formerly landless Mennonites had been attracted in disproportional numbers to the Mennonite Brethren churches of Russia,[2] one could speculate that this accounts at least in part for the fact that many Mennonite Brethren members in Russia attempted work other than farming or in addition to farm labour. Moreover, the Mennonite Brethren in Russia had expanded rapidly in daughter colonies, most of which were geographically distant from Molotschna and Chortiza. A communitarian agrarian culture as Cornies and others had envisioned it was strongest in these centres of Mennonite power.

According to questionnaires filled out by first- and second-generation Mennonites of Yarrow, the general profile just noted was characteristic of Yarrow as well. What had incipiently begun in Russia became more evident in Yarrow, where conditions forced or invited settlers to seek income from work other than farming or in addition to farming. Most of Yarrow's early businessmen did not come out of business backgrounds, but all of them held a high view of business enterprise. It should be added, moreover, that the traditional Russian Mennonite culture many of the early settlers hoped to replicate in Yarrow required a supportive environment—a friendly government, a large Mennonite population, a network of colonies and villages, and some political and economic power. Such an environment never materialized. Indeed, Chilliwack and Sardis, to which Yarrow was politically and economically linked, were already well-established centres of business and agriculture and quickly assumed the big-brother role in terms of influence. What emerged in Yarrow was a community that both proudly claimed and resisted its own most important traditions as well as the influence of nearby communities, while working hard under trying conditions for economic success. These efforts included both traditional and non-traditional business activities. Such activities were a source of satisfaction as well as suspicion in the community.

In the first five years of settlement in Yarrow, the few small businesses that appeared could, in most part, have been predicted: part-time builders, part-time casket manufacturers, two general stores, several tiny gas stations, a shoe-repair business, a blacksmith, and several owner-operators of trucks for local hauling. By 1938 this picture had changed. In an article on the 10th anniversary of Yarrow as a Mennonite community, *The Chilliwack Progress* reported, "There are fifteen places of business now. Three general stores, two woodworking and cabinet building shops, six gas stations, a butcher shop, a shoe repair shop, watch-repair and jewelry store, a blacksmith establishment, machine, general electric and farm implement premises."[3] In fact, the reporter, who seems to have run out of fingers while tallying, also missed a few businesses, including a fruit box and crate manufacturer, casket makers, an incorporated trucking firm, a small consumers' co-operative, a larger fruit growers' co-operative, and a lumber and building-supplies dealer who at this time also developed a lime business outside of Yarrow.

In a report written after his on-site study of Yarrow in 1943, sociologist Winfield Fretz extols the business prowess of Henry Voth, owner of a box factory built in the mid 1930s and greatly expanded in 1938, in seizing the economic opportunity offered by a flourishing new berry economy in the area: "He is manufacturing practically all of the berry boxes for the Fraser Valley at the present time. It should be said that he is perhaps benefiting from the anti-Japanese policy which the Canadian government has been carrying out in removing all the Japanese from the Fraser Valley. ... This is a very profitable and prosperous private industry but is bringing some money into Yarrow and providing considerable employment for a number of local residents." Fretz then enumerates other local Mennonite businesses in 1943: "Two lumber yards, two bicycle shops, one meat market, one electric service and supply store, one general store, a service station, a feed mill, elevator and mixing station, a nursery, three barber shops, a shoemaker, and a rapidly growing Yarrow Growers Co-operative."[4] Like the *Progress* reporter, Fretz missed several businesses.

The number of businesses continued to increase over the next two decades. In her history of Yarrow, Agatha Klassen lists 24 business establishments in Yarrow in 1958.[5] Her enumeration omits several others, including a second fruit-receiving plant, a bank, several building contractors, a cabinetry, a violin-making and -repair shop, a taxi service with routes mostly outside of Yarrow, and a few owners of trucks used for cartage.

What is most significant to Yarrow's business history for the 1940s and '50s, however, is not revealed by these statistics. Several businesses included in the 1938 tally by the *Progress* and the 1943 list in Fretz's report soon developed into relatively large enterprises, other large and profitable businesses appeared, and a few entrepreneurs branched out into several business ventures, only some of which were based in Yarrow. One might characterize this development as the emergence of a business elite. And what escaped the notice of many is the sizable portion of farmers during the late 1940s and '50s who had come to regard their farming as a source of basic or extra income even as they developed small businesses, such as building trades, which in many cases became their principal source of income and satisfaction.

This development of a business class evoked a mixed reaction in the community. Initially, business ventures, especially successful ones, were well received, as they helped underwrite the promise of a successful settlement. Several accounts by settlers refer to these ventures as examples of discipline and sacrifice and a means of addressing practical and immediate community needs. Memoirs and the minutes of the Yarrow Mennonite Brethren Church speak of the first Mennonite general store as one would speak of a good friend. No doubt Johann Derksen's liberal credit terms for patrons influenced this attitude. Yet a similarly favourable view was extended to house and barn builders, woodworkers, casket makers, and to the local nursery business, butcher shop, shoe-repair shop, clock- and watch-repair shop, wood-cutting services, and cartage firms transporting or delivering fuel, farmers' milk, and produce.

Henry P. Neufeldt, one of the early entrepreneurs, served on the fledgling local school board and as second president of the Parent-Teacher Association. Businessmen helped lobby for the introduction of telephone services, and then for improved services. Entrepreneurs John Martens, Henry Sukkau, and Henry Neufeldt successfully negotiated for a local waterworks authority with the water rights bureau in Victoria. Martens was elected to the Chilliwack municipal government and served as councillor for many years. Businessmen assisted in planning community health insurance, fire protection, road improvements, and the like. A few of these individuals also covered the cost of musical purchases, special Sunday School materials, and other encumbrances that the church congregation was unable to assume or unwilling to pay for because it had not done so in the past. Several followed Johann Derksen's example of helping the sick, unemployed, financially strapped, and destitute.

But the Mennonite Brethren Church minutes of the 1940s reveal considerable misgivings about Yarrow's businessmen and allegations of unscrupulous business behaviour, a few of these apparently well founded. As two small co-operatives (a consumers' and a producers' association) merged in the late 1930s into the Yarrow Growers' Co-operative Union, the new Co-op began to expand its operations extensively, and as the number of successful private entrepreneurs and the business share of the local economy increased, tensions between the business community and various other residents, including some influential ministers and Bible-school instructors, became evident. New graduates of the Elim Bible School who had already launched successful businesses were regarded by some of the instructors as unfit for church work. This sentiment was also expressed in sessions of the church council. The suspicion that business enterprise and true piety are incompatible was also reflected in the reservations expressed by more than a few church members about the depth of religious commitment of Co-op administrators. When the majority of Yarrow's most successful businessmen informally organized themselves in the late 1940s as a commercial fraternity that represented their concerns to various constituencies, including the church, tensions increased.

These tensions came to a head in 1948 when this group of businessmen individually and corporately informed the leadership of the Mennonite Brethren Church that they could not agree with the recently instituted two-percent levy on the income of all church members and all businesses owned in part or in full by members. Several other businessmen registered similar views. The new annual assessment, authorized in large part to generate revenues for the new Mennonite high school in Yarrow, had precedents of sorts in Russian Mennonite life. Some communities had paid for public works projects with regular or special assessments, and since the 1880s the churches had paid for the high cost of military alternative programs through "donations" that bore a close resemblance to levies. Nonetheless, the levy in Yarrow produced some consternation. Why, the businessmen asked, was the Co-op exempted from paying this tax? Should businessmen not also receive this exemption, or at least be assessed at a lower rate? And why should businesses only partially owned by one or more church members pay the tax on the total income of the firm? Given the variety of partnerships and the nature and degrees of business indebtedness, how was the tax to be calculated? Besides, many of these businesses had for years extended credit to residents who now, in the face of a collapsing berry market, could not repay their debts and had left businesses with a lot of red ink.

While several other church members openly challenged the levy as a tax not unlike that of a state church and by no definition a voluntary donation, the businessmen questioned the fairness of how the levy had been applied to them. The church council regarded these pleas as efforts to dodge the tax, and at a meeting in September 1948 members not only stated this in so many words, but also decided to call 10 of the most prominent businessmen onto the carpet. One of those named was asked to close the meeting with prayer. Later that month, the church council decided to resolve the impasse by negotiating with each businessman an assessment based on the nature of his business, his investment in it, and his ability to pay a tax at this time. The discussions emphasized the need to re-establish mutual trust, but most of the businessmen were nonetheless required to appear before the congregation to demonstrate the genuineness of their faith in God and commitment to the church, as well as to explain their differences with the church tax.

Written records and anecdotal recollections of the soured relations in the later 1940s between the Mennonite Brethren Church council and the business establishment paint a picture of naïveté, formulaic pieties, and deep suspicions on both sides. Businessmen could not understand why they were treated with little sympathy and understanding. Parties in the church who went after the businessmen were not about to pull in their horns when dealing with them or with related economic issues, which they apparently did not understand and perhaps did not wish to understand. Mediation by several church council members and business leaders, especially Jacob P. Martens, kept matters from getting worse.

On one critical issue, the anti-business factions agreed with the businessmen—no Yarrow business should join a union shop. Labour rights, collective bargaining, and strikes were unthinkable. Undoubtedly, for more than a few residents, news of labour strikes elsewhere conjured memories of the violent strikes in Russia prior to the 1917 revolution, protests that were all too easily viewed in retrospect as agents of anarchy, inhumanity, or perfidious forms of socialism. In the Yarrow Mennonite Brethren Church there was a clear understanding that no church member, and certainly no ordained minister or other church worker, could be a member of a union. When a certain minister discovered that he would be required to join a union in order to retain the job he had had for some time—a job he needed to take care of his family—he withdrew for a time from his church ministries to continue his employment. This decision troubled him, and there were those in the church who believed he should have relinquished his job rather than his work in the church.

Yet with the economic bust in Yarrow, brought on mainly by the collapse of the foreign berry market and the subsequent dissolution of the Co-op and liquidation of its assets in 1949 and 1950, attitudes shifted. The beleaguered community soon began to set stock in entrepreneurs and businesses that could promise solvency, affordable goods, credit, markets for berries, and jobs, thus helping to stabilize the local economy. Several of these businessmen were rightly or wrongly regarded as saviours of the berry industry in the Yarrow area.

In the 1950s, leading businessman Jacob P. Martens assumed a prominent role on the church council. The mistrust that had only a few years earlier characterized relations between businessmen and a number of church educators and ministers diminished noticeably, even though most of the businesses continued to be known for their comparatively low wages, total rejection of the concept of overtime, and minimal benefits. To one looking back, this change of attitude has its ironic aspect in that it coincided with an economic transition that saw several Yarrow businessmen branch out into ventures either not linked to the local community or not based in it. Other businessmen left in the 1950s and early '60s to pursue business interests elsewhere.

There were a few exceptions to the decrease in Mennonite business ventures in Yarrow. The most notable examples were John Guenther's box factory, which diversified its products and developed into a major company, and a small new trucking firm, Vedder Transport, which was soon to grow much larger and leave Yarrow. Nevertheless, by the 1960s it was obvious to everyone that the heyday of Mennonite business

Froese's delivery truck, used to deliver meat locally and in nearby communities.

development in Yarrow was past. By this time, the Mennonite community itself was in decline.

Business operators in Yarrow from 1929 to the 1950s fall into several categories. Following are representative examples of each type.

Farmers Drawn to Other Kinds of Enterprise

These businessmen may have been the most common in Yarrow. John Ratzlaff, Sr., for example, worked a very small farm, but his occupational first love was woodwork, especially the craft of building cabinets and church pews. His brother Henry also owned farming acreage but preferred concrete, plumbing, and electrical work, and machine mechanics. Several farmers were builders at heart, and a few of them established building trades companies. Others established blacksmith shops, a shoe-repair business, a meat market, and a small grocery store. Froese's Meat Market, 1934-1949, is a representative example of this type of business activity.[6]

Jacob A. Froese and his wife, Agnes, arrived in Yarrow with their sons in 1933. In the summer of 1934, Froese decided to test the local market for fresh meat. With his brother-in-law, blacksmith Henry Riesen, he purchased a cow, which he butchered and loaded into a small truck he had borrowed from a friend. Then he sold the meat door-to-door in Yarrow. On his first day he netted $20. Thus Froese's

Meat Market was born. But Froese was also farming several acres on his property on Central Road, near the centre of town. The next year he built a small butcher shop in front of his house and a modest slaughterhouse close to it. In this butcher shop, many Yarrow people purchased some or all of their meat, much of it on credit. When his cash reserves dwindled, he visited those people he thought could pay at least some of the money they owed. Like several other small entrepreneurs in Yarrow, he also accepted bartered goods and services as reimbursement. The poorest were never asked to pay for their meat.

In 1935, his son Aron moved home and began to market and deliver meat in surrounding communities: Tuesday and Friday in Sumas Prairie, Wednesday and Saturday in Greendale. On Thursday, he drove to Vancouver for supplies; Monday was butchering day. He continued in this work for five years. Abram (Ed) filled in for him in the war years until 1943, when he was assigned to work for the war effort at Canada Packers in Vancouver. Except for a basic allowance Ed was permitted from his income, his salary went to the Red Cross. During the next two years, he came home on weekends to do the slaughtering. In 1946, the Froeses built a new and larger meat market on the old site. Ground beef sold at two pounds for 25 cents; soup bones were free. To keep the meat cold, they purchased blocks of ice from the Fraser Valley Milk Producers' plant in Sardis. The ice was covered with sawdust. Later, they installed an ammonia cooling unit. After the war, sons Leonard and Irvin also assisted with the business, the latter acquiring the unpoetic nickname "Wiener."

With the devastating effects of the flood in 1948 and the dissolution of the Co-op in 1949, many families were unable to pay for food and meat they had purchased on credit. Mr. Froese decided not to call in these debts. In fact, his wife made soups and took them along with cuts of meat to families in dire straits. Early in 1950, the Froeses sold their business to C.C. Funk, whose grocery store was adjacent to their meat market.

Full-time Small Businessmen

Most of the proprietors of commercial shops were in this category. Johann Derksen, for example, who was a businessman before he arrived in Yarrow, built a general store that he sold to the Co-op in 1938; John Martens and Henry Neufeldt had each established a small trucking company before they merged in 1934 to form Martens & Neufeldt Trucking. David and Herbert Martens established a successful auto centre, limited dealership, and service station in Yarrow. Jacob Wittenberg, a former teacher, started a jewelry and clock business. John Block established a construction company that Jacob Dyck then joined as partner. David Derksen owned the only radio and electric shop in town; near the front of his shop, he provided fans of major league baseball with their first televised pictures of the World Series. Kornelius Neufeld was proprietor of Yarrow's only printing press. Henry Martens gave new meaning to "Del Monte" by using it as the name of Yarrow's first and only photographic studio. Cornelius Giesbrecht opened his Ronald Allen's clothing store, and his younger brother, John Giesbrecht, purchased and expanded the Yarrow Lumber company.

As Yarrow's first businessman, Johann Derksen was both a unique and representative example of the entrepreneurs just listed.[7] Proprietor of the first and second general stores, Derksen was one of the community's favourite and most generous citizens. He arrived in Yarrow in February 1929, bringing with him stock from a store he had operated in Manitoba and the capital to build a general store. His proficiency in English and prior experience in business made him a valuable link to the outside world of "the English." He ran his store out of a rented house on the corner of Central and Wilson roads while his new store on Central Road was being built (today, the structure houses an insurance firm).

Johann Derksen's general store: Anna Dahl with Mary, Martha, and Annie Derksen. In 1938 he sold his store to the Co-op, and for a number of years Jacob Neumann managed the store.

Derksen's practice was to order syrup and peanut butter in 30-pound pails and resell them in one-pound containers. Other staples of his store included Five Roses Flour, Quaker Oats, white and brown sugar, pharmaceutical products, small items for wedding gifts, rubber boots and rainwear, seed, animal feed, nails, and eventually gasoline from a gravity pump in front of the store. The entire family assisted with the store, which was open mornings and evenings because most people worked during the day. He owned a van, which he used to transport goods from Vancouver and Chilliwack for resale in Yarrow. He negotiated short-term credit with various merchants, such as Eaton's, Woolworth's, Brackman-Ker, and Robinson's Drugstore.

Derksen was more than a storekeeper. He pulled teeth in emergencies, provided early settlers with much-needed transportation to Chilliwack and Vancouver, and, through his business contacts, found reliable families for whom the first Mennonite students to attend Chilliwack High School could work for their room and board: Susie Derksen with the Robinsons who owned the drugstore, Elvira Klassen at the home of dentist Hallman, Sarah Martens at the home of the Watson family, who owned Homemaker's Realty. In those early years, a number of young people in Yarrow sought employment in Chilliwack, and it was often Derksen who located jobs for them.

To the needy and to his children, Derksen was extraordinarily generous and sympathetic, but old-timers also tell of his intolerance for laggards. They still recount an episode when a Mr. McNeal had asked for a ride to Vancouver. Derksen arrived at his house and sounded the horn at the agreed-upon time only to find that McNeal was not ready.

"I'm just shaving," he shouted.

"Go right ahead," replied Derksen, and drove off.

Derksen's children received music lessons, even though commuting to Greendale and, later, to Vancouver for lessons consumed much time. His son David, who later founded a hardware store and then Derksen's Radio and Electric, was sent to Los Angeles to study radio repair.

Major Local Businessmen

In the 1940s and '50s, several of the small businesses begun in the 1930s grew into large and very profitable firms. These include Jacob Martens' lumberyard, Martens & Neufeldt Trucking (later reorganized and renamed Yarrow Freight and Fuels), Guenther's Box Factory, and

C.C. Funk's store, feed mill, and elevator. The most successful of these were the firms established by Cornelius Funk.[8]

From an early age, Funk had assisted in his father's mill in the Molotschna colony of southern Russia. The mill was expropriated after the Russian Revolution. Funk and his family were among the last Mennonites to leave the Soviet Union before Stalin sealed the borders late in 1929 against further emigration. In Coaldale, Alberta, Funk became involved with storekeeping and sausage-making. In 1933, he purchased a farm in Yarrow. Seven years later, eager to return to business, he invested in a hammer mill, following this with the purchase of a feed mixer. Early the next year, he began constructing a feed mill and elevator beside the B.C. Electric Railway tracks, near the south end of Wilson Road. After this facility was completed, he built a store on Central Road. Within a few years, "Funk's" became the principal commercial institution in Yarrow. Funk involved his children in the business. Cornie, the oldest son, managed the feed mill. Henry, the softball star, and Arthur, the complete fisherman, helped to operate the store, which was significantly expanded when they purchased Froese's Meat Market. Several of Funk's daughters worked as sales clerks and office staff in the store.

When the feed mill was destroyed by fire in 1964, the Funks decided to rebuild in Clearbrook, where they established the large and successful Clearbrook Grain and Milling Company. Five years later, they sold their supermarket in Yarrow and built a much larger one in Clearbrook. C.C. Funk exemplifies the modern businessmen who developed substantial local businesses and flourished in Yarrow in the 1940s and '50s.

Major Businessmen With Enterprises in and Beyond Yarrow

A few of Yarrow's entrepreneurs—most notably Jacob Derksen, Jacob Martens, Henry Goosen, and, in the 1950s, Jacob Jantzen—started several kinds of businesses in Yarrow but also invested in businesses elsewhere. Jacob Martens, for example, started a lumberyard that soon became the largest in Yarrow. Somewhat later, he also became a principal partner in a fruit-processing plant in Yarrow, a much larger fruit-processing plant in Clearbrook, and an insurance firm in Yarrow. He also invested in other businesses in the region, including a golf course, and in real estate.

Jacob Derksen's business career is quite similar.[9] In 1932, with a $500 loan from storekeeper Johann Derksen, his uncle, he purchased a truck and began a small hauling business, mainly transporting lime throughout the Fraser Valley and Delta for agricultural purposes. He used his contract with Popkum Lime Company to purchase a 25-percent partnership in the firm. But he also hauled slab-wood, fence posts, hop-pickers, and other loads. After two years he purchased a second truck. In 1935, he and Aron Rempel established Vedder Lumber; a year later he became sole owner. Shortly after the lumberyard began operations, he started a gasoline service (Texaco) on his father's property on Central Road (across the street from where their new home would soon be built). In the early 1940s, he became a shareholder in a sawmill in Mission, which, for reasons of ill health, he leased to Dave Murray, who transformed it into Murray Lumber.

During these years, Derksen also became involved in selling mutual funds and automobiles and in growing raspberries on some 25 acres of land. He developed a close friendship with Earl Pearcy, who operated a raspberry-packing plant in Arnold. In 1953, when construction activity in Yarrow was slow, Pearcy leased Derksen's lumberyard building and converted it into a packing plant. Some years later, Derksen purchased it from Pearcy and expanded it to process strawberries and plums as well. This business provided summer employment for the entire Derksen family as well as many young people of Yarrow.

* * *

A number of the children of early Yarrow businessmen realized greater success in local, national, and international business than their parents could possibly have imagined back in the 1940s. But the majority

Funk's Feed Mill before it was destroyed by fire.

Yarrow Lumber company, begun by Jacob Martens and his brother Herb, began to flourish during the Second World War, when Martens, also known as "Lumber Jack," hauled bricks by government contract to shipyards in Vancouver and returned with reject lumber. Martens sold this business in 1952. In the second photograph are (l-r): Martens and new owners John Giesbrecht, Leonard Froese, and Ben Braun.

of this next generation of entrepreneurs who, from the late 1950s on, found success in business elsewhere did not have business backgrounds. This was not unlike the situation during the early years of the Yarrow community, when only two of the leading businessmen, Johann Derksen and C.C. Funk, had had previous business experience. David Derksen followed his father in business, albeit in hardware and electronics. J.C.

Jacob Derksen's first local business establishment.

Krause appears to have been the only businessman to have studied business and commerce in Russia.

This invites the question of why so many individuals in the relatively closed farming community of early Yarrow chose to go into business. Several memoirs point to one possibility. Some of the young male settlers, having witnessed the loss of their farms in Russia and farming disasters on the Prairies, and having sized up their prospects as farmers in Yarrow, decided to risk failure in private business rather than devote their futures to the hard labour and economic risk of farming in this new settlement. To an outsider like sociologist Winfield Fretz, the success of the Yarrow Co-operative and communal programs in public works suggested a continuation of the way of life settlers had known in their Russian villages. But in his journal, Heinrich Harms notes that only a few years after the pioneers in Yarrow had purchased 200 acres of communal pasture for their cattle, in keeping with their custom in Russia, dairy farmers began to acquire additional private acreage in order to graze their cattle and harvest their hay on their own land. No doubt some of the early promoters of the Co-op had communal designs in mind and foresaw a community in which a thriving Co-op would be the economic engine to link Yarrow with nearby Mennonite communities, with Yarrow dominating them. As it turned out, however, the Co-op was regarded as a marketing outlet for private producers whose loyalty to the Co-op was as dependable as the Co-op's success in selling their produce at a respectable price. Although charity toward others was a centrepiece of preaching and teaching in Yarrow, little charity was shown to the administrators of the Co-op when it failed. As for the businessmen of Yarrow, several of them had benefited directly from the Co-op through relatively lucrative contracts, and others had benefited indirectly in that the Co-op's success, especially in raspberry sales, increased buying power in the community. With the demise of the Co-op, private business ventures almost immediately took its place. These entrepreneurs fared well, and when the Mennonite population of Yarrow went into notable decline, they relocated their businesses elsewhere just as members of the next generation began to enter the entrepreneurial world outside of Yarrow.

Epp Brothers' hardware store in the former Co-op building.

Our Raspberry World

By Thelma Reimer Kauffman

Here and there, like small, colourful dots, we moved over a landscape of green strawberry fields. On our knees and pushing wooden strawberry carriers along the ground, we heard the murmured word being passed from one hunched back to the next—maybe next week, or the following one, raspberries would be ready to pick. Always the two crops overlapped, and there was a tension between harvesting the two. Strawberries were still quite plentiful when the raspberries began to redden and ripen.

As teenagers, if we picked strawberries with our friends on faraway farms, we came home only on Sundays. But raspberry season was spent on home territory. Usually our parents or some relative or neighbour had a raspberry farm, so the choice of where to work was limited or non-existent. Each year was different. If Uncle Pete had acres of berries to pick, we went there, but if we had an acre or more at home, we stayed put. Seldom did a teenager pick at someone else's place to socialize with friends. Rather, it was the other way around: we socialized with whoever worked alongside us—and socialize we did.

It all started when, as children, we were tall enough to reach up into the dark, shadowy, hedge-like line of raspberry bushes and collect the large, red berries that seemed to thrive on concealing themselves inside the bushy plants. Of course, we always ate our fill, and over the years of tasting and testing, we learned just what shade of red or shape of berry tasted best. There is nothing quite like those first, juicy, ripe berries in July, except maybe a rare sunbaked one. When we were little children, the prickly branches seemed a bit hostile to our timid efforts, but soon we and raspberry bushes learned to get along. Actually, we had to, as raspberries were part of our life and survival for so many years of our growing up. Inherently we knew that raspberries were our friends.

When I was considered old enough to pick most of the day along with my cousins in my grandmother's two-acre field, I was thrilled. I got my own lightweight wooden stand, which held an empty shallow wooden flat with 12 small, woven, beechwood boxes, or "hullocks," each box holding about a pound when filled. If we filled the boxes level with the edges, fine and dandy, but if we rounded the flats so that the hullock edges didn't show much except at the border of the flat, we were sure to get more pounds per flat. Early on we learned there was an art to this berry-picking. For example, we would use fewer flats and get the best value for our efforts if we rounded the flats. Sometimes we not only rounded them in the centre, but also filled them to the very border of the flat so that no edges showed. As our rounded flats were stacked, the berries in some of them would be squashed, and juice ran down the sides. Woe to pickers whose flats were dripping, but praise to pickers who filled their flats well and weighed in a goodly sum. My students wonder how I can add triple digit numbers so fast. Why, all day long when picking berries we were estimating, multiplying, and adding in our heads. At the end of the day, we took pride in noting that our estimates were very close to the total weight the scales showed. This math was no textbook learning.

Raspberry picking in Yarrow when raspberry culture was king.

Grandmother's fields were not all of the same quality, and this was true of most farms. The upper or west half had better plants than the lower half. In fact, rows in the south or west areas would usually bear fruit more heavily than would those in the north or east, but in her field, the southern part faced Vedder Mountain, which bordered her land, and so rows there had to wait longer for the sun to rise and ripen the berries. When we youngsters picked in these sparser lower rows, we would ask Grandma for a break. If we had done satisfactory work, she would agree, and then the fun began.

Bordering the berry field was Grandma's orchard. Having come from Russia not 20 years before, my foster grandparents prided themselves on having a beautifully arranged, well-kept farm and orchard. It was an Old World habit. The ground between the trees was always plowed and raked clean. I do not remember any weeds. Numerous varieties of apple trees stood in straight rows next to plums, pears, and apricots. But at the far edge of the orchard, along the border of Jacob Loewen's parents' yard, stood a row of full-grown cherry trees—three Bings, some Montmorency for pies and jam, and one Royal Ann.

It was providential, indeed, that the cherry trees usually ripened at the same time as the raspberries. Several of my boy cousins and I would head for those cherry trees, whooping and racing for the best trees and branches. Sometimes each of us chose a different tree. At other times, we rushed to the same one, climbing up and up to find the perfect spot, the best fork in the tree to nestle into and indulge in those dark, juicy fruits hanging in rich clusters all around us. No one ever told us how much to eat. No one ever restricted us in any way, so we often ate until we were ready to burst and were candidates for diarrhea. The first gorging was the best—and the worst. After that we balanced gorging and restraint. Hiding up in those cherry trees, silently and eagerly eating while watching neighbours and other adults and intermittently chattering with each other, added up to the finest treat we children could have wished for. When the call came to come down and go back to work, we were reluctant, but shortly we were ready to finish what remained of the day. We understood that working long hours was a part of summer life. Eating our fill of cherries and other incidental surprises were vacation moments in our summers.

Now and then the evenness of the day would be abruptly interrupted by a picker's piercing screams echoing through the field. Everyone would rush over to learn what had happened. A sudden garter snake or aggressive bee would have been the cause. For a while my father kept bees. One summer they escaped and followed the queen bee away from home. Father, who rarely wore a bee helmet or gloves, went out in full costume to find the swarm and bring it home. After two days of searching, he found it in a neighbour's raspberry row. Fortunately, the field was not quite ready to be picked—otherwise some unsuspecting picker would have been badly stung.

There are unhappy memories, of course—other than the snakes and bees. Watching the sunrise and knowing there was a l-o-n-g day ahead of lonely picking with no other young people around was a dreaded time. Picking when the berries were too small or too few made the day seem wasted or pointless. Picking in a steady rain or even in a drizzle was a terrible trial, for then the large drops collecting on the leaves and branches would drip into our sleeves, slowly running down itching arms, soaking our clothes and shriveling our whitening fingers. What misery! If, by chance, heavy rains kept pickers indoors for a day or two, the berries would overripen and mould on the stems. Next to picking in the rain, picking soft, gray, rotting berries seemed the most disgusting of tasks.

Although the days often seemed long, there were aspects of raspberry picking that I truly enjoyed, even as a child: the rows that sagged down to me with red clusters that I rolled gently into a hullock, the surprise of enormous solitary berries hiding in the centre or at the bottom of bushes, the joy of accomplishment in deciding that the flat was full, carrying the 15-pound crate to the weigh-station, seeing my stack of flats (or maybe two stacks) slowly rise higher through the course of the day, and noticing when someone else's stack was higher. The satisfaction of a good day's work with an impressive number of pounds of raspberries to one's credit became routine. In retrospect, I realize that this work ethic, with its sense of self-worth, came almost as naturally to us as the summer itself.

The first summer I was allowed to keep an account of my own earnings, I was also promised that I would get them as pay at the season's end. I don't think my father expected my earnings to amount to much. As I diligently picked, I also studied catalogues, dreaming about what I would order. When the season was over and I received my wages from my grandparents, I was amazed at the enormous sum I had, to spend as I saw fit. Proudly, and confidently too, I pulled out the Eaton's catalogue and filled out my order. I recall that when a huge parcel arrived consisting of books, craft kits, and workbooks, I was overwhelmed with the wealth of my new possessions. I still remember the smell of the new books.

There were other new additions. When my widowed father remarried, I gained new cousins, aunts, and uncles. One of my new uncles was an entrepreneur from Manitoba who purchased several farms in the Fraser Valley, replanting them with raspberries. His timing was just right. Prices for berries had been climbing, and his fields were ready to be picked. Both my new mother and I were hired on as his pickers. My uncle ran a tight ship, but he was a first-rate manager. His farms produced wonderful berries, he paid his pickers well, he worked us hard, and he regularly distributed treats. He could gauge quite easily when his pickers needed to renew their energies and attitude, and at such times he would drive into town and buy boxes of ice-cream bars for everyone. When the sun was hot and the afternoons were endless, nothing was more welcome than the opportunity to gather at row's end and rest for a few minutes, ice-cream bar in red-stained hands.

Working for my uncle, I enjoyed the larger crew of pickers; I especially enjoyed picking with a new cousin my age, who was almost as fast a picker as my new mother. Although I couldn't keep up with either of them, if I shared a row with my cousin, each of us picking one side of it, I almost held my own and enjoyed the challenge besides. In time we formed a club called "IT" (her initial and mine), which was also the secret code we used when talking openly of our plans for break time or the evening. IT would climb a great maple in the pasture bordering the berry field or, if time allowed, IT would venture out to the nearby "Jordan" creek.

At the time, the Jordan was a slow stream that widened, pond-like, close to the far end of Sandhill Road. This was the place used by the church as its baptismal site: hence its name. The wide section was a holding place for the water of Stewart Creek, which decades earlier had flowed into Sumas Lake just short of this spot. The Jordan was not deep, but if we stepped in too far, the bottom seemed to slip away, and we were certain that we were in the process of drowning. Most of us couldn't swim at all, yet it was exciting to go in, dare the depth, and narrow the margin of our survival. It was also important that our little group be there alone, so that we could splash and douse each other without others intruding into our world. If other kids, particularly boys, had arrived first, we did little more than stare at them and leave. The Jordan was there for whoever got there first, or for those who aggressively took over with running dives, swimming, and dunking. As often as not, IT found the place already occupied by noisy, boisterous bodies, and IT would return home disappointed yet hopeful about the next time.

The following year, my family was once again signed on at my uncle's. Another of my mother's brothers had moved to B.C. with his family and would be picking there also. This would be a gathering of the clan. Although I was a step-cousin, I was accepted into this larger group of cousins and felt at ease with them. But I was not accustomed to the complaints and criticisms that in-laws sometimes levy against one another. I had assumed that people who were true relatives, members of one family, stuck together loyally and liked each other. One morning, as we were all picking our individual rows, I heard agitated voices nearby. As I picked my way up my row, I began to piece together who the speakers were and what they were talking about. An aunt was complaining to someone, perhaps to my mother, about my uncle, the owner of the farm. She was upset with him and wanted to give him "what for." Raspberry rows will hide people behind curtains of green, and pickers so concealed will intimately reveal themselves to each other, secure in their conviction that no one else is listening because no one else is visible. Quietly I listened and stretched up to look, even as I tried to keep on picking. I picked my way cautiously up my row until I could no longer hear the voices. "What if they don't like each other?" I worried. "What if this new family of relatives falls apart?" I didn't want any family troubles, even unspoken ones, the kind that I had experienced when my sister died.

Always ready to take action, I decided, after a day of high anxiety, that I must do something. I would bring this problem out into the open so that amends could be made and relations restored. Bravely, or so I thought, I went to my uncle and reported to him that the other aunt was unhappy with how he had mishandled things and that family relations were in jeopardy. He studied me severely, asked a few brusque questions, and left. Then he spoke with my mother. The other aunt was confronted, and what happened next was never told to me. But after this there was a pronounced silence in the raspberry patch, and I had the distinct feeling I had stepped onto dangerous terrain. As a teenager, I was just beginning to know a larger and more complicated social world.

But berry picking also marked our youth with heavenly moments. I remember, for example, that pickers would often turn to singing. If a few voices got started, others would join in, and soon a field choir, singing in several parts, could be heard far and wide. When singers moved farther down the rows, their voices would wane and disappear while others joined in, picked up the melody, and kept the singing and song constant: "In the Sweet By and By," "Oh that will be Glory," and "When the Roll is Called Up Yonder." Looking back, I wonder whether we perhaps yearned for a heaven where the workload was not so burdensome and long. We were not slaves in any real sense of that word. Yet could not our wistful singing be compared, in some respects, with the singing of spirituals by black sisters and brothers in the American South, where field hands sang of a heaven that would rescue them from their hard labour and give them the kind of freedom and peace they could barely imagine?

Sometime during my teens, my father joined other latecomers to the new prosperity and plowed under his four acres of pastureland to grow berries. Everybody in the world seemed to be buying raspberries. I could not understand that a market could rise rapidly and then fall even more rapidly. I don't know whether he could understand this. In any event, after the ground was plowed and harrowed, he and my mother went about planting young raspberry shoots, about a foot high, in rows about seven feet apart. Most berries in the Yarrow area were of the Newberg variety, although some growers experimented with Washington and, from the early 1950s on, Willamette varieties. As the shoots began to grow, post holes were dug two feet deep and 15 to 20 feet apart in the rows, then cedar posts were placed into them and tamped tight. A long

Raspberry field, George Epp farm, 1947.

row had 14 to 20 posts in it. Early in the following spring, Father strung galvanized wire strands along the length of each side of the row about 18 inches from the ground, and then fastened these to the cedar posts with U-shaped nails (wire staples). By fall, a second wire was pulled along each side of the row, 24 to 30 inches above the first wire. The rapidly growing shoots, now maturing vines, were then trained and tied to each other or to the wires to keep them erect and manageable. In the first year, the shoots bore little fruit; in the second year, which was the first harvest year, pickers gleaned the relatively few but large berries; by the third year, many pickers had to be hired to harvest the abundant crop. Beginning in January or February, raspberry owners had to cut away the dead vines from the previous year's production, prune the plants down to four or five stalks, and cut these new stalks at chest or shoulder height. This last pruning was referred to as topping. Because raspberry plants are prolific with new volunteer shoots, unwanted vines would be piled every few rows, just beyond the end post.

All in all, managing a raspberry farm was extremely labour-intensive work, yet my father somehow managed to keep his hourly salaried job during the week. Needless to say, I was called on to help with the tying, pruning, and gathering of piles, and, most often, with the hoeing. When it was time for the first full harvest, my parents turned our small garage and storehouse into a makeshift cabin in which they housed pickers from the Prairies who wanted to work in the Fraser Valley berry fields. It was peculiar to have strangers living so close to us day by day. And with no young people in the picking crew on our yard, life became dull—no singing, no socializing, no trouble-making. But I knew that I would soon be moving on to nighttime cannery work, and I could hardly wait.

Late in the next spring, my girlfriends and I decided to earn extra money by hiring ourselves out to hoe raspberry rows. For several Saturdays, we went to work early in the morning and, with heavy hoes, worked the hard clods of lake-bottom clay in the field we had been hired to work. We broke up the grasses and weeds between and around the plants so that they had a better chance of thriving. This was backbreaking work, and the rows seemed endless, miles long. But we endured, and we earned eight to ten dollars a day. We were glad to go to church on Sunday, and school on Monday. Picking berries was pleasant compared to hoeing them.

When the picking season arrived the next year, I was ready to graduate to an hourly job at the Ocean Spray Cannery. Now, no matter if the sun shone, the rain poured, or the weather turned cloudy and chilly, we could work indoors and sit while we worked. Women young and old sat on either side of long conveyor belts that moved the raspberries along. Our job was to remove leaves, stems, dirt, small stones, insects, and the like from the berries slowly streaming by. At the end of the belt, they were funneled into 27-pound pails before being shipped to processing plants. Beginners were seated at the front of the belt, where young men carefully emptied the flats of berries onto the moving belts. There, at the head of the belt, it was easy to find mouldy fruit and other undesirable articles. As the fruit moved down the belt, veteran workers sorted the berries more carefully, especially those below the moving surface of red.

A 16-year-old joining a workforce of older girls or women felt an air of importance. I had to hold my own, working diligently and conscientiously for eight hours or more. The job also had its downside: the tedium of sitting on a stool and focusing on berries sliding by all night, when the need for sleep was often overpowering, especially in the wee hours of the morning. Work began at 8 o'clock in the evening and ended at dawn, around 5 a.m. There were short breaks and a midnight lunch on the cannery dock or steps, where our chatter and laughter echoed in the night air.

The young adult and teenaged men performed a variety of jobs at the cannery: unloading tall stacks of flats from delivery trucks; positioning flats for dumping onto conveyor belts; restacking the emptied flats for delivery to farmers the next day; filling, sealing, and stacking cans of berries; placing cans onto wagons and loading them onto transport trucks; and so forth. Dependable young men, if licensed, would be assigned to drive the loads of cans to the city, often in the U.S., a place that in our childhood and youth conjured images of the distant, foreign, and exotic.

As raspberry season came to a close, the number of flats delivered to the canneries diminished noticeably, and we younger workers were requested to work fewer hours. Only the senior workers now laboured full-time. If we worked only half the night, we slept late and then turned to berrypicking in the afternoon. The rule of summer was never to sit idle if there was work to be done. In fact, it was common knowledge that some girls who worked in the cannery all night would sleep until noon and put in almost a day's worth of picking before heading back to the cannery. Such ambition and discipline were admired in our community.

At the end of the raspberry season, our accomplishments were added up, so to speak, and paid for in full. If we had picked, the pounds were tallied and we were paid about five cents per pound. This usually translated into $100 or more. If we had worked in the cannery, we were paid by the hour, usually earning a little more than we would have as pickers. Now, with hop picking imminent and school not far hence, there was no ordering from the Eaton's catalogue. All earnings went into the family account to pay for school expenses, new clothes for the fall, and a few incidentals badly needed in the home. A weekly or monthly allowance was unknown to most of us. Picking and canning berries was part of the year-round rhythm of survival, and we were proud of our substantial earnings that contributed to our family's welfare. But occasionally we heard others express resentments.

Several days of welcome relief before the start of hop picking provided us with a brief vacation. Even a few free days presented us with alternatives, such as a day trip to picnic at nearby Cultus Lake, a family outing with relatives in Stanley Park in Vancouver, or an excursion to Harrison Hot Springs, where all of us, young and old, bathed in the healing mineral waters. These were the special rewards amid a rapid succession of days of bountiful harvests and hard summer toil in Yarrow, days stocked with work and play, struggle and song, community and friends. Life was full.

Hop Season

By Thelma Reimer Kauffman

In the half-darkness of dawn, a small huddle of people clusters at the side of the road, some leaning on the milk stand next to the driveway. Slowly, another figure emerges from the shadows and the August-night mist and pads softly over to the group. No one speaks, for each is still partly lost in slumber and pays little attention to people or weather. Heads turn and lift as we hear the faraway drone of a truck engine ruining the silence. The truck turns onto our road. Nearer it comes—then roars past us with a gust of wind, only to turn around at the dead end of the street to begin loading the waiting pickers for the Canadian Hop Company's hopyards.

We are the second stop. The driver lowers the short ladder and each of us climbs onto the flat truck bed, where benches on either side rest against the walls. In the centre are two rows of benches on which people lean against one another, no questions asked. We are lucky to get on early and sit farther forward, where we are sheltered by the cab and spared most of the dust and cold morning wind. Each worker is bundled up and loaded down with lunches, jugs, coffee thermoses, blankets, and raingear. After several more stops, the truck is tightly packed and ready to make the half-hour trip to the field. Hop season has begun. The routine is familiar, and yet year after year it is different and exciting, even though the work is terribly tedious and tiring, and the day is so very long.

A new hop field and its "section" of some 200 pickers are always a mystery, but during the ride to it nobody cares. All we want is a good field with large, long hops growing thick on the vines. There is little conversation among us. Despite the jostling and occasional lurching of the truck, we sit in an early-morning stupor, glancing at each other through half-closed eyes. However, precisely at the moment the truck turns off the road and lurches onto the field, we are suddenly awake and ready to rush down and claim our rows, three or four people to a row. It is nearly seven o'clock. Time to begin.

Hop Picking was Skilled Labour

Huge sackcloth or burlap baskets fastened in metal frames stood stacked at the end of each row. The tall, wide rows made a beautiful green design above us, both straight ahead and diagonally. But before any work began, we trekked far up the row to deposit our lunches and extra clothing in the safety of the shade, far away from all the dirt and traffic of the field. Now our work began in earnest. Time was money, so the earlier we started and the later we stayed, the higher our earnings—a wonderful theory that wore thin as the day advanced.

Hop vines were trained along high, thick wires held up by tall posts placed every 40 feet or so. The clinging vines, trained on heavy strings in a zigzag fashion, climbed up to the wires, about 12 feet from the ground. This preparatory work had been done by day labourers who worked in the hopyards year-round or for much of the year. A picker had to pull hard to bring down a vine thick with hops and leaves. It was best if the slasher, a young man hired for the job, came to your aid and cut the vines at the top so they would lie at your feet, fresh and ready to be picked. The idea was to pick, or strip, the feather-light, pale green, cone-shaped hops *without* the leaves. If the inspector came around, as he surely would, and found too many dark green leaves in someone's basket, that unlucky picker was told to clean up his work—a most

The Reverend Jacob Epp and his son, Peter, picking hops.

Nettie Banman, Mary Epp, and Henry Epp at their hop baskets.

time-consuming and embarrassing task. Everything happened out in the open here. Neighbouring eyes and ears saw and heard all. One had only to peer around a hanging vine to eavesdrop on an argument or watch a mother scold her son. Most of us learned to be observant and to communicate more with looks and laughs or subdued voices.

The skills required for hop picking were numerous. You had to know not only how to pick and how to behave, but also how to pick as much and as fast as possible. If you held the vine just right and stripped the hops in clusters, holding back the leaves, the hops fairly flew into the basket, and inch by inch it filled in two or three hours. Then, if weighing time had not arrived, you could push and press on those hops to make room for more. Sometimes a child was coaxed into the basket to stamp down the pile, and this evoked a good laugh as well as looks of admiration. Being an accomplished hop picker required concentration, persistence, and speedy fingers. One season I shared a row with two friends of mine, who are sisters. The older one was so nimble that she literally outstripped me and most of the workers around us. Her younger sister was not far behind. I did my best, but I knew I would never catch up with those two speed demons.

There definitely were downsides to the work. Your hands got dirtier picking hops than at any other job I have known. At first, the dry hops oozed a sticky yellowy green substance that coated your picking hand. This sticky pollen quickly turned brown and then black, so that after an hour's work your hand had a second skin that stayed stuck until evening. It was a real chore to scrub it off. A few pickers wore rubber gloves to protect their hands, but most of us believed that gloves slowed us down, so it was preferable to get our hands dirty. Then there was the rain, in a season that promised mainly sunny days. When it rained, our hands didn't get as dirty, but as the wetness slowly dripped down into our sleeves, even under our raingear, the hoppy drops itched and stung, making the day almost unbearable. The only bright side to such misery was that wet hops weighed considerably more than dry ones.

One year my father had the job of weighing the hops. I was proud of him. For several years, Petrus Martens had had that job in our section. Weighers were powerful people, in my opinion. Somehow, weigh-up always seemed a foretaste of what we imagined Judgment Day might be like. Right there, under God's own heaven, the weighers lifted your sack of hops, hung it on the dangling hook under the wooden tripod, and pronounced judgment on what you had accomplished during the last three or four hours. The number of pounds you had picked was pronounced loudly and clearly enough for everyone nearby to hear, including those standing in line awaiting their own judgments. Once the call was made, a ticket puncher sitting on a fold-up chair like a grand secretary, punched out the number on a small ticket. It was your claim for cash—at the end of the season.

Weighing sacks of picked hops at the Canadian Hop Company hopyards.

David P. Giesbrecht hauling sacks of hops to the drying kiln.

Three times a day, young men came to dump the contents of our baskets into long, wide burlap sacks, which they slung over their shoulders and took to the weigh-up station. If the basket was heaping full, the sack might be half full; if the basket was tamped-down full, or if there were two baskets, the sack was so full that a good grip at the top was difficult, and the carrier might have to get a second sack. A child would be proud just to have picked enough to be allowed to weigh it, which for a child could mean working on one basket all the livelong day. Talk about learning perseverance and fortitude.

If you were lucky, as I was one summer, your boyfriend might be hauling sacks of hops by truck to the kilns, and he would use his break time to come and help you pick. And if your boyfriend was a very fast picker, as mine was, your basket would fill up like a yeasty loaf rising. You would also get to face one another and look at each other to your heart's content, and, perhaps, say a few useless words. What a heady, marvelous feeling, to have a tall, handsome young man spend time generously with you in public. When weighing time came around, there would be smiles and raised eyebrows as my bursting sack was lugged to the weigh-up circle and the pounds were announced.

Lunchtime was always a highlight of the day. Just about everything tasted twice as good outdoors, especially after we'd been working hard for four or five hours. If we had sandwiches, we held them with wax paper, careful not to touch even one corner with our blackened hands. If we had leftovers or pie, a fork helped us to be sanitary. Any food stained with hop residue was bitter and inedible. Cold coffee was a treat with anything. But the tastiest food I recall was a fresh, homegrown tomato that provided an extra juicy zing to any bologna or egg sandwich. Mom's zwieback, *Platz*, and plum *Piroshki* were delicious desserts that completed those picnics under the swaying hop vines. After the lunchkit was empty, the wax paper folded to be reused the next day, and the water jugs and thermoses closed up with a little drink saved for the end of the day, we would sit for a few more minutes. Then it was back to our places in the sun, ready to tear down a new vine or finish an old one.

After the third weigh-up, some time after five, hop picking was done for the day. Or was it? Most of us used every minute to keep on picking and get a head start for the next day. Even a thin layer of green was a gift to yourself for early the next morning. Seldom did we worry that our work would be stolen. But there were also days when all our energy was used up, and the only thing to do was sit on our jackets, ready for the ride home. When the truck lurched onto the field, very few of us would run for a preferred seat. Any seat was good enough now. Sitting on benches, we girls found humour in the most unlikely events and people. Because we were exhausted and a bit giddy, the slightest word spoken in annoyance or disgust would send us into a fit of giggles. If little disagreements mushroomed, this only created greater amusement. Grown-ups riding on those trucks probably considered us silly teenagers, which, of course, we were. Silly, teenage field labourers.

It was a daunting task to leave for work around six in the morning and come home 12 hours later only to face numerous different tasks. When we returned home, Mother's work continued, as did ours. There was supper to be fixed, the garden to be tended, farm animals to be fed, sometimes milking to be done, and always clothes to be washed. First we'd set to scrubbing our hands to take off the tarry layer that had accumulated during the day. Often famished, we still had to pick the lettuce, make the *Rollkuchen*, or fry the chicken before we could sit down and eat. If time was at a premium, supper might consist of several cans of pork and beans, canned salmon, and perhaps peas from the garden. On Saturday evening, the laundry and serious baking would begin. With all the fruit available in August, Mom would bake pies, cookies, and *Piroshki*. She always made zwieback as well, although these had to be baked on Sunday, as the dough needed time to rise. If I had been asked whether I wanted my mom in church on Sundays or at home preparing food for the coming week, I would have been hard pressed to choose. Families in which the mother could stay home all week and take care of the housework and cooking were lucky—and probably not in need of the money, I concluded.

Meeting Another World

The most mysterious, chaotic, and exciting time of hop picking came when we finished picking a field. In those hours, two communities would meet in the middle of the field, each having worked from opposite ends. As young pickers, we were not only excited at the prospect of that day; we were also a little frightened.

About a week before finishing up a field, some brave and curious soul would venture out and run what seemed to be a mile or more in the rough dirt to the end of the row to find out who the pickers were. Perhaps they would be other Mennonites from such communities as Chilliwack, Abbotsford, or Greendale. Sometimes cousins from another community revealed the group's identity. Seldom would the explorer find people he knew from his own community. As a rule, once each season there were pickers at the other end of the row who were different from us, and then the explorer would come back and breathlessly say, "There are Indians at the other end!"

"Indians!"

The rumour would spread like wildfire, and soon other pickers would steal time away from their picking and run up the row to see for themselves. Once I, too, overcome by curiosity, went to look at the strangers. There they were, in long dresses, with shawls and scarves, yet otherwise much like ourselves. How embarrassing to suddenly come face to face with a Native woman quietly picking behind a hop vine at the other end of your own row. In order not to appear too nosy or wide-eyed and open-mouthed, I had to pretend I was looking for something or going somewhere, even as I observed all I could. Then I heard one of them speak, and the language was unintelligible. Imagine that. I, who could speak German, Low German, and English, could not understand a word these people were speaking. What would the finishing day be like?

Closer and closer, day by day, the two groups moved toward each other. Then one day it finally happened—they merged. Pickers in one row met, and that row was done. Now they all went to work in the longest rows remaining. Perhaps the pickers in those rows had missed a day or quit altogether. Perhaps they were just slow. As more and more rows were finished, more people swarmed together to pick the last vines. Soon there was such a buzz and jumble of people and baskets and belongings that every bit of alertness and intelligence was required to know what to do next. Children got lost and began to cry. Lunches and coats had to be protected and collected before the row was done. The hops you had picked needed to be weighed, and by the right weigh-up person. In all the confusion, you didn't dare lose your own partners or the larger group to which you belonged, or you'd end up on the wrong truck, with no way to get home.

Imagine how complicated things got when we Mennonites picked our way smack up against another culture. One minute you'd be busy and safe in your own row, and the next, a Sto:lo man would set his basket next to yours and tear down the neighbouring vine. Few words, if any, were spoken. Indians, as we referred to them, were assumed to be the silent type, and the silence was catching. You could almost hear each other breathe. Children gawked, and grown-ups too did their share of stealthy staring amidst all the disorder. Sad to say, we seldom came away from the experience any wiser or more understanding. It was, in fact, a big muddle of culture shock that gave us only an awareness of another and very different world next to us.

The Payoff

After working three or four weeks, six days a week, we were ready for the end. Mist settled over the hop fields each night now, and the chilly mornings foretold September's weather. In a few days we would finish the last field, and then would come the last truck ride of the season. Picking had been a grueling ordeal, but also a grand, adventurous game. The fields and surrounding mountains were beautiful in the early-morning fog, yet I was thrilled by the mention of school. The prospect of sitting in a classroom and reading books seemed like pure pleasure after a summer of hard physical labour.

At home, we carefully stacked each and every smelly, bent, and dirty ticket. At least once a week I had added up the pounds I'd picked and estimated my total earnings. My friends said they would make $100 or more this year. Whether my total was $90 or $100, I would give it to Mom and Dad for autumn expenses, which included school supplies and new clothes for the coming year. I knew I had contributed to the family fund, and that gave me a sense of accomplishment and relief.

* * *

A year ago, we were driving past hop fields in Oregon. I was so excited, I persuaded my husband to stop and turn off the road. We walked up to the rows, where I showed him the vines and how we had picked them. I pulled down a small branch and smelled it. "Wonderful!" I murmured with eyes closed, but he had no idea what I meant.

THE EVERYDAYNESS OF A DAIRY FARM

By Edward R. Giesbrecht

Any similarity between the city dweller's idyllic dream of farm life and the hard reality of living on a working dairy farm is purely coincidental. Ah yes, fresh air and exercise while one "putters" around plants and animals: these are parts of an alluring pastoral vision. This genial dream makes farming seem so simple and desirable. However, the reality of growing up and working on a dairy farm in Yarrow during the 1940s and '50s was a totally different matter.

It's quarter to five in the morning. Dad stands at the bottom of the stairs and calls up to us in our second-storey bedrooms: "Time to get up, boys." We are two boys in our mid-teens; we groan and roll over for a few more winks. The sound of clattering milk cans invades our semi-consciousness. This is the start of another regular weekday on our farm. The early start is necessary so that we can clean the barn, feed 30 cows (as well as many calves and about a dozen hogs), milk the cows, have breakfast, and get to the bus stop a half-mile away to catch the school bus at eight o'clock for a 40-minute ride to Chilliwack High School.

Two boys and Dad. Dad goes up into the hayloft to throw down the necessary number of hay bales and then begins feeding the cattle. The barn must be cleaned every morning and evening. This involves shoveling manure and putting down fresh straw or sawdust bedding for the cows to help keep their udders warm and dry. The udders are extremely sensitive to cold and susceptible to infections. Cold commonly results in decreased milk production, and infections cause a higher bacteria count in the milk.

My brother and I work on either side of the centre runway to clear the manure gutters. For obvious sanitary reasons, manure deposited overnight must be removed before we can begin milking. A single steel rail is suspended from the ceiling of the barn and extends outside through double rolling doors. Wheels four inches in diameter run on the track. A two-cubic-yard steel tub is connected to these wheels by a system of chains and pulleys. We shovel the manure into the container and move it out the length of the track to dump it on a pile about 50 feet from the main barn. This is a tremendous improvement over loading manure into a wheelbarrow as we used to do, taking the load to the pile over slippery 2 x 12 planks, and dumping it sideways into the sprawling heap of manure. Even with the new system, however, I often end up knee-deep in the smelly slop due to my lack of acrobatic skill in balancing myself and the load on the planks. My rubber boots extend only to mid-calf. When this odious job is done, I wash my hands in hot, soapy bleach-water and assemble the milking machines. Sanitary conditions are paramount to keeping our grade of milk at the highest level. There are financial penalties for any infraction of "A" grade standards.

Using a vacuum-suction milking machine, we now milk 30 cows in the time it used to take us to milk 8 to 10 cows by hand. First we wipe the udder with a warm, wet cloth to get rid of any contaminants and to begin the lactation process. The suction cups are immersed into hot bleach-water between each application to prevent the spread of disease from one cow to the next. Milk is poured out of the machine bucket into a two-gallon galvanized steel pail and carried into the milk

Peter P. Giesbrecht's dairy farm on Boundary Road in 1950s (formerly owned by Pastor J.A. Harder).

house. A strainer sits atop the milk can and removes foreign particles from the milk as it runs into the can. As soon as the can is about half full, it is immersed in cold water to cool the milk as quickly as possible; this helps prevent the growth of bacteria. When the can is filled to the neck, a rotating cooling device is inserted. Cold water runs through stainless steel pipes to help chill the milk more rapidly. As each full can is cooled and the next one filled, the cooled one is set into a refrigeration unit to keep it cold until the milk truck comes to pick up our 15 cans of milk each morning. It is my job to heave them up onto the stand each morning before I leave for the bus stop. The stainless-steel cans, which weigh 25 pounds when empty, hold 10 gallons of milk and weigh 100 pounds when filled to the neck. I am also responsible for the sanitation. This means that I break down all parts of the milking machines every morning and evening, wash them in hot, soapy bleach-water, and turn them over to drain and dry.

We dare not dawdle over any task or we will miss the school bus. And if we miss the bus, we miss school that day. There are days when this would suit us just fine, except that then we would be working on farm chores all day long. Our choice is obvious. We make it to the bus on time.

Our routine schedule does not allow for participation in extra-curricular school activities. We need to get home to do various barn chores before a hearty dinner. Then we hurry back out to clean the barn and feed and milk those same cows yet again. All animals must be fed every day. Twice.

Of course, the bull in his pen requires feed and water too, and he needs to be exercised. Feeding the cats is an amusing diversion from our strict regimen. They are given fresh milk in a bowl or, if Dad is out of the barn, straight from the cow. We get them dancing desperately as they try to stay in the stream of milk we squirt at them directly from the cow's teat. Occasionally the stream wanders from the cats to catch the brother on the other side of the runway. A milk-squirting fight follows. Before Dad gets back, we quickly wipe down the cows' rumps with bedding straw or we will be in serious trouble for wasting precious milk. The watchdog, a black Labrador, steals the milk out of the cats' bowls.

Evening chores are finished by about eight o'clock. This leaves us roughly an hour for reading, homework, and practising piano before we go to bed. Morning will come early.

Mother and my sisters have daily chores in the house. They prepare three substantial meals every day. Added to this labour are activities common to each weekday: washing, ironing, mending, cleaning, and baking for 11 people. Mother is awake when we go to the barn, and she is still up when we go to bed in the evening. Yet, despite her busy routine, she encourages us with a cheerful smile, kind word, and characteristic humour. On Saturday she bakes six pans of zwieback, 12 loaves of bread, butterhorns, cinnamon buns, and pies. Except for the bread, most of these are consumed by Sunday night. Often she bakes biscuits on Monday and pancakes on Tuesday to tide us over until Wednesday, when she bakes another eight loaves of bread. Her baking requires over 200 pounds of flour every month.

On weekends, our schedule varies slightly. We get to sleep in until 5:30 on Saturday and Sunday mornings. However, these are not holidays. Saturdays are spent cleaning out the chicken and pig pens so that disease will not start or spread. Fences and machinery need to be maintained and repaired; feed grain needs to be mixed; wood for the furnace must be chopped and carried into the bin in the basement of the house. So many chores await our Saturday attention that the day is finished before all of them are completed. They will be attacked again a week hence. Saturday night is bath night so that we are clean for church on Sunday. We do not want to wear the farmer's special cologne, "Eau de Bovine," that all-too-familiar fragrance in church.

Sunday is special. We do minimal chores to ensure the animals' comfort. The usual feeding, cleaning, and milking still need to be done morning and evening, but the remainder of the day is devoted to church services and visiting friends and relatives. But we must be home by four o'clock to do the milking before going to the evening service. There is no excuse good enough to justify missing any church service.

Farms in the '50s are models of self-sufficiency. We have at least a dozen hogs—two or three for our own consumption, the rest to be shipped to market. We have chickens—20 laying hens and 100 broilers. Beef for personal use is usually culled from the milking herd; an older cow not producing up to standard is used for hamburger and the beef portion of sausage. We raise calves and heifers continually as replacements for the culls, as well as to increase the size of our herd.

Beyond the daily tasks, each season has its specific activities. Winter has less frantic activity, as cows are confined to the barn and we are confined to school. We follow the regular routine except when a storm leaves snow and ice everywhere. Then emergency measures must be taken to ensure that water pipes remain open and heaters are working efficiently. The yard and access road must remain open so the milk truck can pick up our milk.

In spring, when a young man's thoughts are usually on other pursuits, farm activity increases dramatically. The first job is to clean accumulated manure from the chicken and pig barns and to disinfect the buildings thoroughly. The second job is to spread the manure pile onto the fields, load upon reeking load. The manure is transferred from the pile to the spreader using seven-tine pitchforks—a back-hurting task—but spreading is much easier with a tractor and spreader than with the horse and sled of earlier years. When the spreading has been completed, a harrow is dragged over the fields to break up any manure clumps, which would burn out the grass due to their excessive acidity.

With this task completed, the soil is prepared for planting by plowing, disking, and harrowing. A five-acre field of old pasture is broken up to be planted with corn. The field that was used for corn last year is prepared for seeding this year with a mixture of timothy and clover, for hay. Crops are rotated each year because corn draws too many nutrients out of the soil to be planted in the same field in successive years without heavy fertilizer applications.

The vegetable garden is an important part of farm life, since it provides us with fresh produce throughout summer and preserved fruits and vegetables in winter. It must be planted as early as possible so the vegetables will mature and be ready for harvest in early autumn. In addition, we must attend to pruning, hoeing, and cultivating the raspberry field, strawberry patch, and the orchard with its variety of apple, cherry, plum, and nut trees.

Ditches need to be cleared of weeds that have grown since last spring. This will allow accumulating rainwater to drain away rather than saturating fields and making them unworkable. Ditch cleaning is done by hand, by pulling the long grasses up with rakes and hoes.

Summer is unlike the other seasons because school is out for two months. City folks go away on vacation with their kids. Some children go away to camps to experience the great outdoors first-hand. We stay at home to work harder than in any other season. We labour in the fields under the hot sun from early morning until late in the evening. Since we work without shirts whenever possible, our upper bodies soon take on a mahogany hue. This darkened skin looks fine until we go up to the lake for a swim, where our farm-boy, lily-white legs generate attention and laughter. We throw the offenders into the lake, ungracefully.

In the summer's heat, we also cut the grass and bale it for hay. Often the grass is so thick and so wet from a recent shower that the mower constantly jams. One of us is required to walk behind the cutting bar and remove the matted grass from the mower with a three-tine pitchfork, taking care not to get the tines caught in the mower blade. The grass is left to be sun-dried. The drying process takes three to four warm, breezy days. However, rain can interfere. Too much rain leaches nutrients from the hay and renders it useless for feed. The drying grass is put into windrows for faster haying. Some years earlier, this was done by a horse-drawn rake about eight feet wide. When enough hay had been gathered in the rake, a person riding on top tripped a lever to release the hay onto the ground. Soon thereafter it was gathered into loose piles, or stooks, in the field and then pitchforked onto a wagon or truck bed to be transported to the main yard, where it was stored in the hayloft above the ground floor of the barn. But in the '50s, we use a tractor-drawn side-delivery rake to make continuous windrows for the baler pick-up. When the hay is dry enough, or when rain threatens to ruin the crop, it is packed into 50- to 85-pound bales.

Loading the bales onto the truck to haul them to the barn means that we have to lift each bale at least three feet to the truck deck. Once a base of bales covers the deck, we have to lift subsequent bales higher. We pitch them up with forks until they are stacked on the truck seven layers high in an interlocking pattern so they will not fall off on the way to the barn over the rough fields. Dad arranges the bales remarkably well—we seldom lose any. At the barn, the bales are lifted into the hayloft. The first three layers are hoisted up into the barn by hand so that the floorboards will not crack when additional bales are dropped by the grapple. The first load is easy, but as the day wears on, we soon feel fatigue in our muscles and weariness throughout our bodies.

The grapple is a four-gang-hook mechanism that runs on a steel rail just below the gable ridge of the barn. It grasps a stack of loose hay or bales from the truck or wagon and hauls the load into the upper part of the barn with a track and cable pulled by the tractor. Then the bales are stacked tightly so that no air can get at them. Damp hay can cause spontaneous combustion. If the bales are even slightly wet, as is often the case, we add salt to concentrate the moisture and reduce the heat production.

As soon as we are finished getting our hay safely into the barn, Dad hires out his truck and crew (my brothers and me) to do custom hay hauling for smaller farmers in the area who do not have a truck and crew of their own. Because we do not own a baler, we hire one from our neighbours, the Peter Ungers. They own the only baler in Yarrow. We often haul hay that the Ungers have baled; they are busy baling, and we are busy hauling.

We grow about five acres of field corn for silage. Hoeing the corn during the early stages of its development is a hard task, but we work at it all day long. Teamwork always helps to ease the agony. If one row has a heavier growth of quack grass, the hoer in the lead moves over to help until the other one has caught up. In that way we can work side by side.

Summer quite naturally brings with it various pests. Cats take care of the mice; the dog does the same with rats and trespassers. There are always flies buzzing around the cows, whether they are inside the barn or out. The only weapon the cow has against flies is her tail, which she swishes when they land on her flanks and back. When the milker's head is in line, the tail finds that head and swipes eyeglasses into the manure trough. Sometimes the cow will turn her head on such an occasion and look wide-eyed at the milker.

In spite of all our precautions, flies manage to lay their eggs under the hide on the cow's back. This infestation produces huge welts as the larvae grow. The irritation and pain caused by the welts result in lower milk production. We treat these welts by applying a mixture of motor oil and kerosene to the cow's back to prevent additional flies from settling on the cow and to kill the larvae. Nevertheless, some larvae will survive to breed again the next spring.

As summer shades into autumn, we feel the lure of fishing and traveling. But now is the time when crops such as fruit, vegetables, silage, and a second yield of hay have to be harvested and stored. Perennial plants need to be dressed for winter, raspberries and fruit trees need pruning, strawberries must be bedded. Beef, hogs, and chickens are butchered and processed in this season. We make sausage, ham, lard, and headcheese. At this time, the kitchen is also a beehive of activity: Mother cans fruit, pickles cucumbers, and cooks gallons of raspberry, strawberry, and plum jam while trying to satisfy the hungry gang of harvesters that invades the kitchen three times a day.

One last, arduous job is getting the corn into the silo. Because our corn grows 12 feet high, chopping it down is backbreaking labour. We use hoes with handles cut back to about two feet in length. We hold the hoe in one hand and walk down each row, grabbing the cornstalks with the other arm and chopping as close to the ground as possible. Step ...chop, step ...chop ...a quick rest at the end of the row and back again, all day long—the only break is for lunch. When enough corn has been cut, it is loaded onto wagons and hauled to our two silos, which are 15 and 20 feet high respectively and 10 feet in diameter. The cornstalks are chopped up and blown into the silo by a belt-driven silage cutter. Metal pipes deliver the chopped corn over the top and down into the silo. Making good silage is an art form that requires careful layering and tamping and the right amount of moisture. Two young men guide the corn being blown in and foot-tamp it evenly, going round and round inside each silo. (Today, 50 years later, this is considered an extremely dangerous task requiring breathing masks and safety harness.)

With the hay and silage harvest completed, fall becomes a more enjoyable time on the farm than any other season. The frenetic activity of summer is giving way to a slower, more even rhythm. School is back in session, with new courses and new friends. Soon the steady routine of winter will be here.

Winter. The cows are in the barn 24 hours a day except for the rare warm day, when they are let out for a few hours of fresh air and exercise. In this season, they require significantly more tending than during other seasons, when they are outside most of the time except for milking.

Yet, every day ...EVERY DAY ...at quarter to five in the morning: "Boys, time to get up!"

Recreation Among Young People in Early Yarrow

By Jacob A. Loewen

Recreational opportunities were not readily granted to young Mennonites in early Yarrow. Parents had brought with them a much honoured work ethic and a respect for the sanctity of Sunday, a day that belonged "to the Lord." For many, however, Sunday was the only day in the week that offered any leisure time. Thus, despite opposition, a few of the early settlers actively encouraged recreation among the young people. Because recreation for girls was even more limited than for boys, as early as 1930 Margaret Peters Toews, assisted by Mary Friesen Isaac, organized a club for girls aged 12 and older—the first of its kind in Yarrow. The idea of a club was foreign to many residents and therefore suspect. To help remedy this problem, the club was formally named "Young Girls in Christian Service." Members met Thursday afternoons, Margaret Toews's half-day off from her job as a domestic in Chilliwack. The girls' activities included singing, embroidering, preparing care packages and accompanying letters for people in Russia, making special Christmas gifts for the wives of ministers, going on occasional hikes and picnics, and practising for programs periodically presented in church. When a photo of the club was taken on a Sunday afternoon, not all of the girls in the club were permitted to have their pictures taken.[1]

Margaret Toews did not act in isolation. Her parents, Johann Franz Peters and Maria Loewen Peters, who had moved to Yarrow in 1928, encouraged young men and women to play softball on their property on Sunday afternoons and often invited them to stay for a light evening meal (*Vesper*). Although church leaders disciplined the Peters for encouraging recreation on Sundays, they continued their recreational program.[2]

Yarrow girls' club, 1930s. Back, l-r: Elizabeth Issak, Lydia Siemens, Elsie Peters, Sarah Martens, Cornelia Janzen, Susie Giesbrecht, Elvira Klassen, Elizabeth Epp, Anna Nikkel, Margaret Thiessen. Middle row, l-r: Lena Nikkel, Louise Peters, Annie Derksen, Sarah Neufeldt, Mary Friesen, Margaret Peters, Lena Kroeker, Gertrude Giesbrecht, Mary Epp, Anna Ewert, Mary Thiessen. Front, l-r: Erna Martens, Mary Goosen, Mary Wedel, Helen Reimer, Agnes Isaak, Lena Bargen, Mary Derksen.

The following vignettes, mainly from the 1930s, recall the ingenuity and persistence of those who created their own recreational sports and activities, not all of which were sanctioned in Yarrow but were nonetheless permitted. Informal and more private recreation for young people gradually evolved into community-based team sports open to the general public of Yarrow.

Swimming

Several fairly large holes had been dredged in the Yarrow area. All were deeper than the water level, so, like reservoirs, they filled up with water. They had served as sources of gravel for roadbuilding and other purposes and as water reservoirs for fighting fires. The hole at Peter Kehler's became our first community swimming hole in Yarrow. Located near the corner of First Avenue and Central Road, close to Sukkau's Garage, it was about 25 feet wide and 40 feet long. The middle was about 12 feet deep and it sloped upwards toward the edge to a depth of about three or four feet. This was the hole in which I learned how to swim.

I would get in at the shallow end, slowly back toward the deeper middle, and then try to dog paddle to the shore. One day I walked in too far, and my feet began to slide downward. I was hanging on merely by my toes. The water was at my mouth. I panicked, and inwardly I screamed to God to save me. Then, with one last heroic effort, I tried to swim ashore. Lo, I had learned to swim.

A second such gravel pit was on the property of Peter J. Neufeldt, on Stewart Road next to Stewart Creek. It was about the same width as Kehler's hole, but probably about twice as long and considerably deeper. We had some impediments here, because from noon to 2 p.m. the Neufeldts napped, and it was difficult for 15 to 20 young fellows to swim noiselessly. But the Neufeldts exercised patience with impatient young swimmers who enjoyed the dip precisely when the sun was at its zenith.

Eventually, this swimming hole became useless because the Mennonite Brethren Church decided to convert it into an outdoor baptistery. The church built a 10-by-10-foot square platform, which was sunk to about chest-deep. Steps were built from the shore to the platform. Baptismal candidates walked down the steps to the platform, where the minister received and immersed them. All was well until algae covered the wood with a layer of slime. At one baptism, as the minister tried to receive a particular candidate, they both slipped and were totally immersed. It is said that when a pious old lady observed this fiasco, she intoned in German: *"Ja! Ja! Das sagt meine Bibel auch, 'Und sie stiegen beide hinab ins Wasser'"* (Yes! Yes! That's exactly what my Bible says, 'And they both descended into the water').

Reverend J.A. Harder baptizing David and Louise Rempel, 1937.

Later in the 1930s, the area Drainage Board came to our rescue by lowering Yarrow's water table by several feet. This made a sandy area near Yarrow, along what was then called Sand Road, into a veritable desert. But farmers living along the creek were permitted to dam the creek with abutments, against which they placed planks. When the water level by the dams reached about six feet, the land again got sufficient moisture. If we slipped in another plank, we had a perfect swimming hole, deep enough even for diving. This worked wonderfully until the church again spoiled our fun by using our best swimming hole as its new outdoor baptistery. Soon Stewart Creek was renamed "the Jordan." Luckily, there were several dams, so we could still swim, but diving became a problem because the church had chosen our best swimming hole and had lowered the level of the creek.

Although swimming began as a purely male activity, by the early 1940s girls, especially those with brothers, also began to participate. But the town was changing. As affluence increased and cars became popular, young people abandoned these swimming holes. By the late 1940s, Harrison Hot Springs and especially the beaches of Cultus Lake were taking the place of local swimming holes.

Spring Sucker Fishing

Every spring, Stewart Creek abounded with a bony, local scavenger fish derisively called "sucker" because it has its mouth on its underside and is a bottom-feeder. But in the 1930s, when living was hand-to-mouth in Yarrow, we did not have the luxury of choosing what was best. As bottom feeders, suckers are seldom caught with bait; they have to be snagged. The best pool in which to snag them was on Widow Thiessen's property, several hundred yards downstream from our second swimming hole across from the Peter J. Neufeldt place. With no one to discipline us, we shamelessly exploited the widow's patience. Twenty-five or 30 of us would crowd around the small pool, each with a willow fishing pole, 30 feet of line, a small lead sinker, and a nasty treble hook that we dragged along the bottom until we snagged a fish. As there were far too many lines, we easily and often snagged each others', and violence sometimes erupted. But for about half a decade, a lot of Yarrow's fish protein came from these bony suckers. Later, as the water table dropped, some fishing holes dried up. In addition, suckers gradually lost their attraction, and fishing gravitated to the Vedder and Fraser rivers.

Mountain Climbing

In the 1930s, probably quite early in the decade, a group of young people began to climb Vedder Mountain every Easter Monday. On Easter

Monday, a sacred day, the church would not allow us to engage in many activities, but, for whatever reason, mountain climbing was one of the few activities not specifically forbidden. Thus a tradition was established that some of us faithfully followed until we left Yarrow as young adults. In the early years, there was no pathway up Vedder Mountain. Later, a trail known as Sucker's Trail was cleared nearly straight up from base to summit.

I remember one Easter Monday especially. The day began partly cloudy. We climbed the mountain without difficulty. But at about noon, when it was swarming with climbers, the summit became shrouded with one of the densest fogs I have ever seen. We waited a while for the fog to lift, but it seemed to get worse. Our group selected a leader to take us home down the fog-shrouded mountain. But somewhere he took a wrong turn: instead of seeing Yarrow as we emerged from the fog, we beheld a vast forest. We walked about five miles along an ancient logging road, eventually ending up at a fish hatchery in Columbia Valley at the far end of Cultus Lake. Fortunately, a truck was about to leave for the other end of the lake. We hitched a ride on it and finally walked into Yarrow, thoroughly fatigued.

Ping-Pong at Martens' Lumberyard

At the end of the 1930s, Yarrow's first indoor sports activity was introduced: Ping-Pong at Jake Martens' lumberyard. Martens always found room for enough sawhorses and plywood sheets to accommodate the players who showed up. The plywood sheets might not have been the official size for Ping-Pong, but in those days, who cared? In all the years of playing, I can't remember when anyone could better Martens in the end. Some might beat him in an occasional game, but ultimately he would win the playoffs.

Softball

At first we played softball on the school grounds, but as they were in the middle of town where everyone could observe us, we soon got into trouble. We looked around for something more private. We settled on Yarrow's communal pasture on Dyke Road, across from what later became Dietrich Friesen's farm. Every day a herder would collect the village cows and drive them to this communal pasture for the day, then return them to their owners for the evening milking. On this property, we tried to develop a ball field. But we soon got into difficulties with influential church people, who believed that playing ball on Sunday was a sin. We also got into trouble with the communal bull, who showed no respect whatsoever for the Mennonite doctrine of non-resistance.

* * *

Play Ball: Yarrow's High Summer

By Robert Martens

Ball-playing was often a point of contention in the Mennonite Brethren community of Yarrow. As the playing of the game progressed from an informal pastime to formally organized games on school property and finally to league play, some in the church hierarchy became disturbed by the freewheeling energy exhibited on the diamond. Playing on Sunday was expressly forbidden, and children found attending a game were frequently ordered home. In spite of all this (and perhaps partly because of it), the game prospered, and ball games became a fixture.

The controversy peaked in the late 1940s. After the flood of 1948, Marshall Knox was talked into donating some of his land on Wilson Road for a ball diamond. It was a good park, complete with bleachers,

Yarrow team, B.C. senior league softball champs, 1949. Back, l-r: Leonard Froese, Jake Neufeldt, Peter Ratzlaff, Henry Harder, George Berg, Henry Funk, Alex Rempel, John Adrian, Henry Neufeldt. Front, l-r: George Derksen, Alex Fast, John Giesbrecht (manager), George Thiessen, Peter Wall, George Enns, Irvin Froese (coach). Missing: Ernest Reimer, Al Thiessen.

and crowds of several hundred people showed up to cheer their teams. In the quiet town of Yarrow, the softball game became a major source of entertainment, garnering weekly attention in the *Chilliwack Progress*. And as the talent of Yarrow boys became apparent, the excitement grew. Mennonites traveled from as far as Chilliwack to support the Yarrow squad and razz the opposition. The unlucky army team was a frequent target of catcalls. There were incidents in which the umpire, verbally attacked by the coach and surrounded by hostile Yarrow ball fans, might fear for his safety.[3] The church hierarchy responded to all the commotion by threatening to excommunicate any member who attended or played at a Sunday ballgame. In the late 1940s, the issue came to a head when a player who broke this rule was called onto the carpet. It is reported that George Reimer, a bulwark of the church music community, rose to his feet and excitedly announced that if the talented young outfielder were to be disciplined, "you'll have to discipline me, too. I was at that game" (L. Neufeldt, oral communication). The matter was dropped.

In 1948, sponsored by the Yarrow Growers' Co-op and wearing flashy silk jackets, Yarrow's intermediate team won the league title. John Giesbrecht was both manager and coach. The following year, he coached an unusually gifted Senior B squad, still wearing the jackets of the now defunct Co-op, to the championship. Ball playing continued to flourish in Yarrow for some time. In 1952, a Junior A team under the management of Ed Froese won the provincial championship. The town's Junior A baseball team, also coached by Froese and sponsored by Marcus Urann, the amiable millionaire owner of Cascade Foods, won several league titles in the mid-1950s. But the game was, in John Giesbrecht's words, "never again quite the same."[4] In the years to come, television, the movies, the automobile, and the exodus of residents radically altered the life of the village, and the winning seasons of young Yarrow ballplayers came to be a mere memory tinged with nostalgia.

Part Two

A Gallery of Sketches and Tributes

Aerial view of Yarrow, late 1950s.

Introductory Note

Rarely can individuals and families be said to typify a community, and so the people profiled in this section are not offered as representative types. Rather, in their quite different and sometimes contrasting personalities and lives, they create a cast representing some of the uniqueness and richness of people in Mennonite Yarrow. We have included women and men; early and later settlers; married couples, single parents, and those who chose not to marry or have children; insiders and outsiders; economically successful and unsuccessful; deeply devout and not-so-devout; those who loved their Mennonite heritage, others who coexisted with it or questioned it, and still others who observed Mennonite practices from the outside. Two individuals mentioned repeatedly in both *Before We Were the Land's* and this book, but conspicuously absent in this section of profiles, are Johann and Tina Harder, the most influential pastoral couple in the history of Yarrow. The Yarrow Research Committee has commissioned a separate study of the Harders.

* * *

Recollections of Ethel Irene and Edith Caroline Knox

By Ethel and Edith Knox, with Esther Epp Harder and Lora Sawatsky

We two sisters have always loved our farm near the mountain wilderness. We are the third generation of the Knox family in Yarrow. Our grandparents, Joseph and Margaret Knox, moved to Yarrow in 1905, bought 1,200 acres of land, and immediately began to farm some of it—at the bottom of Majuba Hill on Wilson Road. During high water, they floated logs and lumber on the Fraser River and across Sumas Lake. From the southeastern shore of the lake, eight Clydesdale horses pulled these materials to the farm. The house was completed in 1907. We were told that one day a man came up to my grandfather and asked, "Mr. Knox, what're you gonna call this place?" He thought for a minute and said, "Yarrow, that's what I'm gonna call it, after the flowers that grow here."

Ethel and Edith Knox, daughters of Marshall and Henrietta Knox.

Our father, George Marshall Knox, was born in County Middlesex, Ontario, in the 1880s and two years later moved with his parents to Victoria, B.C. He accompanied them to Yarrow in 1905. In June 1930, he returned to St. Thomas, Ontario, to marry Henrietta (Ettie)

The Knox house. It was built in 1907 for Joseph Knox at the edge of Majuba Hill, where it stands to this day.

Gladys Kirkpatrick, who then accompanied him back to the Knox farm at Majuba Hill.

Our address was 971 Wilson Road. We grew up next to the B.C. Electric Railway tracks and close to the post office on Majuba Hill. Large trees bordered Wilson Road from Gus Landon's place, 964 Wilson Road, almost to the train tracks, which in Yarrow ran alongside Majuba Hill. In spring, white and pink blossoms covered these trees and carried a fragrant scent. We did not play on the hill because we were afraid of the many snakes, but during the winter when it snowed, we had fun sledding with John and Martha Fast. We loved to walk along the tracks and put our ears next to the rail to listen for oncoming trains. We used to take shortcuts across the fields to the elementary school on Central Road, but our father wanted us to walk north on Wilson Road and west on Central Road to the schoolyard, which is now the Yarrow Park.

While we were growing up, we had pleasant as well as challenging days. School days were difficult in more ways than one. We walked to school in all kinds of weather, and when we were cold and wet, studying did not come easily. A large potbelly wood-and-coal stove in the centre of the room heated the classrooms in grades one and two. Students took turns putting wood in the stove to keep the fire burning. Most of the students were Mennonite, but my sister and I were Irish and Scottish; we did not fit in because we were a different nationality.[1]

After school, we loved coming home to the long lane and the large house in which we grew up. This house is almost 100 years old now, and people are still living in it. We have fond memories of it. We remember our large covered veranda, spacious enough to hang our wash. We kept our canned goods in the basement, which had a dirt floor. In our small living room, a potbelly stove kept us warm. In 1949, our parents installed an automatic furnace, which made life more comfortable for us. There were four bedrooms upstairs and one downstairs. We climbed 14 stairs up to the bedrooms. My bedroom was on the right-hand side, facing our long lane, and there was another bedroom across the hall from mine. Mom's and Edith's bedrooms were down the hall, and my sister's bedroom faced the fields.[2]

Our father owned three additional houses. One was a small ranch-style house near the dyke on Wilson Road, another was a one-storey house just beyond the railway tracks on the east end of Majuba Hill, and the third was a nearby cabin we referred to as the grey house. At times, Father rented houses to hunters who came from Vancouver to hunt for ducks and pheasants.[3]

Around our house and barn we had five acres, which we called "our yard," with many tall trees. Our farm had a number of buildings: a barn, milk house, granary, chicken coop, pigpen, and a garage for the car. Near the house, we had four huge walnut trees; Bing, Royal Ann, and sour cherry trees; two pear trees; a small Banana Apple tree; and a winter apple tree. We also had one large Yellow Transparent apple tree. When the apples were ready, the deer would come over and eat all the apples on the lower branches. They were so tame they wandered over to eat apples while we were up in the tree picking them. We were not allowed to pet or feed the deer.

We used to take the cows over the tracks and up "Lovers' Lane" (Old Yale Road) to a field where they grazed until we went to get them around 4 p.m. to be milked at 5 o'clock. We raised chickens and loved to pick up the baby chicks and hold them in our hands. As children, we sometimes had to help catch the baby pigs. It was great fun to run and catch them. When I caught one, I had to lie down on it to hold it until Dad got it from me. After tending to the cows, beef cattle, horses, pigs, and chickens on our farm, we always welcomed the wild rabbits and squirrels, but not the bears that came down from the mountain. It felt good to walk about in our yard, watch the birds building nests in the fir trees, and observe the squirrels with long bushy tails as they looked for nuts.[4]

The creek running through our yard between the house and the milk house was known as Knox Creek. We used to fish in it. Higher up, it was also the source of our running water. As long as we can remember, we had our own reservoir on Majuba Hill, east of Sabo's farm. From this reservoir, built with heavy wood planks, water was piped to the house and from the house to the barn. We had a cold-water tap in the house, and in the barn cattle drank piped water from small metal bowls in their stalls. During cold spells in winter, we helped Father stoke the bonfires to thaw the frozen water pipes on Majuba Hill. Sometimes we had to keep the fires burning for half the night. Later, Yarrow residents built a much larger concrete reservoir using the Knox Creek.[5]

Farming was hard work, but it was our parents' bread and butter, and they loved it. Although they were busy most of the time, Mother also took time for hobbies such as embroidering bedspreads and pillowcases. She quilted, crocheted, and sewed a little as well. We always helped her grow a huge vegetable garden behind the house. She canned vegetables and fruit for the winter. She grew flowers that she loved to pick for bouquets and show to people. From 1939 to 1941, she and 12 to 14 Yarrow women took home nursing courses at Mrs. Siddall's home, so that they would be prepared as medical assistants if disaster struck during the Second World War. Edith was their patient for teaching purposes, and the women demonstrated

Mennonite settlers built their water reservoir on Knox Creek. Construction was supervised by Henry Ratzlaff.

how to treat injuries by putting bandages and splints on her. Edith still has the books Mother used in those courses.

As noted, Father enjoyed farming. We would hear him singing when he milked the cows. Before electricity came to Yarrow in the mid and late 1930s, he got up at three or four o'clock in the morning to milk the cows by hand. When electrical power came, he was able to buy a Surge milking machine. He cared for his Clydesdale horses, riding horses, and young cattle. He liked to train his horses, and he sometimes performed stunts on horseback; we still have a photo of him standing on the back of his riding horse.

The Clydesdales were used to plow the fields, pull the seeder, and pull the mower to cut the hay. The hay was stacked by hand in tent-like piles so it could dry. When it had, the horses pulled the wagons onto the fields, and men loaded the hay. When the wagon was full, the horses pulled it to the barn, where my grandparents had installed a hay pulley. The horses were hitched to this pulley, which pulled the hay up into the barn. The men then spread out the hay, an all-day job. The cows had to be milked again at five o'clock in the evening, and the horses had to be brushed and fed before Father could call it a day. We were expected to help wherever we could with mending fences, stacking wood in preparation for winter, regularly splitting or kindling wood, gardening, canning, haying, and bringing the cows to and from the pasture.

Our father had one of the first cars in Yarrow. Known as the "Knox Car," it was used for trips to Chilliwack and to run the threshing machine and pull others' cars out of drainage ditches. Before Central Road was paved in the 1940s, all roads in early Yarrow were gravel and rocks. They developed large potholes, some so big the kids could jump into them. This was always good for laughs, but the roads were hard on cars and sometimes almost impassable. Every Friday or Saturday, Peter Reimer, one of Yarrow's old-timers, who operated the Chilliwack District road grader, smoothed the Yarrow roads and closed the potholes, making the roads attractive for Sunday.

For some years, we had a special friend, Yee Fong, a Chinese man, whom everyone called Charlie, living on our farm. He was unable to bring his wife and family to Canada. He helped Father on the farm and gave us gifts on special days. In exchange, Father, who empathized with people in need, often helped him in whatever way he could. This mutual assistance was a respected and honourable way of life; money was never exchanged.[6]

Another former Yarrow resident, Peter Wall, recalls how our father was concerned about the welfare of Peter's mother, Elizabeth Wall, a widow with four children. Peter, who delivered the Vancouver *Province* door-to-door, had built his customer count to 75 and covered approximately 15 miles per day on his new bike. He recalls, "One of my memorable customers was Mr. Knox, who with his wife and two daughters lived just opposite the railway station. It seemed he was always at the station to meet me for my daily pickup of papers at 4 p.m. I spent time in summer helping him with farm chores and harvesting produce. I picked ...cherries and gathered potatoes into hundred-pound sacks. Mr. Knox, who thought I was a lucky and happy young fellow, nicknamed me 'Happy.' My close friends and relatives still call me 'Happy' or 'Hap.' Mr. Knox became my friend. So maybe he was a father figure to me."[7]

Our father also assisted the Yarrow community. In 1948, he gave up our hayfield so that soldiers could set up their base camp for fighting the flood. There were 100 soldiers close to our house, and 200 more in the field. They set up large tents for sleeping and another tent as a field kitchen for cooking their meals. Mom baked bread for them. This is the field the Yarrow boys used for playing softball against the soldiers and other teams. Dad gave up the field for three years so these ballgames could be played. Sometimes the Yarrow teams won; sometimes they lost.

Marshall Knox often used his car (free of charge) to tow the vehicles of Mennonite settlers when they were stuck in mud or broken down.

Peter (Hap) Wall and Ethel Knox.

We have good memories of some people in Yarrow. Our love for Sundays began as children, because for seven years Gertie Giesbrecht Abrahams taught Sunday School at our home, which other children in the area also attended. We even had a Christmas program in our home with Lena Kroeker. Gertie would also come over to pick blackberries with us behind our barn. We have good memories of people who befriended us, and of the children who played with us and were our friends at school. We have kept photos of them and remember their names. While we have many good memories of growing up in Yarrow, we also recall how lonely we were because the Mennonites considered us "English" and "not Christian." We found it hard to understand why some of the Mennonites were unkind to our family, as we'd noticed how much our parents and grandparents helped the Mennonites in any way they could by sharing their horses, wagon, farm machinery, and car. While we have good memories, somehow we cannot forget the people who were unkind to us, although we have forgiven them.

We sisters still live in Yarrow, just off Wilson Road North, in a comfortable house that provides us with a view of the mountain we so loved as children. Here we enjoy visiting with friends and working on our hobbies. Both of us enjoy cooking and needlework such as embroidery. Ethel is a member of the Salvation Army, and Edith the Chilliwack Alliance Church. Ethel enjoys carpet bowling, rug-making, gardening, and music (many years ago she took violin and accordion lessons). Edith loves to work on her computer, quilt, and garden. She grows many exquisite roses, herbs, berries, and fruit trees, including her favourite apple trees and espaliered peach trees. In her large greenhouse, she is hoping to grow tomatoes and lettuce all year round. Along her fence are three special perennial plants: pink, white, and yellow yarrow.

From Generation to Generation: The Hooges of Yarrow

By Selma Kornelsen Hooge

At the recent dividing of an estate in Abbotsford, B.C., the item most sought after by 12 siblings was a wooden workbench that their grandfather, Gerhard Hooge, had brought to Yarrow in 1928. Wooden tables, stools, benches, and shelves that he had built were among other treasured items inherited by third- and fourth-generation family members of "old Mr. Hooge."

Gerhard Hooge was 66 when he arrived in Yarrow in February 1928 by train from Pilot Butte, Saskatchewan. He wanted to check out for himself the land that was to become a new settlement. While still in the Ukraine, he had researched Canada's climates, and so he knew he would find the mildest climate in British Columbia. Nevertheless, seeing crocuses and snowdrops blooming in the middle of February came as a delightful surprise. He decided to stay, and immediately he sent word (probably by letter) to his son George to return the partially paid-for farm to the previous owners and to bring all their *Hab und Gut* (possessions) to Yarrow.

Perhaps Gerhard got the idea of renting a boxcar from Nickolai Reimer, who had just arrived in Yarrow and had brought "two horses, four cows, a wagonload of furniture and kitchen utensils" in a boxcar.[1] At any rate, back in Saskatchewan, young George rented a boxcar, into which he loaded two cows, two horses, some chickens and a pig, a wagon, a seed cleaner, a seeding plow, the precious workbench, all the feed and bedding for the animals, all the household items they owned, and a few special keepsakes from the Ukraine. George had to travel in the boxcar with the animals to feed and water them. At the British

Columbia border, the boxcar was pulled into a siding to test the cows for diseases. It is not known whether he came by the Canadian National Railway to Chilliwack or by the Canadian Pacific Railway to Abbotsford or Huntingdon. But eventually his boxcar was switched to a B.C. Electric train, and, in March 1928, brought to Yarrow. Meanwhile, George's mother, Helena Hooge, and his sister, Helena Pauls, had traveled west in a passenger car. Apparently they survived on toasted zwieback and canned meat.

Few of the new Mennonite immigrants had been in Canada long enough to learn the English language. Fortunately, Chauncey Eckert, who was advertising and selling the land in Yarrow, spoke some German. When new families arrived, Eckert provided a place for them to stay. At first, Gerhard Hooge and several others were crowded into a small cabin near Majuba Hill. When George arrived, however, he and the animals stayed at a dairy farm on Wilson Road, near the dyke. Susie Derksen notes that "later, the Nickels bought that farm, and currently a school exists on that property."[2]

Nickolai Reimer (of Reimer's Nurseries) reports in his memoir how pleased he was that "Old Mr. Hooge," who had just settled in Yarrow, had agreed to help Reimer build his house. Gerhard "was a master builder and this was very fortunate for me for I knew nothing about building."[3]

The abundance of wood available in and around Yarrow must have warmed Gerhard's heart. Although he had learned carpentry in the Ukraine and built some furniture in the Prairies, he had never had such a ready supply of wood. As soon as possible, he and George built a house on their 10-acre parcel on Eckert Road. Besides all the necessary furniture, he built a mangle and a *Schloapbentj*, a bench for sleeping on and storing bedding inside, something that every Mennonite home in the Ukraine would have had. Although he preferred to make furniture or build houses, he also kept several cows and shipped milk. Apparently the milk he shipped had the highest butterfat content at Dairyland.

According to grandson Hardy Hooge, "Back in the Ukraine Grandpa was best known for building and repairing wagon wheels. When the Ukrainian villagers heard that he was planning to leave, they begged him to stay and offered to protect him."[4] Although wagon wheels were not in demand in Yarrow, Gerhard's other skills learned in the old country were very useful. He wove baskets from willows, fashioning wooden bottoms for them first. He grew millet, and with it he made his own brooms using split-willow thongs for weaving and tying the spiny straw together.

The home of George and Mary Hooge on Eckert Road.

Gerhard's older grandchildren remember that he built coffins. Hardy Hooge and Mary Janzen speak of their grandpa's workshop, which was "upstairs in his house on Eckert Road. Whenever we went up there, we saw two coffins. They had been built for him and Grandmother. Seeing them gave us a strange, uncomfortable feeling."[5] Those two coffins, although ornate and attractive, were never used for the Hooges. By the time they died—Gerhard in April 1952 and Helena in January 1956—more modern ones were in style. The originals were traded in.

Susie Derksen suggests that Gerhard Hooge may well have been the one who built "a fine little coffin" for the Giesbrecht boy who died of pneumonia on August 2, 1928, a mere 10 days old. Probably the first adult for whom he built a coffin was his niece, Katie Wiens, who died of tuberculosis later that year. Both the Giesbrecht baby and Katie Wiens are buried in the Carman United Church Cemetery on Promontory Road in Sardis. There was, as yet, no cemetery in Yarrow.

If the "old Hooges" weren't the oldest couple to settle in Yarrow, they likely were the first to celebrate their 50th anniversary there (June 10, 1936) as well as their 60th (June 10, 1946). It appears that Gerhard Hooge often visited the Mennonite Brethren Church, but his wife regularly attended the United Mennonite Church (UMC), which later affiliated with the General Conference Mennonites. Their membership was in the UMC church. Their 60th anniversary, celebrated at this church, included five speakers,[6] among them Reverend John Klassen, pastor of the UMC, and Reverend John Harder, pastor of the Mennonite Brethren Church. Gerhard's funeral service was conducted in the Mennonite Brethren Church; again, pastors from both churches presided.[7]

Even as Gerhard's and Helena's health declined, young George's family and possessions increased. When George first arrived in Yarrow in 1928, he farmed with his parents as he had done in Saskatchewan. Before long he took notice of the arrival of several young women. The Giesbrechts, the Epps, and the Wiens/Dahl clan all had girls of marrying age. The Wiens girls were his cousins, but the Dahl girls were only *onjefriede* cousins (cousins by marriage). There was nothing wrong with marrying one of them. He hoped Mary would not refuse him.

George's marriage to Mary Dahl, on June 16, 1929, was the first Mennonite wedding in Yarrow. The evening before the wedding they held a *Polterabend* (wedding-eve party). Susie Derksen, 11 years old at the time, remembers reciting a poem for the couple.[8] It was the custom

Yarrow Mennonites' first wedding: George Hooge and Mary Dahl, June 1929.

among Mennonites to have such an informal social evening at the bride's house on the eve of her wedding day. This was an occasion for people to bring gifts, sing songs, offer good wishes and congratulations, recite poetry and Bible verses, and share a light meal.

In keeping with tradition, the wedding ceremony and reception were held on Sunday afternoon. They took place in Chauncey Eckert's spacious machine shed near the corner of Central and Eckert roads. The Mennonite Brethren congregation was organized by then, but it did not as yet have a building. "I was a 13-year-old lad then," recalls

David Giesbrecht. "I remember that wedding. It was such an exciting event. The English-speaking people had never seen such a wedding—so much singing, so much food."[9] Mary's wedding gown was a pink, calf-length dress that she had purchased in Vancouver shortly before leaving her employment there as a housekeeper. Her sister remembers words of advice given the bridal couple by the minister, Peter Dyck: "Husband and wife should never be angry at the same time. If the wife is upset when the husband comes in, she should wear her kerchief to the left side of the head. If all is well, she should wear it on the right side of the head."[10]

Mary had worked in Vancouver until two weeks before the wedding date, and until the month prior to the wedding she had given her earnings to her parents to help meet other, apparently more pressing, needs. No honeymoon followed the wedding. The next morning it was off to work for both of them, milking cows by hand.

At first, George and Mary lived upstairs in his parents' house. Their own house was finished before the birth of their first child, Ernie, in May 1930. The 10-acre parcel of land was divided into one acre for the parents and nine acres for George and Mary. George recalls that the lumber for his house consisted of one-foot-wide boards shipped on the B.C. Electric from a lumberyard in Abbotsford. He was proud of several features in his new house. The well was in the corner of the basement, but a hand pump over a sink in the kitchen brought the water to the sink. That pump worked so well that a few young boys left unsupervised during milking could flood the kitchen floor. Another feature was his bay window. According to George, "Nobody else had one. Only one other house had a full basement." The wood-burning kitchen stove had a built-in reservoir that held a pail and a half of water. Thus hot water was available whenever the stove was heating.

Before George and Mary got fully established in their own house in Yarrow, they spent one summer on the farm that belonged to the Empress Hotel in Chilliwack. Here they grew produce, looked after the animals, and provided meat as needed by the hotel kitchen. Thereafter, they worked together on their own farm, keeping cows, shipping milk, tending gardens, and looking after the growing family. For a while, they separated the milk and shipped cream. For a few years, they grew strawberries. One year the cannery in Sardis wouldn't accept any more strawberries, and so they advertised their berries for one cent a pound. That brought some unexpected customers from Greendale. Mary recognized the once well-to-do family for whom she had worked as a maid back in the Ukraine.

Even in the years when Mary had a baby almost annually and there were more and more cows to milk, she somehow managed to tend a large garden and raise chickens. When a Chinese man came from Vancouver to buy vegetables, she could provide much of what he needed: rhubarb, cabbages, carrots, beans, and also chickens. Sometimes George made deliveries by bicycle all the way to Chilliwack to a butcher who wanted dressed chickens wrapped in brown paper but with their heads still attached. Eventually, George and Mary discovered that they could increase their income greatly by shipping hatchery eggs. They raised a flock of New Hampshire chickens and shipped the eggs, first to Chilliwack, then to J.J. Hambley's in Abbotsford.

Although Mary thrived on hard work and challenges, her body and emotions undoubtedly were tested to their limits in the winter of 1937. On November 18, 1937, George and Mary's sixth boy was born. The other five boys were sick with pneumonia. Mustard plasters were the only remedy. But Ernie's illness turned into meningitis. He had to be taken to the Chilliwack Hospital, where he remained for many weeks. It was a long time before Mary could visit him: she had her hands full at home. There were, as yet, no electric washing machines or indoor plumbing to ease domestic burdens. Johnny, the four-year-old, was not responding to treatment. He died on December 9, 1937. Meanwhile, Ernie was not improving. When Mary was finally able to visit him, this seemed to be the turning point for his eventual recovery.

The week before George Hooge died, he reminisced about his son Johnny's illness: "He cried when Mom wanted to put on another mustard plaster, 'It hurts too much.' The next year, or maybe only a few months later, when someone else's child had pneumonia, there was medicine already available. That child didn't die. He got better." During those early years, when a new baby arrived every year, Mary's sister, Katie Dahl, as well as Susan Epp and others, were frequent helpers and baby-sitters.

Mary was determined that her children would get an education. Too busy to be of much help to them with schoolwork, however, she had one boy sit at each window in the barn practising his reading while she and her husband milked the cows.

By 1946, the family included six boys and three girls. Although their first house had been expanded and remodeled, it was too small.

They had bought another 10 acres of land "in the bush" east of Yarrow, and 40 more at Tolmie and No. 5 roads on the west side. It was cumbersome taking cows to these pastures and milking them several miles from home. By then, they had a Surge milking machine and milked 15 cows. When George checked out a 100-acre dairy farm on Vye Road in Arnold, the large barn, roomy house, and yard were much to his liking, but the required down payment seemed out of reach. By dividing and then selling their main property on Eckert Road to two other families, and by selling the other acreages, they were able to manage the down payment. But then pressure was on them to come up with the next payment, and the next, to avoid losing everything they had worked for. They kept the farm and increased their family by another three.

Besides this large house, there was a smaller one on the Arnold farm. "Mover Thiessen" of Yarrow was hired to move this cottage to Eckert Road to the Pauls's yard as a home for the aging Gerhard and Helena Hooge. A few years later, Thiessen was hired to move this house again, this time across the fields to Stewart Road to property owned by Mary's father, Johann Dahl, Sr. Today this little house still stands on that property.

In 1966, George and Mary purchased five acres on King and Columbia roads in Abbotsford, where they built a new house for their retirement. Mary died in 1984; George lived in the retirement house and looked after himself until his 97th birthday. At the 70th anniversary of the Yarrow Mennonite Brethren Church in 1999, he was honoured as one of two surviving charter members. He died peacefully on April 21, 2000, with three generations of his family around him.

At the time of this writing, George and Mary Hooge have left behind 12 children, 34 grandchildren, and 35 great-grandchildren.

PIONEERS JOHANN AND SUSANNA BRAUN

By Susan Braun Brandt

My parents, Johann and Susanna Braun, came to Yarrow in March1928 with little money but a strong will to succeed. They were lured to the area by an advertisement placed in the *Mennonitische Rundschau* by Chauncey Eckert. Until their home could be built, they, along with their two sons, John (Harvey) and Menno (Jim), stayed for two weeks in Agassiz and then in Yarrow at what was known as the Nickel home, a vacant house near the dyke on Wilson Road.

Father and Mr. Eckert became good friends, and Father worked for Mr. Eckert for a number of years, supervising a pea-processing plant located on Wilson Road between the B.C. Electric Railway tracks and the Siddalls' grocery store and post office. This plant operated from the early 1930s to 1938 or so, when it was taken over by the Yarrow Growers' Co-operative Union as a raspberry-processing plant. It remained that way until 1944, when the new Yarrow Growers' plant was built on Eckert Road. At that point the Co-op turned it into a feed warehouse for the retail store. Later, until it burned down, it served as a coal-unloading and storage place for Yarrow Freight and Fuels.

During their initial two-week stay in Agassiz, my parents purchased 10 acres, with no down payment, on what a few years later would become Stewart Road, and they immediately built a house while awaiting the birth of a third son. Ben was born the next June. Yarrow was basically unsettled at the time and without roads. Not even Central Road had been constructed, although it had been marked as a future road and brush was being cleared in preparation for construction. To get to their property from the railway station or from another settler's farm, my parents had to cross open fields.

Their house was a wood-frame structure with a small cellar for food storage and, later, a furnace. It had two bedrooms, a large kitchen/dining room, a great room on the main floor, and three bedrooms upstairs. In the front was a covered veranda. Eventually, a separate kitchen and bathroom were added. The lumber for the house was ordered by Mr. Eckert from Vancouver and transported to Agassiz by train, then across the Fraser River at Rosedale by ferry, and across the open country to Yarrow. For Dad, one important feature about the land he had chosen for his own acreage was a stream that ran through it. The banks of the stream in front of our house became lovely slopes of green. My parents immediately planted many trees along what they thought was the property line, but they had to move them when a road (Stewart Road) was put in a few years later.

The house soon became a temporary home for uncles, aunts, and grandmothers who followed as emigrants from Russia. When Uncle Isaac and Aunt Katarina Braun came in November 1929, they brought with them their five children, Isaak, Katie, John, Mary, and Susan, as well as both of their mothers. (My mother and Aunt Katarina were sisters; Uncle Isaac and Father were brothers.) They lived in the house with us, 14 people in all, for approximately five months, during which time, on Dad's advice, their house was built in the neighbouring settlement of Greendale. That area, like Yarrow, was just opening for settlement, with inexpensive land and favourable locations and purchase conditions. Father helped them build their homes in Greendale. Uncle David and Aunt Tina Braun came in 1930 with their two children, Jake and Katie, and they also stayed with our family, which by that time included another child, Martha. So we were 12 people in the house. Uncle David and Aunt Tina also built their home in Greendale.

Although Dad was a miller by profession, not a farmer, he went at farming with gusto. Mr. Eckert advanced Dad $25 to buy a cow. Both Father and Mother worked hard and were willing to try almost anything to make a go of the farm. Raising cattle was a mainstay, but they also tried their hand at geese. They experimented with various crops, often at Mr. Eckert's suggestion, in order to find what was best for the land, climate, and market. They tried soybeans, asparagus, rhubarb, and raspberries. They also experimented with strawberries, beans, sugar beets, peanuts, and peas. In the case of raspberries, they tried six or seven different varieties (one or two rows of each to determine which variety was best suited to the area). In fact, they were responsible for introducing the very first raspberries to the area. Because raspberry plants were imported via rail from eastern Canada at that time, Father had to ride his bicycle more than 20 miles to Agassiz to bring them home. This trip always required a river crossing by ferry.

Harvesting the crops was exacting work. Produce was picked at the peak of ripeness and freshness, packed, and shipped to Vancouver by train. If, perchance, it was not of the quality demanded, the whole shipment was dumped, and the day's labour was in vain. Sometimes, Dad put the produce on his bicycle and rode to Chilliwack, where he would sell it door-to-door. Mother was involved in the farming as much as Dad, but she also looked after the growing family, which came to include twins Mary and David, and Fred and Susan.

Besides cultivating their extensive fruit and vegetable plots, my parents also operated a dairy. On days when Dad had to leave the farm early in the morning to work in the hop fields or elsewhere, Mom milked the cows and made sure they were sent to the communal pasture. Dad and oldest son Harvey would take turns riding the bicycle to the hop fields: one rode, the other walked. They would work all day for 10 cents an hour, then ride and walk the several miles home. They worked as field hands in the Canadian Hop Company fields, but picked hops at Haas, Hulbert, and B.C. Hopyards as well as Canadian at various times.

Father, a hardworking person, was involved in numerous activities within the community. He worked as a carpenter and mason. In later years, when we went for a pleasure ride on a Sunday afternoon or evening, he would proudly point out the houses and chimneys he had built. He was part of a group of 20 farmers who started a wood lot on Vedder Mountain and cut cordwood for heating homes before oil and gas were introduced in the early 1950s as heating fuels. He was also one of the founding members of a number of community ventures. For example, he was part of the first Yarrow Co-op, which supplied members with feed and other farm products and services. It began operating from a small shed on Central Road, but soon grew into a prosperous business for its members, merging with a second Co-op and expanding into a full retail operation with groceries, hardware, dry goods, and feed, and a large egg- and fruit-packing plant. Father was also involved in starting the Yarrow Cemetery in 1931, and for many years he cared for the grounds. Graves had to be dug by hand in those days, and he was responsible for digging many—usually at short notice. Because of his skills as a carpenter, he also built coffins and painted them black.

While Father was initiating various projects, Mother, in addition to raising us and helping run the farm, kept the large gardens and saw to it that the produce was harvested. On summer evenings, after spending all day in the strawberry or raspberry patch, she would pick and then preserve hundreds of jars of vegetables, jams, and fruits. These sustained the family during the winter. In spring, she would often can the fish that the boys caught in the stream that ran through the farm, and in fall she would can chicken, pork, and beef after the annual slaughtering.

In spite of their demanding and time-consuming schedules, my parents enjoyed traveling. They made their first of many trips to California as early as 1945. Later, Dad traveled to South America to visit his only sister, and then to Europe to visit family and attend the Mennonite World Conference in Karlsruhe, Germany. My parents enjoyed bus tours even before these became fashionable for seniors. They took a number of such tours, first to Hillsboro, Kansas when my husband and I graduated from Tabor College. Later, they traveled by bus to California, Texas, Manitoba, and places in between to visit family and friends and enjoy tourist sights.

Always willing to help members of our extended family, my parents, together with Father's brothers, helped a number of cousins come to Canada after the Second World War. In August 1948, many cousins arrived: Anny Klassen with her children, Peter and Anna; Anny's sisters, Margaret, Mary, Katie, and Helen; Lydia Penner; and Helena and Renate Penner. The Klassen family stayed in Yarrow; the others moved either to Greendale or Vancouver. Following Dad's trip to Europe in 1957, Dora Anmueller, a grand-daughter to Dad's sister, came from Germany to be part of our family. In later years, our parents helped care for others by driving those who needed transportation to physicians in Chilliwack, and by visiting people who needed company.

Always active in the church, Father was a lay pastor in the early Yarrow United Mennonite Church for a number of years. In 1937, both he and Mother chose to be rebaptized and join the Mennonite Brethren Church. Although he never preached again, Father did become involved in committees and taught Sunday School, and Mother assumed leadership in a local ladies' sewing circle on Stewart Road.

Mom and Dad were good parents. They taught their children to work hard, but also to relax after a day's work. The youngest in the family, I probably have more recollections than my siblings do of time spent playing games with my parents and of Father taking us to Cultus Lake for a swim after a day of picking raspberries. My parents were good role models, and they showed concern for the spiritual development of each of their children. Bible reading and prayer were essential parts of every day's activities, and Sunday was always a day of rest. Church attendance was expected of everyone in the family. We knew our parents prayed faithfully for each of us.

After the last of the children had left home, my parents sold their farm and retired to a home closer to the church. Here they entertained family and friends until Father's death in 1970. Mother remained in the house for a few more years, then moved to the Menno Home in Abbotsford, where she passed away in 1980.

Dietrich and Anna Friesen

By John E. Friesen

The immigration of our parents, Dietrich and Anna Friesen, to the Canadian Prairies in 1923 was preceded by many losses. They carried the memory of these losses with them to their new home as they faced the challenge not merely of adapting to a new culture, but also of reinventing their lives. Creating a new life in Canada required that they adopt new ways of doing things. It required that they learn a new language, develop new business procedures, arrange for new business contacts, make new friends, and develop new farming methods.

After the economic collapse of the 1930s, our parents faced the onslaught of farming failure. In 1931, just short of declaring bankruptcy in Provost, Alberta, they moved on to Glenbush, Saskatchewan, with their five children and their meagre belongings. In Provost, they had enjoyed a large, beautiful home in which regular Sunday services were held and which offered the opportunity for grand entertaining. Now they lived in a house consisting of a few rooms and constructed out of hand-hewn logs. The cracks between the logs were filled with a mixture of mud and dung. Our parents had invested immense energy in their farm in Alberta, yet they were now destitute. This sudden decline profoundly disillusioned them and threatened their sense of identity and self-worth. It diminished their power over everyday living and increased their feeling of separation from the larger society.

Financial failure was particularly traumatic for our father. It challenged his personal sense of competence. Instead of directing his feelings of failure inward and turning them into despair, he turned them outward, in the form of anger, even rage. Several older children in the family recall our father's unreasonable demands, accompanied by irrational anger. These experiences have left some indelible scars on their personalities. It has been their task to forgive and forget our father's tendency to express his exasperations with such strong passion.

In 1936, after hearing about the new opportunities for farming and for spiritual renewal in Yarrow, our parents left Glenbush with their five children and all their possessions and moved to this place of promise. Here they hoped to find new economic opportunities, social and spiritual support, and better prospects for the educational and vocational development of their children. In large part, they succeeded. It is in the context of suffering, loss, economic deprivation and tribulations, and a stubborn optimism that we offer a tribute to our parents. The legacies they left us—in the areas of religion and spirituality, entrepreneurship, values, and beliefs—were inculcated either by explicit teaching or implicit emphasis in everyday conversations and activities in our home.

The central legacy left by our parents is a spiritual and religious one. All of their cultural activities were tightly linked to the religious, and this left little opportunity for other cultural pursuits with the exception of business ventures. Religion and spirituality spoke to the very heart of our parents' existence and focused on the essential meaning, purpose, and value of life itself. Spirituality was a resource that helped them transcend their personal discouragements, the pressures of poverty, and the oppression of society. As marginalized and disadvantaged people, they found meaning in their struggles through their faith in God. They often spoke of Jesus, who had suffered dreadful pain, isolation, betrayal, and abandonment, but who never ceased to extend himself in love to others. Jesus was the model for our own suffering.

Indeed, our parents believed that suffering is an inevitable part of human life. Their personal losses bore evidence to this fact. Our father frequently spoke of the murder of his first wife, two children, and parents at the hands of Russian bandits. The horror haunted him throughout his life, and his mourning over these losses was never completed.

Jesus' words "In this world you shall have tribulation" capture a predominant spiritual theme in our home. People we love shall die. Things that we hold precious shall be taken from us. Those we love and trust will, from time to time, bring us harm. Things we believe to be permanent will inevitably dissolve, rust, or fall away.

Whereas our mother was committed to an otherworldly perspective, our father had a heart and mind for business. He loved to take financial risks and engage in business transactions. Although he suffered numerous financial losses, he continued to engage in business ventures. Whenever possible, he bought and sold cows, chickens, sheep, horses, and pigs. Or he would buy and sell land, always with the intention of making a profit and improving his financial condition. Making a profit was at the heart of his capitalist instincts. This entrepreneurial interest has been passed on to children and grandchildren and runs considerably deeper than the Vedder River in the Friesen family.

At the core of their being, our parents were hopeful and optimistic. Despite numerous setbacks and losses, and fear of additional losses, they were always ready to face new opportunities and new challenges. They believed that with the help of God they were equal to the tasks that confronted them. Their belief in a personal God furnished them with hope, which helped to overcome discouragement from the world around them and from a battered soul within.

Trying experiences, they were convinced, help to foster mental and spiritual growth. Indeed, problems should be welcomed, not feared. This belief in the value of suffering and tribulation provided a helpful perspective on an everyday life often characterized by intense stress. We almost got the feeling that our parents welcomed hardship; they maintained that those who live with deprivations, pain, and loss often live closest to their spirituality and to their God.

While our parents sacredly guarded and nurtured many core beliefs, a few principal ones will be mentioned here. Perhaps their most central belief was that there is a way through difficulties and trials. Closely linked to this conviction was their view of God as the source of strength, and the corollary that God never permits a greater test than one can deal with. Our parents also believed strongly in the restorative potential of human relationships and the power of love. Ties to spouse, family, children, and relatives, as well as to neighbourhood and society, no matter how complicated and flawed any of these might be, could be maintained by the power of love. They believed that love can heal all.

No less important was the education of their children. As in many immigrant families, education was seen as the vehicle for improving one's situation. We were always encouraged to do well in school and to go on to higher education. Thus we did not approach university studies with fear, but looked forward to them with enthusiasm and optimism.

Applying ourselves diligently in school was, in our parents' view, evidence of a good work ethic, and they strongly encouraged a work ethic. Work was ordained by God. Life should be lived by the sweat of one's brow. Thus work not only provided sustenance for our daily lives; it also brought meaning to life.

We think it important to underscore that our parents also emphasized a philosophy of collective unity rather than of individualism. Times of loss brought together the entire family, extended family, neighbours, friends, members of the church, and members of the community to mourn the loss. To our parents, Yarrow was more than a group of people; it was a supportive community that could offer understanding and reassurance in times of hardship and loss.

Gardening as Beauty and Love: Aron Dietrich Rempel

By Edith Rempel Simpson, with Ruth Rempel Klassen, Charlotte Rempel Shier, Anne Rempel Dyck, and Olga Rempel Peters

September days in Yarrow are the loveliest days of the year—the morning air with its refreshing coolness and the early sun in a cloudless sky that promises a warm day; the smell of autumn in the air; leaves just beginning to turn; the aroma of fall flowers everywhere. It is on such a day in mid-September 1981 that our family has gathered at the Yarrow Mennonite Brethren Church to celebrate our father's life and lay him to rest in the modest Yarrow Cemetery, a mere 15-minute brisk walk from the church. People walking to the cemetery will pass the large home where we all grew up, a Tudor-style house with eight bedrooms and two bathrooms which Father built for us in 1939.

We are gathered in a room downstairs, preparing for the long walk down the aisle accompanying our father on this, his final official church function. For so many years this church had been the focal point not only of the Rempel family, but also of many other Yarrow families. Father loved this church and served both his church and community for half a century.

Memories of Father's presence in our family and his incredible influence on all of us crowd my thoughts. We follow the casket, which is heaped with a spray of 125 orange-scarlet Tropicana roses, beautifully arranged by our sister Hildegarde. Their pungent fragrance fills the air. Walking slowly with the others, I can visualize Father's driveway, which for years he lined with Tropicana roses that, from early summer to late fall, greeted with their extraordinary hue and beauty all who came to our home. He pruned these roses ruthlessly in winter and nurtured them with tenderness in spring and throughout the summer and early autumn.

* * *

Tough and tender. That is how Aron Rempel, our father, lived his life, raising nine children and developing a 10-acre farm that yielded an astonishing variety of fresh fruits, vegetables, nuts, and flowers. Every plant placed in his garden was there according to a mental plan and physical grid, becoming a source of abundant beauty and the finest produce. The varieties in his garden went far beyond the lettuce, cabbage, carrots, potatoes, and cucumbers of the typical garden in our community. The family learned to eat and love unfamiliar fruits, vegetables, and nuts. In winter, he pored over seed and plant catalogues, identifying varieties that he could import from Europe and the United States. He was always experimenting in order to ascertain which varieties would grow a little better, produce a little more, mature a little earlier or a little later.

Father's innovative gardening had its genesis in the estates of his father, Dietrich Rempel, in the Crimea and Caucasus. Dietrich Rempel and his sons were well known both in Russia and Germany for their expertise in budding procedures and grafting techniques, as well as their extensive know-how in growing grapes, soft fruits, and nuts. Horticultural and botanical communities in both countries had high regard for the Rempels' expertise. Besides raising livestock, chickens, geese, ducks, peacocks, and pigeons, Dietrich grew winter wheat, winter and summer oats, corn, and rye. His diverse cultivation also included vineyards, large orchards, and vegetable gardens beautified with lilies and other flowers. This type of mixed farming proved profitable.[1]

Gerhard Rempel, one of Dietrich's sons, remained in Russia and spent his life as an agronomist in Siberia. He achieved national recognition and won numerous medals for developing hybrids and unique cultivation methods for the short growing seasons in Siberia. Working at the Krasnorecenski collective farm in Khabarovsk from 1946 and on, he was responsible for developing the famous hothouses and cold frames that generated about three-fifths of the horticulture department's income. These widely known and highly regarded hothouses gave rise to the practice of growing vegetables in cold frames. Seeds grown in Rempel's novel "cold pots" (freezing the pots rather than drying them out) produced plants that were hardy. As a rule, Gerhard Rempel was able to harvest two crops a year from the forced-growth beds. Before moving to Khabarovsk, he had invented and used this method in the Umylta River area. As a result, workers of that region were eating fresh vegetables much earlier in spring than people in the distant and warmer south.[2]

Gerhard was unable to come to Canada, but on March 30, 1930, Aron, then 26 years old, immigrated to Canada with his oldest brother, Abraham. Dietrich and Katherina Rempel and the rest of their children had come in 1926. On June 15, 1930, Dietrich and his wife and some of the children arrived in Yarrow, starting anew from nothing at the beginning of the Depression, when income was hard to come by and providing for even the bare necessities was a huge challenge. Our parents, Aron Rempel and Olga Hepting Rempel, had experienced a privileged and carefree childhood in Russia on well-managed estates. It was only natural that Aron would work hard to replicate as much of his gardening success as possible in this new country. He had the knowledge, optimism, and enthusiasm.

In the early 1930s, after marrying Olga Hepting, Father went into business with his truck. Sometimes he hauled goods across the border into Washington State. On one such trip, his horticultural eye discovered raspberries growing in Everett, Washington. He learned that these berries, which were producing successfully in the Everett area, were Newbergs. It was clear to him that as the climate and soil in Yarrow were about the same as they were in Everett, some 70 miles south, Newbergs could be grown in Yarrow. He purchased a truckload of young starts, brought them home, and planted them on his newly purchased farm on Dyke Road.

The result was a strange and, for some, unsettling scene. When the wife of Father's mortgage holder saw these many rows of twigs sticking out of the ground like dead spikes, she fretted, "Now he's poked his land full of sticks, and when he defaults on his mortgage payments, we will have the additional burden of pulling them out." As people soon found out, however, those sticks greened into thick, mature bushes that bloomed every May and June and that, summer after summer, produced large crops of delicious berries. In fact, for some time Newberg raspberries were the most popular variety in Yarrow. Many years later, Yarrow school children offered a program on the history of their community, and in a skit they portrayed our father as the grower who brought the first raspberry plants into the area. At the conclusion of the performance, he was called on stage and crowned "Raspberry King."[3]

Although it was mainly our father's raspberry crops that became a local legend, he experimented with as many kinds of plants as time and garden space allowed. He soon learned that soft fruits were the most productive in our area. He collaborated with personnel at the Agassiz Provincial Experimental Farm, sharing his findings and testing their suggestions. He soon became known for his expertise in growing raspberries and strawberries. His strawberries were a special treat, and with great enthusiasm he would take us to discover the first ripe berries. I always believed that I had the best eye for seeing them, and so it was my singular delight to find them for my birthday in early June, the beginning of the season. Beehives were placed strategically throughout the gardens to assist in the pollination. In autumn, it was exciting for us to help extract the honey from dripping honeycombs.

Although soft fruits were Father's specialty, he also grew a variety of nuts. Early on, he attempted a few crops of peanuts, but our climate did not provide adequate hours of sunlight. So the peanuts were removed, and he concentrated on walnuts, hazelnuts, and almonds, all good producers in our part of the Fraser Valley.

It seemed there was nothing he couldn't grow and nothing he wouldn't share. From early spring until late fall, there was an abundance of fresh vegetables and fruit, and no one who came to our farm left empty-handed. What was not given away was canned. Mother usually preserved well over 1,000 jars every summer, and she gave these away as readily as Father gave away fresh produce.

Father's vineyard was a favourite place for me. We were assured of fresh grapes from early September to late November, from his 10-plus varieties, and throughout the winter we had grape juice that our mother had preserved. The first grapes of the season were a small green variety; our favourite was the deep purple Concord grape. As a rule, my school lunch bag was heavy with grapes for all of my friends and me. We grew up assuming that generosity was part of daily living.

Fall was a time for shipping fruit to relatives and friends in the Prairie Provinces. We helped our father fill box after box with half-ripe plums, pears, and apples, nailing them shut and loading them into the car. It was difficult, tiring work for us, but the reward was a trip to the train station, where the boxes were unloaded from our car and prepared for shipping. As a child, Ollie, a younger sister, often wondered what those homes on the Prairies were like and if the recipients knew how much work all our growing and shipping entailed. And did they enjoy their delicious fruits?

In addition to being a practical and knowledgeable gardener, our father had an eye and a heart for beauty, and he always managed to add a little loveliness to the ordinary. During the time when his raspberries were producing heavily, he hired pickers, who were lodged in a summerhouse that he had built on our property. This house was both practical and aesthetic, from its wallpapered bedrooms to the vegetable garden planted for the pickers' exclusive use. We knew not to touch their garden when Mother sent us out to fetch vegetables for dinner. To lift the spirits of his often weary pickers, Father also planted arrangements of flowers in their garden. When they entered their communal kitchen after a long day's work, they could usually delight in the fresh flowers he had placed on the big oak table or in their rooms.

Father was a romantic, sister Charlotte recalls, and flowers were his language of love. He cherished, loved, and honoured our beautiful mother. She received the first of each flower variety as it bloomed, beginning with snowdrops in January. She received the last rose in December. Without fail, there was a bouquet of fresh flowers beside her bed. Every birthday, Mother's and ours, was celebrated with a bouquet at the breakfast table. It was exciting beyond words to be the special person for the day in a family of nine very lively children; it felt good to be special at least once a year. One of Charlotte's earliest memories is of Father taking her by the hand into the garden early in the spring to a small plot under an apple tree. There he showed her a cluster of green spikes poking up from the cold ground. He told her that if she watched the progress of this green growth, she would have a lovely surprise in a few weeks. So with great anticipation she watched her little garden grow, and one day, to her delight, the green stalks were capped with the purest of white flowers called narcissus. She enjoyed this little plot for years to come. One of my sisters had a plot of violets, another a plot of snowdrops, and so each of us individually shared this special joy with our father.

Each spring he planted a half-acre with gladiola bulbs. July, August, and September brought a profusion of colour to our front yard. These summer months were given to weddings at our church. Brides would come during the week to choose the flowers that best suited the wedding, and early Sunday morning Father would cut them, place them in buckets, and carry them to the church.

The service has ended with the singing of yet one more of the old, well-known hymns, and we rise to follow our father, one last time, out of the church. It seems as though we have never left this place: the sanctuary, with its well-worn, solid-wood pews, the beautiful hardwood floors, still in excellent condition, the chandeliers hanging from the peaked ceiling like so many upside-down wedding cakes, the lovely pipe organ, a later addition through the efforts of our brother, and the most amazing acoustics. This is the church that Father and other craftsmen like him built in the 1930s. Outside, we are ushered into the cars for the drive to the cemetery. It is a short drive, past our family house and to the next corner, where we turn left, heading west on a narrow road.

At one time, mourners used to walk behind the casket all the way to the cemetery. Even now, numerous people are going by foot, and when we arrive many are already waiting. The sky is blue, and the sun is warm. After a brief service we are urged to take home a rose from the large spray on the casket. A number of friends and relatives who have gathered with us at the graveside also take a flower. Finally everyone leaves, and as we drive in our car past all those people walking, I am overcome by the sight of so many mourners, each carrying home a Tropicana rose. A final gift from Aron Rempel—a gift of both knowledge and beauty, given in a spirit of generosity and love.

"Widow" Epp

By George H. Epp

Our mother, Gertrude Rempel Epp, usually called Trude, was born September 24, 1892, to Katharina and Dietrich Aron Rempel in the Kuban of Russia. She married Heinrich Epp, a farmer six years her senior. As newlyweds, they settled in the Caucasus region along the banks of the Terek River. Soon they were a family of six, with three boys—David, Dietrich, and Abraham—and, by adoption, a sister, Ella Martens. With the growing political and economic uncertainties, the entire Dietrich Rempel clan, except for Mother's brother Gerhard, immigrated to Canada in 1926. They all settled in southern Manitoba, the Heinrich Epp family in the farming community of La Rivière. Mother's brother Gerhard made his peace with the new Bolshevik regime, studied botany in the USSR, and eventually gained national and international distinction for his pioneering work on growing vegetables in cold temperatures.

Until 1932, our parents struggled in Manitoba under trying conditions. During some of that time, our grandparents, Dietrich and Katharina Rempel, and their youngest daughter, Tina, lived in the same small house with our parents. Our grandfather found the adjustment from considerable wealth to poverty a difficult one. In her introduction to her translation of his journal, granddaughter Helen Rempel Klassen makes this pointed observation: "Grandfather was a man of many good qualities, but some of us, his grandchildren, rarely got to see them." A cantankerous patriarch was not what the Epp family needed at this time. During this brief stay in Manitoba, another four children were born to Gertrude and Heinrich: Henry, George, Frieda, and, shortly after our father's sudden and untimely death in 1932, Bruno. Adding to the domestic tension were mounting financial problems, made even more difficult by the collapse of the Canadian economy in 1929.

The harsh Manitoba winters, combined with financial failure, had the Rempel clan casting about for more pleasant climes. Soon they heard of the Fraser Valley of British Columbia, where land was becoming available in the Abbotsford and Yarrow areas. In 1930, most of them moved west. After a short stay in Abbotsford with the Abram Rempel family, who also had recently settled in B.C., Grandfather Rempel acquired 10 acres of land in Yarrow. Chauncey Eckert, a local land speculator, offered land to the new arrivals for a down payment of one dollar per acre. Our uncle, Aron Rempel, tells the story of Mr. Eckert, barely conversant in German, cruising into Yarrow in his 1929 Model A Ford. He would say, in an attempt at Low German, "*Hascht een Dolla* (Do you have a dollar)?" If you dared to venture, you had an acre of Yarrow soil.

Grandfather Rempel's 10 acres fronted on the south side of Yarrow Central Road and stretched west in a narrow band almost up to the Yarrow Mennonite Brethren Church. This land was settled by several family members. Grandfather's yard was at the corner of Eckert and Yarrow Central roads. Adjoining his was the Peter Thiessen parcel (his wife, Anna, was Mother's sister), then Mother's, and, finally, her brother Aron's. When Mother arrived in Yarrow with her eight children, Grandfather gave her almost an acre of land. My brother Dave, assisted by Aron Rempel, built our simple frame structure at 1016 Yarrow Central Road. A small barn sufficient for a family cow and hay storage was also added at this time. During these construction days, we lived together with a number of other new Yarrow arrivals in a temporary shelter adjacent to the David Heinrichs's dairy farm.

Our new house was actually too small for a family of eight. There were only two bedrooms; Mother shared one of them with Frieda. The bedroom upstairs was for my brothers, Abraham (Abe) and Dietrich (Dick). The other half of the upstairs, never finished, served as storage and emergency nighttime accommodation. It was also the place where the hams and sausage from the annual fall hog-butchering were hung. The sausages, especially, had a way of mysteriously shrinking, due only in small part to dehydration. The living room was also used as a sleeping area. It contained a *Schlaffbank* (bench-bed), which, as the word implies, is a dual-purpose bench. The lid that functioned as a place to sit could be folded back. Below it was a drawer with bedding. When pulled out, this drawer became an extension of the bottom of the bench and formed a bed wide enough for two persons. Making the bed in the morning was simple: you merely pushed the drawer back in and dropped the lid-seat back down on the bench.

Because our house lacked insulation and the windows were single-pane, with snow sifting in on window ledges and in the attic, we were always very happy to hear the first robins in spring. Frozen water pipes were never a problem, as we had no indoor plumbing. Once it became available, we did have electrical power and at least five wall plugs, but no electrical appliances. We never had a telephone. For heat, we had two wood-burning stoves: the cooking stove in the kitchen and a shaky potbelly stove in the living room. The upstairs received some heat through a hole cut in the ceiling of the living room just above the stove. Our domestic water source was a shallow well immediately behind the house. We shared our well with the frogs.

The crowded living conditions were soon alleviated. Ella found housework in Vancouver, as was customary for many of the young women of Yarrow. Dave left to find work in Peace River, Alberta. He soon returned to Yarrow with a new wife, Jessie, to start a family and establish a bicycle shop and trucking business. For their home, he acquired a plot subdivided from the Epp property. His business later grew into a hardware, plumbing, and heating business that developed into a partnership with Dick known as Epp Bros.

Our small parcel of land, about an acre, some of which was marsh and drainage ditch, was large enough to grow various vegetables, gooseberries, raspberries, and fruit trees. Given our severe living conditions, it was crucial to pickle, can, and dry fruits and vegetables. One of our first cows, an Ayrshire heifer given to us by Frank Dyck, Sr. of Boundary Road, was herded together with others' cows to the common pasture on Dyke Road, now known as No. 3 Road, and led home again each evening. I mention Mr. Frank Dyck in this context because he was a member of the United Mennonite Church and we were Mennonite Brethren. No distinction was made among cows, but as Mennonite Brethren we considered ourselves more spiritual than people like him. This foolish distinction was general in Yarrow.

Family income was accumulated in various ways. Soon after school classes were dismissed for the summer months, the raspberry-picking season was upon us. We had only a few rows, but enough to fill several flats each day or two for shipping to the Co-op receiving and processing plant at the end of Eckert Road. But Uncle Aron offered us berry-picking jobs. He was always meticulous about the quality of picking—you had to search each bush carefully. He allowed me to operate his garden tractor, one of the first such implements in Yarrow. It was a decided improvement over the horse-drawn cultivator. Being an innovative person, he also built a *Haxelmaschine*. With it he chopped the year's spent raspberry canes and spread them on the soil, replenishing it.

A few days after berry picking ended, the hop picking season arrived. Aboriginals from the Fraser Canyon and beyond were the first hop pickers to arrive, rumbling along Yarrow Central Road on horse-drawn wagons. They were on their way to the Canadian Hopyards in Sumas Prairie. When we as children saw these darker-skinned people passing through with their loads, we scooted into our houses and peered from behind drawn curtains, hoping that they would keep on going. Our tolerance for what to us was unfamiliar and unknown was slight.

Picking hops required getting up very early. Mother always packed lunches the night before. After our hurried breakfast of porridge, she would hustle us out to the road to catch the transport truck for pickers. The ride to the hop field was bumpy, dusty, and cold in the early hours, and often it was wet. Our mother had the privilege of riding in the cab with her brother Aron, owner-operator of the truck. A long day of picking ensued. We stood beside our baskets, tearing branches off the vine and hops off the branches. To relieve our day-long tedium, we kids would play pranks on each other and on families in neighbouring rows. Thus one of the challenges for Mother was to concentrate on the task at hand while also mediating disputes. She really did not need the additional task of reconciler. Hard as she tried, she never excelled as picker. On the other hand, she was a great peacemaker.

After the berry and hop seasons, Mother, with some cash in hand, joined several other women in shopping for winter clothing in Vancouver at "the Old Church," as it was called. How this place, basically a large thrift store or rummage centre, got its name I don't know, but it was clear that for us, brand-new clothing would have to wait until we reached a higher standard of living. There was a choice of "taxis" in Yarrow: one could get a ride to Vancouver with either Isbrandt Riesen or Johann Derksen, usually for a small fee.

As our mother was the only parent, she had to assume the role of disciplinarian. I do not recall the misdemeanour I committed on one occasion that called for corporal punishment. Whatever it was, my brother Abe, also known as "Apple," was instructed by Mother to administer the punishment, since he was the oldest of the brothers living at home at the time. I was told to find a stick, which I dutifully did. Then he led me into the barn, asked me to bend over a chopping block, and let go with one whack of moderate force, no more. My understanding was that this is what an elder brother does. He was a kind of surrogate dad—in this case, gentle, rather like Mother. I do not recall any feelings of animosity toward him or Mother.

Somehow, our widowed mother persevered. In her view, it was the church that sustained her. Fortunately, we lived within easy walking distance of the church. No matter what the weather, Mother attended services regularly: Sunday morning, Sunday evening, and mid-week. Although generally inconspicuous in church, she never really felt neglected. She had only the highest esteem for the pastor, Reverend Johann Harder, and his wife, Tina, who gave Mother much pastoral care. It was important for us as children to observe this kind of concern; it made us feel more secure. The Harders were also very generous in practical ways, as was the family of David Rempel. The ladies from the church sewing circle were another source of stability in our mother's life. When it was Mother's turn to host their meetings, there were bonuses for us children, as goodies were often left for us to munch on.

In the church community, Mother was known as *Witwe* (Widow) Epp. This name gave her a sense of identity. It was good for us as children to know that she had a status, albeit this simple one. Although she never spoke up at church meetings—women simply did not do so—she compensated for this during the period for public prayer. Because the sanctuary was huge, it was often the case that those praying aloud could not hear each other—at least, not at first. But when they became aware of others praying, a kind of competition

Gertrude Epp, daughter of Katharina and Dietrich Rempel, came to Yarrow as a young widow and raised her eight children as a single parent.

would develop. At such times Mother turned up the volume and left the competition behind.

Mother was very zealous in nurturing a relationship with the Lord. Her Bible reading and audible prayers and singing could be heard from any room in our house. She did her best to cultivate in us a respect for scripture and a conscientious practice of prayer and devotion. Although lacking in material goods, she was very generous. At times, we felt that she was too otherworldly. For instance, when she was given a gift of money she would often place it into the Sunday collection at church. Or if she was given a gift of clothing, say a sweater or scarf, she would give it to someone whom she regarded as more needy than herself. More than once, Frieda expressed annoyance with these acts of generosity. The image still vivid in my mind is that when doling out soup, eggs, potatoes, hamburger, or chicken, Mother would make sure we all had enough before she ate. Invariably she kept the smallest portion, or nothing, for herself. A very stark reminder of her otherworldliness is a Russian, mustard-coloured, plywood trunk that easily contained all of her belongings at the time of her death. She hoarded nothing.

Every year, Mother went all out to make Christmas as much of a highlight for us as she could. At least a week before Christmas, we would find a candy, a cookie, or peanuts in our shoes. She would sneak these items into our room between the time we fell asleep at night and woke up in the morning. After the Christmas Eve program at church, we came home to a decorated Christmas tree mounted on the kitchen table. Under the tree was a plate for each of us, with peanuts, Brazil nuts, Russian candy, walnuts, a Japanese mandarin orange, and a Neilsen's chocolate bar. We always had to wait until the next morning to discover what Santa had left for us under the tree, which by then had been moved by the same Santa to the living room. We woke early to find our gifts under the tree, illuminated by real candles. What we received had been clandestinely ordered from the Eaton's catalogue. The tree remained in the living room until New Year's Day. Then, with a feeling of loss and regret, we helped Mother dismantle it and pack away the decorations for another year.

Mother's health was no doubt affected by our father's tragic demise, which seemed to have started or aggravated an asthmatic condition that plagued her until about 10 years before her death. For virtually all of those years, she inhaled a putrid smoke produced by smouldering Rexall asthma powder. She also suffered bouts of depression, but the good

Lord and caring people and siblings looked after her, and this condition improved. I cannot remember her ever complaining or being discouraged. Her prayers were always suffused with praise, gratitude, and expressions of hope.

It seems that in the final decade of her life, her sense of humour and desire for adventure came alive. In 1962 she traveled to Goshen, Indiana, to visit my wife and me and our children, Mark and Annette. At this time, my wife, Adelaide, and I were enrolled at Goshen College and Elkart Seminary, two Mennonite institutions of higher education in close proximity to each other. Here Mother enjoyed a very different Mennonite culture and the large grain farms of the American Midwest. As the friends with whom she had traveled needed to return to Canada earlier than she did, she was quite prepared to return to B.C. alone by train. What is noteworthy about this decision is that, although she'd lived almost half a century in Canada, she could communicate very little in English. How she ever managed this long train ride home to Yarrow without as much as a hint of fear before embarking still astounds us. My simple explanation is her implicit faith that her God would always look after her.

In 1968, Mother moved from Yarrow to the Tabor Retirement Home in Clearbrook, B.C. For her, this change was easy. She enjoyed the socializing, service, and personal assistance. Five years later, on Sunday, March 18, 1973, she died of a stroke. The simple faith, hope, generosity, and perseverance of this single parent continue to encourage those of us who intimately shared her life.

Building the Community, Exploring the World: Julia and Jack Wittenberg

By Lora Sawatsky

A steady rain trickles along our arms and settles into our sleeves. It drips from the back of our hats and saturates our jackets. It runs down our slacks to form puddles around our feet, which squish water in rubber boots too big or too small. This is a slow drizzle, not enough to warrant a reprieve from the everyday routine of raspberry picking. We notice the cloud cover lifting: the bottom half of Sumas Mountain is clearly outlined. Anxiously we look to the west, where dark clouds are gathering. How we pray for a downpour over our raspberry field. Then, totally miserable, we might be allowed to leave dripping bushes, step out of boots weighted with mud, wash our scratched and red hands, flex our stiffened fingers, and rush to the jewelry shop before closing time to ask Julia Wittenberg about the latest acquisitions of the Yarrow Public Library.

We were among the lucky ones: we lived close to the Wittenberg shop, and if we ran fast we could perhaps still get there before closing. What better way to spend part of a rainy evening than curled up with *My Friend Flicka*, *The Green Grass of Wyoming*, another Zane Grey western, the latest adventures of the Hardy Boys or Nancy Drew, or a Jack London story. Numerous early Yarrow homes held small libraries, a shelf or two with several Bibles, a copy of *Evangeliums-Lieder*, a German *Fibel*, perhaps a concordance, a commentary, an atlas, sometimes a copy of John Bunyan's *Pilgrim's Progress*, and a biography or two of missionary heroes like David Livingstone. Fewer homes may have had devotional books like *The Christian Secret of a Happy Life* by Hannah Withal Smith, *My Utmost for His Highest* by Oswald Chambers, or *In His Steps* by

Charles M. Sheldon. The Book of Knowledge series, usually purchased second-hand at a rummage sale in the Vancouver "Old Church" basement, was popular in any number of homes, as was Harriet Beecher Stowe's *Uncle Tom's Cabin*. Somehow, most young girls had access to *The Virtuous Woman*, by John R. Rice. Few, if any, of these private libraries would have included *The Swiss Family Robinson*, Sherlock Holmes mysteries, *Tom Sawyer*, *Anne of Green Gables*, *Helen of Troy*, or *How Green Was My Valley*. These treasures were available only at Wittenbergs' library.

In early Yarrow days, we looked forward to seeing Julia's sparkling hazel eyes, hearing her laughter and humorous comments, and getting her help in finding just the right books. We wanted those that would keep us awake nights, reading by flashlight or dimmed hall light, or even by overhead light if we lowered the window shades and turned the light on ever so quietly. We felt special when Julia pulled a book from the shelves and declared, "I think you will like this one," or "I have a new book just for you," or "I think you should try *Little Women*. Now that's a good book!" With books, she encouraged Yarrow children to see beyond clock- and work-governed village life to a world of experiences foreign to them.

Julia and her husband, Jack, moved to Yarrow in 1937 from Fife Lake, Saskatchewan, where they had been accustomed to an endless horizon. "Yarrow," Julia observed, "is geographically bound to the south by Vedder Mountain, to the north by the Vedder River, to the east by the B.C. Electric Railway and to the west by Sumas Municipality ... and by Boundary Road, dividing it from the rest of the province."

"Yarrow was a limited settlement, territorially speaking," Jack concurred.[1] And so he, like Julia, understood the importance of seeking wider horizons. Like his wife, Jack was interested in nurturing Yarrow's cultural life. He championed a strong school system and was a major supporter of Walter Neufeld's string orchestra. "Jack was so proud whenever he heard of Yarrow's young people achieving success in their field of expertise," comments Julia.

Jack was born in Samara, a Mennonite settlement in Russia, on June 3, 1904.[2] After completing his college studies in Russia, he immigrated to Rosthern, Saskatchewan, in 1924. He and Julia met in Kipling, Saskatchewan, where he was teaching. They were married December 26, 1929. Almost immediately, he left his teaching position in Kipling for a new situation in a community near North Battleford and the North Saskatchewan River. Soon thereafter, he and Julia moved to Fife Lake, an arid region south of Moose Jaw, where Jack continued his teaching.

Julia and Jack remained in Saskatchewan, but Charles and Julianna Sabo, Julia's parents, moved first to Sardis, where they lived for several years, and then to Yarrow in 1932. Here they purchased the Broe farm on Majuba Hill.[3] "My mother, Julianna Csizmadia, later changed her name to Shoemaker, which is the meaning of the word Csizmadia," says Julia. In 1898, at age 12, Julianna had emigrated from Hungary, eventually settling with her family near Kipling, Saskatchewan. Julia's father, Charles Sabo, had also emigrated from Hungary and settled near Kipling, where his family homesteaded. Julia was born on October 2, 1908. She still sings Hungarian songs, and for several years she served as translator for the Hungarian refugees who arrived at the Vancouver airport in 1957 and were billeted at the Abbotsford airport until they found living accommodations and work. Yarrow residents offered work and provided housing for a number of these refugees.

When the Sabos moved to Majuba Hill, they cleared land on the Hill and grew raspberries, but deer jumped the fences and ate the young plants. The Sabos also raised cattle and shipped milk. "Most people in Yarrow had a cow or two," says Julia. "After Jack and I arrived in Yarrow in 1937, I used to observe pioneers taking turns every morning herding their cows along the main path in Yarrow to a common pasture on No. 3 Road. I was fascinated watching cows being herded back along the same path every evening, as each cow knew exactly at which yard to turn in for the night. I wore out many pairs of shoes walking up the Hill through gravel and mud to visit my parents in their home. A bear with cubs homesteaded near the path I used, and deer regularly crossed the path. At that time, my younger brothers, Charlie and Steven, lived with our parents on the Hill."[4]

Always interested in prose and poetry, Julia wanted to engage more people in Yarrow in reading. She writes:

> The development of the book depository begins in the early months of 1947. It was in this year that my husband was appointed a School District #33 Chilliwack representative on the Fraser Valley Library Board. For some time before a Book Van had called periodically at the old Yarrow Post Office, which was at that time also a grocery store close to the B.C. Electric tram station and a stopping point for the Chilliwack-Vancouver bus. ...

> By 1947, people were well established, younger people fairly well schooled, and we observed that the inconvenient calls and stops of the Book Van were to some extent responsible for the small number of readers. My husband, therefore, suggested to the Board, respectively Mr. P. Grossman—Librarian, that a small depository in Yarrow should be tried out.[5]

The Wittenbergs offered space in their jewelry shop on Central Road, and so the Yarrow Public Library began—with two shelves of books. The Yarrow Waterworks minutes for May 1947 record a decision that "Mrs. Julia Wittenberg be appointed as librarian to replace J.J. Wittenberg. The monthly fee is to remain at $10.00." At first the library was open only three days a week, during jewelry-shop hours. The Wittenbergs soon relocated their shop to a more central site to accommodate an expanding library: in 1950 to Menges' Café, then in 1952 to a room between the Ronald Allen clothing store and a Canadian Bank of Commerce in the former Co-op building.

Always searching for innovative ideas for their shop, the Wittenbergs had opened Yarrow's first ice-cream parlour before the Second World War. Because sugar was rationed during the war, they were forced to close their confectionary. Jack spent 1942-46 in North Vancouver, working in the office of a firm that built Liberty Ships. In 1947 he moved back to Yarrow, where his parents, Jacob and Agatha Wittenberg, had lived since 1930. Once back in Yarrow, he started his business as a jeweler. "'There was a jewelry shop, a public library, and the Waterworks all in one office,' he chuckled."[6] Since most Yarrow settlers had incurred debts with their transportation to Canada and land purchases in Yarrow, Jack frequently found himself repairing used watches, clocks, and electrical equipment rather than selling new merchandise. Besides running the jewelry shop and serving as the Yarrow correspondent to *The Chilliwack Progress*, he was an active member of the Yarrow Waterworks Board, which was granted its charter in 1944.[7] It was not unusual for a parent and children to enter the jewelry shop together, the parent to pay the family Waterworks bill, the children to examine the library shelves. Both Julia and Jack usually engaged parents and children alike in lively conversation.

If Julia sought to widen mental horizons with books, the Waterworks Board sought to transform Yarrow's infrastructure. In 1944, the Yarrow Waterworks received permission from Victoria to tap into Volkert and Knox creeks to provide a sanitary and independent water source for

Yarrow residents. In the same year, John Block was elected foreman of this project, and Henry Neufeldt secretary-treasurer for its duration. Henry Ratzlaff was in charge of installing the water lines. Although the Board was granted five years to complete this project, it was completed before the year ended.[8]

Jack Wittenberg provided continuity on the Waterworks Board, serving as its secretary-treasurer for 30 years. He worked with at least eight chairpersons, including, in the early years, William Schellenberg, Henry Sukkau, John H. Martens, Henry H. Goosen, Isaac J. Epp, and Cornelius H. Penner, and, in later years, Peter Reimer and Art Kurz.[9] As the only committee in Yarrow enjoying official status, the Waterworks Board became the unofficial governing body of Yarrow after 1944, representing Yarrow in all civic matters. In 1947 and 1948, for example, the board oversaw the completion of the fire hall and appointed Henry Ratzlaff as fire chief and John Langeman as chief mechanic. It also decided that the fire chief and mechanic be paid $2 per practice, and that such practices should be held no fewer than six times per year. Furthermore, it placed Henry Ratzlaff in charge of repairs to school-bus shelters. Municipal authorities were petitioned to install streetlights and construct concrete sidewalks. During this time, the board also decided where sidewalks and streetlights should be placed. A tender by McKenzie Brothers for the sidewalk construction was accepted in April 1948, and by the end of that year sidewalks along Central and Wilson roads (on one side of the road only) were completed. Then the board decided to make these walkways safe for pedestrians by requesting a "by-law banning bicycles, cattle and other unusual traffic" from sidewalks. In addition, board members collected the signatures of Yarrow citizens interested in extending the telephone system and persuaded Ottawa to move the post office to a more central location. In the midst of all this development of Yarrow's infrastructure, the local softball team was not ignored. Increasingly successful in local and regional competition, it was given a $25 donation by the Waterworks Board.[10]

Always involved in building a more inclusive community, Julia and Jack managed to cross boundaries, including those of religious denominations. Julia was raised Presbyterian, and her family remained Presbyterian, joining the Abbotsford Presbyterian church after moving to Majuba Hill. Julia and Jack, on the other hand, were members of the Sumas United Church (Adams Road), where Jack conducted a young people's choir. Later, the Wittenbergs attended the Carman United Church in nearby Sardis. They also participated in the Hillcrest United Church on Majuba Hill, although to a lesser degree than did the Sabos. At times, Julia and Jack attended the Yarrow Mennonite Brethren Church, which had become the religious home of Jack's parents after they had transferred their membership from the United Mennonite Church.

After 30 years as secretary-treasurer of Yarrow Waterworks, Jack retired in 1976 and closed his jewelry shop.[11] One year later, at age 73, he died of a heart attack. Julia retired in 1974, having spent 27 years as community librarian of Yarrow's only public library and serving the Fraser Valley Regional Library under three directors, "including the late Peter Grossman, Ronald Ley and Howard Overend."[12] For a short time, Patricia Heighton replaced her. Then Gail Berger, who for many years owned "The Apple Farm" in Yarrow with her husband Klaus, became the community librarian, a position she still held as of October 2002. When the new library opened in the community centre October 1, 1977, Julia was asked to cut the ribbon. She was also honoured by a plaque permanently placed in the Julia Wittenberg Room of the library, a room which, at the time of this writing, is being renovated as part of a new community centre.

Julia celebrated her 93rd birthday in October 2001 still living independently in her apartment in Chilliwack. With her characteristic smile, she remarks pointedly, "I still don't like Harlequin romances;

Presentation to librarian Julia Wittenberg at her retirement.

they are a waste of time. I like historical novels and a good who-dun-it."[13] Among her favourite authors are Nellie McClung and such poets as E. Pauline Johnson, Tennyson, Kipling, and Robert Service.

For those of us who go back to the earlier years in Yarrow, Julia has a personal and significant place in our lives. By offering books to children and young people, she encouraged many to envision a world that stretched far beyond raspberry fields and the everyday routine of village life in Yarrow.

Move the Choir to the Centre of the Chancel: George Reimer and Choral Music

By Leonard Neufeldt, with Robert Martens

In 1953, the voting members of the Yarrow Mennonite Brethren Church approved plans to renovate the church building. Most of the funds for this work had come into the church coffers in the form of a small and controversial windfall from selling the new and ill-fated Sharon Mennonite Collegiate high school building to the Chilliwack School District. A number of families in Yarrow were still seeking to recover from the collapse of the Co-op, soft markets for berries, and the swift demise of the high school. Yet the church was now in a position to make physical improvements that some thought long overdue. Among other changes, these plans called for remodeling the front of the sanctuary by removing the right choir, until then the exclusive preserve of Yarrow's many ordained ministers and a few other highly regarded aging men. This choir would be replaced by a new pulpit that was smaller, more attractive, and much closer to the congregation than the old one. The erstwhile ministers would now have to find their place down in the pews.

When the remodeling was completed, there were several other notable changes in the chancel area. Gone was the balustrade at the front of the chancel. Also gone were the raised alcove and its massive pulpit at the centre rear of the chancel and as far removed from the main sanctuary as was physically possible. No longer did the leading minister or his associates rise from an elevated throne-like chair, step forward, grip the lofty pulpit with strong hands, halt for a moment before looking up to the balcony and across the congregation below, and then, from that stronghold of physical withdrawal and spiritual authority, call for the opening hymn or announce that it had pleased almighty God to bring a new child into the community or take away someone known to everybody by name and life. Gone, too, was the chair beside the pulpit, where the very deaf Reverend Peter Jacob Neufeldt, the last of the hard-of-hearing pulpit flankers, sat with his hand cupped to his large right ear so as to capture the words spoken. He, too, had been relegated to the pews below. Here, destined to develop respect for the new-generation listening device he could hold to his ear, he sat on his initialed pillow in the fourth row.

To the eye of anyone facing the front and familiar with the old configuration, the most notable change was the relocation of the left choir, where for many years the singers and conductor had sat. This precinct had been moved to an elevated stage at the very centre, taking the place, as it were, of the now-vanished pulpit alcove and its high, small windows of streaming morning light. A sensible new design, many will have agreed, and certainly the acoustical effect was much improved. But one can argue that this change symbolized the increased importance and authority of presence that George Reimer's choir and its music-making had gradually assumed during the previous decade.

Even before the early Mennonites of Yarrow formally organized their two respective congregations, the Mennonite Brethren and the

Noted senior choir of Yarrow Mennonite Brethren Church: conductor, George Reimer; pianist, Martha Plett.

United Mennonite followers had formed choirs and made them an integral part of church and community life. In 1929, when members from the two denominations changed their meeting place for joint services from private homes to the one-room schoolhouse on Central Road, a choir was formed, and singers, whether baptized members or not, took pride in participating. Peter Giesbrecht, Sr. was the first conductor. Shortly after the Mennonite Brethren congregation was organized in late 1929, David Friesen, whose home had been the site of choir rehearsals, assumed the position. He was followed by Johann Derksen, proprietor of the first grocery store in the Mennonite settlement. With the success of his business and construction of a new and larger store, he resigned in favour of Peter Jantzen, Sr. Two or three years later Nickolai Boschman, a talented musician and popular conductor, assumed the helm and served until he moved to Laidlaw for employment. Jacob Froese stepped in briefly, and Jacob Neufeldt, director of the junior choir, also provided some assistance; then Peter Jantzen returned as conductor for a while. But at the church business meeting on December 19, 1938, Jantzen's decision to resign was announced. A month later, the church elected a committee of three to search for a new director. Their choice was George Reimer, a young and, in their view, very promising successor to Jantzen.

A tenor with a shock of wavy black hair, an operatically large voice, and enormous emotional energy, Reimer initially declined the invitation to become the next choirmaster. But he was finally convinced that in accepting the position he would not have to abandon his role as soloist. He was also assured that the congregation would offer him strong moral support. For almost 25 years thereafter, he and choral music in Yarrow were synonymous. During this time he took only one leave of absence, early in the 1950s, and Henry P. Neufeldt, a longtime friend, filled in for a year. He and Reimer had commuted to Vancouver for two years at the beginning of the 1940s for lessons with noted voice instructor John Goss. At that time, Reimer was a Sunday-afternoon fixture at the Neufeldt house, rehearsing with Neufeldt and sometimes with a pianist. They worked on music assigned by Goss, as well as songs Reimer planned to introduce into his choir's repertoire. As evening approached, Reimer's spouse, Lena, would send over one of the children to fetch him home.

Reimer was an unabashed romantic, as his musical tastes, interpretations, conducting style, and life revealed. At home he could be quietly reflective for hours, but not so on stage. This "natural musician"[1] who referred openly to "heavenly choirs"[2] loved hauntingly simple and plaintive melodies, soaring anthems, and texts and musical themes filled with ardour and religious devotion. As he conducted, singers watched his brown eyes go wide, then half-closed, and sometimes briefly closed before fluttering open under his dark and bushy eyebrows as he surveyed his choir left to right, his arms powerfully engaged and his impassioned breathing and whispered words of text audible to the singers, especially during passages sung in pianissimo. Those who knew him well recognized a similar gusto and powerful feeling in his personal life. He loved sports as much as music. During the winter, Saturday nights were spent with his children around the radio, listening to Foster Hewitt describe the hockey action from Toronto's old Maple Leaf Gardens. On summer evenings, he could be found at the softball games and later at the baseball games, cheering with the kind of intensity his singers witnessed and, in turn, felt within. When his work as carpenter took him far from Yarrow, he would write his wife what one of his children has described as "incredible love letters."[3]

He was not a stern lawgiver bent on bringing home the strict demands of the church and community he loved. Church proscriptions against swimming on Sunday, especially at Cultus Lake beaches, were quietly left unattended, but not the sheet music he sometimes took along. In the summer, the Vancouver Symphony Orchestra featured Sunday afternoon concerts in the Malkin Bowl in Stanley Park. Not infrequently, Reimer's wife would slip out of the morning service early to pack a picnic lunch so that the family could leave for Vancouver immediately after the service to take in the performance, meet with friends, enjoy a picnic, and take photographs. Occasionally, the family enjoyed a warm Sunday afternoon at Cultus Lake. He loved life, he loved music, and he could not understand how people could utter harsh and demeaning words about others, or how they could remain passive in the presence of good music, which he viewed as sacred regardless of whether it was overtly religious or not.

Less than two years before Reimer assumed the position of church choir conductor, the congregation had purchased its first piano, despite some opposition to spending money on such an instrument. Presumably guitars, a few violins, or a small brass group had filled in adequately; besides, using a piano in the Sunday-morning services was viewed by some with deep suspicion. Nonetheless, after several congregational business sessions on the matter, a piano was purchased for $110, and almost immediately old Mr. Dietrich Rempel walked from his house to the unlocked church to spend the morning limbering his fingers and spirits on the keyboard.[4]

For Reimer, the question was not whether to have a piano, but how to acquire a better one. Two years after stepping in as conductor, he offered any encouragement he could to the purchase of another instrument. With the shrewd assistance of several young choir members, a few donors were cajoled into pledging more than they had expected to—indeed, more than half of the purchase price of a new piano—and so a better piano was acquired. A few years later, Reimer convinced the church to purchase a small grand piano and, in 1956, a Steinway concert grand piano. In the 1950s, he occasionally arranged to rent organs and hire organists for special performances of cantatas such as Stainer's *Crucifixion* and Dubois' *Seven Last Words of Christ* and selections from oratorios such as Handel's *Messiah*. Several times in these years, he also used a small string orchestra to accompany the choir in special performances. These string players, led by his own talented sons William and Rudolph, were students of violin teacher Walter Neufeld. On the cello was their younger brother, John.

Virtually from the outset of his tenure as choir conductor, Reimer insisted on personally auditioning prospective singers, rigorously training the choir, expanding the repertoire, and holding periodic choral workshops in Yarrow and other nearby Mennonite communities for conductors and individual or mass choirs. His predecessors had sought to build a choir of four sections through a policy of open invitation and special invitation. Abram Esau recounts how he, a mere 15-year-old newcomer, was approached by the first choir director because he was the younger brother of a respected bass singer. "Whether my voice was ripe enough to handle that part, at least I stood proudly ... and did the best I could."[5] The steady growth of the congregation seemed to assure an adequate reservoir of singers. Numbers were not Reimer's problem. He was concerned about lack of blend and balance within and among the sections. Lack of sight reading skills also troubled him, in that teaching the choir new music consumed too much rehearsal time. But his chief concern was the tendency of some singers to sing off pitch—several of them normally a little flat—several quite sharp during events or music that excited them. This problem had its ironic aspect, since he very much wanted his singers to be excited about rigorous choir workouts and the music he was teaching them. It was not long before he found ways of auditioning voices he regarded as prospects for the choir. Because the problems of blend, balance, and singing slightly off-pitch did not vanish despite his best efforts, he dissolved the choir in the fall of 1949 and reorganized it within a week with old and new singers who could carry out the mission of the choir as he understood it. This action prompted a few words of reproof at the year-end church business meeting. Apparently, he did not respond.

Reimer's success in developing and maintaining a distinguished choral program issued, in part, from the congregation's enthusiasm for his choral ministry. At the year-end congregational business meetings, it became commonplace for the church to express its delight in the choir's music and to request that the choir sing at more Sunday-evening services, conferences, funerals, and the like, and that more time be allotted to the choir in the Sunday-morning services. The latter request presented problems for the ministers, who were accustomed to their monopoly on the more than two hours devoted to morning services in those days. Yet gradually the leadership acceded to requests that the congregational singing receive greater attention and that the choir become a mainstay of the service. For baptismal services, held at church-owned property on Stewart Creek—or "the Jordan," as it was waggishly called—Reimer had a flatbed truck driven to the site, complete with piano. The choir would mount a ladder and perform from the truck bed.

The positive congregational response to the choir's ministry gave Reimer the opportunity to negotiate better financial support for the choir. From the time of the first choir under Peter Giesbrecht until during Reimer's second year as conductor, singers and a few other donors had paid for all musical supplies. The financial burden had gradually increased, and under Reimer it rose significantly. In his view, the costs for songbooks, cantatas, sheet music, duplication, and so forth should not have to be borne by conductor and singers. In December 1940, the congregation delegated one of its members to collect money on a voluntary basis to cover mounting music costs. A year later, the congregation agreed to assume the cost of duplicating music. Over the next few years, the budget and finance committee was directed by the church, at Reimer's urging, to pick up a number of expenditures for music and to pay the balance remaining on the piano. Eventually, the annual church budget included a line for the music program, including choir costs.

A major factor in the notable cost increases was Reimer's persistent effort to expand the choir's repertoire. The congregation could always expect an assortment of familiar favourites and largely or totally unfamiliar music. He and the choir were pleased to see that some of their new anthems soon joined the congregation's list of favourites. There was resistance to the expansion of the repertoire, especially to music that struck a relatively small number of parishioners and several influential ministers as undesirable. In the presence of such resistance, Reimer was cheerfully stubborn, as he was on more than one occasion with leading minister Johann A. Harder, who observed to him and Henry Neufeldt that pleasant and simple "*Jesus Lieder*" were sufficient.[6] Good cheer could not survive all of these encounters. One notable example was the response to the choir's magnificent performance in the early 1950s of the "Hallelujah" from Beethoven's oratorio *The Mount of Olives*. The rousing conclusion gave way to clasped hands, stunned silence, smiles, and nods of appreciation in the audience. Yet after the service, the pastor telephoned Reimer, who had just sat down for Sunday dinner, to inform him that such a piece should not again be performed since it was too artistic. Shaken and hurt, Reimer walked the Vedder dyke for hours before rejoining his family. Nevertheless, at the next opportunity, the Chilliwack Rotary Club's annual Christmas Carol Festival for choirs of the region, he conducted the choir in Beethoven's "Hallelujah," and he repeated it in a live broadcast from the Chilliwack radio station, his entire choir crowded into Studio A. Within a few years, the pastor, by then recognized for his capacity for change, had become one of Reimer's champions.

The enthusiastic response of the audience at the Rotary Festival to the rendition of the Beethoven anthem did not surprise Reimer or his singers. Since the inaugural Festival in 1950, they had performed annually at this event, and their participation had helped to establish their reputation for excellence among the many church choirs in the Central and Upper Fraser Valley. The Yarrow correspondent for *The Chilliwack Progress* had been partly responsible for putting the choir on readers' mental maps in the first place. Reimer's early success with the choir and his strong efforts, together with Jacob Harder of Greendale and Henry Neufeldt and (later) Cornelius D. Toews of Yarrow, to institutionalize periodic week-long choral workshops for conductors and church choirs resulted in expanded and favourable coverage of the Yarrow choir's activities. Prior to the Reimer era, the most extensive report in the *Progress* on the choir was the following: "Thanksgiving services were observed in the German church Sunday. After morning service lunch was served in the schoolroom. In the afternoon another service was held, with special music by the choir."[7] But on the occasion of the workshop for choirs in Yarrow in January 1941 and a choir festival hard on its heels, the *Progress* ran two prominent reports, the second one a lengthy column under the large headline "Nearly Two Thousand Hear Song Festival at Yarrow."[8] This kind of reporting by the *Progress* on choral music in Yarrow became routine for years to come.

The church music festival just noted was referred to in the Mennonite Brethren Church as a *Sängerfest*—a festival of singers. Throughout the 1940s and early 1950s, the church hosted choral workshops featuring noted Mennonite guest choral conductors and music educators. Having been charged with upgrading choirs, choir conducting, and musical repertoires in the churches, the provincial Mennonite music association invited the flamboyant K.H. Neufeld of Winkler, Manitoba, to the Fraser Valley in 1939 for a little more than two weeks to train conductors, choirs, and individual singers. Neufeld, a well-known educator and representative of the Manitoba Music Festival in Winnipeg, spent several of these days in Yarrow as a guest of Henry and Margaret Neufeldt, but how many singers from Yarrow participated in this inaugural event is not known. Two years later, however, the Yarrow Mennonite Brethren Church served as host of another such workshop with the same educator. This event concluded with the choir festival prominently announced and reported on in the *Progress*. One of Neufeld's tasks was to teach conductors and singers to make the transition from their Old-World habit of singing by numerals, or *Ziffern* (numbers representing simple and compound musical intervals) to reading regular musical notation. He was invited back for one more choir workshop. In his second and third visits, he stayed at the Reimer home.

Other notable music educators to hold choral workshops in Yarrow—and, in several cases, to serve as guest conductors of individual and mass choirs performing at a closing festival—were Franz C. Thiessen of Abbotsford, Benjamin Horch of Winnipeg (the latter at least twice), and Paul Wohlgemuth of Tabor College, Kansas. Horch, even more than the others, sought to introduce conductors and singers to classical music, and it was he who fueled Reimer's desire to perform selections from several oratorios, including Handel's *Messiah* and *Judas Maccabeus*, Haydn's *Creation*, and Beethoven's *Mount of Olives*. Prior to the Second

World War and in the war years, workshops were usually held in the winter; in the late '40s and early '50s the timing varied. In these later years, when Horch brought his college choir to Yarrow for concerts, Reimer would encourage his singers to regard the event as a workshop, and he himself was known to place large orders for music in Vancouver after these performances. On a few occasions, the choir festival was independent of the workshop, the workshop having taken place months earlier or not at all. A number of us who grew up in Yarrow can remember festivals in the Yarrow church sanctuary and also on a mowed, tree-flanked field off Wilson Road, where bleachers for the mass choir were erected against the south side of a large barn that also served as home court for the Sharon Mennonite Collegiate Institute men's basketball team. The acoustics at these outdoor festivals were surprisingly good, as was the weather.

Eventually, Reimer's oldest son, William, followed Ben Horch of Winnipeg and Victor Martens of Yarrow to music studies at the distinguished Detmold Musikakademie in Germany, and he became a professional musician and music professor in Hanover, Germany. Daughters Holda and Irene trained as vocalists and became lead singers, and Holda has served as music educator and conductor in several places in Canada. Elfrieda sings in choirs and has directed a church choir. Rudolph, the second son, became concertmaster of the Fraser Valley String Orchestra and then a church choir director. John continues to play the cello in ensembles and orchestras in the Fraser Valley, and he and his younger brother Robert sing in various choirs. None has stayed in Yarrow. Among the successors to Reimer as conductor in Yarrow, perhaps only Walter Rempel showed Reimer's degree of passion for choral and repertorial excellence. But Rempel presided at a time of rapidly declining membership in the Mennonite Brethren congregation and rapidly changing musical tastes in the younger generation.

As long as Reimer was conductor, his tastes reigned supreme in the church for the simple reason that his work was so deeply loved and admired. Although the position of choirmaster was unsalaried, the church saw fit to provide him with occasional stipends. In 1956, as the date of the Reimers' silver wedding anniversary approached, the congregation decided to host and underwrite a large anniversary celebration that would include a meal and a generous gift.

Reimer's efforts on behalf of choral music in Yarrow were pioneering in more ways than one. Having arrived in 1928, the first year of

Mennonite settlement, he himself was one of Yarrow's true pioneers, and his marriage to Lena was the second Mennonite wedding in Yarrow. When he died unexpectedly in 1963 at the age of 55, the coroner's observation that there was not an ounce of fat in his body was little consolation to his devastated family and friends. More comforting to memory was (and continues to be) the decision of the pastor of the Mennonite Brethren Church, the Reverend Henry Brucks, to honour Reimer's long and popular service on behalf of church music. He did so a few weeks before Reimer's death by asking "witnesses" from the congregation to step forward and speak words of commendation and thanks for almost a quarter of a century of music ministry. The many expressions of admiration and affection comprised one of the strongest tributes ever paid to anyone in Yarrow since the coming of the Mennonite settlers.

Music for Life: Walter and Menno Neufeld

By Robert Martens

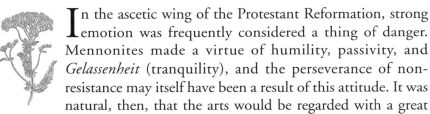

In the ascetic wing of the Protestant Reformation, strong emotion was frequently considered a thing of danger. Mennonites made a virtue of humility, passivity, and *Gelassenheit* (tranquility), and the perseverance of non-resistance may itself have been a result of this attitude. It was natural, then, that the arts would be regarded with a great deal of suspicion. The Mennonites in Russia, however, included many who were well educated, and who rubbed shoulders with the more progressive individuals of the day. Mennonites studied literature, in particular the great German writers, and music eventually became a sophisticated and much-loved social activity, especially among the Mennonite Brethren. Although the attitude toward the arts was clearly one of ambivalence, the affection for music managed to survive the horrors of the Bolshevik Revolution and the mass migrations that followed.

It was into this milieu that Walter and Menno Neufeld were born. Their father, John Neufeld, was a highly intelligent minister and teacher who spoke several languages, including Russian. Low German, however, was seldom spoken in this family, as High German remained the primary choice of educated Mennonites. Because of the peripatetic nature of John Neufeld's profession as teacher, the family was often in transition. Menno was born in Churnhill, Saskatchewan, and Walter, the younger of the two, in Dallas, Oregon. Altogether there were nine children. In the 1930s, the family lived briefly in Yarrow, working in hopyards and residing in workers' cabins. Here, Walter and Menno took some of their first schooling. The Neufeld family was already preoccupied with "music, music, music,"[1] but a contentious streak surfaced when John found himself at odds with the church over religious issues. Possibly as a consequence, Walter and Menno would later decide not to take out church membership, although their deep commitment to church and sacred concerns would never waver. Throughout their lives, they also remained conservative and somewhat anti-elitist. The Neufeld family left Yarrow after a hopyard workers' strike and took up residence on E. 49th Avenue in Vancouver, where Walter and Menno spent much of their early lives.

John Neufeld, a profoundly "patriarchal" but "gentle and methodical" man,[2] was also deeply devout. He was fond of greeting people with, "*Wie steht es zwischen dir und dem Herrn Jesus?*"[3] (How is your relationship with the Lord Jesus?) Anna Neufeld, his wife, was a quiet and submissive woman. She would serve raisin bread and butter at the musical sessions, which occurred frequently at their home. When the family moved to Strawberry Hill (later Surrey, B.C.), relatives and friends were often invited to visit the Neufeld home, where Bible reading and hymn singing took place. There were also simple instrumental collaborations—John Neufeld played the guitar and had taught himself his own way of fingering.

It seems natural, then, that Walter and Menno, with their innate talent, should pursue musical careers and receive the best training possible. They made early decisions to be "real musicians," as a brother-in-law from Austria advised.[4] Walter was trained in violin first by Frederick Greaves, who "laughed at his own jokes," and later by Harold Berkeley in New York, and Joachim Chasman in Los Angeles. Chasman had only the best of students and "liked to put his arms around everybody."[5] Menno's early piano training was with Ken Ross, a professional musician who sometimes performed on radio, and then later with Marshall Sumner, an Australian concert pianist, who was "fantastic at technique but was still relaxed."[6] Both Menno and Walter had perfect pitch.

In the early 1940s, while still living in Strawberry Hill, Walter began traveling to Yarrow to teach violin, as well as viola, cello, and bass. A man named Dunn had cornered the teaching market in Yarrow, renting instruments cheaply and instructing in groups. Once Walter had achieved his degree at the London Royal School of Music, however, he became more available to Yarrow residents, and very quickly, anyone who was serious about music acquired Walter as teacher. Over the years, he gave lessons in various locations: in a berry-pickers' shack on Dyke Road, a fact that reflects on the poverty of the times; in a school building situated near the front of the Mennonite Brethren Church property; and in the residence of a certain Mr. and Mrs. Bergen. Later, Henry Neufeldt, one of several musical leaders in Yarrow, asked Walter how many students he needed in order to teach on a regular basis. When Walter replied that he would need about 15, the necessary students were found, and instruction then took place in the home of Henry and Margaret Neufeldt. In lieu of payment for use of the home, free lessons were offered to members of the Neufeldt family. Students would sit in the hallway and sometimes the kitchen, awaiting their turn. Lessons took place every Friday, and invariably Walter would phone the nearby Bright Spot Café to order his lunch. There were rarely more than two items, and the selection often remained the same for some length of time. An apparent favourite of Walter's was sauerkraut and sausages.

The musical teaching career of the Neufeld brothers was beginning to expand rapidly. Some instruction took place in Chilliwack, Clearbrook, Strawberry Hill, and Vancouver, but the real growth was happening in Yarrow. Menno, who was then teaching in a church basement in Clearbrook, followed Walter to Yarrow, "the centre of civilization," about one year later.[7] As soon as there were enough students, Walter started a small orchestra, and a tradition of camaraderie began that was to last for many years. Orchestra practices took place at the Bible school building behind the Mennonite Brethren Church, and recitals were held on a regular basis. One participant in the very first "concert," really more of a recital, writes that he "played in only a few simple numbers, including 'Twinkle, Twinkle, Little Star.' I think the audience numbered no more than 50 people. Yet in that room the audience seemed large to a young kid."[8] But there was resistance to the efforts of the Neufeld brothers. Some vowed that they would never buy tickets to any Neufeld musical function as long as the brothers were not members of the church. Students, who were encouraged with prizes (such as records) to sell tickets, were sometimes turned down flat—one little boy came home crying, bewildered that anyone would not choose to attend a concert.[9] The issue may well have been poverty—a 50-cent ticket was unaffordable for some in those days. But others, like Peter Neufeldt, later minister of the Yarrow Mennonite Brethren Church, were simply unimpressed with the importance of the arts: surely a church meeting or Bible study should take priority. It was, however, a tribute to the Neufeld brothers' quiet persistence that over the years opposition broke down. George Reimer, the best-known promoter of music in Yarrow, admired them from the beginning: "Music was more important than politics."[10] In the end, Walter and Menno were welcome members of the Mennonite community, and Peter Neufeldt eventually made his own home available for Menno's piano lessons. In the years that followed, Menno gave instruction at various venues: the home of Jake and Sarah Martens, the home of Aron and Olga Rempel, and in a business block in downtown Yarrow.

Walter's string orchestra was prospering. At one point, it performed Mozart's "*Eine Kleine Nachtmusik*" at the Chilliwack Music Festival and

Walter Neufeld's string orchestra performing in Chilliwack, ca. 1952.

received raves from adjudicator John Avison, later conductor of the CBC Orchestra in Vancouver. "Outsiders" were often impressed by the quality of music emanating from a seemingly insignificant farming town. This was certainly due to Walter's intensity and meticulous concern for his music: "A single mistake could be a terror."[11] No doubt he exercised a kind of control over his students that might not be feasible or readily acceptable today. As for orchestra practices, there were "no excuses; a rehearsal could not be missed." He is remembered by students as having "pitch black hair" and being "very tall."[12] When basketball season arrived, he would "lay down the law,"[13] insisting that music take priority. Both

Menno and Walter, in keeping with the ethos of the day, regarded music as earnest and noble, as "work"; Walter "built determination into a person."[14] They were single-minded, "very frugal, spending their lives on music."[15] One archetypal story, which is still told by many with relish, including Walter himself, runs as follows:

> Walter was quite strict about attendance at orchestra practices. On the occasion of the heavyweight championship fight between Jersey Joe Walcott and Joe Louis, a number of us decided our interest in the fight was greater than our interest in practising *Eine Kleine Nachtmusik*. We convinced ourselves that Walter should work more diligently with the less advanced students who would be at orchestra practice since they still had the fear of Walter in their hearts. Four of us more mature students settled in to hear the fight called that evening, in our separate homes to be sure. Suddenly there was a knock at the door. The fight was still in the early rounds. There was Walter standing at the door with a serious demeanour, several of the other hooky players already in his car. "You're late for orchestra practice," is all he said. I quickly retrieved my violin and followed him to his car. All four of us sat quietly and glumly as we were chauffeured to the place where all the younger players had already assembled and were waiting for us with a certain hostility in their hearts.[16]

Years later, struggles also occurred when students endeavoured to set up their own playing groups.

At the same time, Walter won the respect of his students through his gentle patience and tolerance. He was demanding and meticulous, lessons were "intense and scholarly," but there was "an extended family feeling," and students "felt very connected."[17] Examinations (which were almost always Royal Conservatory of Music of Toronto) were nerve-wracking, but Walter was always there to coach and to tune instruments, if necessary. On occasions like this, his presence was quiet but reassuring. His teaching style was clear and rather unemotional, but he sometimes liked to impress his students by playing some "fancy music" at the beginning of lessons.[18] He also loved to talk. Some students, who perhaps had neglected to practise quite hard enough, learned to take advantage of this fact by engaging him in long conversation. As for technique, he went with, in his own words, "whatever works." He would sometimes advise students, "You have to play more Jewish," perhaps reflecting his own experience with Jewish teachers. His dedication to classical music was absolute; he once said of the Beatles: "some people actually believe that this is good music." And his persistence was legendary. One winter day, for example, when snow blanketed the village and fields of Yarrow, Walter was dropped off by the bus on the highway exit to town. He walked all the miles into Yarrow only to find that because no one was expecting him, no one had shown up for lessons.

Menno, unlike Walter, was rather thin, with a frizzy shock of hair. Although he also exercised a great deal of control over his students, he was a sociable and considerate man. He would make such demands as "no basketball until next year." But he was also known, as was his brother, for making arrangements to balance music and a demanding lifestyle. He "had the patience of Job" and "never lost his cool."[19] Invariably he had a pat on the back for a student coming offstage after a performance. Like Walter, his discipline and clear teaching style paid off with some excellent results from his pupils. He had access only to an upright piano, yet his students were gaining their musical degrees.

At the same time, Menno was studying with world-class choral instructors such as Robert Shaw and Helmut Rilling. In 1952, he formed the Bethel Choir, and, although "he couldn't sing his way out of a paper bag," he managed to lead the group into winning the CBC Choral Competition in the early 1960s. Rehearsals, which always began with prayer, were frequently held on Sunday afternoons, a fact that rankled some singers. But his famous dry sense of humour, which contrasted somewhat with Walter's rather more acerbic approach, won them over. He often ended choir rehearsals with "Okay, everyone take your vitamins and eat your raisin pie." His sense of perfect pitch frequently had him waving his finger in the air, usually pointing up to indicate a flat note. On one occasion, he announced that an alto singer was off-key and asked the altos to sing the section by themselves. Trying to narrow down the problem, he asked the third row of the altos to sing by themselves. Then: "Now, second row." But after hearing the second row perform, he quipped, "Now that alto isn't singing."[20] He thus managed to both resolve and defuse the situation through laughter.

In the mid-1960s, the Neufeld brothers were proud to record an LP with Hildor Janz, who, together with his brother Leo, worked in an evangelical ministry in Europe. The recording sessions took place in the Yarrow Mennonite Brethren Church, where the acoustics were very fine. Both orchestra (including young children) and choir participated. A difficulty arose, however, with street noise, and the Neufeld brothers called for a session at three o'clock in the morning, when the town would be quiet. It was a characteristic gesture for two men who believed in the priority of their art. One witness remembers Walter listening to playback in the recording room of the church, sitting cross-legged, shoeless, and with enormous holes in his socks.[21] Like Walter, Menno typically dressed several years out of fashion.

These were two men who had built something important out of independent-minded perseverance. Each year saw spring concerts; each year choir and orchestra went on oratorio tours. Walter traveled to Italy to buy violins, and to Japan, where he met the famous Suzuki of the violin school.

But by the mid-1960s, the Mennonite community of Yarrow was in decline, and Menno and Walter were about to move out. Years before, in the early 1950s, they had constructed a studio in Clearbrook, based on a design they had seen in Langley, B.C. Their studio had been built modestly, as money was tight, and the builder jokingly called it a *Klubutje* [shed]. The front-entrance waiting room, complete with magazines, opened to the left to Menno's teaching room, and to the right to Walter's. Living quarters were to the back, and it was a lucky student who could ever catch a glimpse. Students were also denied access to washroom facilities, and for some time used the outhouse in the backyard. The rehearsal room for orchestra was downstairs, and Walter, who had worked as a machinist when young and was something of an inventor, had covered the ceiling with paper egg cartons in order to enhance the acoustics.

By the late 1960s, the Neufeld brothers had ceased teaching in Yarrow, and all lessons took place at the Clearbrook studio. They engaged in real estate, buying a hamburger stand near the freeway and an old hall in the Matsqui Flats that students jokingly called the "Philharmonic Hall." Their caution in making decisions may have exasperated some businessmen. They became a fixture on the streets of Clearbrook, making their daily walk to the local restaurants where invariably they ate their meals. In 1974, for a variety of reasons, the Bethel Choir folded. Eventually, Walter and Menno sold their studio, which was then demolished, and moved to a new house in Abbotsford. In 1989 a dinner and concert were arranged in their honour.

As of this writing in 2001, they are retired and suffer health problems. Menno still plays on his Schimmel grand piano, and Walter loves to edit scores, tinker with his large collection of violins, and play Bach's music for unaccompanied violin. They both retain a superb memory for music and for the lives of musicians. And their legacy is large: they "have many grandchildren."[22] At one point, for example, all the piano teachers in Abbotsford were former students of Menno.[23] "Music study exalts life," reads their advertising caption in the 1954 edition of the Sharon Mennonite Collegiate yearbook. It is a slogan that articulates both their ethical and musical principles. A recent incident exemplifies the ideals that galvanized their lives. At the funeral of their sister, Hulda, Menno and Walter played a duet that was warmly received. After the number was finished, Walter, suffering from the effects of a stroke, was having difficulty climbing down the stairs, but he imperiously dismissed an offer of aid. Menno looked out over the congregation and remarked, "Fiercely independent, you might say."

Menno's and Walter's persistence, kindness, and sense of humour won over the Mennonite community through the years. Barriers were broken; music was made. They never married, but they lived out the values they considered of supreme importance. They stuck to their principles to the end, and in this shifting world, that may well be more than enough.

[Menno Neufeld died on May 5, 2002.]

Heinrich Friesen, Violin Maker

By Robert Martens

In an increasingly individualistic yet generic world, the very idea of community has become, for many of us, remote, even nostalgic. But for those who have experienced life in a genuine community, such as Yarrow was for several decades, the double-edged nature of its character is well known. On the one hand, there is daily mutual support; on the other, a sometimes suffocating demand for conformity. The talented violin-maker Heinrich (Henry) Friesen lived as an outsider during the years he spent in Yarrow. There was certainly generous support for him and his family, but he was never fully accepted and was frequently truly alone. Nevertheless, his rich inner life and his ardent love for violin-making rendered him relatively impervious to the politics of community. He lived in the private sanctuary of his heart, and here he seemed to find peace.

Heinrich Friesen, one of a family of nine children, was born east of the Crimea in Russia in 1892. It is reported that he was fascinated by the violin music of gypsies at a very early age and that his first violin was a crude toy made of bamboo-like wood. As a boy, he came across a book on violin-making, and thus began a lifelong passion. When his father died, Heinrich was obligated to work as a clerk in a store, but he pursued his hobby of making violins during the nights. In 1914 he was drafted into the Russian army and served as a member of the medical corps in a Turkish hospital. In 1918 he returned home, and life remained relatively normal until the famines of the early 1920s and the collectivization programs of a few years later. Stalin's reign of terror was just beginning. Many people starved or were executed; many simply disappeared into the gulag. Friesen was briefly assigned as a musician at a club, which was used more for propaganda than entertainment. Later on, from 1930 to 1933, he served on a collective farm, but he was finally sent to Stavropol to make violins for the government. In 1937 and 1938, he took advanced training at the Moscow Institute of Music. About this time he learned from newspapers that he had won a national prize of 5000 rubles for violin-making. "I did not get any word about winning the prize and I did not get any money," he recounted. "But that was not important. The important thing was that I was wise enough to tell everyone that I had given the 5000 rubles to Stalin because I loved him."[1]

Friesen had married and had a son and daughter. In 1941, however, any semblance of a normal life in the USSR was permanently disrupted: the secret police invaded his home and arrested him as a German spy. He was jailed and interrogated. He shared his cell with another prisoner in penal uniform, with whom he talked all night, airing some of his political grievances. When he finally stood before a judge, he discovered that the "prisoner" was actually a professional informant. Friesen was tortured, reportedly left standing for days in a tiny enclosure about the size of a phone booth. It was an attempt by the authorities to force him to deny God, and they succeeded; this experience permanently scarred Friesen's psyche. Meanwhile, he remained under arrest, nearly dying from hunger.

Some 18 months later, in the fall of 1942, Friesen was part of a column of political prisoners retreating before the German advance. A sympathetic NKVD officer gave him a travel document, and Friesen was finally able to return home, only to learn that his son was in the Red Army and his wife and daughter were in prison somewhere. His son was later arrested, and then he disappeared, as had the others, and his siblings. But a few months later the German army captured Friesen's home town, and in January of 1943 he was taken to Germany, where he spent six months in a hospital. Upon his release, he met one of his sisters, who had already resided in that country for 12 years. Friesen decided to go to Mittenwald, in Bavaria, where he took further instruction in violin-making.

It was here that he met a young woman, Margarete Fink, a kindergarten teacher who was 28 years his junior. A relationship blossomed, and a child, Ulrike, was born in 1948. Friesen, apparently still fearing the long reach of the Soviet secret police, decided to immigrate to Canada. In January 1949, he arrived in Yarrow, without his family but with a substantial supply of European maple and spruce. He lived on Boundary Road with his sister Anna, the only of his siblings to emigrate from the USSR, and her husband, Cornelius Janzen. He pleaded with Margarete to join him with their child. Her family, however, was intractably opposed to the marriage. Religious objections intruded: Margarete was Catholic and at one point had even considered becoming a nun. Moreover, her two brothers had died in the war, and the family, quite naturally, was reluctant to lose another child. Friesen's unhappy prospects as a violin-maker may also have influenced them.

But in the early 1950s, Margarete, after a great deal of agonizing, followed Friesen to Yarrow. They were still unmarried; Cornelius D. Toews, however, even while recognizing that Heinrich had been previously married in the USSR, kindly consented to perform the ceremony. Not much later, Friesen was shocked to learn that his former family, whom he had presumed dead, had resurfaced. This was a scandal that Yarrow could not readily accept. Because he had been married in the USSR and then remarried without having the proper death certificates, "the church didn't know how to handle the case."[2] He was to become a loner in the community. Perhaps under the influence of a helpful man named Harder, who was a talented machinist and a Jehovah's Witness, Friesen took on the faith of his new friend; this decision alienated him even further from the townspeople of Yarrow. He was to claim later on that the Mennonite Church had not been able to provide the strong faith that he needed to prevent him from denying God under torture. But although he would proselytize for his new religion, his beliefs seemed to be a mixture of Mennonite and Jehovah's Witness: in other words, "a Friesen religion."[3]

Meanwhile, Friesen persevered, living and working in Yarrow and continuing to correspond with his first wife. (The daughter of his first marriage later immigrated to Germany and met some of his second family.) It was apparent, however, that he would need his own home if he wished to continue violin-making. One day he announced to his wife and daughter that he had "found a nice little house" at the end of Eckert Road. It turned out to be "not exactly nice"[4]; in fact, it was nothing more than a rough two-room cabin. But they lived in this shack until it was clear that a family of five (two more children had been born) could not comfortably reside there. Friesen had loyal acquaintances in the community, and he received a great deal of material support from the church membership. Henry Spenst, who worked with Cornelius Regehr for Modern Building Movers, suggested that "Friesen should have a house."[5] At this time, in the late 1950s, some houses in

New Westminster were being cleared away for business development and could be had for a bargain. Regehr and Spenst identified a house that was not selling, drove to Vancouver, and cut a deal for $300 rather than the asking price of $1,000. Peter Friesen had a hydraulic system and a one-ton truck, and an application to move the house to Yarrow was made to the government. Permission was finally granted; Regehr cut the rafters, the roof was lifted off with a crane, and the move was on. It took place, according to regulation, between 1:00 and 6:00 in the morning. John Esau, labouring under a physical disability, volunteered to put in the foundation; costs (the moving alone amounted to $1,000) were borne by the community. It was a good house, and Friesen lived there for the remainder of his days. It was located next to his old cabin, which could now serve as his workshop.

Violin-making was, it sometimes seemed, his whole life. "They are my children," he once said.[6] He referred to the belly and back of the violin as "he" and "she," and talked of "marrying the belly to the back, so they're compatible." He told one young friend that "he could imagine building violins for the next 1,000 years."[7] And he became known in Yarrow as "Fiddler Friesen," an epithet that, like many of Yarrow's nicknames, was partly derogatory. But Friesen was largely oblivious to

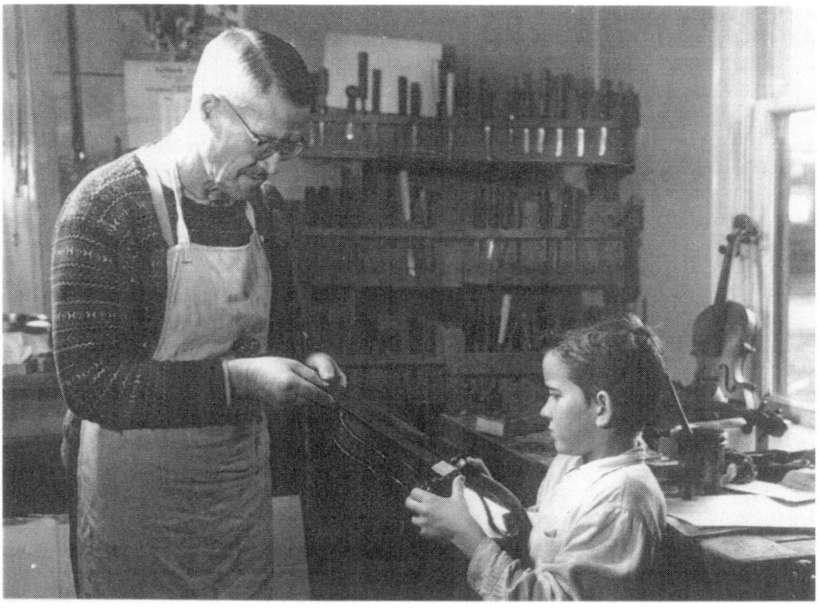

Heinrich Friesen and son Walter. Friesen refused any compromise with time and imperfection.

the opinions of others: he had an overriding purpose in life—he had been placed on earth to use his talent. A perfectionist, he pulled apart violins that disappointed him and started over. His tools, made of steel salvaged from everything from clockworks to hacksaws, were razor sharp. "And the top of the instrument, you didn't even have to put sandpaper to it. It was just like glass. That's how sharp he had those tools."[8] Typically, his violins had a distinctive sweet smell resulting from his use of propolis, a byproduct of honeybees that is used to seal the hive. The propolis, in a process known as a French polish, was rubbed onto a violin that had been dabbed with linseed oil. In Friesen's case, the result was often an instrument with very little varnish at all. He had an intuition regarding suitable wood; he could feel a piece of wood and know its qualities. John Ratzlaff, for some years Friesen's neighbour, recalls that "for hours, he would talk to me about how you pick a tree that would produce the right wood. A tree that has as much sunlight as possible, not a shade tree, and it … can't just be on the north-facing side, or on the south-facing side; it has to be up high, almost standing by itself."[9] Friesen preferred to stick with his own inventive techniques, often rejecting suggested improvements. He had calipers, but the final test for thickness was done with glass and resin—"he was a genius, careful and slow."[10] Several young people, including Bill and Rudy Reimer, were often privileged to play a nearly finished instrument for him, sometimes outdoors as Friesen walked around the yard, smiling.

Although repairwork was a potential major source of income, Friesen considered it the bane of his life. He simply wanted to build violins, and he often charged almost nothing after working on a damaged instrument that he considered inferior. In one instance, upon being asked to repair a violin that was, in his opinion, useless, his puckish sense of humour offered a solution in the following largely untranslatable pun: "*Darf ich diese Geige besitzen?*" (May I have this violin?) he asked. Upon receiving assent, he sat (*sitzen*) upon the violin.[11] "I do not make business, I make violins," he said. "I want nothing more than to make violins. It is my life."[12]

With an attitude like this, it is no wonder that Friesen never became comfortably well-off. Friends, however, sought to improve his economic condition. For example, an American concert violinist was scheduled to appear in Chilliwack, and Friesen, in an uncharacteristic mood to advance his career, asked Cornelius Regehr what he could do to present one of his instruments to the performer. Regehr phoned the musician's representatives but received the cold shoulder. He decided to drive Friesen to Chilliwack. It was a cold rainy day, and Friesen, lacking a carrying case, held a violin under his coat as he stepped into the lobby of the Empress Hotel. After making several phone calls to the performer's room, Regehr finally reached him. "We have a man here who makes violins; we might have something good to show you," he said.

"Alright, but no more than five minutes," was the reply.

In his hotel room, the performer alternately played his own violin and the Friesen. Five minutes turned into half an hour, and the violinist asked if he could keep the instrument for the evening's performance. Friesen agreed. That night, the concert violinist stepped forward with three violins: his own Stradivarius and Guarneri, and the Friesen. He played all three instruments, asking the audience to applaud for their favourite. Friesen's violin attracted the greatest applause, and he was invited onstage to receive congratulations. He strode forward in high boots and long coat and flashed a typical crinkly smile. It was to be a high point of his life.[13]

Friesen continued to live what seemed to be a placid existence. He hated the cold, loved the summer, and greatly enjoyed swimming. When his oldest daughter was still young, he would bicycle with her to Cultus Lake. Later, friends would drive him to the lake, where he liked to lie in the water, arms outstretched, in quiet rapture. One acquaintance admired his ability to lie on his back in the water and read the newspaper at the same time.[14] He loved to hike and often refused offers of car rides. "No, he wanted to walk. Many times, in the summer almost on a weekly basis, he would walk distances like 10 kilometres. He would climb up to the railroad grade, go east along it where it circles around the mountain to Cultus Lake, dip in the water, come back again and on the way he'd pick the berries he could find. ... Exercise for soul medicine."[15]

Friesen exerted the same kind of care in making strong, clear blackberry wine as he did in making violins. The wine was regularly stolen by young boys from the town. He always dressed casually, almost indifferently, and often wore clogs in summer. An impractical man, according to a friend, Friesen "couldn't figure out how to turn on a water tap."[16] His work area was normally in a state of chaos, with bread drying on window shelves and violins drying outside on the clothesline.

But Friesen was an intelligent man, living in a world of his own. It was a world of dreams and music. In Frank Dyck's view, he had "the idiosyncrasies of a fanatical and gifted artist."[17] "Some people live inside themselves," says a daughter, "and that's where they stay."[18] His artistic temperament extended far beyond violin-making: "When he expressed himself about nature," Dyck states, "you just had to be quiet and listen; it could bring tears to your eyes."[19] He was a moody man, usually high-spirited and jocular, then, suddenly, pensive. At such times one knew he had something important to say.

But his deep inwardness and lack of business sense cost his family dearly. He "never had a budget, never thought that was necessary."[20] His family suffered the consequences, being forced to accept support from government and community. The lack of a car placed severe restrictions on his wife and children. On his part, Friesen continued his unruffled existence and was seemingly happy with very little. Despite his relative poverty, he produced a large family, fathering his last child at age 70.

Friesen's rather harsh old-school sense of discipline also elicited the inevitable resentments from his children. It was his wife, Margarete (Gretel), who possessed the love, devotion, and energy that held the family together: "As far as I'm concerned, she could do no wrong," declares daughter Norma.[21] Never approving of Heinrich's conversion to the Jehovah's Witnesses, Gretel remained a Catholic, but she greatly appreciated the Yarrow community's support, and sometimes attended the Mennonite Brethren Church out of gratitude. She was a positive person, who sang when she did the housework. Yet in some ways, her isolation was greater than her husband's. High German (or English) had to be spoken in the home, as she did not know any Low German. Because of the rift with her parental family, she avoided even mentioning the birth of her children in the letters she wrote to Germany. Twice, she traveled "back home" to renew family ties. Then, while still relatively young, she contracted a brain tumour, and her short-term memory was badly affected. In those final years, the children took to hiding their atlas; if Gretel were to find it, she might be found staring at a map of Germany and weeping. She never ceased agonizing over her decision to come to Canada.

But despite Heinrich Friesen's incompetence in economic and family matters, and the unintentional difficulties that resulted, his friends knew him as a gentle, observant man. He loved to play violin duets and would often cry over the beauty of the music. A non-confrontational man, he liked to slip unnoticed into the back of the Mennonite Brethren Church to hear George Reimer's choir rehearse. Later, he developed a liking for the Reverend Henry Brucks, who himself was non-confrontational by nature. Yet Friesen also loved to talk and debate issues of the day—using speech that was fast and sometimes hard to understand (his English was always broken). He developed a routine of walking to Jake's Shoe Shop, where a special chair was set aside for him. This was a venue for energetic discussion; it attracted a variety of open-minded and vigorous men, such as Isbrandt Riesen, Henry Dahl, Gerhard Derksen, Petrus Martens, and Jake Barwich. "I learned more in that shop than anywhere else," says Jacob Barwich. Friesen "was the one that got me thinking about the various aspects of life, religion, and philosophy," reports William Reimer.[22]

Friesen's reputation as a violin-maker continued to prosper. At about age 70, however, he suffered a severe heart attack, and his skills deteriorated with illness and age. "His latest instruments were such bad handiwork, I felt sorry when I saw them," says Frank Dyck, who served as his student for some months. "He knew what to do, he knew what to expect, but his hands weren't steady anymore." Friesen was aware of the problems, but his sense of humour did not desert him: upon suffering dizzy spells, he joked, "*Man sagt die Welt dreht sich. Je älter ich werde, desto mehr kann ich das glauben.*"[23] (They say that the world turns. The older I get, the more I believe it.) But Friesen's dream of beauty was coming to an end. In 1976, he passed away, with no apparent regrets; "*Lass mich nur sterben*" (Just let me die), he said.[24] His wife followed him three years later and is buried at his side in Musselwhite Cemetery in Abbotsford. The inscription on his headstone is simple: "Heinrich Friesen—Violin Maker."

"I Was Left Alone with My Little Children": Elizabeth Wall

By Elizabeth Wall Dyck

Elizabeth Wall, our mother, lost her husband shortly after arriving in Yarrow. As a single parent, she raised her four children, managed the little family farm, worked locally at various jobs, and, like several other women in similar situations, became a symbol of personal strength, faith, and perseverance to many in the community.

Our mother, born on May 25, 1897, in Rudnerweide, Ukraine, to Heinrich and Anna Kliewer, was brought up in a Christian home. In April 1919, she married Martin Harder from Mariawohl, Molotschna colony. Shortly thereafter, he was drafted into the Russian army. Three months later, he came home on a brief furlough but soon had to return to the front. He never came home again. She inquired wherever and whenever she could if, perchance, someone had heard of his whereabouts, but to no avail. A year later, word came to her that he had been seen in a battle area with his team of horses, and that one of these horses had been killed by a bomb. Presumably he also perished, as he was never heard from again. For six years she waited, sought information about him, and grieved for him. Eventually, she received a new assurance from a passage in the Old Testament: "How long will you mourn…?" (I Samuel 16:1). In January 1925, she married Hermann Wall. The newly married couple lived with Hermann's parents, and their son Henry was born in December of that year.

Storm clouds had been gathering over Russia, and, with the revolutionary turmoil, many Mennonites began to make plans to immigrate to Canada. Our parents were able to book passage on the ship *Montroyal*, which arrived in Saint John, New Brunswick, on

November 28, 1926. Their first place of residence was Hochfeld, Manitoba, at the Peter Plett farm. The small Plett house consisted mainly of a kitchen and large living room, and the Pletts' six children still lived at home. Mother used to say, "Some slept on the table and some under it." Here, on December 15, just over two weeks after their arrival in Canada, I, their only daughter, was born. Soon they found a residence in Morden, where Father also found work, and our brother Pete was born two years later. A year or two after that, our parents decided to move to Foam Lake, Saskatchewan, where they rented a farm in partnership with two other families. When this contract expired, Father re-contracted for another three years. It was here that two more children were born, Johnny in 1932 and Victor in 1936. Johnny died of pneumonia in 1935.

These were the mid-1930s, the hardest period of the Great Depression, and many people were searching for opportunities to make a better living. A Mennonite periodical had been carrying advertisements regarding inexpensive land, job opportunities, a milder climate, and a German-speaking community in the Fraser Valley of British Columbia. Because these prospects appealed to our parents, they decided in 1936 to venture to the West. When they had completed the harvest and auctioned their animals, farm equipment, and personal goods late that year, they boarded the train for B.C. with their remaining possessions. Upon arriving at the B.C. Electric station in Yarrow, they and their four children were welcomed by David and Elizabeth Heinrichs, who provided accommodation for all in their modest farm home. Father

Elizabeth Wall and children.

immediately began to look for property. He selected a two-acre plot on Wilson Road, where he planned to build a house and, later, a barn for a cow and some chickens. Since we had arrived in blustery November weather, he was unable to start on the house immediately. But he found employment cutting cordwood, as well as other odd jobs. As soon as possible, he began to build the house. We must have stayed with the Heinrichses for at least three months. At the time, there were no houses for rent in Yarrow.

In the spring of 1937, Father found a job in the hopyards. After four days of work, he realized he needed some rainwear. And little Victor, 15 months old, needed shoes. Mother traced Victor's foot on a piece of cardboard, cut it out, and sent it along with Father, who rode on his bicycle (our only mode of transportation) to Chilliwack to do the shopping. On the way home, he was hit by a drunk driver and killed instantly—after only six months in Yarrow. The children remember that fateful day when he was not home in time for supper. Mother, although concerned about his failure to arrive, realized that he could be late because of the various kinds of shopping he had planned to do. Two of the children, Henry and I, had been singing "*Es geht nach Haus, zum Vaterhaus;/ Wer weiss, vielleicht schon morgen*" (We're going home to the Father's house; who knows, perhaps tomorrow). Apparently, this song was beginning to trouble Mother; however, she did not order us to stop, and we sang it over and over. Shortly after supper, she sent us to bed. Later that evening we were ushered downstairs to the kitchen and met by a police officer, who informed us of the tragic death of our father. At ages 11, 10, 8, and 1, we children could not comprehend the enormity of this catastrophe. We do not recall the effect it had on our mother at that time, but it must have been devastating. In one of her papers she writes, "He was 40 years old, and I was left alone with my little children. The pain was indescribable. But the Lord had a word for me that greatly comforted me: 'Beloved, think it not strange concerning the fiery trial which is to try you, as though some strange thing happened unto you. But rejoice, inasmuch as ye are partakers of Christ's sufferings; that, when his glory shall be revealed, ye may be glad also with exceeding joy'" (1 Peter 4:12-13).

Although she repeatedly found spiritual comfort in the Bible, Mother had a very difficult time financially. Besides trying to provide her family with food and clothing, she was also making payments to the Canadian Mennonite Board of Colonization on the debt incurred through the journey from Russia. In those early years, everyone earned money by picking hops. In our case, hop picking produced the best income of the year. We children all helped. The highlight of this season was a trip to Vancouver at the end of hop picking. Our neighbours, John and Helen Block, who owned a pickup truck, invited us to accompany them to shop at the "Old Church" thrift store, where we rummaged through second-hand goods, mostly clothes. Mother made some of these over into "new" clothes for us. Usually each of us found an inexpensive item that we particularly liked: a softball and glove, children's books, a small ornament, a piece of clothing that we were allowed to buy as our reward for our diligent work during that summer.

As for Mother, she got by with wearing the same clothes repeatedly. On one occasion, when she was wearing a dress that she had already worn a number of times, someone said to her, "And now you have a new dress again." Mother, a sensitive person, found such comments offensive, and this statement truly annoyed her. After all, she was wearing an old dress. But she had attractive features, was of petite stature, and had an eye for what suited her. Thus she always seemed to dress well and always looked good, even in old dresses.

We were fortunate to live on two acres of land, which provided us with both food and a little money. Mother laboured hard planting and caring for raspberries, strawberries, plums, rhubarb, and various vegetables. Whatever fruit was not needed was shipped to the cannery. She also raised chickens and livestock to feed her family, and she sold butter, milk, and eggs to people in Yarrow.

Mother had her challenges and exasperations as she endeavoured to raise her children. During these years, for example, the government provided her with a widow's allowance of $18 per month. We don't recall what the stipulations were, but when we purchased a 1928 Model A car in 1943, the allowance was discontinued. Although this loss was a blow to Mom, we badly needed transportation. Somehow we managed without the $18, but not without her garden. I recall one day when Mother went out berry picking and I stayed at home to look after my younger brother. The neighbour girl was also at home, looking after her younger siblings, and so we played together. We hopped around the garden pretending we were rabbits. The corn patch was a wonderful place in which to hide from each other. The cabbage was at the stage where it had headed out beautifully, and we started to nibble on the cabbage heads. By the time our game was done, all the cabbage had been chewed at. Mother came home, inspected her cabbage patch, and couldn't believe her eyes. How could the neighbour's cow have gotten into her lovely garden? I had to confess that it was not a neighbour's cow, but we kids who had browsed the cabbage. She was not happy, to say the least.

Despite our lack of means, Mother was always a generous person. For example, her nephew and his wife had been forced to emigrate from Russia to Paraguay because, at the time they emigrated, the Canadian government had frozen all immigration to Canada except for residents of a few, select countries, like England. Because living conditions for new settlers in Paraguay were extremely harsh, Mother periodically sent her nephew $20 from her hard-earned income. Eventually he became quite prosperous, in large part because a generous, caring widow in Yarrow had sacrificed on his behalf. Moreover, Mother always contributed regularly to the Sunday church offering, and she was also mindful of needy people in the community. Often we had to take soup or other foodstuffs to someone who was ill or had experienced some other misfortune.

Mother was a deeply spiritual believer, and she prayed for her children, always reminding the Lord of His assurance that "all your sons will be taught of the Lord; and the well-being of your sons will be great" (Isaiah 54:13). Church services were the highlight of her week. After successive days of tiring labour, she found in these services rest for both body and soul. She had been baptized by sprinkling in her youth; in Yarrow, however, she became affiliated with the Mennonite Brethren, and membership required baptism by immersion. She took this step of re-baptism in the year that Father was killed, as an act of obedience to the Lord and the church. She greatly appreciated the church and the community, where she enjoyed friends and fellowship. Many times she must have thanked the Lord for bringing her to Yarrow, where she had the opportunity to bring up her children in a closely knit community of like-minded folk.

Several occasions gave Mother a special sense of accomplishment. November 17, 1941, was a memorable day indeed, as it was the day on which she was able to make her final payment to the Board of Colonization for providing passage to Canada and transportation to Yarrow. She had accomplished this in a mere four and a half years after her husband's death and five years after arriving in B.C. The purchase of a car that allowed us to get around was also an important achievement.

Later, she was able to purchase a piano so that her children could have the same opportunity to take lessons as their friends did. Years later, during the 1960s, she had her first and only experience of flying when her cousin accompanied her on a commercial airliner to visit relatives in Ontario. This trip she truly enjoyed.

When the property in Yarrow became too much for her to manage alone, she moved to a smaller place in Clearbrook (Abbotsford). Here she diligently worked in her garden and enjoyed her new neighbourhood. After suffering a stroke in 1970, she relocated to the Tabor Home. Eventually, she needed extended care and so was transferred to the Menno Home, another Mennonite care facility in Abbotsford, where she passed away on December 22, 1985. For almost half a century, she had raised her family as a single parent. She was stalwart yet self-effacing, and these traits were valued in a woman, particularly in a widow. She left her community, and especially her children, a wonderful legacy: a strong work ethic, a refusal to give up when sorely tried, a love for her neighbours, and, most important, a quiet and unshakable faith in God.

"A Dream Come True": Frida Nachtigal, First Mennonite Teacher

By Agatha E. Klassen

A dream come true!" was Frida Nachtigal (Nightingale) Johnstone-Langton's reaction when the Chilliwack School Board offered her a teaching position in Yarrow in 1945. Teaching school was a dream—and a far-fetched one—when Frida was a little girl in Russia. She recalls that as a child she could not go to sleep until her mother had sung at her bedside. The words and melodies always touched her. Little did she know that one day she would teach children and direct school choirs. Her parents emigrated from Russia in 1924; secretly, and only rarely, did she revisit her childhood dream during the tough years of the 1930s, when she tried to get her education in Manitoba.

Because of the nature of her early school days in Manitoba, Frida speaks of them reluctantly. As a young child, she had known no English. At that time there was often a dearth of trained teachers in rural schools. Typically, a teacher had little education, no pedagogical qualifications, and usually worked with a special permit. Frida did learn to read and write, but comprehension of concepts and written texts was not taught. When her parents moved to Arnaud, Manitoba, her schooling did not improve because her teacher offered little instruction and seemed uninterested in whether she and her fellow students were learning anything. All the while, she applied herself to disciplined study. One could say that she was self-educated. Then, while still in elementary school, she had the opportunity to attend school in Winnipeg, where her sister lived, and this turned out to be a milestone in her educational journey. She remembers with gratitude a Mrs. Thompson, who taught her proper phonics and thus greatly enhanced her reading ability and comprehension of the English language. By the time she completed grade eight at Gordon Bell School in Winnipeg, she had begun to blossom intellectually and was well on her way to acquiring the kind of education for which she had yearned. One of her favourite recollections of grade eight is a course in millinery, for which she had to walk many city blocks. Artistically inclined, she enjoyed that class immensely.

Since the Nachtigal family was large and without means, the parents could not afford to send their children to a private school or pay for their room and board in Winnipeg so they could attend public school there. In fact, several of Frida's older siblings had taken jobs to help support the family, and she had to earn her way through school, mostly doing housework for well-to-do families in the city. This difficult labour and the frequent changes in place of work added to her frustration, but she was not about to give up. She completed her final two years of high school at the Mennonite Educational Institute in Gretna, Manitoba, one of two Mennonite high schools in Canada at the time. Because it was widely regarded as a first-rate academic institution, she considered herself fortunate to graduate from Gretna.

In 1935, the Nachtigal family moved to Yarrow. Frida worked for six years as a domestic for a family in Vancouver. Eventually she enrolled at the Vancouver Normal School and graduated in 1945 with a first-class teaching certificate. One can imagine her delight when the Chilliwack School Board accepted her application for a teaching position—the first Mennonite ever to be hired by the district. Her first school was Atchelitz Elementary. In rain, sleet, snow, or sunshine, she resolutely walked four miles to school each morning that year, following the B.C. Electric Interurban railway tracks, which took her within

Ethel Knox and instructor Frida Nightingale, who taught in Yarrow in the 1940s and '50s.

a mile or so of her school. She recalls occasionally getting a ride home in a car in the evening.

At the end of her first year of teaching, Frida asked to be transferred to Yarrow. Was it difficult to get approval for the transfer? "Oh no," she states. "My credentials were good, and the chairman of the Chilliwack School Board was very compassionate when I told him that I was supporting my elderly parents in Yarrow." In Atchelitz, she had taught a split grade two and three class, and she was delighted with the age-level of the grade four class assigned to her in Yarrow, starting in September 1946. Although the Yarrow Elementary School was relatively new, the desks in her classroom had seen better days. They were scratched, paint had peeled away, and former students had carved their initials into the wooden tops. With such badly defaced furniture, she clearly could not teach her students to be tidy. Frida and her grade four students laboured for months to restore the desks, devoting after-school hours several times a week to this purpose. It was an ambitious project that should not have gone unnoticed. To her disappointment, no one gave her class any recognition for this undertaking, not even the principal, Carl Wilson. "Nevertheless, we were very proud of our achievement," she recalls. "It made for good rapport with my students, and they learned a practical lesson in the rewards of good housekeeping. I was told that my room was the most attractive one in the school, and the students made sure it was kept that way."[1]

Frida's students were expected to have a Bible or New Testament on their desks so they could follow along as she read the Bible passage for the day. (In those days the Department of Education prescribed daily reading from the Bible.) Sometimes her students dramatized a Bible story. Children did not misbehave, show boredom, or ask to leave the room during Bible reading. Her conservative upbringing—her father was a preacher—was evident in her teaching and her aspirations for her students. When a problem arose, she was not embarrassed to pray with a student after school. Often she visited the homes of her students, thereby establishing rapport with parents and gaining their respect. When asked whether she was a strict teacher, she conceded that she was, that she belonged to the old school. Good cheer and amusement were all right, but she tolerated no nonsense. When corporal punishment seemed absolutely necessary, she administered the strap herself even though other teachers asked the principal to take over this particular duty. On one such occasion, a grade eight student whom she had just strapped remarked, "Boy, Miss Nightingale, you sure can wallop." Another student remembers that Frida, while strict, was not a typical disciplinarian. What she was implying, perhaps, is that Frida felt badly when she punished her students.

Frida excelled in—and is most remembered for—her outstanding accomplishments with school choirs and drama.[2] When the short-lived Sharon Mennonite Collegiate Institute on Wilson Road in Yarrow was purchased by the Chilliwack School Board, it became an Elementary and Junior High school. This was good news for the community since students no longer had to be bussed 11 miles to Chilliwack for grades seven to nine. It was also good news for Frida because it offered a new dimension to her work. Several teachers, including Frida, were offered the opportunity to teach advanced grades if they were qualified and so inclined. Her childhood dream of teaching children music was realized. Her love for music motivated her to undertake difficult operettas such as *The Pirates of Penzance* and *The Mikado*. Fortunately she had some very talented students to work with, including choirmaster George Reimer's daughters, Holda and Frieda, who sang and played accompaniment on the piano, and tall and handsome Ed Barkowsky, who had shown no interest until he was offered the role of a pirate. When Frida uncovered his hidden talent and his exuberance on stage, she was as elated as he was. Although a number of teachers felt that she was too ambitious in attempting such complicated productions, she had no reservations. Indeed, she was in her glory, and the community enthusiastically rallied around her. She recalls how mothers sewed costumes and fathers constructed stage props. Her performances were a rousing success.

Elfrieda Krumhols, a niece, and a former student of Frida's, wrote her a letter in October 2000 in which she reminisced about her school days and the joy she found in Frida's musical projects. "I remember," she writes, "the old school on Central Road in Yarrow. The children were lined up on the wide staircase and we sang many of the songs you referred to, like Cherry Stones and Mockingbird Hill. I know that you were ahead of the times when you arranged for a bus to take your students to Vancouver to see and hear a production of the Makado [*sic*] by Gilbert and Sullivan. What excitement! You and the colourful Mrs. McCutcheon were very brave to tackle not just one but two operettas with grade VII and VIII students who really didn't understand the magnitude of the project. I know that I perk up when I hear music by Gilbert and Sullivan and I'm sure there are many others like me. Thank you for that gift to us."[3]

When Frida's father died, the old house in Yarrow was sold. Frida purchased a house in Chilliwack, and her mother came to live with her. While attending summer school at the University of British Columbia, Frida met William Alexander Annandale Johnstone, and their acquaintance developed into friendship and then romance. Three years later, on June 18, 1957, she and Alexander (Lex) were married. By that time she had moved to White Rock, where she now taught school in the Surrey District, and where they became members of the Baptist church. Both were active in the deaconate, and she also conducted a children's choir. Their marriage ended with Alexander's death after a little more than 10 years. It was a happy marriage, she reflects, and all too short.

It was during her years with Alexander that Frida, eager to upgrade her teaching certificate and having enrolled in summer school courses at the University of British Columbia for a number of years, obtained her Bachelor of Arts (1962).

The year 1970 began yet another chapter in Frida's life. This was the year she completed 25 years of teaching. It was also the year she married Wenman Langton, another member of the White Rock Baptist congregation. She completed a final year of teaching but then accepted the opportunities retirement offered. As she and Wenman were in good health and loved to travel, they made numerous excursions in Canada and the United States and abroad. For six years, they resided in California, where they enjoyed the warm climate, but then they returned to White Rock. Wenman died in 1990. Looking back on those years, she observes simply that they had 20 wonderful years together.

With Wenman's death, Frida sold her property in White Rock and moved to Trethewey Towers in Abbotsford. From here she sends frequent letters to siblings, nieces, and nephews, keeping in touch with them, educating them about history and their particular ancestral roots, and reminding them that God has been good.

Building a Life Through Necessity: Cornelius Regehr

By Cornelius (Chuck) Regehr

Cornelius Regehr had several reasons to move to Yarrow from his home in Coaldale, Alberta. The climate in southern Alberta was playing havoc with his health, and his in-laws, David and Katharina Klassen, were already in Yarrow, having left a hard life on the Prairies for the promise of a new start in British Columbia. The question of whether to move was settled when Cornelius (Cornie) was offered a job at a service station just being opened by Aron Klassen at the corner of First Street and Central Road. In 1941, Cornie put his wife Katie and their son John on the train to B.C. and drove to Yarrow with his brother-in-law, David Klassen.

Cornie was 30 years old when he made the move to the community that was to be his home for the next 52 years. This, however, was not his first big move. He had been born in 1911 in the village of Talma in the Terek Settlement in Russia, where his father taught school in one of the Mennonite villages. The family enjoyed a comfortable life, but that changed with the First World War and the Russian Revolution. At the end of 1925, the Regehr family left by ship for Canada, docked in Saint John, New Brunswick, and immediately boarded a train for Rosthern, Saskatchewan. In 1927, the family moved again, this time to Lethbridge, Alberta, and then to a farm in nearby Coaldale. In 1940, Cornie married Katharina Klassen, and a year later they moved to Yarrow.

Cornie's first job in Yarrow didn't last. Aron Klassen was a relative newcomer in a community that wasn't quick to embrace change—few residents of Yarrow chose to patronize the new service station. Within six months both the business and Cornie's job were gone. But Canada was at war, and there was a lot of demand for skilled labour. He took a welding course in Vancouver, then quickly landed a job at the North Vancouver Ship Repair Company, which was building Liberty Ships. That job lasted about a year. Katie visited occasionally but spent most of the year in Yarrow.

In addition to looking after their son, Katie worked in the hopyards. One morning on her way to work, one of the men pointed out to her that her husband, a pacifist Mennonite, was aiding Canada's war effort by working in the shipyard. Not one to take such criticism quietly, Katie pointed out to this man that he was picking hops used to make beer. He quickly replied that the hops he picked were used for yeast.

After a year at the Vancouver shipyard, the shift work and the separation from his family started to wear on Cornie. Returning to Yarrow, he accepted a job as truck driver for the firm of Martens & Neufeldt. Much of the time he was hauling cordwood from Chilliwack Lake Road. The road was rough, and the trucks were not always in top mechanical condition. One night, on the way down the mountain, his truck lost its lights. The road could not be safely negotiated in the dark, so he stopped at a farmhouse to borrow a lantern, which he hung on the front of the truck, and carefully worked his way down the narrow, twisting road.

In 1944, Cornie took a job as clerk with the Yarrow Growers' Co-operative Union. Peter Friesen, the former president of a co-op in Russia where Cornie had worked as a clerk when he was 13 years old, hired him. This position might have been a career for him, but shortly after the end of the war, the Co-op fell on hard times. Yarrow's main crop at the time was raspberries, and production was up sharply just as overseas markets started going into decline. By 1948, the Co-op was in trouble—it had 6,000 tons of berries with no market in sight, and when the berries were finally sold, the proceeds were eaten up by storage costs. The Co-op was involved by then in processing and selling much more than berries; it owned and operated a two-storey department store and office complex. Most of the members had a hard time distinguishing between the Co-op's flourishing retail business and its troubled berry-processing plant. Rather than work through the hard times, the shareholders voted in the spring of 1949 to disband the Co-op. When all the assets were sold, berry growers were left with 41 cents on the dollar, and, after five years as clerk, Cornie was once again unemployed.

Cornie took the loss of his position at the Co-op in stride. Like many others in Yarrow, he was prepared to do whatever was necessary to support his family of four, and there was no shortage of work in the Fraser Valley. He spent the next 20 years working on construction projects in Yarrow, throughout the Chilliwack and Abbotsford districts, and as far away as New Westminster. Often he worked with Henry Ratzlaff on Waterworks projects, and with John and Sam Klassen on other construction jobs. These entailed hard physical labour and long days, but he was known for his work ethic and the wit that he brought to every job. Invariably he came home at the end of the day with a story about something humorous that had happened at work. He built a chicken barn for Peter D. Loewen, a barn and feed tower for the Wiens brothers, and a feed shed for the Heinrichs's farm. He also helped build the Coqualeetza Hospital in Sardis. In addition, he worked as an enumerator in 1951 and 1961. The family berry patch on two acres of land at the end of Walnut Road also provided some income. In 1956, he and his wife purchased the stately Petrus Martens home on Eckert Road.

During his years in construction, Cornie had opportunities to join the carpenters union, which would have meant substantially higher wages and perhaps more work. But he was opposed to unions and their propensity to strike over what he regarded as trivial issues, and the union was not prepared to provide any guarantees of work. So when the union arrived on a job to sign up new members, he would pack up his tools and go home.

But Cornie was innovative and always willing to try something new. During the late 1950s, when the new way to control weeds and pests in farming was to spray with herbicides and pesticides, he designed and built a small commercial sprayer and spent a number of years spraying berry farms in Yarrow and Chilliwack. The sprayer tank, which held 150 gallons of liquid, was made by welding together sheets of steel; inside, blades kept the contents properly mixed while the sprayer was in operation. The tank was mounted on a couple of tail wheels from small aircraft. The sprayer heads could be mounted horizontally to spray a field of strawberries or vertically to go up and down raspberry rows. This contraption was hitched to Cornie's Farmall A tractor.

He also experimented with different crops on his Eckert Road farm. In addition to raspberries, the family grew blackberries, corn, cucumbers, and beans. To irrigate his crops, he bought a pump and motor and had the two pieces built into one unit at a machine shop. After walking around the farm with a water witch, he found an underground spring feeding into a slough that ran through the property. A well dug on that site provided the water for his irrigation system.

On the job, he was always looking for ways to save a step. For example, for shingling a roof, he fashioned a nail dispenser out of sheet metal that he attached to his carpenter's overalls. It gave him a steady supply of nails, which came out of the dispenser right side up and ready for pounding, so he did not have to reach into a pocket for a handful of nails every few minutes.

In 1970, Cornie embarked on a new career as the rural mailman for East Chilliwack. He loved this job since it provided a vital service while allowing him to interact with a wide variety of people. He delivered the mail until 1982, when he reached the mandatory retirement age of 71. During that time, the number of people on his route grew from 330 to 480, all of whom he knew by name.

Throughout his time in Yarrow, Cornie was active in both the Mennonite Brethren Church and the community. In the 1940s and early 50s, he was the timekeeper and treasurer for the Sunday School. In 1950, he became the secretary-treasurer for the church, a position he took over from his father-in-law, David Klassen, and he served in this capacity as a member of the church council for 25 years. Devoted to the church, he was always ready to offer assistance, whatever the need. After his retirement, he took responsibility for much of the building maintenance and any other odd job that needed to be done. He was also a strong supporter of Sharon Mennonite Collegiate in Yarrow, a small private school run by a society within the Mennonite Brethren Church. All four of the Regehr children attended Sharon High, and both Cornie and Katie were active in the affairs of the school, working as fundraisers and serving on committees.

However, the highlight of his more than 50 years in the Yarrow church was the five he spent as director of the German choir, from 1984 to 1989. During that time, he kept any vacations to visit his children short so that he would miss as little choir time as possible. He always spent hours selecting the right mix of songs, then memorizing them. Not all of the voices in his choir were the kind a conductor would normally seek out, but what mattered most to him was what was in the hearts of his singers. His favourite song was *"Der Friedensfürst"* (Prince of Peace), an anthem he directed with the whole church at Christmas 1988.

His retirement also gave him time to enjoy something he had loved since he was a child—poetry. At the age of 90, he was reciting poems during church services, by heart and from the heart, but no longer in Yarrow. In November 1993, he and Katie moved to Abbotsford, where they joined the Clearbrook Mennonite Brethren Church, a congregation that still offers some traditional Mennonite services in German. Ninety years of age at the time of this writing, Cornie remains active in the church as a member of the German choir, a volunteer worker with the church's indispensable tape-duplicating ministry, and a man of many skills, always alert to needs around him and willing to help.

Anna Bartsch (1897-1989)

By Arthur Bartsch

My mother, Anna Bartsch (nee Funk), was the 10th in a family of 18 children, of whom 13 grew to adulthood. She was born in Russia in 1897, immigrated to Canada when she was 29, joined her husband, Henry G. Bartsch, as a missionary in the Congo and, with her four children, returned to Canada in 1938, quite weakened and exhausted by her ordeal in the tropics of Africa. Then 41 years old, she was unwell and needed treatment for what was thought to be a cancer of the skin on her scalp, nose, and ears. Her husband went back to Africa for another three years, and the children had to be "farmed out" among friends and relatives. One would have thought her life was over, but she lived another 50 active years, surviving her husband by more than two decades.

An active member of the Mennonite Brethren Church in Yarrow, Mother conducted Bible classes, led the Ladies' Choir, and taught in both the Sunday School and the German Religious School. At the same time, she cultivated a large and productive vegetable and fruit garden. Our yard on First Street in Yarrow was distinguished by a 200-foot white picket fence covered with brilliant red roses. How she managed to raise a family of four school-aged children and manage house, yard, and church-related work when Father was often away reporting on mission work is still a mystery to me.

In Russia, Mother had closely studied large portions of the Bible, particularly the Psalms and the Book of Romans. Indeed, while waiting for her emigration papers, she memorized the entire Epistle to the Romans. This early regimen bore fruit as she conducted regular Bible studies, often in the home of her friend, Susie Konrad. These meetings were regularly attended by one of the many women's groups of the church.

Mother also taught Sunday School. For years, she had an active group of teen-age girls in her classes. I don't know what they talked about, but the girls, some 20 or 30 in number, seemed to enjoy their lessons. They studied the Psalms and memorized their favourite ones. One of the girls thought this was too demanding. She asked if she could be exempted from the requirement to memorize Psalms. When the teacher persisted, this very intelligent girl asked if she could substitute Psalm 117 for the one she had been assigned. Psalm 117, she had discovered, was the shortest one in the Bible. "Shame on you!" came the response. "You should have chosen Psalm 119!" (the longest Psalm). Mother could be very direct.

The Mennonite tradition has learned to perpetuate itself and part of this tradition was the cultivation of the German language, first in Russia, then in Canada. This study was encouraged and conducted in Yarrow by the German School—even during the war years, when in Canada everything German was suspect. I remember how, on Saturday mornings, the entire community of school-aged children ambled to the Mennonite Brethren Church basement, Bible School building, or the Sharon Mennonite Collegiate on Stewart Road to study German. German school was referred to as *Religionsschule*, and this name may have had some war-time advantages. Mother was one of the teachers. Characteristically, she threw herself wholly into the work. On Saturday mornings, our house was a flurry of activity. As soon as the breakfast dishes were cleared, she was busy mimeographing papers, drawing, scheduling, and selecting music. She seemed never to be quite ready—there was always something more to do. Her briefcase bulged with materials. She appeared to enjoy her work enormously. Her various duties included leading the singing and other musical activities. When she returned home after 1 p.m., she would collapse into an armchair.

I would like to elaborate a little on my mother's method and teaching style, for which she is often remembered by her students. The classes we recall her teaching were held in some of the Sunday School buildings (long since removed) of the Mennonite Brethren Church and later in the Sharon High School. The mornings were divided into several parts: reading, writing, and memory work, with great emphasis on speech. Mother made a point of using the *Wort und Satz Methode* as she called it. By this she meant that the pupil does not learn by studying the letters of the alphabet as much as seeing the whole word to get its meaning in a context. To do this, she developed, very much on her own, a handwritten primer known as the *Fibel-Leselust* (Reader's Delight). Each school day students received another page that emphasized the use of a particular letter in short sentences. These pages were carefully scribed with a stylus in a gothic (Old German) script on a Gestetner stencil. I often saw her make corrections the very morning of the class. Most of the pages were illustrated simply. She described the genesis and purpose of the *Fibel* in the following way:

> This *Fibel* emerged within a few weeks and grew out of a desire to awaken an interest in the German language and to make it easier for the student to learn. It was prepared for 20 Saturdays. …
>
> Even though every lesson begins with one letter of the alphabet one should pay close attention to the meaning of the word and the sentence. Before long the pupils will rival each other in writing the sentences on the blackboard. No drilling here, but only an encouragement and a sense of accomplishment, which will inspire even the weaker students.[1]

Because it was necessary to give more reading practice to the students, Mother also prepared a small reader, *Deutsches Lesebuch*. She notes that the idea for this work first came to her in 1915, when she was a young girl in Russia. Eventually she wrote down stories and poems from her childhood memories, then imaginatively elaborated them. The *Lesebuch* appears to have had its successes, for even in recent years, while walking through the mall with Mother, I have met persons who introduced themselves to her by saying, "I remember you as my German School teacher, when we read those funny stories." That was part of the legacy of the German Religious School in Yarrow in the 1940s. Tuition was free to all children of the Yarrow community; the teachers received a very modest honorarium.

My mother was also involved in a ladies' choir, which performed regularly in church events for many years. This group of about 30 women sang in four-part harmony; Mother usually sang alto. Their songs, ones that they had learned in Russia, were scored in *Ziffern*, or cipher notation, familiar to Mennonites but rarely used at that time in Canada. I don't know if any recordings were ever made, but I have always thought it would be wonderful to hear this music again.

In her later years, Mother joined a group of women from Yarrow who visited the Tabor Home for the aged in Clearbrook. Their visitation was usually in the form of a service consisting of singing, prayers, and scripture readings. This service continued for many years on a weekly basis.

Interestingly, and far beyond our expectation, Mother spent her last years writing a memoir reconstructing and summarizing aspects of her life. Already 85 years of age, she was concerned that if her children ever wanted to get on record any of her personal reflections about her life, they would have to be written down soon. I often visited on weekends and observed her at her work—typing away with the old portable typewriter on her lap. She was blessed with an excellent memory. I was surprised at the things she could recall, details of events in her life that went back more than 80 years. She had kept diaries, which helped her significantly. She was surprised that her account was going to be published by a Mennonite publishing house; after all, she had intended it only as a "family memoir." On the day that it was submitted to the press, however, a cogent entry appeared in her diary. It read, "The Lord can make water into wine." She was referring to her life, work, and memoir.

She had outlived all her siblings, but at 92, she was having difficulties with her health. One evening when I visited her, I kissed her goodnight as usual, and she said, "I'll see you in heaven." Her plain and simple comment shocked me. A strange way to say goodnight, I thought. She died that night.

Take Counsel from Strength and Duty: Agatha Klassen

By Cornelius (Chuck) Regehr

A new beginning! That's how Agatha Klassen describes her move to Yarrow—a move to a community that was to be her home for more than 50 years, and a church that would be her spiritual foundation for almost 60 years. A gifted teacher, an influential church leader, a noted historian, and a person with a strong commitment to her community and her family, Agatha Klassen will always be inseparable from Yarrow, present and past.

Agatha was just two years old when the Klassen family arrived in Canada from Russia in the early 1920s. They settled in Hepburn, Saskatchewan, but within two years they moved on to Coaldale, Alberta. Life in Alberta wasn't easy. In the Dirty Thirties, the economic depression in Canada took its heaviest toll on the Prairies. For Agatha, Coaldale holds good memories, but also memories of poverty. Those were difficult years to live through, she says, even though she was just a child and not exposed to some of the hardships that her parents and older siblings experienced. The hard times and harsh climate were a far cry from what the family had envisioned when they decided to leave Russia for a land of new opportunity. So the family decided to move again.

At the end of the decade, some of the Klassen family's friends moved from Coaldale to Yarrow and sent back reports of a land of milk and honey. In August 1941, Agatha's mother decided to go and see for herself. She came back with stories of a land that included not only milk and honey but also fruit trees, fertile soil, and a climate in which one could grow more than just turnips and beets. As evidence of what Yarrow could produce, she brought back a suitcase full of fresh plums and other fruit. Within weeks, the family was on its way to Yarrow.

Yarrow felt like home to Agatha almost from the moment the family arrived. Several good friends were already there, and compared to Coaldale, Yarrow had more freedom for young people. Teenagers were actually allowed to go out together in mixed groups (of boys and girls) on Sunday afternoons. They visited places like Harrison Lake and Stanley Park, even Cultus Lake, although that was considered taboo because other men and women were together in bathing suits on the beach and in the water.

Agatha flourished in her new surroundings. She loved the church, she was developing a circle of new friends, and shortly after her arrival she was back in Bible school. Starting school in Yarrow with students who had been together for one or two years was a challenge, because other students studied and socialized in well-established groups. Her only friend in school that year was another outsider, a girl who had also transferred to Elim Bible School for her third and final year of studies.

The following year, Sharon Mennonite Collegiate Institute opened, and Agatha resumed her high school education. She was a little older than many of the students, but several other girls in their late teens were also going back to school, and she made several lifelong friends there. The decision to return to school was another step toward her goal of being a teacher. Her determination to become a teacher had already set her apart from some of her friends in Coaldale, where she was one of only two Mennonite girls in her class to stay in school through grade 10. The rest dropped out after grade eight. They were at home, baking cakes, helping on the farm, finding boyfriends, and hoping to get married.

Librarian and historian Agatha Klassen with bouquet of Yarrow flowers.

Agatha always loved school. She remembers every one of her

teachers, from grade one through university. Her first-grade teacher in Coaldale, a Miss Porter, made the Mennonite children feel loved and accepted with hugs and kisses. A grade five teacher, Jenny King, had fiery red hair that matched her disposition, but she was a brilliant music teacher and gave Agatha her first opportunity to sing in choirs. A grade eight teacher, Lloyd Elliott, was another favourite. He told the class that only two or three of them would ever make it to university, and she was determined to be one of them. Since the age of three, she had known that one day she would be a teacher, and nothing would stand in the way of that dream.

Her early inspiration had come from her aunt, Agatha Warkentin, her kindergarten teacher in Hepburn, Saskatchewan, who had always told her that she, Agatha, would be the teacher in her family. For Agatha, her aunt became an early role model. Her other inspiration came from her father. David Klassen had been a teacher in Russia before immigrating to Canada, and he was the one who insisted that Agatha continue her education both in Coaldale and in Yarrow. Teaching was a wonderful and rewarding career, he told his daughter, and that's what he wanted her to do.

The move to Yarrow gave Agatha the opportunity to return to school, but her decision to become a teacher left her with a difficult personal choice. During her year in Bible school, she was engaged to be married. In those days, getting married and pursuing a career were not compatible for women in Mennonite communities. Marriage at the age of 20 would have meant the end of her dream to have her own career. Just before going back to school for grades 12 and 13, she called off the engagement.

After completing grade 13 at Sharon Mennonite Collegiate Institute, Agatha took a year of teacher's training, or "normal school" as it was called at the time. That year didn't really give her the qualifications she felt she needed for her new career, but shortly after graduating she was in the office of W. Chidlow, the secretary-treasurer for the Chilliwack School District, applying for a job. The district needed teachers, but this did not mean automatic placement. Mr. Chidlow told her that the district liked to hire locally, but preference was given to teachers who had gone to public schools in the district. Agatha was a graduate of a private school in Yarrow, a school that took students out of the public system. Perhaps he was trying to scare her. He then asked her what kind of a student she had been. She told him to call her former principal,

Jake Friesen, who was still teaching in Yarrow. He immediately picked up the phone and called Friesen. Apparently he liked what he heard. After he hung up the phone, he hired Agatha on the spot. Her first school was in Rosedale.

Looking back on her first year of teaching, Agatha says she was ill-prepared to be a teacher. However, she was determined, and she devoted all of her energies to making sure that her students were well versed in the three "Rs." More precisely, that was her main focus in her early years of teaching. She taught classes from grades one to six in a number of different schools in Sardis, Cultus Lake, and Chilliwack.

After about five years of teaching, Agatha had an experience in the classroom that changed her. She was teaching a grade three class at the time. One of the boys in the class wasn't paying much attention either to her or to his schoolwork. When she asked him what was wrong, he replied with just two words: "home problems." Those two words had a profound impact on her for the rest of her career. Her approach had been to teach to the best of her ability and to make sure everyone in her class was a good student. Non-academic problems were usually left to the school nurse. But the little boy with "home problems" opened her eyes and heart. She became more sympathetic and attentive to the various needs of her students. She wanted them to remember her as more than just someone who taught them to read and write well.

In the late 1950s, Agatha embarked on a new teaching adventure. Along with her good friend Erma Wiebe, she volunteered for a year of duty with the Mennonite Central Committee as a teacher in Newfoundland. Her school was on the South Island of the Twillingate Islands. Teaching in Twillingate was a major adjustment—both a joy and, at times, a nightmare. The joy came from the interaction with children who lapped up the attention they got and responded eagerly to what to them was a new way of teaching. She was the only fully trained teacher in the school; many of the others had gone directly from the classroom in grade 11 or 12 to the teacher's desk without any further training. The nightmarish aspects included the conditions under which she had to work. There were virtually no supplies—no paper, no copiers, no crayons, no glue, no scissors, not even any library books. The school also had no electricity, and that meant a short teaching day during the winter months, when the light started to fade by 2:30 in the afternoon. And being a teacher from "the mainland" meant that her every move was scrutinized. But she was well liked by both the students and the school personnel. For years after she left, letters arrived from the school superintendent asking her to come back, even if only for one more year.

Village life in Newfoundland was also quite a change for Agatha. Many residents of the community had never been to the village in the next bay, much less crossed the bridge to the other island. Since she had occasional access to an MCC car, she decided one Sunday afternoon to take her landlords, the Earles, for a ride on the 17 miles of the South Island's unpaved roads. This experience was quite a novelty for the Earles. On one of the stretches in this drive, the car lurched through a pothole and stopped dead. Agatha was not mechanically inclined, but she jumped out of the car, confidently opened up the hood and peered down at the engine, pretending to know what she was doing. Then she spotted a loose wire sticking straight up. She knew the wire should be attached to something, so she wrapped it around a knob on the battery, closed the hood with a loud bang, and jumped back into the car. The engine started like a shot, and away they went. The Earles simply stared at her in disbelief. "You Canadian women are some smart," Wilson Earle remarked. "Not only can you drive a car, you also know how to fix it!" The story got a good laugh when she told it to friends that night.

Upon her return to Yarrow, Agatha went back to university to complete her Bachelor of Arts, specializing in Library Science, and when she graduated, she had a job waiting for her in Chilliwack as district librarian. Six years later, she became the librarian at the Chilliwack Senior Secondary School, a position she held until her retirement in 1985. Trying to keep teenagers quiet and focused on their studies in an understaffed high-school library proved to be a challenge. But she states that working with high-school students helped keep her young.

Throughout her years as a teacher, Agatha remained in contact with a circle of close friends, many of whom she got to know as a teenager in Coaldale and Yarrow. There were 10 or 15 women in this group, most of whom had chosen to be single. All cherished the freedom to pursue their careers and interests. One of Agatha's interests was traveling. One summer, shortly after she had started teaching, she and three friends left on a trip the day after school closed. They criss-crossed the United States, driving all the way to Florida, and returned to Yarrow the day before school started.

There was another love in Agatha's life in addition to her teaching career—her church work. She started as a Sunday School teacher at a time when "women knew their place" in the Yarrow churches. She was quite shy at the time. But as her teaching career blossomed, so did her self-confidence, and she was no longer content to serve quietly and unobtrusively while less-qualified people made the decisions. She recalls a committee she was on which had to have at least one male member so that he could report to the all-male *Vorberat*, the church council, what the committee was doing. That did not sit well with her. Her frustration was shared by other professional women in the church, who felt they were fully qualified to assume leadership positions. The Sunday School superintendent, Peter D. Loewen, let them know how much their work was appreciated, but the church and the conference had rules, and these had to be followed.

Agatha chose to work for change from within the church, pushing for more responsibility. Apparently her attitude at the time was considered aggressive by some in the church, though in a man, that kind of initiative would have been considered progressive. Her hard work did not go unnoticed. In the early 1970s, she was nominated by another woman at a church business meeting to serve as Christian Education director. Agatha rose to declare that she would accept the position, but only if she were also appointed to the church council. That had to be approved by the other members of the council and it was put to a vote. There was one dissenting voice, but just over 10 years after women in the Yarrow Mennonite Brethren Church had finally been given the vote, the church had its first female council member.

Some influential families in the church resented having a woman on the council, but Agatha received strong support from all of the pastors with whom she served and from some of the old guard. One of her staunchest supporters was Peter Loewen, who, according to her, was more progressive in his views than even he would sometimes admit. The first female member of the council, she also became the first female Sunday School superintendent and the first woman to serve on the pulpit committee.

In addition to her work with the church, Agatha found time to write a book on the history of Yarrow, the first such work on this subject. The idea for the book stemmed from a conversation with Jacob C. Krause in the 1950s. Krause was concerned that Yarrow's rich history would be lost unless someone made the effort to put the community's stories into print, and said that she was the perfect candidate to do just that. It took more than 20 years for that seed to begin to germinate but in 1971, she began work on *Yarrow: A Portrait in Mosaic.* The life of this community is recounted in short essays accompanied by hundreds of photographs of the times. The stories vividly picture the various stages in Yarrow's development. Each essay contributes to a mosaic of community life: from the arrival of the first settlers to the early days of picking hops and tobacco, from the early experiments in agriculture to the community response to natural disasters, from the community's attempts to control the education of its children to the changing role of the Yarrow churches and their members. For Agatha, the book was a labour of love that took all of her spare time for the better part of five years. This book went through two editions, each of which quickly sold out. Today it is unavailable except in libraries. For anyone who grew up in Yarrow, the book recalls a simpler time and a homogeneous community.

Retirement, to Agatha, meant more than spending time in a rocking chair reading books. She immersed herself in church work and community service. One morning in 1993 she received a call from her pastor. A group of 25 people was scheduled to travel to Russia in July to conduct door-to-door evangelism, telling about the ministry of Jesus. The group was short by one person, and she was urged to join. The invitation took her by surprise but she was intrigued by the thought of going back to the country where she had been born. She wasted little time making up her mind. It was an opportunity to combine her love for adventure and travel with service to God. The trip also laid the groundwork for a much longer and more challenging trip to Russia.

One of the sightseeing excursions during that first visit took Agatha to the Christian University in St. Petersburg. She became acquainted with the librarian, who, with his wife (both of them Canadian), was just completing the first three months of a project to computerize the library. As a professional librarian, Agatha was keenly interested in what they were doing. Clearly it was a difficult job, given the inadequate equipment and resources, and the austere living conditions. She felt sorry for them but, other than wishing them well, there was little she could do. Her group returned to Canada in August.

Just before Christmas, Agatha received another unexpected telephone call. It was from St. Petersburg. The couple working on the library had returned to Canada, and the university needed a new librarian. Once again she accepted the invitation, but this time she was going to Russia with her eyes open. A friend from Abbotsford, Lydia Reimer, offered to accompany her to help with the cooking and shopping. They arrived in St. Petersburg on February 1, 1994, in minus-25-degree weather, carrying two computers, a printer, some library supplies, personal belongings, and a suitcase filled with $10,000 (U.S.) in cash that churches, family, and friends had donated. Most of it went to the university and to students living on the equivalent of about $20 a month.

Agatha declares that in all her years of teaching she never worked as hard as she did for the next 13 months in St. Petersburg. She was at the library from 8:30 every morning until 5:00 every evening and usually again after supper. One month into her stay, the university president decided to change the library cataloguing system from Library of Congress to Dewey Decimal. She was trained in the Dewey system, but all of her material was in Library of Congress. Her sister tried to send Agatha's Dewey material, but it was lost in the mail. Eventually she received Dewey material from an American who had visited the university. By the time she left, she had processed 12,000 books.

In 1992, Agatha and her sister Anne moved from Yarrow to Abbotsford, but they continued to attend the Yarrow Mennonite Brethren Church for another eight years before transferring their membership to the Bakerview Mennonite Brethren Church in Abbotsford.

She had arrived in Yarrow almost 60 years earlier as a shy teenager, the daughter of conservative and tradition-minded parents. She came to Yarrow with a faith in God that was firmly rooted in the historic values of the Mennonite Brethren Church. Never did she question those values, but she did question the community's interpretation of a creed that equated the true church with second-class membership for women. In her firm but gentle way, she worked from within the structure of the community and the church for equal status for women, a status which her life has exemplified. Her actions and bearing also brought respect and equal status to professional and non-professional women who chose not to marry. For the important roles she has served, she belongs to Yarrow pioneers.

M Hank

By Harvey Neufeldt

"You should buy this place.... You need roots. If you don't have roots, you can just pick up and leave."[1]

When one thinks of individuals who best represent Yarrow's history, a number can be mentioned. But if one were to ask which individual best represents longevity, a long and deep rootedness in Yarrow's history, the name that rises to the top is Hank the barber—Henry Giesbrecht or, as he was affectionately known, "M Hank."

Former residents returning to the Yarrow barbershop have no trouble recognizing M Hank, the same man who cut their hair three or four decades ago, or, as the welcome mat reads, "Hank da Barber." The returnee will invariably be introduced by M Hank to another customer, who, whether a regular or a visitor, also feels like a welcome guest in this shop. "Do you recognize him? Think back 40 years." Often the people being introduced by Hank do not recognize each other.

Hank Giesbrecht was a latecomer on the Yarrow scene: by the time the Giesbrechts arrived in the Fraser Valley, Yarrow settlers were just beginning to pull themselves out of the poverty that had threatened their survival as a viable community during the Depression.

Giesbrecht was born in 1926 in Omsk, Russia, a few months before the family immigrated to Canada. He was part of a large family, 11 children in all. There were two daughters from Walter's first wife and one daughter and eight boys, including Hank, from Sarah, his second wife. In this home Hank learned the values of family, companionship, loyalty, and hard work. Upon arriving in Canada, the Giesbrechts settled briefly in Rosemary, Alberta. The section of land they received from the

Canadian Pacific Railway proved too difficult to till, so the Giesbrechts relocated to Coaldale, Alberta. They resided there for the next 15 years, subsisting on mixed farming that included sugar beets. In Coaldale, Hank was introduced to the Mennonite Brethren Church, which prepared him for what he would encounter upon entering the Yarrow Mennonite Brethren Church as a 15-year-old lad. When asked to compare the Yarrow church with the one in Coaldale, Hank remarked that they were "exactly the same."

The move from Coaldale to Yarrow was prompted by reports Walter Giesbrecht had received concerning economic opportunities in the Fraser Valley. One friend wrote enthusiastically: "In Yarrow you can go to the hopyard and earn as much as $2.50 a day for only ten hours a day. … Father and son are making $5.00 a day." In addition, "we can pick hops and even kids one year old can pick hops." The Giesbrechts arrived in Yarrow in 1941 and purchased a small dairy farm on Boundary Road, not far from the home of Reverend Johann Harder; in 1945 they moved to a dairy farm in Chilliwack. When he arrived in Yarrow, Hank was struck by the greenness of his world, the many trees and lush vegetation—so different from the Prairies.

Hank's education in Yarrow proved to be of short duration. He completed grade eight in Yarrow and enrolled the following year in grade nine at Chilliwack High School. Part way through that year he dropped out. He had to sit at the back of the classroom, he explains, and because of his poor eyesight and hearing problems, he had difficulty keeping up with the work. Instead of moving him to the front, the teacher would stand beside him and poke him on the head with a pencil, all the while saying, "C'mon, Giesbrecht, hurry up, hurry up." This so infuriated Hank that one day he picked up his books and walked out. When the teacher asked him where he was going, he replied, "I am leaving." In recounting this event, he adds, "I never came back." It was fortunate that he had begun grade nine—the barber school required a

Henry Giesbrecht ("M Hank") and his first barbershop.

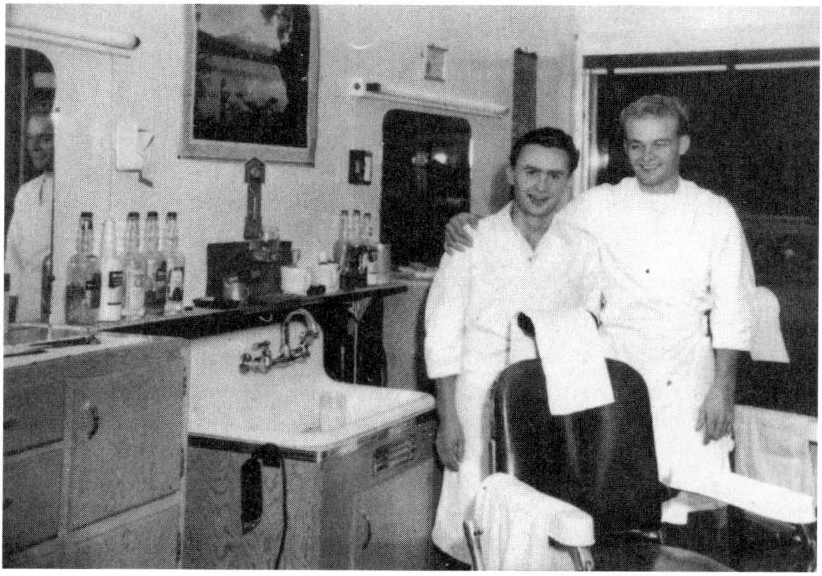

Barbers Henry Giesbrecht and Leonard Froese.

ninth-grade education. "I probably entered nine [completed] grades of school when applying for admission," he confesses.

Upon leaving school, Hank quickly found a job at the Yarrow Co-op. He is proud of his work record, which includes some 29 jobs. "I've never been unemployed in my life," he is quick to point out. At age 16, he drove to Vancouver with his father and brother Jake to look for work. His first job there was with Burns and Company, but he soon switched to the shipyard, where he could earn up to $1 an hour, double the salary Burns and Company was paying him, for doing piece work. Hank and Jake kept only the coins in their pay envelopes; the rest went home to the family. If their earnings were some 70 cents beyond the whole dollar amount, they felt that they were fortunate; if only a dime was in the envelope, they had little spending money until the next pay period.

While he was at the shipyard, Hank received his military draft notice. He had an older brother who had registered as a conscientious objector, who was now stationed in England, but Hank decided to sign up. He never seriously considered applying for CO status. He hadn't joined the church or become involved in its activities, nor had he attended the Mennonite high school or the Bible school. "I just had other interests," he explains, "and I don't think they were all bad things. ... I just didn't do some of the things that ... [went with] the general flow." And so, he admits, in early Yarrow he was considered a rebel. Unable to join the navy because of his age, he enlisted in the army. The war soon ended, however, and his stint in the military was over after nine days.

It was during his time working in a logging camp near Powell River in 1945 that Hank decided to take up barbering as his life's profession. He had begun cutting his brothers' hair when he was only seven or eight years old. At the logging camp, he observed the camp barber's work and decided he could do a better job, so he had his clippers mailed to him and began cutting hair at the camp. One of the men remarked: "You're a pretty good haircutter; you should take it up professionally." Hank followed this advice and enrolled in barber school in Vancouver.

Hank opened his first barbershop in Yarrow in the fall of 1945. He found a 12-by-8-foot shed, on the present site of Cherry Motors in Chilliwack, that would serve as his shop. His father purchased it for him for $35, and Hank paid Martens & Neufeldt Trucking $5 to haul it to Yarrow. The plumbing, wiring, and carpentry work, performed by Dick Epp and Henry Ratzlaff, cost $382, which he covered with a $400 loan from the local bank. Moving and renovating the shop took one week. For the first week, the shed stood on oil drums, eliciting disparaging comments from curious bystanders. He opened for business on a Friday, and after several hours his first customer, John Fast, arrived. Fast was soon followed by Reverend Peter D. Loewen. Hank used the 35 cents he received for the first haircut to buy his lunch at the Bright Spot, Yarrow's only café. Business was slow at first, so he took several other jobs, including firing kilns at the hopyards at night and working at a Chilliwack cannery. Nineteen years old now, he stopped sending his money to his parents. There just wasn't enough income to continue doing so.

For the next several years, Hank struggled to develop the business. In 1948, he entered into a partnership with Leonard (Len) Froese. To supplement their income, Hank worked five days a week as a barber at Camp Chilliwack, the army camp at Vedder Crossing, and Saturdays in Yarrow. Leonard supplemented their income in the summer by looking after a friend's berry crop. Everything Hank and Len earned they split 50:50; they even jointly purchased and owned a car, a Morris Minor. During the hop-picking season, Hank set up shop at the hopyards. Their dream of opening several barbershops failed to materialize, however, and in 1951, when Len went into the lumber business, they dissolved their partnership. By this time there was enough business for one barber and Hank no longer needed much outside employment, although he still returned on occasion to the army camp. For his first vacation, he simply posted a sign in his shop—"back by 4 o'clock." The sign didn't indicate which day.

Around this time, Hank decided to broaden his business to include a beauty salon for women. He returned to Vancouver for a week's training in hairdressing at the Vancouver Vocational School and his brother, an apprentice barber, ran the barbershop while he was away. The opening of a beauty salon signaled a change in the Yarrow Mennonite culture. Throughout the 1930s and '40s, short, curled hair on adult women had been considered a mark of worldliness, and few women wished to be seen entering the shop. His first female customer wore a shawl to and from the barbershop so people would not see that Hank had done her hair. After a time, she said, "I am not going to do that any more; now I am going to advertise for you. You are doing such a fine job."

Another woman, who had injured her back, asked if Hank could wash her hair. She inquired whether it could be done after hours, and if there was a side entrance so she would not be seen coming in. She arrived with a pillow for her back and a blanket to cover her legs to the floor. When he was finished, she apologized; she had brought the blanket for a specific reason—"How do I know that you are not looking where you shouldn't be looking when I have my head back?" Over time, some 300 women patronized his shop, but after several beauty salons had opened in Yarrow, his establishment once again became primarily a barbershop for men.

To many today, Hank Giesbrecht is known simply as M Hank; some people probably do not know his last name. He accepts the name with pride, and it is ironic that it began as a short version of "Mennonite Hank." Although he never joined a Mennonite church, he decided to operate his shop by carefully observing Mennonite customs. As he explains: "I wanted to be on the good side of everybody, so whenever there was any ... church holiday—*Himmelfahrt* [Ascension Day], or something like that—I would probably be closed. ... So they started calling me Mennonite Hank. Well that name stuck. ..." Eventually, it was simply abbreviated to M Hank. Despite the name, some of the church people did not consider him a Christian believer and tried to convert him whenever the Mennonite Brethren Church held revival meetings. Aware that he had engaged in activities that many Yarrow folk found questionable, he didn't take offence at efforts to bring him into the fold, and, in general, he felt well accepted over the years. He never once suspected people of questioning his place in the Yarrow community; they, in turn, never suggested that he didn't belong. "I am a people person," he explains. "I want to be accepted, and I work at it."

In 1951, M Hank strengthened his Yarrow ties by purchasing the building that had housed the Del Monte photographic studio. By this time, he had moved his barbershop to a rented space in the Epp Block. Henry Martens approached Hank to suggest that he buy the studio building. As Martens explained, "You need roots. ... If you don't have roots, you can just pick up and leave and we'll never see you again." Martens gave Hank $1 for a down payment and sold him the building for $4,000. Hank has never left Yarrow, and the building still serves as his barbershop today.

What is particularly striking about M Hank's ties to the Mennonite community is that his wife and children have not shared this loyalty. He met his wife, Kathleen Hunt, who was born in New Westminster, when he and Len Froese were rollerskating at Cultus Lake. At first, his father had concerns about Hank and Kathleen's relationship and asked him if he knew what he was doing. He was the first in his family to marry outside the Mennonite circle, and at that time marrying into the Anglo community was still frowned upon by many in the church community. He and Kathleen were married in the Chilliwack United Church in 1955 (also questionable in the view of many), and his children were baptized in the United Church. Social life for Kathleen remained primarily in Chilliwack. When their children approached school age, Hank and Kathleen moved to Chilliwack so the children could attend kindergarten. In 1971, the family moved back to Yarrow, settling on Majuba Hill, where they remained until 1987. Throughout the years in Yarrow and Chilliwack, Hank remained a Yarrow fixture, proud of being Mennonite Hank. Asked why he insisted on establishing his business in Yarrow, he replies, "I think it was a little bit of pioneering spirit in my blood. I just wanted maybe to be the first."

Today Hank cannot imagine not being a barber. Looking back on being the community's barber for 55 years, he observes: "I can't give this up. It hasn't even entered my mind, not even for a second, that I should quit this effort." Ironically, M Hank, whom local Mennonites tried to transform, is still a Yarrow fixture, while many of his would-be Mennonite rescuers have long since left the community and become assimilated into the larger North American culture. He is one of the few first- and second-generation Mennonite immigrants still to be found in Yarrow. In a real sense, he has earned the right to be called Yarrow's Mennonite Hank.

Yee Fong

By Robert Martens

On the quiet streets of Yarrow, children were met by a strange, shabbily dressed Asian. Strange to them, that is. "Him good," he might say, handing out gifts of oranges or grapefruit as he gesticulated and smiled broadly. He sometimes wore a traditional conical straw hat, especially in his younger years, and on his shoulder he often balanced a pole with a bucket on each end filled with vegetables. To some children in this tightly knit Mennonite community, he could be an alarming figure. Who was this man who spoke a simple, broken English, who approached them with seemingly random gifts, who lived alone in a shack? Yee Fong, often called Charlie Fong and sometimes referred to by the racially tinged epithet "Chinaman Charlie," was known to friends as a mild and warm human being. Yet even to Yarrow residents who were close to him, this gentle man remains largely a mystery. He survived a solitude and poverty that many might find unendurable. He chose to stay in a small Mennonite village where, despite the support he received from friends and community, his existence would inevitably be lonely. And indeed his choice of Yarrow was rather odd, living as he did in cultural and linguistic isolation among Mennonite immigrants who themselves were often similarly estranged from the culture surrounding them.

Yee Fong lived in a Canada that was frequently hostile to Chinese immigrants. Chinese first came to the "Golden Mountains" of British Columbia during the gold rush of the late 1850s. These mostly male newcomers were hardworking and ambitious, and they were welcome as long as they seemed valuable to a booming economy dominated by new European and American settlers. Many were killed doing the dangerous work of constructing the Canadian Pacific Railway. By 1884, 10 percent of British Columbia's population was Chinese.[1] But their very success was soon perceived by the mainstream population as a threat, and the reaction was swift and racist. The Asiatic Exclusion League was created. Laws were passed that severely restricted jobs for Asians. Race riots took place in Vancouver. In 1875, the British Columbia government prohibited anyone of Chinese racial origin from voting. The first head tax on Chinese immigrants was imposed in 1885; by 1943, the enormous sum of $23 million had been collected. The most extreme measure against these newcomers was the Chinese Immigration Act, passed by Canada's Parliament in 1923. Among other things, it closed Canada's borders to any "persons of Chinese origin or descent," excepting diplomats, merchants, students, or children born in Canada.[2] This law, not rescinded until 1947, resulted in a generation of "married bachelors," men who supported wives and children back in China but who had virtually no hope of reuniting with them in Canada. Due to such legislation as well as other circumstances, Yee Fong lived in B.C. as a "married bachelor."

He was born on March 20, 1891, in a village outside the city of Guangzhou (Canton). China was in turmoil, disintegrating under brutal exploitation by foreign powers and the ruthless ambitions of local and regional warlords. The result was widespread economic ruin, resentment, and violence, culminating in the Boxer Rebellion of 1900. In this chaotic milieu, Chinese seeking to improve their lives often imagined North America as a land of limitless opportunity. Indeed, Yee Fong's father had already worked in the San Francisco area for some years by the time Yee Fong was born. In 1908, Yee Fong was married to Yuet Ying Lee Yee, one year younger. Their first child, a daughter, was born in 1909. Even though his wife's family members were educated and prosperous, Yee Fong decided about 1912 to immigrate to Canada, influenced, perhaps, by the advent of major new civil strife, which involved the reformer Sun Yat-sen.

Yee Fong had hoped to enter the United States but was denied access, and it was this turn of events that brought him to B.C. He settled in Chilliwack, probably somewhere outside of its Chinatown. He must have paid the current head tax of $500, a huge sum in those days. In his early years, he apparently supported himself by working in laundries and restaurants. The Chinatowns of that era were social and ethnic enclaves, unlike the commercial districts of today. They originated as a retreat from racial hostility and as a refuge from direct economic competition with white Canadians. Ironically, however, although living quarters for working Chinese men were often cramped and squalid, business seemed to flourish. The Chilliwack Chinatown, located on Yale Road between the city and Sardis to the south, was no exception. It was busy and well developed, with sidewalks and porches to shelter customers from the rain, and it boasted seven or eight businesses, an infirmary, and a Masonic temple.

In 1934, this Chinese district went up in flames and was almost totally destroyed. A local newspaper report speculated that the fire may have been started by smoking transients,[3] but the Chinese population suspected arson. In anger, several of the families, or clans, left for Vancouver. Among those who stayed was Yee Fong. For a time he may have worked in the hopyards, where many Mennonites from Yarrow also made their living. This seems unlikely, however, as he possessed an independence and tough-mindedness that made him reluctant to work for others. In his own quiet way, he would develop a rather ingenious way to stay alive.

By the time of the Chinatown fire, many so-called married bachelors were living in shacks on affluent farms around Chilliwack, farming small plots of land with the landowners' permission. The shacks were most primitive, about 10 feet by 10 feet, with earthen floors, cutouts for windows, sacks for curtains, a simple stove and bed, and apple or orange boxes for shelving.[4] In exchange for tenant land use, the Chinese farmer might sharecrop or work a designated period of time for the property owner.

Yarrow, lacking in wealthy estates, presented Yee Fong with a novel opportunity. It is unknown when he first crossed the Vedder River to explore prospects in Yarrow, but he was already living there in the early 1930s. At that time, he was working with two Chinese friends. Within a few years, however, they disappeared from the scene, and he remained to farm alone. There was no shortage of acreage in the village, and Mennonites offered him small parcels of land already ploughed but lying fallow. In a sense, then, he was doing the owners a favour by working the land. His shacks were extremely basic, with a simple bunk for sleeping and potato sacks for covers. There was no outhouse, and he may have continued the Chinese tradition of utilizing excrement as fertilizer.

He resided in several locations but seemed to prefer living close to where the railway crossed the Vedder River, perhaps because of the quick access to the railway bridge and the tracks beyond, which served as a personal highway to Sardis. Here he still had friends such as On Lee, who owned a market. And here was one of several potential buyers of produce he sometimes sold outside of Yarrow.

In Yarrow, Yee Fong lived his life by a system of gift exchange: as he farmed various plots of land, he reciprocated by offering fruit, vegetables, and herbs to property owners. In his earlier days, he also possessed a horse, which he used not only for his own purposes but also for cultivating the land of people who had helped him out. In summer, he regularly slept in the open air near his vegetable gardens. Sacks served as blankets. It was a life style that seemed to satisfy both him and the landowners who were the recipients of his gifts and who often became Yee Fong's close acquaintances.

Apparently, affection for this kind-hearted man came easily to the people who knew him well. He readily reciprocated such affection. When George Reimer, one of the musical leaders of Yarrow, died suddenly, Fong approached a friend and pulled some herbs from his pocket, saying, "George Reimer not die, he get up."[5] He was deferential toward women, and rarely looked them directly in the face. Another cultural distinction was bringing gifts such as oranges for good luck to celebrate the birth of a male, but not for that of a female. Several women, however, were among his warmest supporters. On Saturdays, the traditional Mennonite baking day, such people as Katharina Ratzlaff (on whose land Yee Fong farmed for a time) would send him freshly baked goods (zwieback or *Platz*) and might be rewarded with a sack of vegetables in return. Surprise gifts of cabbage, herbs, or incense were sometimes left by Yee Fong on a friend's porch or windowsill.[6] And with certain men, Yee Fong had a special rapport. Although this Cantonese-speaking man conversed in an English so fractured that few could understand him, several long-time acquaintances, such as Ed (Abram) Froese and Peter Williams, understood him well. They gave him rides to Chilliwack, where he might visit with friends or purchase goods, and even to Vancouver, where he bought rice and Oriental medicines. Froese's Meat Market supplied him with offal, which he apparently then dried.

Although he lived near the Vedder River, Yee Fong rarely fished, preferring to live off the land. In China, he might have been a peasant farmer, thus a member of a respected and proud class of people. In Yarrow, he was a shrewd farmer. Indeed, "he was smart," says a friend. "He survived very well." Potatoes and cabbage seem to have been his chief market vegetables, and he chatted to himself in Cantonese as he worked. He also planted bamboo near the river dyke for his personal use. When working in his fields, he subsisted on uncooked rice, reaching into his shirt or jacket pocket, pulling out a handful without spilling a grain, and popping the rice into his mouth. To store his crops, he built root cellars. These were lined with lime, boards, leafless branches, and sacks, then covered with sod and cedar shakes. Above the cellars, he constructed lean-tos. On one occasion, he erected a lean-to against the wall of the house of friends, who were consequently surprised by a sudden stream of customer traffic to their property. He had advertised by leaving two potatoes on the desk of the Yarrow post office.[7]

Winters must have been difficult for Yee Fong. He had very little wood—"a stick here, a stick there"—because he lacked the tools to cut cordwood. During one snowstorm, his cabin was so inadequately heated that friends found him in bed, half-frozen and taking the occasional swig from a bottle, hoping to last out the bad weather.[8] It should come as no surprise, then, that he spent days at a time in Chinatown, where opium, gambling, and prostitutes were available, but where one could also visit friends, including individuals from one's village or region in China. Such visits were traditional outlets for easing the pain of loneliness, poverty, and racial antagonism among Canada's immigrant Chinese.

Of the money he made from farming, Yee Fong sent what he could to his wife. Tragically, his sacrifices were not always rewarded: much of the money that he mailed to his family never reached its destination. Perhaps due to the Chinese Immigration Act of 1923, he had been unable to bring his wife to Canada. He did, however, return to Guangdong three times. On each occasion, he remained there for two years because, as stipulated by the Chinese Immigration Act, any Canadian resident of Chinese descent who left the country for more than two years would be registered as a new immigrant.[9] He was in China from 1916-18 and fathered his first son; from 1926-28, when he fathered a daughter and another son; and again, from 1935-37.[10] Each time, he returned to a homeland torn by warfare, with the Japanese, the Kuomintang, and the Communists struggling for control. Then, around 1949-50, when Mao Zedong was in power, he made one last attempt to reach his family. What happened next was an experience he was reluctant to discuss, and therefore remains, like much of his life, in shadow. Apparently he was thrown into prison at the border; perhaps he was tortured. He returned to Canada "skin and bones," a frightened man.[11] He was never to see his family again.

Politics were not the only tragedy in his life. A shack in which he was living, on the property of Dave Schellenberg, burned down. Since Yee Fong had been in the habit of hiding his money beneath piles of newspaper in his cabin, it is possible that his life savings were destroyed.[12] Without money, he lost any chance of being reunited with his wife. He desperately missed his family. Occasionally he sat on the steps of the house of Ed and Mary Froese, staring at a picture of their son, and muttering, "Nice, nice." When a Froese family member was married, he became depressed.[13]

However, friends came to his aid after the fire. He was invited to stay in Dave and Agnes Schellenberg's basement, and here he lived and cooked for a few months until alternative arrangements could be made. A shed was bought, and it was moved by friends, including Henry Ratzlaff, Dave Giesbrecht, and John Langeman, to Dave Schellenberg's property. Here Yee Fong lived for many years, isolated, but to all appearances reasonably content. Contact with his family was limited to letter-writing. From time to time he attended a service at either of the two Mennonite churches in Yarrow, but he would have understood little. Besides, he had been raised a Buddhist.

As Yee Fong grew older, his eccentricities may have increased. To some people, a friend observed, he could be a "frightening figure" as he dropped off gifts of sacks or vegetables at 10 or 11 o'clock at night.[14] He loved to talk, to chat in a kitchen or on a porch, but on the other hand seemed reclusive. Seldom, if ever, did he allow himself to be invited in for dinner. Chinese custom required that if he was invited to dinner, he was expected to reciprocate, something he could not do given his meagre diet and primitive shack; possibly, also, he felt bound by the customary practice of refusing initial offers.[15] It was a rare individual who was permitted a glimpse inside his cabin. His habits were largely a result of his poverty and cultural differences. He brushed his teeth with bamboo twigs and used a foul-tasting toothpaste that "looked like ashes."[16] He refused offers of washing his laundry. He wore rubber boots with no socks on his feet, never used gloves, and went to bed without undressing.

As he aged, this man, who had been so strong, grew stooped and arthritic. He had health problems, starting with his prostate and progressing to his kidney and heart. On one occasion, he was taken into the X-ray laboratory at Chilliwack General Hospital. Suddenly, this gentlest of human beings became violently berserk and had to be restrained. A friend later asked him about it. "You know what they do," he replied, "they let you die, pick your bones, hang you up." It turned out that he had seen a human skeleton hanging from the wall of the X-ray room and had drawn his own conclusion.[17] This reaction was a result, perhaps, of kidney failure, which can play tricks with the mind. But it may be indicative, as well, of the fears and alienation he must have felt as a Chinese living alone in Canada.

Personal harassment was growing as many Mennonites left Yarrow and the homogeneity of the community was breaking down. Young people, both Mennonite and non-Mennonite, yelled, "Chinky, chinky," as Yee Fong passed by on the street. At night, they sometimes gathered to throw rocks at his shack and shout, "Come on out."[18] And then, on April 25, 1968, there was a fire in Yarrow:

> Elderly occupant of a small home in Yarrow, Yee Fong, died in a blaze which severely damaged the building on Thursday evening. A fire official said cause of the blaze is unknown but it is believed to have started toward the front of the building. Yee Fong did not smoke, said the official, and there was no electricity. His body was found on a bed in the house, which is at the rear of 42691 East Walnut Road, Yarrow. Members of Yarrow brigade answered the call which came in at around 8:50 p.m. The brigade was notified by D.D. Schellenberg of Yarrow, who owns the property. Flames destroyed the roof of the building but the walls are still standing. Loss has been estimated at somewhere around $650.[19]

The funeral was held a few days later at Henderson's Funeral Home in Chilliwack. Mary Froese, who had some connections with Henderson's, was able to arrange the best of ceremonies for her friend. He was given a Christian burial and lies in the Carman United Church Cemetery in Sardis.

The fire was considered suspicious. Several young people were questioned at length, and in June of 1968 an inquest was held in Chilliwack. Evidence was given to support the position that the conflagration was accidental: a piece of wood was sticking out of the stove; the ash receptacle for the stove had been removed and placed on some sacking near the door; there were no signs of pre-death injury on Yee Fong's badly burned body; and Yee Fong's habit of using the door, rather than the chimney, as an outlet for smoke was recounted (Inquest

Report). Close acquaintances also knew that occasionally Yee Fong smoked opium. But although the fire may have been accidental, suspicions remain. A series of fires had burned down several of Yarrow's businesses over the years, and there seems to have been a British Columbian tradition of burning Chinese "married bachelor" homes: "There were several old Chinese bachelors … that died of very mysterious circumstances," relates one Chinese-Canadian, "but I don't think records were kept."[20]

Yet the sadness of this story does not end here. In 1956, Yee Fong's wife, Yuet Ying Lee Yee, had finally been granted permission to leave the People's Republic of China. She was evidently given her release because of her advanced age and the food shortages in China following the Korean War. Yuet Ying Lee Yee crossed the border into Macao, where she lived with her eldest son. Her eldest daughter, Mary, then immigrated to the Bahamas in hopes of later entering either Canada or the United States. In 1969, two grandsons of Yee Fong, Louis and Warren Lee, traveled from the Bahamas to Yarrow in search of their grandfather. They discovered a burned-out shack. Uncommunicative neighbours merely confirmed that Yee Fong was dead and advised them to go to the authorities. In 1976, the grandsons decided to try again. This time they were successful. They inquired at the post office, where the postmaster, Myrtle Kehler, directed them at once to Mary and Ed Froese, who had known Yee Fong well. The grandsons came bearing the news that Yuet Ying Lee Yee had managed to enter Canada in 1973 and that she was desperately ill in a Burnaby hospital. Heartbreakingly, she died the very next day, before Mary Froese was able to reach her.

Gravesite of Yee Fong, Carman United Church Cemetery: Grandson Louis Lee with Ed Froese.

Yuet Ying Lee Yee was given both Christian and Buddhist funeral services and was buried beside her husband in the Carman United Church Cemetery. They share a single tombstone. The family, says one witness, was "thankful that they were connected again. She came all this way, and she was laid to rest beside Yee Fong."[21] At the gravesite, incense was burned to ward off evil spirits, and duck was left behind to honour the dead. Fortuitously, and to the delight of the family, Yee Fong had been buried facing the rising sun. This "mild" and "distinguished gentleman,"[22] who lived in obscurity and apart from his wife, leaves behind grandchildren and great-grandchildren, who now reside in the Lower Mainland of British Columbia. And the bamboo that he planted near the Vedder River still flourishes.

Special acknowledgments to Louis Lee, who honoured his grandfather by telling his story, and to Mary and Ed Froese, who still speak of their friend with fondness.

Yarrow's War Dead

By Harold J. Dyck

They shall not grow old, as we that are left grow old:
Age shall not weary them, nor the years condemn.
At the going down of the sun and in the morning
We will remember them.
Laurence Binyon, "For the Fallen"

Sixty-six of Yarrow's young people served in Canada's armed forces during the Second World War; more than 40 were posted overseas; four died and did not return home:

Trooper Douglas M. Rexford
8th Reconnaissance Regiment

Private Norville Nowell
Seaforth Highlanders of Canada

Corporal Abe Wittenberg
Loyal Edmonton Regiment

Private Rudolf Goetz
Royal Canadian Army Medical Corps

These four are at rest in cemeteries close to where they died, in England, Italy, and Holland. Norville Nowell and Abe Wittenberg were infantrymen, Rudy Goetz was a stretcher-bearer, and Doug Rexford a dispatch driver.

By any measure these men were ordinary. They had little more than an elementary school education; they were marginal members of their community before the war; none achieved high rank in the military; and none received medals for bravery or heroism while they were still alive. But they served their country, patrolling England's historic Sussex coast, logging in Scotland's northern forests, carrying the dead and wounded off numerous battlefields from St. Pierre-Sur-Dives in France to Xanten, Germany, and fighting for the ridges, towns, and valleys from Sicily's Costa Dell' Ambra to Ravenna in Italy. Three of the four saw battlefields carpeted with human bodies and landscapes turned into grotesque and silent images of destruction after a battle. The infantrymen fought hand-to-hand and house-to-house battles; the Medical Corps' stretcher-bearer ran across spaces unprotected from enemy fire to try to save wounded fellow soldiers.

Like most of their comrades, many of Yarrow's soldiers undoubtedly had dreams of an end to the war and fervent hopes of returning home to see their parents, siblings, and friends. Four were not granted this privilege. They deserve a firm place in our "community of memory."

In Memoriam

On a visit to his sister in Edmonton in October 1939, a month after Canada had declared war on Germany, Douglas Milton Rexford presented himself at the Edmonton Armories and enlisted in the Loyal Edmonton Regiment. He was the first from Yarrow to join Canada's

Canadian War Cemetery, Ravenna, Italy. One of two Yarrow soldiers killed in Italy lies buried here.

armed forces during the Second World War. But Doug was back home for Christmas that year, discharged for being underage. His father, Roy, believing his fourth of seven children too young for military duty, had informed the army of his son's true age, 16. Within another two months, however, the persistent and adventuresome young Rexford had persuaded his father to allow him to rejoin the military. On March 11, 1940, Doug was back in uniform, still under the required age for military duty.

The Rexfords were an old Fraser Valley family. Roy had grown up in the Vedder River flats alongside Vedder Mountain. After marrying, he and his wife, Daisy, had made their home in Mission, B.C. In 1932, they moved to the family farm at the corner of Lumsden and Vedder Mountain roads, just east of the new Mennonite settlement of Yarrow. Here they were again close to friends on Majuba Hill and at Vedder Crossing; Roy was able to fish, hunt, and operate his trap line close to Chilliwack Lake, and the children attended the Sardis Elementary School. It was evident to the new Yarrow settlers who passed the Rexford farmstead on their occasional trips to Sardis or Chilliwack that Roy and Daisy kept their yard tidy, their orchard well-cultivated, and their house and barns neatly painted.

Doug's elementary school chums remember him "for his red hair and outgoing personality ... friendly, easygoing, and fearless; a rascal, a daredevil, and a tease; and as a young man who wanted to experience everything."[1] An avid outdoorsman, he dropped out of school after grade eight and took full-time work at Eddie's Nurseries in nearby Greendale. His salary was sometimes partly paid with fruit-tree saplings, and, until a few years ago, some of the mature trees that these saplings became still stood in what was once the Rexfords' orchard.

Doug celebrated his 17th birthday at home, a few weeks late. He had been posted overseas and was home on furlough. From Yarrow, he traveled across Canada by train to the east coast to board a ship to Britain. He landed in England on June 28, 1940, just after France fell to the Germans, when the German air force was stepping up its bombing campaign against British cities. He was, reportedly, a member of the Seaforth Highlanders of Canada, and a photograph of him from that time[2] shows him in a Highlander uniform with a soldier's balmoral bonnet that proudly sets off the square of the Mackenzie tartan. His carefully trimmed, thin-line moustache contributes to his suave appearance, and his long, handsome jaw lines give him a more mature appearance than his 17 years. Curiously, there is no record of his service to the Highlanders in the archives of that infantry brigade, nor does his name appear on its comprehensive nominal roll. He may have served in the 72nd Seaforth Highlander Cadet Brigade for a few months, a service that would not have been registered in the annals of the Seaforth Highlanders Regiment. It is also possible that he was a member of another Highlander corps during his early military service. Much more certain is the record of his assignment to the 8th Reconnaissance Regiment once he arrived in England.[3]

The 8th Reconnaissance Regiment was part of the 2nd Canadian Infantry Division, which was being mobilized in early 1940 for service overseas. As the various units of this division arrived in Aldershot, southwest of London, they were immediately put to work on various large-scale military maneuvers, mock battles, exercises, and "schemes" on the assumption that Germany would invade England from across the English Channel. These activities led the troops to conclude that they would soon be properly equipped and engaged directly in the war. With the collapse of France, this conclusion was not without foundation.[4]

One can imagine the disappointment of someone like Doug Rexford, anxious for adventure, when the Canadian troops were put on reserve status. This status was maintained until the autumn of 1941, more than a year after Doug had arrived in England. The Canadian Corps was now assigned a tactical function—the defence of the coast of Sussex. If the Germans tried a land invasion of Britain, they would probably make the attempt in this sector. The corps, including young Rexford's regiment, now believed that they would have the opportunity, given their new role, location, and special training, to undertake raids on German-held beaches and towns across the channel. Instead, as the *War Diary* notes repeatedly, they were given further training—course after course in various matters related to the conduct of a war. Although sorely disappointed not to have a more active role in the war, the Canadians found the change in scenery from Aldershot to Sussex agreeable.

The duties of the 8th Reconnaissance Regiment, in which Doug's role was that of dispatch driver, were serious and real—to watch day and night for the enemy and discern his movements. Though being on watch was boring, Doug and his fellow troopers could observe the Battle of Britain. Night after night they would hear the drone and watch the swarms of German bombers emerge from the eastern horizon to unleash their destructive force on England's cities while the Royal Air Force engaged the enemy aircraft in dogfights. Occasionally this battle would become more than a spectator experience—when a German bomb smashed the Canadian regiment's mess hall or storage depot.

The level of activity of the 8th Reconnaissance Regiment diminished as it became clear that London and other British cities would not succumb to Germany's bombing. The *War Diary* of the regiment records no major events for the last several months of 1941, only weather reports and the words, "All is quiet." It was on one such "All-is-quiet" day that a regimental "Order," issued at 1730 hours, reported:

> K-53330 Tpr Rexford, D. M. s.o.s. to No. 1 C.A.C.H.U. on being admitted to Royal East Sussex Hospital w.e.f. 13 Dec. '4, [1941].[5]

This part of the diary, written late in the same day, includes the following entry: "An unfortunate accident occurred today when Tpr. Rexford crashed into a lorry and lost a leg. His condition is critical and he was taken to the Royal East Sussex Hospital in Hastings." Doug was riding a motorcycle and, according to one account, his accident took place during a blackout, and he actually lost both legs.[6] The regiment's *War Diary* entry for the next day announces simply: "Tpr Rexford died today as a result of injuries on the previous day. 14 Dec. '41 0600."

Trooper Douglas Milton Rexford was 18 years old, the first and youngest of Yarrow's soldiers to die. He is buried in the Brookwood Military Cemetery in Woking, Surrey, England.

* * *

The news of Doug Rexford's death came as a shock to the closely knit community of Majuba Hill-Vedder Flats. The grieving Rexford family must have been particularly anxious about their other son, Tom, who was also serving overseas. Other families with children in the armed forces, those of Gordon Cameron, Charles Sabo, and the Nowells, were doubtless dismayed when they heard the news of Doug's untimely death. Norman and Maud Nowell, neighbours to the Rexfords on Lumsden Road, had three children in the Canadian armed services by this time: sons Norville ("Bud") and Reuben in the army, and daughter Geraldine in the Royal Canadian Air Force—the first woman in the Chilliwack district to join the Armed Forces. A third son, George, would join up later. Any fears the Nowells harboured were warranted. Norville never came back; he was killed in Italy near the end of 1943 during what some Canadian military historians refer to as "Bloody December."

After dropping out of school, Norville had gone to work in a gold mine in Jonesville, B.C. His job was terminated, at least temporarily, when he was found guilty of burglary in 1938 and sentenced to a one-year jail term. On his release from the Young Offenders Unit in Oakalla Prison, he returned to mining. In 1940, during the Christmas holidays, he and a number of his friends, including his brother Reuben and Henry Fast from Yarrow—Fast's testimony was partly responsible for Norville's incarceration—traveled to New Westminster and enlisted in the Canadian Forestry Corps.

The Canadian authorities had arranged with Britain to provide 20 companies, each with 200 men, for the production of lumber needed for military purposes—for example, for the construction of barracks, hangars, storage depots, ships, and rafts. By late 1940, it was clear that ten additional companies would be needed for this work. Where better to recruit foresters than in British Columbia? The Yarrow boys were told that they would produce lumber, but they would also be trained as infantrymen.

In June 1941, after basic and infantry training, Norville and Reuben Nowell and Henry Fast were sent to work in the forests of Scotland. Here Norville learned to perform every task required in the self-contained community of 200 young men living in a forest—cooking, cleaning barracks, clearing snow, high rigging, doing laundry, cutting bush and trees, and all manner of construction. So when the opportunity arose to transfer to a fighting unit of the military (the Forestry Corps was being reduced in strength by ten companies), Norville jumped at the chance. On June 4, 1943, after two years of service in the Forestry Corps, he joined the Seaforth Highlanders of Canada, an infantry brigade of the 1st Canadian Infantry Division. The Highlanders, one of several brigades stationed in Hamilton, Scotland, were training for the so-called "African" campaign.

On June 15, the battalion boarded the HMT *Circassia*. The next day the ship was loaded with cargo of "tons after tons of mortar bombs, Bangalores, S.A.A. [small arms ammunition]," notes the officer who wrote the Intelligence Report. "The coming exercise will be the noisiest the [Battalion] has yet experienced." Much to the dismay of the troops, the ship lay at anchor for another two weeks. Mid-morning on the 29th of June, an announcement was read over the ship's public address system: "A signal has been received from the Admiralty. It reads 'You are going to the Mediterranean to take part in the biggest combined operation the world has ever seen.' "[7]

Here was Norville, a kid from Yarrow's Vedder River Flats, now a member of a distinguished battalion sailing for the Mediterranean and about to take part in what could be an historic military campaign, the largest such operation in the history of warfare. One can imagine the feelings Norville's father, now the reeve of Chilliwack Township, would have experienced had he known about his son's mission, but all information about the operation was censored.

By July 7, the Allied armada of hundreds of ships reached the North African coast. The heat was oppressive, and sleeping below deck was almost impossible. German submarines were lurking in the depths of the Mediterranean, gathering intelligence on the movements of the armada. The Highlanders' diarist wrote, "The presence of enemy U-boats caused a 'little flutter' for some of the allied troops in the armada. No damage." What caused the real excitement among the troops was the news that their destination was Sicily. They would finally engage the enemy. Some had waited for three years for this moment. On July 9, as the Allied armada was drawing closer to Sicily, a gale-force storm struck during the night, tossing smaller ships around "like corks" according to the *War Diary*. "We would like to fight Germans, not Father Neptune," was the wry comment of the diarist. However, by midday the storm was over and the sea calm. The landing on the Costa Dell' Ambra took place on schedule with little opposition from the enemy.[8]

The assignment of the Canadian troops was to take control of the heart of Sicily: Caltagirone, Piazza Armerina, Leonforte, Nicosia, Agira, and Regalbuto. This meant clearing out tens of thousands of German and Italian troops. For 38 days, the Canadians fought a stubborn enemy, climbing the Sicilian hills in the intense summer heat and marching dusty roads from town to town only to fight again. Often the troops moved forward at night to avoid the heat, but in danger of enemy snipers. After a long march, the men, caked with limestone dust and sweat, usually had nowhere to bathe. A few weeks of fierce battles and marches of up to 30 miles a day meant that they began to suffer exhaustion. In a letter home, Norville revealed, "I never thought a man could march so far on two hours sleep and one meal a day, but you never even worry about it until they give you a couple days rest, then you can certainly sleep."[9]

The weeks in Sicily gave the Canadian troops an introduction to the perils and miseries of waging war in Italy, but they had yet to move through a number of formidable lines of defence established by the

German and Italian forces on the mainland: the Bernhard Line about a third of the way up the Italian boot; the Gustav and Hitler lines in the Liri Valley; the Caesar Line intended to protect Rome; and the redoubtable German defenses on the Lombard Plain. It would be another 18 months before the Seaforth Highlanders and the other Canadian regiments would leave Italy. Norville Nowell and 5,789 other Canadians would not be among them.

Rains and mists came with autumn. The Canadians pushed northward up the centre of the Italian peninsula to Potenza, and up to Campobasso and Colle d'Anchise. With each passing mile, the German resistance became stiffer.

A major military operation awaited them at the Bernhard Line. Breaching this line on its Adriatic side required three weeks of fighting as bitter "as any to be found in the long grim chronicle of this war ... the bitterest and costliest the 1st Division had yet experienced. ..."[10] Beginning on the night of November 28, the Allied forces began to fight their way across the Sangro River. By December 6, the Seaforth Highlanders found themselves at the gates of San Leonardo. At great cost in Canadian lives during the next several days of house-to-house fighting, San Leonardo was cleared.

The next military objective was to push the German troops back from the road to Ortona. This meant first clearing a valley beyond San Leonardo which lifted to a ridge that supported the main road. The Gully, as it became known, had formidable bluffs on its seaward side and moderate contours farther inland. It was heavily fortified by the Germans. The fields around The Gully and its ridges and contours were mined and booby-trapped, and rain had softened the ploughed soil, making it difficult for tanks to maneuver and tortuous for troops to move. "The landscape was bare, with an occasional battered stone farmhouse and its usual small orchard of gnarled naked olive trees, worthless for cover, and the usual straggle of vine poles and wires, a curse to men laden with arms and equipment and moving in the dark."[11]

The German Panzer Grenadiers had dug deep shelters on the near side of The Gully where they were largely safe from bombardments by artillery. When a company of Canadians scaled the ridge, German gunners rose out of the earth, almost magically, unloaded their fire, and disappeared again into their bunkers. By December 11, it was clear to the Canadians that there would be no easy way to penetrate the enemy's defences. Yet on this day, the Seaforths, already greatly reduced in strength by the fighting of previous days, were ordered to seize the western ridge of The Gully. The fighting was ferocious, unrelenting small-arms and mortar fire keeping the Seaforths in their soft, muddy slit trenches. The fields reeked of cordite and death. With the backup assistance of a tank regiment, the Seaforths took the ridge shortly after midnight.

Private Norville Nowell died in this battle for the ridge, on December 11, 1943. How he was killed—whether by an exploding mine, machine-gun fire, or shrapnel from an enemy shell—is unknown. While he was engaged in battle, perhaps at the very time that he lay dying in the mud, his mother and father were at home, on Lumsden Road in Yarrow, offering special prayers for him and toasting his 23rd birthday.[12]

Norville's name is listed in the nominal roll of the regiment. He was a plain boy from Yarrow doing the dirty work of war. He is buried in the Canadian War Cemetery in Ortona, Italy, along with dozens of his fellow Highlanders killed during that dreadful week in December 1943.

* * *

In addition to Norville Nowell, Yarrow had four more of its young men (there may have been more) in the Italian campaign: Mrs. Elizabeth Wiens' three sons, Henry, John, and Victor, and Abraham Wittenberg, son of Abram and Katherine Wittenberg.[13] Abe died of wounds he sustained on December 13, 1944, a year and two days after Norville Nowell met his fate. Like Nowell, Abe belonged to the 2nd Infantry Brigade, which included both the Seaforth Highlanders and the Loyal Edmonton Regiment. Abe served in the latter.

Abe was born on August 1, 1919, into a Mennonite family in Gnadenheim, Slavgorod District, Siberia. In 1925, the family immigrated to Canada and settled in Drake, Saskatchewan. Within a year or two, they relocated to Winnipeg, where Abe attended school. He left school in 1935 when the Wittenbergs moved to Yarrow, settling in a house on Central Road close to Boundary Road. Like most Mennonite young people whose parents had emigrated from Russia, he immediately sought work after quitting school in order to help support the family. Initially, he found employment in the hopyards near Yarrow and in a variety of other seasonal jobs. Though required to work long hours, he always had time to develop his athletic skills, and he became a formidable softball pitcher.

In 1942, Abe, his brother Jacob, and their friend Jacob Wiebe were employed by Mackenzie Barge and Derrick in Vancouver. For no particular reason that Jake Wittenberg can now remember, except, perhaps, desire for adventure, the three young men decided to enlist in the Canadian Army. "We just went to the Little Mountain Army recruiting offices and joined up."[14] They enlisted on February 5, 1943. This act was hardly unusual for draft-age Mennonite men of Yarrow. During the war, the majority of them joined the fighting forces.

But the Wittenberg brothers and Jake Wiebe had decided to join the infantry, not the Medical Corps. Their choice would have been questioned by the leadership of the Yarrow Mennonite Brethren Church, the congregation to which the Wittenberg and Wiebe families belonged, because the ministerial leadership appealed to its members to encourage their sons to register as conscientious objectors. They should seize the opportunity afforded by the Government of Canada to perform alternative service, mainly in forestry and agriculture. Failing that, the church council insisted, they should be encouraged to enlist in the special Medical Corps in which they would be exempted from bearing arms. Despite the church community's advice and pleading, more than two-thirds of the young Mennonite men from Yarrow who entered military service joined one or another of the combatant services. As Abe's brother Jake explained, "We weren't thinking about the church much at that time. Conscientious objection? We just weren't involved in that kind of thing then."[15]

Abe and Jake and Jake Wiebe reported to Vernon for their basic training and, after three months, were transferred to Currie Barracks, Calgary, for more advanced infantry training. In August of 1943, six months after enlisting, they sailed to England on the *Queen Mary* and were stationed in Aldershot. In less than a month, Abe was posted for active duty in "Africa," seemingly a code name for the Allied invasion of Italy. His brother Jake received the same orders. Just before he was to leave for the Mediterranean, Jake was notified that he would be stationed on one of the Channel Islands. In September, Abe left for his assignment with the Loyal Edmonton Regiment (the "Eddies") of the 1st Canadian Infantry Division.[16]

It appears that Abe joined the Eddies in southern Italy, in Catanzaro or Crotone, or later in Potenza, after the campaign in Sicily had been completed. It is entirely possible that he and Norville Nowell, both from Yarrow, met that autumn and chatted about their war experiences and home as their respective battalions, the Eddies and the Seaforth Highlanders, were camped beside each other. The two units had participated in many of the same military maneuvers and fought side by side in the same battles in the Italian campaign.

Norville did not celebrate Christmas that year, and Abe may have had his Christmas in a military hospital. At some point (it is unclear when or where), he was wounded, although the wounds were not serious enough to send him back to England or Canada. He recovered and, as a corporal and seasoned infantryman, rejoined the Loyal Edmonton Regiment by December 1944, in time for the battle of the Canale Naviglio, close to Ravenna.

On December 11 and 12, the Eddies were camped about a mile east of the Canale Naviglio. Abe's unit had struck across the Lamone River on the moonless night of the 10th. The German forces, meanwhile, seeing the advance of the Canadian infantry regiments, withdrew behind the banks of the canal. During the evening and night of December 12, several Canadian regiments made a determined effort to clear a part of the far side of the canal north of the town of Bagnacavallo. On the other side, regiments would be up against perpendicular, 20-foot-high flood banks. However, the bed of the canal was not flooded, and one of the Canadian units proceeded to cross over to the north side. Within several hours, the Canadian bridgehead was more than 1,000 yards wide and 700 yards deep. But with dawn, the German divisions counterattacked in full force with tanks and infantry to take back the bridgehead. By noon, the Canadian regiments trying to keep this bridgehead were in trouble.

The bridgehead had to be saved if Ravenna was to be taken, and this task was given to the Loyal Edmonton Regiment. At 1600 hours, with the gloom of the cold evening settling on the canal, the Eddies began their advance. German tanks and self-propelled guns roamed the area. Gunfire shattered the gloaming, and "Long strings of tracers slit the darkness, followed by a series of detonating Jerry potato-masher grenades, the eye-blinking pinpoints of flame scarring the ground mists. ... The slow, rhythmic thump-thump-thump of a Bren gun, spouting incendiaries, sprayed the faint outline of the dyke, followed by the intermittent harsh crack of our own 36 grenades."[17]

According to the battalion's *War Diary*, as the Eddies took up their positions, they were hindered by fire from three roadhouses along the canal. They managed to take the first two houses without much difficulty, but they suffered casualties attempting to capture the third. "An enemy sniper was behind the third house and firing on B Coy [company]."[18]

Hours later the third house was finally cleared, but German troops still held positions between the second and third houses. These were finally cleared by 2215 hours.

Abe Wittenberg was involved in a house-to-house battle when he was wounded.[19] Sometime during the evening he and the men in his unit were probably ordered to enter one of the enemy-occupied roadhouses (most likely the third one) in an effort to clear it. As corporal (leader of the group), he would have entered the house first, and was met with enemy fire to his legs. As he fell forward, he was strafed across the chest. He died sometime thereafter, but exactly where and at what time we can only speculate. He was the only one of the Loyal Edmonton Regiment to die on December 13, but the 301st of the regiment to die in Italy since it had landed on the Costa Dell' Ambra a year and a half before.

The Wittenberg family was notified of the death of their eldest child a few days before Christmas. For Abe's parents and siblings, that Christmas celebration was turned to mourning.

Cpl. Abraham Wittenberg lies in the Canadian War Cemetery in Ravenna, Italy.

* * *

Rudy Goetz was, by all accounts, a personable and devout young man. Like Abe Wittenberg, he was born in Russia of Mennonite parents, on March 10, 1921. An only child, he came to Canada with his father and mother, Gerhard and Anna Goetz, in 1924. After living in Dalmeny, Saskatchewan, for about a decade, the family moved to Yarrow in the mid-1930s, settling on Eckert Road near Central Road. Here Rudy's father was able to take up his profession as a veterinarian. Rudy, having dropped out of public school at age 15, worked at various seasonal jobs. During the winter months, he continued his education in the Elim Bible School, graduating in 1941.

Rudy had a reputation for boxing. He was fast, wiry, and relatively short—the perfect build for a welterweight. In their small barn, he and his father built what was perhaps the only boxing and wrestling ring that Yarrow ever had. Here Rudy would take on all comers. At wrestling he could be beaten; in boxing he always had the upper hand, even against much bigger and stronger opponents.[20]

Rudy enlisted in the Royal Canadian Army Medical Corps on December 12, 1943, part of a rush between December 1943 and January 1944 of military-aged Yarrow men to join the Medical Corps. Eleven of the 17 Yarrow recruits to the Medical Corps joined during those two months. These enlistees, including Rudy, declared to the military recruitment and selection boards their conscientious objection to war. Mennonite young men who made such a declaration were usually granted their petition to serve in the non-combatant Medical Corps and, after September 1943, conscientious objectors like Rudy were no longer required to train with weapons.

Rudy received his basic training in Trenton, Ontario. Here, he and the other boys from Yarrow were grouped in Medical Corps units with other enlisted conscientious objectors to war—Quakers, Jehovah's Witnesses, Plymouth Brethren, and a number of Mennonites from across Canada. To the great amusement of some officers and taunting soldiers from the infantry units, these "conchies" used stretchers instead of guns in their basic training routines.[21] After completing basic training, Rudy and his fellow Medical Corps enlistees were transferred to Camp Borden, also in Ontario, for their medical training. In May 1944, before he was scheduled to go overseas, he was given furlough, which he spent in Yarrow with his parents and friends. He departed for Britain on June 25.

By the time Rudy arrived at his overseas destination, the 11th Field Ambulance had been serving various regiments in France since D-day (June 6, 1944) on the beaches, cliffs, and hedgerows of Normandy. After two months of intense fighting, the 11th desperately needed reinforcements. It was not unusual to transfer men from one unit to another according to need, and among the unit's Daily Orders dated August 16, 1944, is the following: "Strength—Increase/ Pte Goetz, R. TOS from #12 Bn 2 CBRG wef 16 Aug. 44."[22] Rudy had been transferred from the 12th Battalion to the 11th Ambulance, joining his new unit in Saint-Pierre-sur-Dives, France. His assignment: stretcher-bearer.

Undoubtedly, he was happy to meet young men with names like Funk, Tessman, Wiebe, and Jantzen, who were already members of the unit. Their backgrounds were similar to his, most of them having grown up in Christian homes and in Mennonite communities. These were young men with whom he could participate in Bible study and prayer meetings. They would be able to laugh together at the in-group ethnic jokes they told in Low German when they were alone. They could share news from back home, from Winkler, Manitoba, Glenbush, Saskatchewan, and Yarrow. When the news was good, their spirits soared, and when it was bad, they supported each other.

For several weeks after Rudy joined it, the 11th Field Ambulance was on the move every two or three days due to the rapid advances of the 1st Canadian Army to the north, in the direction of Belgium and Holland. During Rudy's first two weeks, the 11th Ambulance moved five times, from Saint-Pierre-sur-Dives to Falaise to Orbec to Brionne and on to Dieppe. During this time, in addition to adapting himself to the procedures of his new unit and to the new military and physical environments, he would have carried wounded and dead civilians from the dwellings bombed by the Germans in Falaise. He would have struggled with fatigue and grime in his efforts to take the wounded, shellshocked, and dead off the battlefields in the Falaise Gap. He would have carried the wounded on the run to the advance dressing station. The Gap, a 12-mile-wide natural bottleneck just outside of Falaise where the German and Allied Forces met head on, was literally layered in places with dead and wounded soldiers during a battle that raged from August 19 to 21. His quite sudden introduction to the horrors of war must have been overwhelming.

Goetz may well have administered first aid to German POWs at Brionne. Given his beliefs, he would not have defined them as enemies. He may have engaged captured German troops in conversation in their own language, which had been his before he developed proficiency in English. He may have served as translator for his commanders and for doctors in his unit who were treating the German wounded.

From Dieppe, where the 11th Field Ambulance was camped on September 1, the unit traveled up the coastline to Dunkirk, crossing the France-Belgium border at Dixmude, moving on to Ostend, and arriving in Antwerp on the 17th. From Antwerp, the 11th served various infantry units trying to clear the Germans out of the Schelde and South and North Beveland, and to free the city's port for the transport of military supplies. With this military objective accomplished by early November, Rudy's unit was relocated to Groesbeek and Nijmegen in Holland. Here it remained until the major Allied offensive into the Rhineland in early February 1945.

At times, the operation was hampered more by weather than by German troops. The sudden thaw and flooding that year reduced most roads to corridors of mud. The various German Panzer divisions were well dug in and had had ample time to fortify their positions, particularly in the forests southeast of Nijmegen. The Canadian divisions (2nd, 3rd, and 4th Armoured) moved toward the Rhine and the famous

Siegfried Line through the city of Kleve to the north of the Reichswald. On February 16, the 11th Field Hospital was able to establish the first advanced dressing station on German soil, in Kleve. It would take another three weeks, however, before the Canadians took Xanten, the birthplace of the legendary Siegfried, and then only after suffering large numbers of casualties.

By March 6, the Hochwald and the Balberger Wald were clear. Another two days of strenuous battle by both Canadian and British troops were required to secure Xanten and its south ridge facing the German town of Wesel and the Rhine River. There was heavy shelling on March 7, and the 11th Field Ambulance lost several of its personnel—an ambulance driver among them.[23] On March 8, the ambulance unit was overwhelmed by 160 casualties from the brigade to which it was assigned.

Hour after hour Goetz and his fellow medical corpsmen heard the howl of shells from a distance, listened as some howls turned into shrieks, and took note of how far away the shells were exploding. On hearing a shell fired in the distance, infantrymen and stretcher-bearers alike threw themselves down, clutched the ground, crawled toward slit trenches if there were any nearby, and took the explosions with bodies pressed to the earth. Between volleys of incoming shells, their call came, "Stretcher-bearer, stretcher-bearer, over here." And responding to the call, the stretcher-bearers would make their way to the wounded, over and under the retreating enemy's barbed wire, through water and mud, over the bodies of soldiers, some dead, some alive, some in a stupor of shell-shock, some praying, and others crying for their mothers.

Each stretcher-bearer had a limited supply of medical items—bandages, sulpha, and morphine. When these ran out, he had to make do with whatever was available to deal with gaping wounds, missing limbs, or blood spurting from holes in the chest. Half-rotten leaves were used to try to close a bleeding wound; clothing was taken from the dead to blanket the wounded or was torn into strips for bandaging. For those wounded who were conscious, there was often an encouraging word from stretcher-bearers. And if there was time, Rudy would undoubtedly have tried to calm a young soldier screaming with glazed eyes to drown out the eerie sounds of the shelling.

By March 9, after the month-long battle for the Rhineland, in which over 5,000 Canadians were killed or wounded, the troops were exhausted. Stretcher-bearers, drivers, and medical officers had been on duty around the clock, sometimes for 36 consecutive hours. These men, including Rudy Goetz, were required to stay out in the field. They were cold, wet, dirty, and desperate for sleep, sleeping when and where they could, always with their clothes and boots on. Their joints were stiff and painful; their voices hoarse; their brains dull and insensitive. Even fears and anxieties were suppressed for lack of sleep.

By March 9, enemy weapons' fire in the Xanten area was spasmodic. Occasionally there were volleys of muffled thumps at a distance or the rat-tat-tat of machine gun fire, and sometimes the air still erupted with the screech of shells and loud explosions. Then all was quiet again. On this day, the frantic call for a stretcher-bearer was seldom heard, but after a sudden volley of shells, one stretcher-bearer was calling for help for another. Rudy Goetz had been hit.

In the 11th Field Ambulance's operations centre, Major Barney Bucove hurriedly scribbled a message to his superiors dated 09 at 1730 hours: "Cliff was in about an hour ago and informed us that Pte Goetz bad." An entry written later that day, records the following:

> Germany 9 Mar 45
> MR055413
> Sheet Xanten
> Cool cloudy day. Fairly quiet during the night. … Pte Goetz, R. and Pte Sauve, R. A. have both been killed in action while acting as S. Bs [stretcher-bearers] with the Infantry Regiments. Things are quiet this evening.[24]

A German shell had exploded close to where Rudy, Frank Sawatsky, his friend from Yarrow and fellow Bible-school student, and a non-commissioned officer were resting. Assuming the immediate area to be safe, they had apparently decided to nap under a demobilized German tank, a shelter from weather and mortar fire. The shell landed closest to Rudy, exploded, and wounded him fatally. Shrapnel injured the sergeant and hit Frank Sawatsky as well. Frank was hit in the chest, but was not injured. The shrapnel ripped his jacket and penetrated the New Testament he always carried in his vest pocket. Miraculously, it did not enter his chest. Rudy lay there near death,[25] and he was delivered to the regimental aid station with major wounds to his stomach.[26] There is no mention in the documents of the 11th Field Ambulance of the circumstances of Rudy's death. Exactly how Rudy Goetz died can only be imagined.

On the following day, the personnel of the 11th Field Ambulance were notified of his death in the Daily Orders:

K1553 Pte Goetz, R SOS deceased—Killed by enemy action.[27]

That day, March 10, 1945, would have been Rudy Goetz's 24th birthday. According to the War Diary, it was a quiet, cold, and dreary Saturday.

The announcement of their son's death reached the Goetz home in Yarrow two weeks later, and a memorial service for Rudy was held on April 2 in the Yarrow Mennonite Brethren Church.

The war in Europe ended a month later.

Rudy is buried in the Groesbeek Canadian War Cemetery at Nijmegen in the Netherlands. The inscription on the marker for his grave is succinct:

Goetz, Pte. Rudolf, K/1553.
11 Field Amb. R.C.A.M.C.
8th March 1945. III. H. 10

* * *

War meant something different to each of these four young men—as they enlisted, underwent training and indoctrination, waited to join battles, fought in their various ways in the face of the "enemy," and then passed through the moments from suffering a mortal wound to slipping from this life. What did war mean to the conscientious objector struggling to bring the Medical Corps' humanity to the killing fields? To the boy who was so anxious to serve in the military that he lied about his age, was decommissioned, and enlisted again before he was 18? What did war mean to the youth

Anne Ratzlaff at cousin Abe Wittenberg's grave, Ravenna, Italy. She received a letter from Wittenberg after his family had been notified of his death.

who had laboured in gold mines with other men, served a term in prison, worked in the forests of Scotland, and fought for five months in a land entirely foreign to him, yet in the end his resting place? And what did war mean to the handsome young infantryman from a gentle and loving home, brought up in a Mennonite church, popular in the Yarrow community and eligible for conscientious objector status had he desired it?

These men did not have an opportunity to grow old. Their lives left few traces in their community. They left no widows behind, no children. Of those they did leave—parents, siblings, lovers, close friends —few now remain. For us, these war dead remain forever the age of their last photograph. And those few still living who knew one or another of the four remember only fragments of the way they were in life. These fragments are the "pleasant voices, the Nightingales" that time, not death, will take.

I would like to express my gratitude to Marlene Sawatsky for her valuable suggestions on the stories presented here. This text is an abridged version of the original.

Conclusion: So Close, So Far Away

By Leonard Neufeldt

Early Yarrow remembers her own like a mother's body, whether they are still there in familiar sites, have taken their place in the row-upon-row chronology of graves in the Yarrow Cemetery, have retired and died elsewhere, or left years ago for careers that Yarrow could imagine but not provide. The deep lines and folds of Yarrow's former life have not vanished as swiftly as the traces of Yarrow's war dead buried in cemeteries overseas. Since rent was cheap in Yarrow in the 1960s, '70s, and '80s, a number of people seeking low-cost housing, including talented artists of several kinds, were attracted to it. For some of them, and no doubt in some of the expensive new homes on Majuba Hill,

Yarrow Cemetery as it appears today.

Susie Derksen and Mary Froese in Yarrow Cemetery. They have led the effort to renovate this graveyard.

history is what happened five days or five years ago. This is hardly surprising, since so much of our contemporary culture focuses relentlessly on the present and a future oblivious to what once happened.

Nonetheless, we still have more than just fragments of the Mennonite centre Yarrow once was and the heritage its pioneers brought with them. Most of the old streets have retained their names, and few new streets have been added. The large slab of concrete that marks the site of the former Co-op store has been weathering for years as weeds and grasses fill its chinks and cracks. Several of the local businesses that once flourished remain, although under new ownership. There are two notable exceptions: "M Hank's" barbershop is still an informal centre for history and old friendships, and Nickolai Reimer's grandsons run Reimer's Nurseries. The two Mennonite churches continue to serve their parishioners, but they are eclipsed today by the much more contemporary church building belonging to the Christian and Missionary Alliance and the recently completed church of the Dutch Reformed denomination. Several canneries have vanished; the Sun-Ripe cannery has been turned into a pottery and ceramics business. The former elementary school property has been transformed into an attractive three-acre park. There is a historical marker where early settlers went for their mail or to catch the rail tram to Sardis or Chilliwack. Susie Derksen and Mary Froese have spearheaded a major effort to renovate the Yarrow

Cemetery. There are a few surviving pioneers in Yarrow and they, like most of the children of pioneers who stayed, live in fine houses, some on Majuba Hill overlooking a valley that is rapidly urbanizing.

If one stands on the dyke just before dusk, one can still hear the Vedder River flowing over river rock deposited by the last ice age and worn smooth since then. Here the feelings of being both insider and remote outsider become one. To the south, Vedder Mountain, logged in several stages, offers a familiar outline, its clear-cut areas now filled with green. "Study this," the wordless evening world between river and mountain seems to entreat. This village was wondrous in that its frailty was the source of its urgency. Here, in this temperate place, many of our parents sought to bracket off not nature, old learning, new knowledge, technology, and economic advancement per se, but the way of life of cultures around them. Here, years ago, we spoke of the future in an inflated way, as a heroic frame, perhaps partly to avoid noticing that so much of our vision and perseverance would go for everything, and also for naught.

Nothing validates us more than our history; nothing humbles us more than history. And writing one's history is not like rebuilding the old home until it is a perfect copy of what it once was. Sometimes our chronicles may seem to be that, but in reality, the task of trying to recount what Yarrow was is often more like painstakingly cleaning out

Yarrow from the site where the ashes of Elizabeth Goosen Menges are buried on Vedder Mountain.

a house until familiar rooms begin to grow large with empty space and to echo when you step into them. That's a sound one doesn't forget. But there's another kind of sound in these two volumes, one much more obvious to readers. Taken together, the contributors of essays have written not simply about themselves or on behalf of themselves: they have written about and for others and about a time and place inexorably growing more remote. In doing so, they have become ventriloquists, giving a voice to aspects of a particular past that really happened but cannot speak for itself.

To the extent that our study is historical, *Before We Were the Land's* and *Village of Unsettled Yearnings* are such a narrative. We have asked the past to speak from memoirs, family papers, our memories, others' recollections, community albums, newspaper accounts, published and unpublished historical, sociological, and religious studies, and records of many kinds in small and large archives across Canada. We have tried to listen to what these various sources are telling us, but we have also put questions to them, aware that the past has words but no voice. Here and there, even the words have been supplied by us. And, in the words of Frances Mayes in *Under the Tuscan Sun*, "We can walk here, the latest little dots on the time line." We have spoken for a past that the reader will recognize as very close to us, even though it may also be far away.

Giving voice to the past has always been, and will always be, governed more by relation to what happened than by the span of time that separates us from it. We sincerely hope that our attempt to speak for the past confirms our respect for the cultural moment created by the settling of Yarrow, British Columbia.

Endnotes

RITES OF DYING, DEATH, AND BURIAL

1. "Death and Dying," *Canadian Mennonite Encyclopedia Online.*
2. Edith Knox, interview, 4 Oct. 2000.
3. M.K. Neufeld, "My Grandmother was an Undertaker," 2.
4. *Zionsbote*, 23 Mar. 1949, 12; *Mennonitische Rundschau*, 13 Apr. 1949, 1.
5. Ibid.

MIDWIFERY: A MINISTRY

1. Jacob Sawatzky, "Ein Familien Register," n.p.
2. "Biographical Sketch: Thielman," p 1; see also Thielman, *Book About Gynecology*, n.p.
3. Friesen, *Mennonite Brotherhood*, 815-20.
4. Derksen Siemens, E-Mail Communication, 26 Mar. 2001.
5. Bergen, "Dr. Katherina Born Thiessen," 8; Bergen, interview, 23 Mar. 2002.
6. M. Neufeldt, interview by Epp, 9 Nov. 2000.
7. Lillian Harms, "Biographical Recollections," 1; J. Martens, interview.
8. Halseth, "Mrs Kipp," n.p.
9. Young, et al., "Medical History," n.p.
10. Denman, "A Victorian Love," n.p.
11. Young, et al., "Medical History," n.p.; S. Martens, interview by Sawatsky, 9 Apr. 2002; M. Neufeldt, interview by Sawatsky, 8 Apr. 2002.
12. Fretz, "Recent Mennonite Community Building," 16.
13. Lena Neufeld, interview.
14. Agatha Klassen, interview by Sawatsky, 4 June 2001; S. Derksen, interview by Sawatsky, 3 Aug. 2000.
15. Agatha Klassen, interview, ibid.
16. Johnstone-Langton, interview by Klassen; Nightingale, interview; E. Giesbrecht, interview.
17. Derksen Siemens, E-Mail Communication, 20 Dec. 2000.
18. Hildebrandt, interview.
19. S. Derksen, interview by Sawatsky, 3 July 2000.
20. Lillian Harms, "Biographical Recollections," 1; "Elizabeth Harms" [obituary], *Mennonitische Rundschau*, 24 Aug. 1983, 26.
21. Lillian Harms, "Biographical Recollections," 1-2.
22. Ibid.; Elizabeth Harms, Diploma.
23. Schroeder, *Miracles of Grace*, 46-56.
24. "Elizabeth Harms" [obituary], *Mennonitische Rundschau*, 24 Aug. 1983, 26.
25. Ibid.
26. Heinrich Harms, *Journal*, n.p.
27. Lillian Harms, "Biographical Recollections," 3.
28. Heinrich Harms, *Journal*, n.p.
29. Lillian Harms, "Biographical Recollections," 4.
30. Heinrich Harms, *Journal*, n.p.
31. Lillian Harms, "Biographical Recollections," 4-5 (expanded by authorial addition).
32. "Funeral Service of Elizabeth. Harms."
33. M. Froese, interview by Sawatsky, 23 Jan. 2001; Lillian Harms, "Biographical Recollections," 6.
34. Lillian Harms, ibid.
35. Lillian Harms, "Lebensverzeichnis," 2.

36. Margaret Neufeldt, Written Recollections: Margaretha Enns, 1996, 3; 1999, 1.
37. Ibid.; K. Durksen, interview.
38. Sarah Martens, Written Recollections, 2.
39. Schroeder and Huebert, *Mennonite Historical Atlas*, 134.
40. "Margaretha Enns" [obituary], *Mennonitische Rundschau*, 30 Mar. 1977, 12.
41. Sarah Martens, Written Recollections, 2.
42. *Yarrow M.B. Church, Family Register*, n.p.
43. Schroeder and Huebert, *Mennonite Historical Atlas*, 132.
44. Margaret Neufeldt, Written Recollections: Margaretha Enns, 1996, 3-4.
45. Ibid., 1999, 1.
46. S. Martens, interview by Sawatsky, 10 Apr. 2002; M. Neufeldt, interview by Epp, 14 Nov. 2000.
47. G. and H. Enns, interview, 10 Apr. 2002.

LIVING EAST OF EDEN

1. Agatha Klassen, *Yarrow*, 19.
2. *Chilliwack Progress*, 10 June 1958, B1.
3. Ibid., 19 Apr. 1905.
4. Ibid., 23 Feb. 1938, B1.
5. B. Schmidt, interview.
6. Steinson, *Community Events Timeline*, 60.
7. J. Loewen, interview by Giesbrecht.
8. B. Schmidt, interview.

THE EARLY YEARS OF THE MENNONITE BRETHREN CHURCH

1. Agatha Klassen, *Yarrow*, 80.
2. Esau, *Memoirs of Abram J. Esau*, 24.
3. *Mennonitische Rundschau*, 21 Nov. 1928, 5.
4. Agatha Klassen, "Historical Sketch," 2.
5. Esau and Abrahams, *Memoirs of Yarrow Residents*, 3.
6. *Minutes of Yarrow M.B. Church*, 14 May 1938, 15 Apr. 1939.
7. Agatha Klassen, "Historical Sketch," 5.

HISTORY OF THE YARROW UNITED MENNONITE CHURCH

1. *Minutes of the Yarrow U.M. Church*, 26 Nov. 1979, 173.
2. Agatha Klassen, *Yarrow*, 78.
3. *Churches in Profile*, 59.
4. Hildebrandt and Fast, *Des Bestehens*, 6.
5. Ibid., 8.
6. *Minutes of the Yarrow U.M. Church*, 25 Oct. 1938, 2.
7. Anna Klassen, interview.
8. Rempel, comp, *History of B.C. Mennonite Women*, 89.
9. Ibid., 9.
10. *Minutes of the Yarrow U.M. Church*, 14 Jan. 1945, 46.
11. Hildebrandt and Fast, *Des Bestehens*, 15.
12. *Minutes of the Yarrow U.M. Church*, 14 Jan. 1945, 50.
13. Ibid., 25 Aug. 1957, 62; 25 Sept. 1979, 171.
14. Ibid., 27 Nov. 1949, 142.

THE FOREIGN MISSIONARY AS HERO

1. Harder, E-Mail Communication.
2. J. Loewen, *Culture and Human Values*, 405.
3. S. Brucks, *To God be the Glory*, 80; H. Brucks, *God's Hand on My Life*, 29.
4. *Missionary Album*, n.p.
5. Ibid.; J. Loewen, *Culture and Human Values*, ix, xvii, 400-443.
6. *Missionary Album*, n.p.
7. Pettifer and Bradley, *Missionaries*, 23.
8. Kane, *Understanding Christian Missions*, 60-62; Carpenter and Shenk, *Earthen Vessels*, 252; P. Penner, *Russians*, 303, note # 25.
9. H. Brucks, Correspondence Files, J.B. Toews to Henry Brucks.
10. P. Penner, *Russians*, 164.
11. S. Brucks, Congo Correspondence Files, A.E. Janzen to S. Brucks, 27 Mar. 1852.
12. Ibid., S. Brucks to A.E. Janzen, 30 Jan. 1946.

13. Ibid., Brucks to Janzen, 27 Apr. 1947.
14. See S. Brucks, Congo Correspondence Files, 7 Mar., 26 Aug. 1959.
15. Ibid., S. Brucks to J.B. Toews, 22 Apr. 1956; Toews to Brucks, 9 Mar. 1957.
16. Ibid., 10 Mar., 21 Oct. 1955.
17. S. Brucks, *To God be the Glory*, 71, 73, 82, 86-87, 95-96.
18. S. Brucks, Congo Correspondence Files, 12 Apr. 1953.
19. J. Loewen, *Culture and Human Values*, 430.
20. Harvey Neufeldt, E-Mail Communication.
21. J. Loewen, *Culture and Human Values*, 400-01.
22. H. Brucks, Correspondence Files, 1955.
23. Kane, *Understanding Christian Missions*, 16; P. Penner, *Russians*, vi-vii.

WE DARE NOT LOSE OUR LANGUAGE

1. A. and S. Funk, interview.
2. E. Klassen, interview.
3. Harms, interview by Klassen.
4. C. and K. Regehr, interview.
5. Matties, interview.
6. John Toews, "Russian Mennonite Intellect," 24.

GLIMPSES OF ELIM BIBLE SCHOOL

1. P. Penner, *No Longer at Arm's Length*, 25.
2. P. Loewen, *Memoirs*, 78-79; Warkentin, "Elim Bible School, 89.
3. P. Penner, *No Longer at Arm's Length*, 24-26.
4. Pries, *A Place Called Pniel*, 17-19.
5. P. Penner, *No Longer at Arm's Length*, 24-26; P. Penner, *Reaching the Otherwise Unreached*, 23-24, 110, 114.
6. Lenzmann, interview.
7. P. Penner, *Reaching the Otherwise Unreached*, 55, 100; Warkentin, "Elim Bible School," Agatha Klassen, *Yarrow*, 91-92.
8. Penner, ibid., 28.
9. Harder, interview, 29 May 2000.
10. P. Penner, *No Longer at Arm's Length*, 22-23.
11. J. Loewen, *Only the Sword*, 254.

"THEY HAD TO LEARN TO BE CANADIAN"

1. Wilson, interview by Neufeldt.
2. *Vancouver Sunday Province*, 20 July 1930, Miss. 366, file 1.
3. Wilson, interview by Grainger, # 443.
4. Ibid., # 409, # 443.
5. Wilson, interview by Horricks.
6. Wilson, interview by Neufeldt.
7. Wilson, interview by Horricks.
8. Wilson, interview by Grainger, # 443; Wilson, interview by Neufeldt; Johnstone-Langton, interview by Neufeldt.
9. Wilson, interview by Neufeldt.
10. *Chilliwack Progress*, 22 Apr. 1903, 5; 13 Oct. 1937, 9.
11. Wilson, interview by Horricks.
12. Wilson, interview by Grainger, # 443.
13. Wilson, interview by Neufeldt.
14. Wilson, interview by Grainger, # 443; Wilson, interview by Neufeldt.
15. Wilson, interview by Neufeldt.
16. Ibid.
17. *Minutes of the Chilliwack School Board*, 25 Nov. 1952, 88.
18. Wilson, interview by Neufeldt.
19. Ibid.

YARROW'S SOLDIERS

1. *Chilliwack Progress*, 25 Oct. 1939, 4.
2. Ibid., 20 Sept. 1939, 8; 27 Sept. 1939, 1.
3. Ibid., 11 Nov. 1942, 1; 12 May 1943, 1.
4. Ibid., 21 Nov. 1945, 4; 19 Dec. 1945, 1.

5. Ibid. See, for example, 4 June 1941, 9; 24 July 1946, 1.
6. H. Epp, Compilation of Data; see also Appendix at conclusion of this essay.
7. M. Froese, interview by Sawatsky e-mailed to Dyck.
8. Buehler, interview; J. Block, interview.
9. J. Wittenberg, interview, 23 Oct. 2000.
10. J. Dyck, interview.
11. *Chilliwack Progress*, 4 June 1941, 9.
12. J. Block, interview.
13. J. Wittenberg, interview.
14. See, for example, *Chilliwack Progress*, 24 Mar. 1943, 1; 12 May 1943, 1, 2; 26 May 1943, 1.
15. Hepting, interview.
16. A. Penner, interview; Sawatsky, interview; J. Block, interview.
17. J. Dyck, interview.
18. J. Loewen, interview by Dyck and Sawatsky.
19. M. Froese, interview by Sawatsky e-mailed to Dyck.

DISPLACED LIVES: INFLUX OF EUROPEAN REFUGEES

1. F. Epp, *Mennonite Exodus*, 372-73.
2. Quapp, interview.
3. G. Martens, interview.
4. Hooge, *Thanks to the War*, 158.
5. F. Epp, *Mennonite Exodus*, 413.
6. Claassen, interview.
7. F. Epp, *Mennonite Exodus*, 413.

ARTISANS AND ART

1. Margaret Neufeldt, Written Recollection.
2. S. Derksen, interview by Sawatsky, 6 Dec. 2000; Agatha Klassen, interview.
3. Buschman, "Katie's Christmas Miracle," 8-9.
4. Martin, interview.
5. "Jahresbericht vom Frauenverein," n.p.
6. D. Epp, *Johann Cornies*, 51.
7. S. Derksen, interview by Sawatsky, 6 Dec. 2000.
8. Hopes, "Artist's work," B1.

"PICK THE BERRIES, DON'T PAINT THEM"

1. Polson, interview.
2. Siemens, interview; Kaetler, interview; Wipf, interview; F. Derksen, interviews 17 June 2000, 13 Nov. 2001.
3. Kaetler, interview.
4. Sims, interview.

A COMMUNITY OF VERSE

1. *Unter dem Nordlicht*, 26-27.
2. R. Martens, *Full Moon*, n.p.; H. Dyck, "A Lament," 5.
3. L. Regehr, "War's Aftermath," 7.
4. L. Neufeldt, *Yarrow*, 51-52.
5. M. Toews's "Mothers Only" section appears in her *Five Loaves*, 131-72.
6. See Jantzen, *A Poetic Summary*; M. Toews, *Five Loaves*, 173-96, and Louise Rempel's poems (unpublished), among others.
7. L. Neufeldt, *Raspberrying*, 36-37.
8. Nightingale, "riding freehand," *W 49*, 21-22.
9. Ibid., "Aganetha Against the Wind," 65.
10. L. Neufeldt, *Car Failure*, 42-44; J. Harder, Harder Book of Poetry, 2.

THE DYNAMICS OF BUSINESS IN YARROW

1. J.A. Toews, *History of the Mennonite Brethren Church*, 52.
2. P. Klassen, "Historiography of the Birth," 116; Klaus, *Unsere Kolonien*, 259-60; Nafziger, "Economics," 256; Smith, *Story of the Mennonites*, 435.
3. *Chilliwack Progress*, 23 Feb. 1938, 1.
4. Fretz, "Report of My Trip to Canada," 33-35.
5. Agatha Klassen, *Yarrow*, 77.

6. Discussion of Froese based in large part on A. and L. Froese, interview by Neufeldt and Sawatsky, and M. Froese, interview by Sawatsky, 23 Nov. 2001.
7. Discussion of Johann Derksen based largely on Jack Derksen's personal recollections and oral communications from Derksen family members.
8. Discussion of Funk based in part on C.C. Funk, *Escape to Freedom*, 105-23, and H. Funk, interview.
9. Discussion of Jacob Derksen is based largely on Jack Derksen's personal knowledge of his father's business activities and on family records.

RECREATION AMONG YOUNG MENNONITES IN EARLY YARROW
1. Toews, interviews, 19 Oct., 5 Dec. 2001.
2. Peters, interview.
3. M. Froese, interview by Martens, 23 Sept. 2001; A. Froese, interview by Martens, 23 Sept. 2001.
4. J. Giesbrecht, interview; A. Froese, interview by Martens, 23 Sept. 2001.

RECOLLECTIONS OF ETHEL AND EDITH CAROLINE KNOX
1. Edith Knox, Written Recollections, n.p.
2. Ethel Knox, Written Recollections, n.p.
3. Ibid.
4. Ibid.
5. Edith Knox, Written Recollections, n.p.
6. Ibid.
7. Wall, "Short Summary of My Early Teen-Age years," single page.

FROM GENERATION TO GENERATION: THE HOOGES OF YARROW
1. N. Reimer, *Story of My Life*, 48.
2. M. Janzen, interview; S. Derksen, interview by Hooge.
3. N. Reimer, *Story of My Life*, 50.
4. H. Hooge, interview.
5. Ibid.; M. Janzen interview.
6. *Der Bote*, 26 June 1946.
7. *Zionsbote*, 7 May 1952.
8. S. Derksen, interview by Hooge.
9. D. Giesbrecht, interview by Hooge.
10. K. Hooge, interview.

GARDENING AS BEAUTY AND LOVE: ARON DIETRICH REMPEL
1. R. Klassen, "The Rempel Art of Gardening," 1-2.
2. Wiedemeier, "The Sower: Gerhard D. Rempel," 1-4.
3. A. Dyck, "The Raspberry King," single page.

BUILDING THE COMMUNITY; EXPLORING THE WORLD
1. Julia Wittenberg, Acceptance Speech, 1; *Chilliwack Progress*, 22 Dec. 1976, C3.
2. *Chilliwack Progress*, 5 Oct. 1977, A12.
3. Agatha Klassen, *Yarrow*, 108.
4. Julia Wittenberg, interview by Sawatsky, 9 Feb. 2000.
5. Julia Wittenberg, Acceptance Speech, 1.
6. *Chilliwack Progress*, 22 Dec. 1976, C3.
7. *Yarrow Waterworks Minutes*, 1944.
8. *Yarrow Waterworks Minutes*, 1944; *Chilliwack Progress*, 27 May 1953, 5.
9. *Yarrow Waterworks Minutes*, 1944; *Chilliwack Progress*, 22 Dec. 1976, C3; Unger, interview.
10. *Yarrow Waterworks Minutes*, 1944, 1947-48.
11. *Chilliwack Progress*, 22 Dec. 1976, C3.
12. *Chilliwack Progress*, 5 Oct. 1977, A12.
13. Julia Wittenberg, interview by Sawatsky, 6 June 2000.

MOVE THE CHOIR TO THE CENTRE OF THE CHANCEL: GEORGE REIMER
1. R. Reimer, interview, 8 Nov. 2000.
2. Plett, interview.
3. Redekopp. Interview.
4. Rempel, *Journal*, 70.
5. Esau, *Memoirs*, 24.

6. H. Neufeldt, interview by Neufeldt, 8 Oct. 2000.
7. *Chilliwack Progress*, 20 Oct. 1937, 8.
8. Ibid., 29 Jan. 1941, 3; 19 Feb. 1941, 11.

MUSIC FOR LIFE: WALTER AND MENNO NEUFELD

1. Neumann, interview.
2. R. Reimer, interview, 24 July 2000.
3. S. Martens, interview by Martens, 12 May 2000.
4. Hal Neufeld, interview.
5. W. Neufeld, interview.
6. M. Neufeld, interview.
7. Ibid.
8. L. Neufeldt, E-Mail Communication, 5 Feb. 2000.
9. M. Neufeldt, interview by Martens.
10. R. Reimer, interview, 24 July 2000.
11. F. Dyck, interview by Martens, 8 May 2000.
12. R. Reimer, interview, 24 July 2000.
13. W. Neufeld, interview.
14. F. Dyck, interview by Martens, 8 May 2000.
15. J. Neufeldt, E-Mail Communication.
16. H. Dyck, E-Mail Communication.
17. F. Dyck, interview by Martens, 8 May 2000.
18. R. Reimer, interview, 24 July 2000.
19. Ibid.; H. Reimer, interview, 24 July 2000.
20. Thiessen, interview.
21. F. Dyck, interview by Martens, 8 May 2000.
22. Thiessen, interview.
23. H. Reimer, interview, 24 July 2000.

HEINRICH FRIESEN, VIOLIN MAKER

1. *Chilliwack Progress*, 23 Jan. 1952, 1.
2. Barwich, interview.
3. F. Dyck, interview by Martens, 28 Oct. 2000.
4. Johnston, interview.
5. C. Regehr, interview by Martens.
6. Ibid.
7. *Abbotsford Free Press*, 15 June 1976, 1; W. Reimer, E-Mail Communication.
8. F. Dyck, interview by Martens, 28 Oct. 2000.
9. Ratzlaff, interview.
10. R. Reimer, interview, 8 Nov. 2000.
11. C. Regehr, interview by Martens.
12. *Chilliwack Progress*, 23 Jan. 1952, 1.
13. C. Regehr, interview by Martens; S. Martens, interview by Martens.
14. P. Reimer, interview.
15. Ratzlaff, interview.
16. Barwich, interview.
17. F. Dyck, interview by Martens, 28 Oct. 2000.
18. N. Friesen, interview.
19. F. Dyck, interview by Martens, 28 Oct. 2000.
20. Johnston, interview.
21. N. Friesen, interview.
22. Barwich, interview; W. Reimer, E-Mail Communication.
23. F. Dyck, interview by Martens, 28 Oct. 2000; W. Neufeld, interview.
24. Johnston, interview.

"A DREAM COME TRUE": FRIDA NACHTIGAL, FIRST MENNONITE TEACHER

1. Johnstone-Langton, interview by Klassen.
2. McCutcheon, interview.
3. Krumhols, Letter to Frida Nightingale Johnstone-Langton.

ANNA BARTSCH

1. From Preface, Bartsch, *Fibel-Leselust*, n.p.

M HANK

1. This quote, as well as all other quotations and the contents of essay are from H. Giesbrecht, interviews by Neufeldt, 10 Aug. 1990, 9 Aug. 1999.

YEE FONG

1. Wilson, Notes on Chinese Immigration, 1.
2. Li, *The Chinese in Canada*, 23, 38, 30.
3. *Chilliwack Progress*, 30 Aug. 1934, 1.
4. Kostzrewa, interview.
5. A. Froese, interview by Martens, 4 Dec. 2000.
6. M. Froese, interview by Martens, 4 Dec. 2000.
7. Ibid.
8. D. Giesbrecht, interview by Martens.
9. Li, *The Chinese in Canada*, 31.
10. Lee, interview.
11. A. Froese, interview, 14 Nov. 2000.
12. Lee, interview.
13. M. Froese, interview by Martens, 6 Dec. 2000.
14. Williams, interview.
15. Mark, E-Mail Communication.
16. M. Froese, interview by Martens, 4 Dec. 2000.
17. Williams, interview.
18. A. Froese, interview by Martens, 4 Dec. 2000.
19. *Chilliwack Progress*, 1 May 1968, 1.
20. Kostzrewa, interview.
21. M. Froese, interview by Martens, 6 Dec. 2000.
22. Williams, interview.

YARROW'S WAR DEAD

1. Grainger, *The Mountain Project*, 45.
2. Ibid., 16.
3. See *War Diary of the 8th Reconnaissance.*
4. Ibid.
5. Ibid., 13 Dec. 1941.
6. Grainger, *The Mountain Project*, 46.
7. *War Diary of the Seaforth Highlanders*, 15 June, 29 June 1943.
8. Ibid., 7 July, 9 July 1943.
9. Grainger, *The Mountain Project*, 63.
10. Stacey, *The Canadian Army*, 116-17.
11. Dancocks, *D-day Dodgers*, 166.
12. Nowell, interview, 9 Feb. 2001.
13. L. Ratzlaff, Written Recollection.
14. Jake Wittenberg, interview, 15 Oct. 2000.
15. Ibid.
16. Biography of Cpl. Abe Wittenberg, n.p.
17. Cederberg, *Long Road Home*, 201.
18. *War Diary of the Seaforth Highlanders*, 13 Dec. 1944.
19. Jake Wittenberg, interview, 23 Oct. 2000.
20. J. Block, interview.
21. Ibid.
22. *War Diary of the No. 11 Field Ambulance*, vol. 15871.
23. Ibid., 7 Mar. 1945.
24. Ibid., 9 Mar. 1945.
25. J. Dyck, interview.
26. J. Block, interview.
27. *War Diary of the No. 11 Field Ambulance*, vol. 15688, Daily Orders, 10 Mar. 1945.

Bibliography

Written Works:

The Abbotsford Free Press.

Abrahams, Jacob, Jr. "Aron and Helena Martens and Family," n.d. Typescript.

Bartsch, Anna. *Deutsches Lesebuch.* Yarrow, BC: Columbia Printers: 1945.

———. *Fibel-Leselust.* Personal textbook, n.d. Trans. Arthur Bartsch.

———. *The Hidden Hand.* Revised and expanded. Trans. Arthur Bartsch. Winnipeg: The Christian Press, 1987.

———. *Die Verborgene Hand.* Winnipeg: The Christian Press, 1982.

Bergen, Shirley. "Dr. Katherina Born Thiessen: A Woman Who Made a Difference." *Mennonite Historian* 23.3 (Sept. 1997): 8.

"Biographical Sketch: Sarah Dekker Thielman," n.d. Staff document, Sarah Dekker Thielman Fonds. Centre for Mennonite Brethren Studies, Winnipeg.

Biography of Cpl. Abe Wittenberg. K49935. Chilliwack Archives, Chilliwack, BC.

Blackburn, George G. *The Guns of Victory.* Toronto: McClelland and Stewart, 1996.

Der Bote [Canadian Mennonite biweekly newspaper].

Brucks, Henry. Correspondence Files, 1950-1962, A 250-10-2. Center for Mennonite Brethren Studies, Fresno, California.

———, and Elsie Brucks. *God's Hand On My Life* [autobiography]. Henry Brucks, n.d.

Brucks, Susie. Congo Correspondence Files, 1945-1960, A 250-10-2. Center for Mennonite Brethren Studies, Fresno, California.

———. *To God be the Glory! My Life as God's Servant in Africa.* Winnipeg: Christian Press, 1983.

"Burial." *The Mennonite Encyclopaedia*, ed. Cornelius Krahn, et al. 5 vols. Scottdale, Pennsylvania: Herald Press, 1955-1990. 1: 473-75.

Buschman, Rose Friesen. "Katie's Christmas Miracle." *The Christian Leader* 55 (1 Dec. 1992): 8-9.

Carpenter, J.A., and Wilbert Shenk. *Earthen Vessels: American Evangelicals and Foreign Missions, 1880-1980.* Grand Rapids, Michigan: Eerdmans, 1990.

"Cemeteries." *The Mennonite Encyclopaedia*. 5 vols. 1: 539-40.

The Canadians in Britain, 1939-1944. Ottawa: King's Printer, 1945.

Cederberg, Fred. *The Long Road Home*. Toronto: General Publishing, 1984.
The Chilliwack Progress.

Churches in Profile. Clearbrook, BC: Conference of Mennonites in B.C. 1978.

Constitution, By-Laws and Statement of Faith, Yarrow United Mennonite Church. Rev. Apr. 19, 1999. United Mennonite Church, Yarrow, BC.

"Cremation." *Canadian Mennonite Encyclopedia Online*. 2 Oct. 2000. http://www.mhsc.ca/encyclopedia/contents/D358ME.html.

Dancocks, Daniel G. *The D-Day Dodgers: The Canadians in Italy, 1943-1945*. Toronto: McClelland and Stewart, 1991.

"Death and Dying." *Canadian Mennonite Encyclopedia Online*. 2 Oct. 2000.

Denman, Ron. "A Victorian Love." *Chilliwack Museum and Historical Society Newsletter* (Jan. 1987): n.p. Chilliwack Archives, Chilliwack, BC.

Derksen, Jacob G., and Susie Alice Giesbrecht Derksen. "As We Remember Something Of the Past," 1987. Typescript.

Derksen Siemens, Ruth. E-Mail Communications to Lora Sawatsky, 20 Dec. 2000, 26 Mar. 2001.

Dyck, Anne Rempel. "The Raspberry King," 2000. Autograph page.

Dyck, Harold. E-Mail Communication to Robert Martens, 14 June 2000.

———. "A Lament." *Mennonite Historical Society of BC Newsletter* 6 (Summer 2000): 5.

The Elim Palm. Annual [Yearbook of Elim Bible School]. Yarrow, BC: Columbia Press. Issues 1951-53.

Epp, David H. *Johann Cornies*. Rosthern, SK: Echo Verlag, 1943.

Epp Family Records [Tina Epp Dahl, Elizabeth Dahl Giesbrecht, Susan Epp, Esther Epp Harder], n.d. Typescript.

Epp, Frank H. *Mennonite Exodus: The Rescue and Resettlement of the Russian Mennonites Since the Communist Revolution*. Altona, MB: D.W. Friesen, 1962.

Epp, Helen. Compilation of Data on Canadian Mennonite Military Service Personnel during World War II, n.d. *Canadian Armed Forces Records*, National Archives of Canada, Ottawa.

Esau, Abram J. *Memoirs of Abram J. Esau*. Abram Esau, [1999].

———, and Jacob and Tina Abrahams. *Memoirs of Yarrow Residents*, n.d. Typescript.

Ewert, Henry. *The Story of the B.C. Electric Railway Company*. Vancouver: Whitecap Books, 1986.

Fretz, J. Winfield. "Report of My Trip to Canada to Study Mennonite Colonization," 1943. Prepared for the Mennonite Central Committee. Typescript photocopy.

Friesen, Heinrich. Private Notes, n.d. Autograph pages.

———. "Recent Mennonite Community Building in Canada." *The Mennonite Quarterly Review* 18 (1944): 5-21.

Friesen, Peter M. *The Mennonite Brotherhood in Russia* (1789-1910). Rev. ed. Trans. J.B. Toews, et al. Fresno, California: Mennonite Brethren Publications, 1980.

"Funeral Customs." *The Mennonite Encyclopaedia*. 5 vols. 2: 419-20.

"Funeral Service of Elizabeth Harms," 20 July 1983, Vancouver, BC. Audiocassette.

"Funerals." *The Mennonite Encyclopaedia*. 5 vols. 5: 320.

Funk, Cornelius C. *Escape to Freedom*. Trans. and ed. Peter J. Klassen. Hillsboro, Kansas: Mennonite Brethren Publishing House, 1982.

Giesbrecht, Elizabeth, and David Giesbrecht. "Anna Bartsch: 1897-1989." *Profiles of Mennonite Faith*. Fresno, CA: North American Mennonite Brethren Conference Historical Commission, no. 16, 2001.

Grainger, Neil. *The Mountain Project*. Chilliwack, BC: Rapid Abbot Instant Printing, 1998.

Halseth, Regine. "Mrs. Kipp, the first trained Medical Person in the Valley." *Chilliwack Museum and Historical Society Newsletter* (Jan. 1987): n.p. Chilliwack Archives, Chilliwack, BC.

Harder, Esther Epp. E-Mail Communication to Peter Penner, 3 June 2001.

Harder, Johannes A. Harder Book of Poetry # 2, n.d. Bound autograph manuscript.

Harms, Elizabeth. Diploma for completion of Midwifery Certification Program, 11 July 1912. Trans. Katie Peters.

Harms, Heinrich. *Journal, 1898-1948*, n.d. Excerpts trans. Agatha Klassen and Leonard Neufeldt. Autograph manuscript.

Harms, Lillian. Biographical Recollections: Elizabeth Harms, 2000. Autograph pages.

———. "Das Lebensverzeichnis meiner lieben Mutter Elizabeth Harms," 1983. Typescript.

Harris, R.C. "The Old Yale Road 1875." *British Columbia Historical News* 17.1 (1984): 2.

Hildebrandt, H.H., and H.J. Fast. *Des Bestehens Der Vereinigten Mennonitengemeinde Zu Yarrow, B.C., 1938-1963*. Yarrow, BC: Columbia Press, 1963.

Hooge, Jake. E-mail letters to Selma Hooge, 3 Aug. and 22 Aug. 2000.

Hooge, Selma Kornelsen. *Thanks to the War*, 1982. Typescript.

Hopes, Vikki. "Artist's work history in the making." *The Abbotsford and Mission News* 28 July 2001, B1.

Isaac, Lena. Written Recollections, 2001. Typescript.

"Jahresbericht vom Frauenverein 1960-61." *Records of Ladies Aid Society of Yarrow MB Church*. File Box 7—992.12.7. Archives of the Mennonite Historical Society of British Columbia, Abbotsford, BC.

Jantzen, Helen Matties. *A Poetic Summary of God's Hand in Old Testament History*. Yarrow, BC: Columbia Press, 1967.

J.K. Janzen Family Records [J.K. Janzen, Henry J. Janzen, Helen Janzen Kroeker, Elizabeth Janzen Epp, Esther Epp Harder], n.d. Typescript.

Johnstone-Langton, Frida Nightingale. Letter to Nieces and Nephews, 12 Dec.1999. Typescript.

Kane, J. Herbert. *Understanding Christian Missions.* Grand Rapids, Michigan: Baker, 1978.

Klassen, Agatha E. "Historical Sketch of the Yarrow Mennonite Brethren Church," 1999. File Box 11—992.12.11, file 13. Archives of the Mennonite Historical Society of British Columbia, Abbotsford, BC.

———. *Yarrow: A Portrait in Mosaic.* Abbotsford, BC: Blairhouse, 1976.

Klassen, A.J. *Alternative Service for Peace in Canada during World War II, 1941-1946.* Abbotsford, BC: Mennonite Central Committee (BC) Seniors for Peace, 1998.

Klassen, Peter. "The Historiography of the Birth of the Mennonite Brethren Church." *P.M. Friesen and his History*, ed. Abraham Friesen. Fresno, California: Center for Mennonite Brethren Studies, 1979. 115-131.

Klassen, Ruth Rempel, comp. "The Rempel Art of Gardening from Crimea, Russia to Yarrow, B.C.," n.d. From *Journal of Dietrich Aron Rempel*, n.d. Trans. Helen Rempel Klassen.

Klaus, Alexander. *Unsere Kolonien. Studien and Materialien zur Geschichte und Statistik der ausländischen Kolonization in Russland.* Trans. J. Toews. Odessa, Russia: Odessaer Zeitung, 1887.

Knox, Edith Caroline. Written Recollections, 2001. Autograph pages.

Knox, Ethel Irene. Written Recollections, 2000. Autograph pages.

Kornelsen, Anna Goosen. *Diary of Anna (Goosen) Kornelsen*, 1958. Excerpts trans. Leonard Neufeldt. Autograph manuscript photocopy, 2 notebooks.

Kostzrewa, Dorothy Chung. "Oral history interview." Add.Mss. 419, Tape 1, Chilliwack Archives, Chilliwack, BC.

Krumhols, Elfrieda. Letter to Frida Nightingale Johnstone-Langton, 11 Nov. 1999. Typescript.

Lehn, Cornelia, comp. *The History of the Development of the Conference of Mennonites in B.C. and Their Churches.* Clearbrook, BC: Conference of Mennonites in B.C., 1990.

Li, Peter S. *The Chinese in Canada.* Toronto: Oxford UP, 1988.

Loewen, Gladys. E-Mail Communications to Lora Sawatsky, 8 Aug. and 2 Sept. 2001.

Loewen, Jacob A. *Culture and Human Values: Christian Intervention in Anthropological Perspective.* Pasadena, California: William Carey Library, 1975.

———. *Only the Sword of the Spirit!* Fresno, California: Mennonite Brethren Historical Society, 1997.

Loewen, Peter D. *Memoirs of Peter Daniel Loewen*. Trans. Agatha Klassen. Abbotsford, BC: Fraser Valley Custom Printers, 1999.

———. "My Experiences in the Yarrow Sunday School," n.d. File Box 11—992.12.11. Archives of the Mennonite Historical Society of British Columbia, Abbotsford, BC.

The Loyal Edmonton Regiment, Memorial Booklet. Nijkerk, Holland: C.C. Callenbach, 1945.

Mark, Nancy. E-Mail Communication to Lora Sawatsky, 28 June 2001.

Martens, Petrus. Report on the German School. File Box 11—992.12.11, file 1. Archives of the Mennonite Historical Society of British Columbia, Abbotsford, BC.

Martens, Robert. *Full Moon*. Lake Errock, BC: Penny-a-Line Promotions, 1998.

Martens, Sarah Enns. Written Recollections: Margaretha Enns, 1996. Typescript. *Die Mennonitische Rundschau* [Canadian Mennonite Brethren weekly newspaper]. *Minutes of the Chilliwack School Board*. Add.Mss. 752 Chilliwack School District 33, Chilliwack Fonds. Chilliwack Archives, Chilliwack, BC.

Minutes of the Yarrow Mennonite Brethren Church, (1929-1950). File Box 1—992.12.1. Archives of the Mennonite Historical Society of British Columbia, Abbotsford, BC.

Minutes of the Yarrow United Mennonite Church, 1938-1952; 1953-1964. United Mennonite Church Archives, Yarrow, BC.

Missionary Album. Hillsboro, Kansas: Mennonite Brethren Board of Foreign Missions,1954.

Nafziger, E. Wayne. "Economics." *Mennonite Encyclopedia*. 5 vols. 5: 255-56.

Neufeld, Margaret Klassen. "My Grandmother was an Undertaker: A Tribute to Aganetha Dyck Baerg (1859-1942)." *Mennonite Historian* 24 (1998): 2, 9.

Neufeldt, Harvey. E-Mail Communication to Peter Penner, 31 May 2000.

Neufeldt, Henry P. *A Brief History of My Life*, 1996. Autograph manuscript, 4 notebooks.

———. Recollections of Music in Yarrow, 2000. Autograph pages.

Neufeldt, Jerry. E-Mail Communication to Robert Martens, 17 May 2000.

Neufeldt, Leonard. *Car Failure North of Nîmes*. Windsor: Black Moss, 1994.

———. E-Mail Communications to Robert Martens, 2 Jan., 5 Feb. 2000.

———. *Raspberrying*. Windsor: Black Moss, 1991.

———. *Yarrow*. Windsor: Black Moss, 1993.

Neufeldt, Margaret Enns. "A Brief History of the Ladies Aid Society of the Yarrow MB Church 1930-1989." File Box 7—992.12.7. Archives of the Mennonite Historical Society of British Columbia, Abbotsford, BC.

———. Written Recollection, 2001. Typescript.

———. Written Recollections: Margaretha Enns, 1996, 1999. Typescript.

Nicholson, G.W.L. *The Canadians in Italy, 1943-1945*. Vol. II. Ottawa: Queen's Printer, 1957.
Nightingale, Larry. "Aganetha Against the Wind (Lines on Paging Through the Family Albums)." *The Dry Wells of India*. Ed. George Woodcock. Madeira Park: Harbour Publishing, 1989: 65.
———. "riding freehand." *W 49*. 7 (2001): 21-22.
Papers for the 60th Anniversary of the Yarrow Mennonite Brethren Church: "A Brief Outline of Historical Events"; "Building Projects of the Yarrow M.B. Church"; "Membership and Baptism Profile"; "Milestones in the 60-Year History"; "Pastors, Assistant Pastors and Interim Pastors"; "Sunday School . . . 1929-1989." File Box 11—992.12.11, file 32. Archives of the Mennonite Historical Society of British Columbia, Abbotsford, BC.
Penner, Cornelius H. *The Story of My Life*. Cornelius Penner, 1997.
Penner, Peter. *No Longer at Arm's Length: Mennonite Brethren Church Planting in Canada*. Winnipeg: Kindred Press, 1987.
———. *Russians, North Americans, and Telugus: The MB Mission in India, 1885-1975*. Winnipeg: Kindred Press, 1997.
———. "Life of Herman and Tina (Wiens) Lenzmann," 2001. Work in progress. Typescript. Yarrow Research Committee.
———. *Reaching the Otherwise Unreached: An Historical Account of the West Coast Children's Mission of B.C.* Clearbrook, BC: West Coast Children's Mission, 1959.
Pettifer, Julian, and Richard Bradley. *Missionaries*. London: BBC Books, 1990.
Pries, George D. *A Place Called Pniel: Winkler Bible School, 1925-1975*. Altona, MB: D.W. Friesen, 1975.
Quapp, Helen Froese. *Instructive Guide in Flat Design*. David Friesen, n.d.
Ratzlaff, Agatha Enns, comp. *Ratzlaff: Our Family Heritage*. Clearbrook, BC: Agatha Enns Ratzlaff, 1992.
Ratzlaff, Lydia. Written Recollection, 2000. Typescript.
Redekop, John H. *Anabaptism: The Basic Beliefs*. Canadian Conference of Mennonite Brethren Churches. Winnipeg: Board of Faith & Life, 1993.
———. "Reflections on a Bible School." *Mennonite Brethren Herald* 36 (29 Aug. 1997): 4-7.
Regehr, Lydia. "Russia's Mennonites." *The Mennonite* 95 (29 Jan. 1980): 79.
———. "War's Aftermath." *Mennonite Brethren Herald* 18 (Oct. 1979): 7.
Regehr, T.D. "Lost Sons: The Canadian Mennonite Soldiers of World War II." *The Mennonite Quarterly Review* 66 (1992): 461-480.
———. *Mennonites in Canada, 1939-1970*. Toronto: University of Toronto Press, 1996.
The Register of names of those who fell in the 1939-1945 War and are buried in *Cemeteries in the Netherlands*, n.d. National Archives of Canada, Ottawa.

Register of Pupils, Yarrow Public Schools. Add.Mss. 752, School District 33, Chilliwack Fonds. Chilliwack Archives, Chilliwack, BC.

Reimer, George. "Meine Lebensgeschichte," n.d. Autograph manuscript.

Reimer, Nickolai N. *The Story of My Life*. Trans. Henry S. Neufeld. N.N. Reimer, 1986.

Reimer, William. E-mail letter to Robert Martens, 27 Oct. 2000.

Rempel, Dietrich Aron. *Journal of Dietrich Aron Rempel*, n.d. Trans. Helen Rempel Klassen. Typescript.

Rempel, Martha, comp. *History of B.C. Mennonite Women in Mission, 1939-1976*. Altona, MB: D.W. Friesen, n.d.

Sawatzky, Jacob. "Ein Familien Register für uns und unsere Eltern, Kinder, Grosskinder und Urgrosskinder," ca 1910. Autograph manuscript.

Sawatsky, Lora Neufeldt. E-Mail Communication to Robert Martens, 23 May 2000.

Sawatsky, Roland. E-Mail Communication to Robert Martens, 23 May 2000.

Schroeder, Gerhard P. *Miracles of Grace and Judgment*. Kingsport, Tennessee: Kingsport Press, 1974.

Schroeder, William, and Helmut T. Huebert. *Mennonite Historical Atlas*. Winnipeg: Springfield Publishers, 1996.

Smith, C. Henry. *The Story of the Mennonites*. Third edition, rev. Cornelius Krahn. Newton, Kansas: Mennonite Publication Office, 1950.

Stacey, C. P. *The Canadian Army, 1939-1945*. Ottawa, King's Printer, 1948.

Steinson, Doug. *Community Events Timeline: 1873-1926*. Chilliwack Archives, Chilliwack, BC, 2000.

Thielman, Sarah Dekker. *A Book about Gynecology, and Records of Thielman's Activity as Midwife in Russia and Canada, 1909-41*, n.d. Sarah Dekker Thielman Fonds. Centre for Mennonite Brethren Studies, Winnipeg.

Thiessen, Veronica. "Yarrow United Mennonite Church." *Churches in Profile*. Clearbrook, BC: Conference of Mennonites in B.C., 1978.

Toews, John. "The Russian Mennonite Intellect of the Nineteenth Century," *P.M. Friesen and his History*, ed. Abraham Friesen. Fresno, California: Center for Mennonite Brethren Studies, 1979. 1-33.

Toews, John A. *A History of the Mennonite Brethren Church*. Fresno, California: Mennonite Brethren Board of Christian Literature, 1975.

Toews, John B. *The MB Church in Zaire*. Fresno, California: Mennonite Brethren Board of Christian Literature, 1978.

Toews, Margaret Penner. *Five Loaves and two small fishes . . . .* Yarrow: Milton and Margaret Toews, 1976.

Toews, Reginald. "Story of Johann H. and Aganetha Toews," 19 Nov. 2000. Typescript [sermon]. Greendale Mennonite Brethren Church, Greendale, BC.

Unter dem Nordlicht: Anthologie des deutschen Schrifttums Der Mennoniten in Canada, ed. Georg K. Epp. Winnipeg: The Mennonite German Society of Canada, 1977.

The Vancouver Daily Province.
Wall, Peter. "Short Summary of My Early Teen-Age years in Yarrow," 2001. Typescript page.
War Diary of the 8th Reconnaissance Regiment, RG24, vol.14221, Serial No. 581, microfilm reel, T-12683. National Archives of Canada, Ottawa.
War Diary of the No. 11 Field Ambulance, Royal Canadian Army Medical Corps,1943/08-1945/06, vol. 15871, Serial No. 199; vol. 15688. RG 24, National Archives Canada, Ottawa.
War Diary of The Seaforth Highlanders of Canada, 1943/08-1944/07, RG 25, vol. 15256, Serial No. 37. National Archives of Canada, Ottawa.
[Warkentin, Henry]. "The Elim Bible School," in Klassen, Agatha E. *Yarrow: A Portrait in Mosaic*. Abbotsford, BC: Blairhouse, 1976. 89-93.
Wiedemeier, Kurt. "The Sower: Gerhard D. Rempel," 1970. Trans. Helen Rempel Klassen. Typescript photocopy.
Wilson, David. Notes on Chinese Immigration. Add.Mss. 419. Chilliwack Archives, Chilliwack, BC.
Wittenberg, Julia Sabo. Acceptance Speech at Award Ceremony, Yarrow Library, 1974. Typescript photocopy.
Yarrow Mennonite Brethren Church: Family Register # 1. File Box 11—992.12.2, file 1. Archives of the Mennonite Historical Society of British Columbia, Abbotsford, BC.
Yarrow Waterworks Minutes, 1944-1973. Add.Mss. 690 C51. Chilliwack Archives, Chilliwack, BC.
Young, Archie D., M.D., et al. "A Medical History of the Upper Fraser Valley," 1999, Vertical File, "Health Care—Chilliwack." Chilliwack Archives, Chilliwack, BC.
Zionsbote [American Mennonite Brethren weekly newspaper].

Interviews:

Barwich, Jacob. Interview by Robert Martens, Yarrow, BC, 9 Aug. 2000.
Bergen, Shirley Penner. Interviews by Lora Sawatsky, Brandon, MB, 26 Feb. 2001; Abbotsford, BC, 22 and 23 Mar. 2002.
Berger, Gail. Interview by Lora Sawatsky (telephone), 17 Oct. 2000.
Block, Arthur J. Interview by Leonard Neufeldt, Vancouver, BC, 27 Mar. 2001.
Block, Jack. Interview by Harold Dyck and Marlene Sawatsky, Surrey, BC, 4 Aug. 2000.
Buehler, Les. Interview by Harold Dyck and Marlene Sawatsky, Abbotsford, BC, 2 Aug. 2000.
Buschman, Rose Friesen. Interview by Lora Sawatsky (telephone), 7 Dec. 2000.
Claassen, Henry. Interview by Selma Hooge (telephone), 21 Aug. 2000.
Derksen, Freda Brucks. Interviews by Ruth Derksen Siemens, Abbotsford, BC, 17 June 2000, 13 Nov. 2001.

Derksen, Susie Giesbrecht. Interview by Jack Derksen and Leonard Neufeldt, Yarrow, BC, 28 Dec. 2000.
Derksen, Susie Giesbrecht. Interview by Selma Hooge, Yarrow, BC, 21 July 2000.
Derksen, Susie Giesbrecht. Interviews by Lora Sawatsky, Yarrow, BC, 3 July, 3 Aug., 6 Dec. 2000.
Durksen, Kaethe. Interview by Irma Epp, Winnipeg, MB, 18 Oct. 2000.
Dyck, Frank. Interview by Jacob A. Loewen, Abbotsford, BC, n.d., 2000.
Dyck, Frank. Interviews by Robert Martens, Abbotsford, BC, 8 May, 28 Oct. 2000.
Dyck, Jacob A. Interview by Harold Dyck, Richmond, BC, 13 Dec. 2000.
Eitzen, Sara. "Tips for Women: Radio Interview." Interview by Kaethe Durksen, [daughter of midwife Anna Duerksen], Radio-ZP-30, Filadelphia, Paraguay, 25 Nov. 1998.
Enns, George. Interview by Lora Sawatsky (telephone), 1 Nov. 1999.
Enns, George, and Helen Enns. Interviews by Lora Sawatsky, Chilliwack, BC, 8 Jan. 2000; 9 and 10 Apr. 2002.
Enns, Henry. Interview by Irma Epp, Winnipeg, MB, 13 Oct. 2000.
Friesen, Gabriela. Interview by Robert Martens (telephone), 24 Sept. 2000.
Friesen, Jack. Interview by Robert Martens (telephone), 12 May 2000.
Friesen, Norma. Interview by Robert Martens, Abbotsford, BC, 23 Sept. 2000.
Friesen, Rudy. Interview by Robert Martens, Denman Island, BC, 20 June 2000.
Froese, Abram (Ed). Interviews by Robert Martens, Yarrow, BC, 14 Nov., 4 Dec 2000; 23 Sept. 2001.
Froese, Abram (Ed), and Leonard Froese. Interview by Leonard Neufeldt and Lora Sawatsky, Yarrow, BC, 13 Nov. 2000.
Froese, Mary Ratzlaff. Interviews by Robert Martens, Yarrow, BC, 14, 17, 21 Nov. and 4, 6 Dec. 2000; 23 Sept. 2001.
Froese, Mary Ratzlaff. Interviews by Lora Sawatsky, Yarrow, BC, 2 Nov. 2000; 23 and 27 Jan. 2001.
Funk, Anne, and Susie Funk. Interview by Agatha Klassen, Orchas Island, WA, 17 Jan. 2000.
Funk, Henry. Interview by Jack Derksen, Abbotsford, BC, 19 Feb. 2000.
Giesbrecht, Cornelius. Interview by Robert Martens, Abbotsford, BC, 7 Dec. 2000.
Giesbrecht, David P. Interviews by Selma Hooge, Abbotsford, BC, 5 Apr. and 13 Apr. 2000.
Giesbrecht, David P. Interview by Robert Martens, Abbotsford, BC, 21 Nov. 2000.
Giesbrecht, Elizabeth Dahl. Interview by Agatha Klassen, Abbotsford, BC, 4 June 2001.
Giesbrecht, Henry. Interview by Harold Dyck, Yarrow, BC, 13 Oct. 2000.
Giesbrecht, Henry. Interviews by Harvey Neufeldt, Yarrow, BC, 10 Aug. 1990, 9 Aug. 1999.

Giesbrecht, John. Interviews by Robert Martens, telephone, 8 Dec. 2000; Chilliwack, BC, 22 Sept. 2001.
Giesbrecht, William. Interview by David Giesbrecht, Abbotsford, BC, 12 June 2000.
Harder, Peter. Interviews by Peter Penner, Chilliwack, BC, 10 May 1999, 29 May 2000.
Harms, Lillian. Interview by Agatha Klassen, Abbotsford, BC, 10 Mar. 2000.
Harms, Lillian. Interview by Lora Sawatsky and Irma Epp, Abbotsford, BC, 14 Sept. 2000.
Harms, Lillian. Interviews by Lora Sawatsky, Abbotsford, BC, 16 Jan. 2001; 1 and 19 Mar. 2001.
Hepting, John. Interview by Harold Dyck (telephone), 13 Nov. 2000.
Hildebrandt, Hedy. Interview by Lora Sawatsky (telephone), 7 Mar. 2001.
Hooge, Hardy. Interview by Selma Hooge, Mission, BC, 7 Apr. 2000.
Hooge, Katie Dahl. Interview by Selma Hooge, Sardis, BC, 10 Aug. 2000.
Janz, Margaret. Interview by Selma Hooge, Abbotsford, BC, 17 Apr. 2000.
Janzen, Henry. Interview by David Giesbrecht (telephone), 20 Aug. 2000.
Janzen, Katharine. Interview by David Giesbrecht, Vancouver, BC, 15 Oct. 2000.
Janzen, Leona Sawatsky. Interview by Lora Sawatsky, Abbotsford, BC, 28 Oct. 2000.
Janzen, Mary Pauls. Interview by Selma Hooge, Abbotsford, BC, 18 May 18 2000.
Johnston, Ulrike Friesen. Interview by Robert Martens, Yarrow, BC, 27 Oct. 2000.
Johnstone-Langton, Frida Nightingale. Interview by Agatha Klassen, Abbotsford, BC, 16 Mar. 2000.
Johnstone-Langton, Frida Nightingale. Interview by Harvey Neufeldt, Abbotsford, BC, 8 Sept. 2000.
Kaetler, Sarah Brucks. Interview by Ruth Derksen Siemens, Abbotsford, BC, 2 Aug. 2000.
Klassen, Agatha. Interviews by Lora Sawatsky (telephone), 19 Mar., 4 June, 26 July 2001.
Klassen, Anna Dyck. Interview by Veronica Thiessen, Abbotsford, BC, 25 July 2001.
Klassen, Edward. Interview by Agatha Klassen (telephone), 15 May 2000.
Knox, Edith Caroline. Interviews by Esther Epp Harder and Lora Sawatsky, Yarrow, BC, 4 Oct. 2000, 18 Apr. 2001.
Knox, Ethel. Interviews by Esther Epp Harder and Lora Sawatsky, Yarrow, BC, 4 Oct. 2000, 18 Apr. 2001.
Konrad, Elfrieda Neufeldt. Interview by Lora Sawatsky, Abbotsford, BC, 28 Oct. 2000. Kostzrewa, Dorothy Chung. Interview by Robert Martens (telephone), 18 Nov. 2000.
Langeman, John. Interview by Robert Martens, Abbotsford, BC, 28 Nov. 2000.

Lee, Louis. Interview by Robert Martens, Mission, BC, 28 Nov. 2000.

Lenzmann, Herman. Interview by Peter Penner, Winnipeg, MB, 20 May 20 2000.

Lockner, Charlene, M.D. Interview by Gertrude Martens (telephone), 12 Mar. 2001.

Loewen, Anne Enns. Interview by Lora Sawatsky, Abbotsford, BC, 9 Jan. 2000.

Loewen, Jacob A. Interview by Harold Dyck and Marlene Sawatsky, Abbotsford, BC, 2 Aug. 2000.

Loewen, Jacob A. Interview by David Giesbrecht, Abbotsford, BC, 10 Apr. 2001.

Loewen, Jacob A. Interview by Leonard Neufeldt, Abbotsford, BC, 28 Oct. 2000.

Martens, Gertrude. Interview by Selma Hooge, Abbotsford, BC, 30 May 2000.

Martens, Jacob Aron. Interview by Lillian Harms, Abbotsford, BC, 8 Mar. 2001.

Martens, Melvin. Interview by Robert Martens, Abbotsford, BC, 18 Oct. 2000.

Martens, Sarah Enns. Interview by Robert Martens, Abbotsford, BC, 12 May, 18 Oct. 2000.

Martens, Sarah Enns. Interview by Leonard Neufeldt, Abbotsford, BC, 11 Sept. 2000.

Martens, Sarah Enns. Interviews by Lora Sawatsky (telephone), 9 and 10 Apr. 2002.

Martin, Hildegarde Klassen. Interview by Lora Sawatsky (telephone), 30 Aug. 2001.

Matties, Linda. Interview by Agatha Klassen, Abbotsford, BC, 19 May 2000.

McCutcheon, Dorothy. Interview by Agatha Klassen, Abbotsford, BC, 6 Apr. 2000.

Neufeld, Ernie. Interview by Robert Martens, Abbotsford, BC, 5 July 2000.

Neufeld, Frieda. Interview by Robert Martens (telephone), 29 May 2000.

Neufeld, Hal. Interview by Robert Martens (telephone), 29 May 2000.

Neufeld, Lena Kroeker. Interview by Lora Sawatsky (telephone), 7 Mar. 2001.

Neufeld, Menno. Interview by Robert Martens, Abbotsford, BC, 27 July 2000.

Neufeld, Walter. Interview by Robert Martens, Abbotsford, BC, 27 July 2000.

Neufeldt, Henry P. Interviews by Leonard Neufeldt, Abbotsford, BC, 4 July, 8 Oct. and 29 Oct. 2000; 6 Feb. 2001.

Neufeldt, Leonard. Interview by Lora Sawatsky, Abbotsford, BC, 28 Oct. 2000.

Neufeldt, Margaret Enns. Interviews by Irma Epp (telephone), 9 and 14 Nov. 2000.

Neufeldt, Margaret Enns. Interview by Robert Martens, Abbotsford, BC, 5 June 2000.

Neufeldt, Margaret Enns. Interviews by Leonard Neufeldt, Abbotsford, BC, 8 and 29 Oct. 2000.
Neufeldt, Margaret Enns. Interviews by Lora Sawatsky, Abbotsford, BC, 8 and 10 Apr. 2002.
Neumann, Erna Martens. Interview by Robert Martens (telephone), 29 May 2000.
Nightingale, James. Interview by Lora Sawatsky (telephone), 7 Mar. 2001.
Nowell, Reenie. Interviews by Harold Dyck (telephone), 9 Feb., 6 Mar. 2001.
Penner, Anne. Interview by Harold Dyck (telephone), 6 Mar. 2001.
Penner, Peter D. Interview by David Giesbrecht (telephone), 20 Aug. 2000.
Peters, Pete, and Anne Rempel Peters. Interview by Lora Sawatsky (telephone), 28 Nov. 2001.
Plett, Martha Derksen. Interview by Robert Martens, Abbotsford, BC, 4 Nov. 2000.
Polson, Judith Reimer Wills. Interview by Ruth Derksen Siemens, Burnaby, BC, 27 Nov. 2001.
Quapp, Jacob, and Elizabeth Quapp. Interview by Selma Hooge (telephone), 18 Apr. 2000.
Ratzlaff, John, Jr. Interview by Jacob Loewen, Abbotsford, BC, n.d. 2000.
Redekopp, Holda Reimer Fast. Interview by Robert Martens, Abbotsford, BC, 17 Nov. 2000.
Regehr, Cornelius. Interview by Robert Martens, Abbotsford, BC, 23 Oct. 2000.
Regehr, Cornelius, and Katherine Regehr. Interview by Agatha Klassen, Abbotsford, BC, 6 June 2000.
Reimer, Hilda Martens. Interviews by Robert Martens, Abbotsford, BC, 24 July, 8 Nov. 2000.
Reimer, Nick. Interview by Robert Martens, Abbotsford, BC, 21 Oct. 2000.
Reimer, Peter. Interview by Robert Martens, Abbotsford, BC, 19 Oct. 2000.
Reimer, Rudolph. Interviews by Robert Martens, Abbotsford, BC, 24 July, 8 Nov. 2000; telephone, 21 Sept. 2001.
Reimer, William. Interview by Leonard Neufeldt, Abbotsford, BC, 26 May 2001.
Sawatsky, Leona Warkentin. Interview by Harold Dyck and Marlene Sawatsky, Richmond, BC, 1 Aug. 2000.
Schellenberg, Alvin. Interview by Robert Martens (telephone), 27 Nov. 2000.
Schmidt, Ben. Interview by David Giesbrecht (telephone), 4 Nov. 2000.
Schmidt, Jacob. Interview by David Giesbrecht, Winnipeg, MB, 6 Aug. 2000.
Siemens, George. Interview by Ruth Derksen Siemens, Abbotsford, BC, 13 May 1999.
Sims, Hanna Nikkel. Interviews by Ruth Derksen Siemens, Burnaby, BC, 6 July 2000, 1 Feb. 2001.
Thiessen, John. Interview by Robert Martens, Abbotsford, BC, 7 June 2000.
Toews, Margaret Peters. Interviews by Lora Sawatsky (telephone), 19 Oct., 5 Dec. 2001.

Unger, John. Interview by Lora Sawatsky (telephone), 19 Oct. 2001.
Warkentin, Henry. Interview by Peter Penner, Chilliwack, BC, 29 May, 2000.
Williams, Dorothy. Interview by Robert Martens (telephone), 23 Jan. 2001.
Wilson, Carl. Interview by Neil Grainger, 1983. "Carl A. Wilson Interview." Add.Mss. 409, Chilliwack Archives, Chilliwack, BC.
Wilson, Carl. Interview by Neil Grainger, 1983. "Carl A. Wilson Interview." Add.Mss. 443, Chilliwack Archives, Chilliwack, BC.
Wilson, Carl. Interview by Marcia Horricks, 1981. "Carl A. Wilson Interview." Add.Mss. 345, Chilliwack Archives, Chilliwack, BC.
Wilson, Carl. Interview by Harvey Neufeldt, Vedder Crossing, BC, 26 Aug. 1985.
Wipf, Elizabeth Brucks. Interviews by Ruth Derksen Siemens, Abbotsford, BC, 4 Dec. 2000, 24 Jan. 2001.
Wittenberg, Jake. Interviews by Harold Dyck, Vancouver, BC, 15 and 23 Oct. 2000.
Wittenberg, Julia Sabo. Interviews by Lora Sawatsky, Chilliwack, BC, 16 Sept. 1999, 9 Feb. 2000, 6 June 2000, 17 Oct. 2000; telephone, 11 Jan. and 16 Feb. 2000.

Notes on Contributors

ARTHUR BARTSCH was born in Bololo, Belgian Congo, resided in Yarrow 1943-1965, took his graduate degrees in history, and spent many years as a professor of history. He lives in retirement in Nelson, B.C.

ARTHUR BLOCK was born in Mullingar, Saskatchewan, of Mennonite émigrés from Russia, moved to Yarrow in his boyhood, completed degree programs at the University of British Columbia and Harvard Business School, and in the 1950s began to build a corporation engaged mainly in real estate, steel, and agribusiness.

SUSAN BRAUN BRANDT lived her first 22 years in Yarrow. At the college level she studied humanities at Tabor College in Kansas and theology at several seminaries. For many years on the staff of the Canadian Mennonite Brethren Conference, she is currently managing editor of the *Mennonite Brethren Herald*.

MARY LENZMANN BRAUN moved as a child from Saskatchewan to Yarrow, where she spent 17 years. After completing degrees in music, religious education, and education, she developed a dual-track career in music (piano, theory, and music history) and public school teaching. She has retired in Calgary.

DOROTHY LOEWEN DERKSEN was born and raised in Yarrow. After university studies she worked many years in administration in industry and as a college instructor in adult education. Retired, she lives in Winnipeg.

JACK DERKSEN was born and raised in Yarrow. After university studies he taught high school before serving as an officer of the Canadian Foreign Service in several countries. Eventually he and his wife, Jeanette, and children settled in Santa Cruz, Bolivia, to ranch and develop a business.

ANNE REMPEL DYCK spent the first 19 years of her life in Yarrow, took further studies in Winnipeg, and for 13 years served as foster parent at a children's treatment ranch in Ontario. She lives in Abbotsford.

ELIZABETH WALL DYCK was born in Manitoba two weeks after her parents had emigrated from Russia. She spent the years 1937 to 1947 in Yarrow, where she received her high school education and attended Elim Bible School. After many years in pastoral work, she and her husband semi-retired to Abbotsford.

HAROLD DYCK has served as Senior Executive, Housing and Urban Affairs, Government of Canada; Deputy Minister, Urban and Municipal Affairs, Government of Saskatchewan; Executive Director, Ontario Association of Independent Schools; and professor in education at the University of California, Berkeley, and the University of British Columbia. His immigrant family moved from Saskatchewan to Yarrow when he was a child. He has retired to Vancouver.

GEORGE EPP was born in Manitou, Manitoba, of Mennonite parents from Russia and lived in Yarrow 1932-1948. Trained both in the humanities and divinity, he served many years as a school instructor — in Prince George, Paraguay, and Chilliwack.

IRMA NEUFELDT EPP served many years as high school English teacher and counselor in Winnipeg and in recent years as associate pastor. Prior to that she spent 16 years in the Congo as a missionary. She was born and raised in Yarrow.

JOHN FRIESEN was born in Alberta of Mennonite immigrants and grew up in Yarrow. His vocation has been in psychological counseling, first as Supervisor of Psychological Services in the Ministry of Education in the Government of Alberta, then as professor at the University of British Columbia.

DAVID GIESBRECHT was born of immigrant Mennonite parents and moved as a child from Elm Creek, Manitoba, to Yarrow, where he resided 1948-1960. He received his master's degree in Library Information Services and, except for the years he and his wife, Betty, spent abroad with the Mennonite Central Committee, has been a college librarian.

ESTHER EPP HARDER was born in Yarrow and, 21 years later, moved to Greendale. Today she and her husband reside in Chilliwack. For many years a medical office assistant, she now teaches courses in this field at the University College of the Fraser Valley.

LILLIAN HARMS's background is briefly detailed in the essay "Midwifery." She trained in clinical microbiology technology and worked for more than two decades for the Centre of Disease Control. She has retired to Abbotsford.

SELMA KORNELSEN HOOGE has briefly recounted her early years in the Ukraine and her experience as a war refugee (see "Displaced Lives" in this volume). Besides teaching pre-school, she has published essays and several children's books. In 1990, she and her husband retired to a farm in Greendale.

LENA GIESBRECHT ISAAC was born in Russia and arrived in Yarrow as a four-year-old in 1928 with her pioneer family. She graduated from the Mennonite high school in Yarrow, attended Elim Bible School, and took further studies in Winnipeg. She writes poetry and has published articles in denominational magazines.

THELMA REIMER KAUFFMAN was born in Greendale and a year later moved across the Vedder to Yarrow. After college studies, she served with the Mennonite Central Committee in Ohio and Vienna, Austria. Later she completed graduate studies in library science. Recently retired (in Issaquah, Washington), she has been a teacher and librarian.

AGATHA KLASSEN, "Yarrow's historian," was born in the USSR and moved to Yarrow from Coaldale, Alberta, in 1941. Her biography is briefly detailed in this volume in "Take Counsel From Strength and Duty."

RUTH REMPEL KLASSEN resided in Yarrow for her first 20 years. A retired piano teacher, she lives in Richmond, B.C.

ETHEL and EDITH KNOX have always lived in Yarrow. For more biographical information, see "Recollections of Ethel and Edith Caroline Knox" in this volume.

GLADYS LOEWEN was born in Kansas and lived most of her early years overseas but spent many summers in Yarrow, several of these with her grandmother. She is currently manager of a provincial program, having served previously as a teacher, counselor, and Coordinator of Disability Services.

JACOB LOEWEN, a prolific author, emigrated from Russia to Canada as a young boy in 1929 and moved to Yarrow in 1934. In 1947, he and his wife, Anne, entered missionary work in Colombia. After completing his doctorate, he taught college before spending two decades as a supervisory translation consultant for the United Bible Societies. He retired to Abbotsford in 1984.

ROBERT MARTENS, poet and essayist, was born and raised in Yarrow, completed his degree program in English at Simon Fraser University, then joined the Canadian Postal Service. He lives in Abbotsford.

HARVEY NEUFELDT, a retired university professor, lives in Cookeville, Tennessee. His publications include work in history of adult education,

African-American studies, history of immigrant education, and the history of Yarrow. He was born and raised in Yarrow.

LEONARD NEUFELDT, born and raised in Yarrow, is a retired university professor and administrator. His published work includes monographs in American Studies and books of poetry.

PETER PENNER, Professor Emeritus of History, has published widely on Mennonite subjects and on Colonial India. He left Siberia for Canada as an infant in 1926, and he resided in Chilliwack and Abbotsford in the 1950s. He lives in Calgary, Alberta.

OLGA REMPEL PETERS spent her first 20 years in Yarrow. After completing the degree program of the Toronto Conservatory of Music, she made piano instruction her profession. She lives in Delta, B.C.

CHUCK REGEHR lives in Calgary, Alberta, where he is a senior producer and broadcaster for CBC Radio. He was born and raised in Yarrow and studied at the University of British Columbia.

LORA NEUFELDT SAWATSKY, a high-school English and adult-education teacher in Kansas and Winnipeg, retired to Chilliwack. She was born and raised in Yarrow.

MARLENE SAWATSKY's connection to Yarrow is through stories told by her parents, who resided in Yarrow for several years. Marlene, who was born in nearby Abbotsford, is a faculty member in the English Department of Simon Fraser University, where she previously took her graduate studies.

CHARLOTTE REMPEL SHIER spent her first 18 years in Yarrow. She lives in Tsawwassen, B.C., in the house where she and her physician husband raised their three children. She enjoys gardening.

RUTH DERKSEN SIEMENS was born in Vancouver but spent many summers on her grandparents' raspberry farm in Yarrow. After completing her training with the Toronto Conservatory of Music, she spent several years as a music instructor before taking her graduate education in English. She is a faculty member at Simon Fraser University.

EDITH REMPEL SIMPSON, a Yarrow resident for 19 years, was born there with midwife E. Harms in attendance. She attended a business college in Chilliwack and worked many years for the T. Eaton Company. She has a small garden design business.

VERONICA BARKOWSKY THIESSEN was born in the Ukraine, survived the long trek westward in the latter part of the Second World War, arrived in Yarrow in 1948, trained in computer accounting, and made accounting her profession. She is vice president of B.C. Mennonite Women in Mission.

JOHN WIENS was born in Winnipeg of immigrant Mennonite parents and resided in Yarrow 1942-1949. After a number of years as professor in education at several universities (including the University of Alberta and the University of British Columbia), he concluded his career as Superintendent of Schools in British Columbia.

ABOUT THE ARTIST

Huibert Van Drimmelen's paintings have been purchased locally and internationally by private and corporate collectors. He painted about five renditions of the Vedder: *Vedder River*, published in 1978, is the first of them and is his last painting in oil. After completing it, he began working in arylic and watercolour.

Huibert was born in Zeist, Holland, on November 18, 1950. Seven years later, he immigrated with his parents to Burnaby, B.C. In 1972 he and his wife, Karen, moved to Chilliwack, B.C., where they purchased and still operate a small gallery called The Artisan.

Photo and Map Credits

Cover, front and back: Courtesy Huibert Van Drimmelen, limited-edition print of his oil painting *Vedder River*

p. ix: Map: Courtesy Ron Brass. "Welcome to Chilliwack Map, 2001-2002." Source modified

p. x: Map: Courtesy Herbert Hooge, private collection. "TP 22" [Township 22]. Source modified

p. 1: Gertrude Esau Martens

p. 2: Esther Epp Harder

p. 4: Roland Sawatsky

p. 6: Esther Epp Harder

pp. 17, 18: Lillian Harms

p. 22: Margaret Enns Neufeldt

p. 26: Roland Sawatsky

p. 35: Esther Epp Harder

p. 38: Elizabeth Epp

pp. 45, 49: Veronica Barkowsky Thiessen

p. 80: Sarah Enns Martens

p. 83: Margaret Enns Neufeldt

p. 88: Susan E. Epp

p. 90: Susie Giesbrecht Derksen

p. 91: Agnes Banman Letkeman

p. 98: John H. Enns

p. 100: Abram J. (Ed) and Mary Ratzlaff Froese

pp. 103, 104: Mary Ratzlaff Froese

p. 110: John Wiens

p. 118: Selma Kornelsen Hooge

p. 122: Top left: Roland Sawatsky; top right: Margaret Enns Neufeldt; middle right: Agnes Braun Loewen; bottom right: Gladys A. Loewen

p. 123: Agatha Klassen
p. 127: Edward R. Derksen
pp. 131, 134, 137: Courtesy Ruth Derksen Siemens
p. 156: Abram J. (Ed) and Mary Ratzlaff Froese
p. 158: Agatha Klassen
p. 161: Dorothy Funk Fast
p. 162: Top: Sarah Enns Martens
p. 162: Bottom: John Giesbrecht
p. 163: Susie Giesbrecht Derksen
p. 164: Agatha Klassen
p. 166: John H. Enns
p. 171: Esther Epp Harder
p. 176: Courtesy Chilliwack Archives (P. Coll 109, file 32)
p. 177: Agnes Banman Letkeman
p. 178: Esther Epp Harder
p. 179: Susie Giesbrecht Derksen
p. 185: David P. Giesbrecht
p. 193: Margaret Peters Toews
p. 194: Esther Epp Harder
p. 197: Hilda Neufeldt Rempel
p. 199: Courtesy Chilliwack Archives (P4751)
pp. 201, 202, 204, 206, 207: Ethel Irene Knox and Edith Caroline Knox
pp. 210, 211: Helmut and Selma Kornelsen Hooge
p. 234: George H. Epp
p. 242: Courtesy Chilliwack Archives (P. Coll 106 Chilliwack Progress Photos, Acc. No. 199923)
p. 245: Margaret Enns Neufeldt
p. 257: Leonard N. Neufeldt
p. 265: Anne Rempel Dyck
p. 271: Elizabeth Wall Dyck
p. 277: Ethel Irene Knox and Edith Caroline Knox
p. 291: Agatha Klassen
pp. 299, 300: Henry Giesbrecht
p. 312: Abram J. (Ed) and Mary Ratzlaff Froese
pp. 315, 330: Anne Ratzlaff
p. 332: Esther Epp Harder
p. 333: Courtesy *Chilliwack Progress*, Rick Collins, photographer
p. 334: Robert Menges and Bonnie Menges Coutu

INDEX

Names

Topics